AF661047

About Pearson

Pearson is the world's learning company, with presence across 70 countries worldwide. Our unique insights and world-class expertise comes from a long history of working closely with renowned teachers, authors and thought leaders, as a result of which, we have emerged as the preferred choice for millions of teachers and learners across the world.

We believe learning opens up opportunities, creates fulfilling careers and hence better lives. We hence collaborate with the best of minds to deliver you class-leading products, spread across the Higher Education and Test Preparation spectrum.

Superior learning experience and improved outcomes are at the heart of everything we do. This product is the result of one such effort.

Your feedback plays a critical role in the evolution of our products and you can contact us - reachus@pearson.com. We look forward to it.

Construction Quality Management and Control

Kumar Neeraj Jha
Professor of Civil Engineering
Indian Institute of Technology
Delhi

Amarjit Singh
Professor of Civil, Environmental and
Construction Engineering
University of Hawaii, Manoa

Sreedevi A. R.
Assistant Professor
College of Engineering Trivandrum

Pearson

Senior Manager—Product: Harsha Singh
Senior Editor—Production: C. Purushothaman

ISBN 978-93-671-3755-0

First Impression

Published by Pearson India Education Services Pvt. Ltd, CIN: U72200TN2005PTC057128.

Head Office: 1st Floor, Berger Tower, Plot No. C-001A/2, Sector 16B, Noida - 201 301, Uttar Pradesh, India.
Registered Office: Featherlite, 'The Address' 5th Floor, Survey No 203/10B, 200 Ft MMRD Road, Zamin Pallavaram, Chennai - 600044, Tamilnadu, India.
Website: in.pearson.com, Email: companysecretary.india@pearson.com

Compositor: SRS Global, Puducherry.
Printed in India by Rajkamal Electric Press, Kundli, Haryana-131 028.

Contents

Preface

Quality, cost, and time are traditionally significant factors that determine the success of a construction project. It has been observed on many projects that cost and time factors are given far more importance than quality. The time taken and the cost incurred for construction at each milestone can be measured relatively easily. Since time and cost components directly affect the profit, these factors are often taken seriously. Though it is widely agreed that the quality component of a project affects the cost and time of a project, it has not been given the significance it deserves. It may be because quantifying quality is complex, unlike cost and time.

Most of the common construction contracts in current times are awarded to the lowest bidder. This practice often leads to substandard quality of work, as contractors try to cut corners to be competitive. If quality could be quantified accurately, then it would be possible to specify the required quality threshold in the contracts.

We have come across numerous news articles that report the failure of structures such as buildings, bridges, and roads due to substandard quality. In many instances, such failures have even led to the loss of lives. It also leads to wastage of resources due to rework. If proper care is taken regarding quality during the construction process, a significant amount of resources can be saved by avoiding rework. Though it is difficult to accurately quantify all the losses due to inferior quality of construction activities, researchers have found ways to determine the major costs associated with poor quality.

The most common way of quantifying quality is by determining the cost of quality which is otherwise known as the cost of poor quality. Even in this method, measuring the cost of external failures such as loss of reputation and revenue losses is difficult. The number of research works that have been done in this area of the construction industry is minimal, primarily due to the lack of sufficient data in this regard. Construction is an industry where multiple stakeholders are involved, but most construction participants do not track the cost of quality failure. At the contractor level, they fear that disclosing it may affect their reputation. However, not all the quality costs are borne by the contractors. Some researchers have found that poor quality costs or quality failure costs may vary from 1 to 20% of the original contract value.

The construction industry in India as per the government of India contributes 8% to its GDP, which is around 23.83 lakh crores Indian Rupees, considering the GDP in the financial year 2023–2024. However, the authors believe that a considerable amount of additional construction is undertaken in the sectors of power, agriculture, defence, mining and industries, which are not included in the above data. And if we consider all those expenditures, the actual construction expenditure might be many times more than the reported figure[1]. Even if we consider the government of India data and the cost of poor quality to be approximately 10% of the project cost in India, then the financial loss is nearly 2.383 lakh crore Indian Rupees in the FY 2023–2024 alone. If the quality were good, this much money would not have been wasted and could be used for developing 10 AIIMS at ₹3,000 crore per AIIMS, 10 IITs at ₹2,000 crore per IIT, 40 solar power plants of 500 MW at the estimated cost of ₹2,500 crore, and 3,500 km of 6-lane expressways at ₹25 crore per km. These figures are only approximations.

The loss due to poor quality deprives the public from enjoying better essential services. If we determine this accurately, it might be an enormous financial loss. However, this has been happening for decades and will continue for years to come if left undetermined. It is high time we educate our young engineers to bring about a change that puts quality as the paramount factor in construction. Following stringent quality standards and implementing quality management will be an enabler to achieve this change.

The manufacturing and service industry has benefitted immensely from the effective implementation of quality management techniques. However, the construction industry has a long way to go.

This book aims to introduce quality concepts to construction engineers and give insights into various quality management techniques that may be adopted in construction projects to improve the quality of construction.

A book of such a nature would not have been possible without the active support of our students and research scholars. We are thankful to all research scholars who contributed to the development of this book. We also extend our gratitude to our family members for their understanding and for sacrificing their share of time during the process of writing this book. We look forward to the comments of our readers for the improvement to the subsequent editions of this book.

Kumar Neeraj Jha
Amarjit Singh
Sreedevi

---

1 According to the *Report on Economies in Construction Costs, Planning Commission 1968*, the reported outlay in construction was nearly 50% of the total outlay.

Synopsis

In the dynamic and demanding world of construction, delivering high-quality projects on time and within budget is essential. *Construction Quality Management and Control* is a comprehensive guide that equips construction professionals, project managers, engineers and students with the tools and knowledge to ensure excellence in every phase of a construction project.

This book delves into the principles and practices of quality management, addressing critical topics such as quality planning, assurance, control processes, and continuous improvement strategies. It provides practical insights into implementing quality control measures, conducting inspections and managing risks that can compromise project integrity.

Real-world examples and case studies illustrate the challenges faced in construction and how effective quality management techniques can lead to superior outcomes. Focusing on modern tools and technologies, the book covers topics such as reliability, availability, operating characteristic curves, process capability, Six Sigma, and data-driven decision-making, effectively bridging the gap between traditional practices and emerging innovations.

Whether you're managing small residential projects or large-scale commercial developments, this book provides actionable guidance to achieve high standards, minimize rework, and foster a culture of quality within your team. Packed with valuable insights, it serves as an essential resource for those striving for excellence in the construction industry.

About the Authors

Kumar Neeraj Jha, PhD is a Professor of Civil Engineering at the Indian Institute of Technology Delhi. He started his career with Larsen and Toubro Ltd. and was instrumental in the successful completion of a number of construction projects. He has published more than 160 papers in international and national journals and conference proceedings. He has supervised 24 PhD Students and more than 120 MTech students. He was included in the list of the World's Top two per cent Scientists in 2024, published by Elsevier and Stanford University. His books on 'Construction Project Management: Theory and Practice' and 'Formwork and Scaffold Engineering' published by Pearson Education and 'Determinants of Construction Project Success in India' are widely accepted as textbooks and reference books in different universities. He has also co-authored books on 'Construction Safety Management' published by Pearson Education and 'Construction Company Management'. He teaches courses in construction engineering and management. He has conducted numerous training programs both offline and online. His online program on project management has trained more than 2,000 professionals. He has been involved in a number of consultancy and R&D projects. His research interests focus on project and organisation success factors, formwork, project risks, and construction quality and safety.

Amarjit Singh, PhD, PEng, CEng, FICE, FASCE, FIE is a Professor of Civil, Environmental and Construction Engineering at the University of Hawaii at Manoa. He graduated from IIT Delhi with a BTech degree, worked in the construction industry for 10 years in responsible positions in India, Nepal, and Kuwait, and then earned an MEng degree from Texas A&M University, College Station, TX, USA, followed by a PhD from Purdue University, West Lafayette, IN, USA. He worked another year as a consultant in the construction industry in Canada before joining academia. He received ASCE's 2024 Richard R. Torrens Award; the 2019 ASCE Construction Management Award; the 2012 College of Engineering

Service Award; and the 2009 University of Hawaii Board of Regents Medal for Excellence in Teaching; and 10 best paper awards. He was on sabbatical as a Visiting Professor at IIT Delhi and as a Visiting Associate Professor at the University of New South Wales, Sydney, Australia, as well as at Cornell University, Ithaca, NY, USA. He was also a visiting scholar at Reading University, England, and City University of Hong Kong. He serves as the founding President and Chairman of the International Structural Engineering and Construction Society and as the Founding Editor-in-Chief of the ASCE Journal of Legal Affairs and Dispute Resolution in Engineering and Construction. Dr Singh was Chairperson of the Hawaii Council of Engineering Societies, Director at the University of Hawaii Professional Assembly, and Co-Chair of the University of Hawaii's All Campus Council of Faculty Senate Chairs. He wrote a textbook titled 'Quantitative Risk Management and Decision Making in Construction', and co-wrote books titled 'Area Cost Factors Method Methodology in Construction Cost Estimating' and 'Construction Safety Management'. He teaches quality control and applied probability and statistics, among other subjects in engineering management. He is a fellow of the Institution of Civil Engineers (UK), the American Society of Civil Engineers, and the Institution of Engineers (India).

Sreedevi A. R., MTech has been an Assistant Professor in the Department of Civil Engineering at the College of Engineering Trivandrum, since 2019. She holds a BTech in Civil Engineering from Government Engineering College, Thrissur; and an MTech in Construction Technology and Management from the National Institute of Technology Karnataka, Surathkal, for which she was awarded the Gold Medal. She is currently pursuing her PhD degree at the Indian Institute of Technology Delhi. She has over eight years of professional experience in the construction sector, having worked with Sobha Developers and the Government of Kerala as an Assistant Engineer. Sreedevi's primary research interest lies in the area of quality management in construction, a subject she has explored extensively as part of her PhD research.

CHAPTER 1 Introduction

1.1 MEANING AND ETYMOLOGY

The term quality originated in the 14th century from the Middle English *qualite*, from Anglo-French *qualité*, from Latin *qualitat, presumably* translated from the Greek word '*poiotē*[1]'. It means a particular property or feature. The word 'quality' came into vogue when craftsmen started guilds in the 13th–14th century, which prescribed quality for work done. The Oxford Dictionary gives the definition of the term 'quality' as 'the standard of something measured against other things of a similar kind' and this definition is amplified by explaining quality as 'the degree of excellence of something'. This definition does not mention the person making the judgment. Quality has different meanings for different users. It varies with the users' requirements and purposes in accordance with the interests driving it. For an owner in the construction sector, quality is getting all the needs fulfilled within time and budget. In contrast, for the contractor, it is fulfilling the requirements within time and satisfying the customer. Though some might say that the concept of quality is similar to the concept of beauty, i.e., it exists in the eyes of the beholder, that is not quite true in engineering. For instance, if the machining error of a Rolls Royce engine must be 1/787th of a millimetre, there's little about beauty in this, but it is all about accuracy. The specifications are driven by the needs that are fulfilled by the technologies available. Nevertheless, some quality features are partly subjective, such as the cover to rebar, where 30 mm to 50 mm might be sufficient, based on the designer's recommendation.

A building constructed in good quality may not be perceived in the same way by two different stakeholders for aesthetic reasons. But where some level of quality may be acceptable to one person, it may be deficient to another. Rather than being driven by perception and subjectivity, it may be driven by a perception of the needs and capabilities available. Overall, the word quality is mainly associated with a process and the processes adopted, but what matters is the outcome based on the context. It depends on the regulations of the country and is dynamic in nature. The building that has been called a quality construction today may not remain in the same category tomorrow.

---

[1] But as in many other English words that trace their roots to Arabic and Sanskrit, the authors find considerable causation for the root word '*qual*' of '*qualita*' to come from the Arabic '*kul*', or 'qul' meaning 'total', which implies 'completeness', which implies 'perfection', which is what quality is about..

In the manufacturing industry, quality is a distinctive competency that increases sales and profitability. After World War II, the completely shattered Japanese economy was revived by adopting the new quality concepts advocated by Edward Deming and Joseph Juran (Burati *et al.,* 1991). They focused on statistical quality control (SQC) as the underlying principle of specifying quality. When the growth of the Japanese economy led to a crisis in the United States, U.S. companies gradually started launching initiatives to improve the quality of their products (Love, 1995). Though this concept of SQC has been well established in the manufacturing sector, it was not – and is not – very popular in the construction industry due to its diverse nature and culture. But whichever way anyone looks at it, quality is something that has far-reaching consequences (Collins, 1996).

1.2 DEFINITION OF QUALITY

Quality is defined distinctly by different researchers based on their work context. Due to the fact that different stakeholders interpret it differently, there is no universally accepted definition for quality, but they all deliver us to a higher level. The common definitions for quality are (Jha, 2015):

- fitness for purpose
- conformance to specifications
- meeting or exceeding the needs of the customer
- value for money
- customer satisfaction/customer delight
- doing it right the first time and every time
- the reduction of variability

The concept of quality has been interpreted by various experts as given in Table 1.1. These are important to understand the underlying philosophy and drivers behind trying to get quality.

TABLE 1.1 Definitions of quality

Definition	Source
'Quality is a customer determination which is based on the customer's actual experience with the product or service, measured against his or her requirements – stated or unstated, conscious or merely sensed, technically operational or entirely subjective and always representing a moving target in a competitive market'.	Feigenbaum, 1961
'In the final analysis of the marketplace, the quality of a product depends on how well it fits patterns of consumer preferences'.	Kuehn, 1962
'Quality consists of the capacity to satisfy wants'.	Deming, 1986
'Quality is the degree to which a specific product satisfies the wants of a specific consumer. Quality is the degree to which a specific product conforms to a design or specification.'	Gilmore, 1974
'Quality (means) conformance to requirements'.	Crosby, 1979

Definition	Source
'Quality is the degree of excellence at an acceptable price and the control of variability at an acceptable cost'.	Broh, 1982
'Good quality means a predictable degree of uniformity and dependability at a low cost with a quality suited to the market'.	Deming, 1986
'Quality is fitness for use'.	Juran, 1988
'Quality is meeting the customer requirements, and this is not restricted to the functional characteristics of the product or service'.	Oakland, 2003
'Quality is the extent to which the customer or users believe the product or service surpasses their needs and expectations.'	Gitlow, 1989
'Quality - is to satisfy customers' requirements continually; Total quality - is to achieve quality at low cost; Total Quality Management - is to achieve quality at low cost by involving everyone's daily commitment'.	Kanji, 1990
'The totality of features and characteristics of a product or service that bear on its ability to satisfy stated or implied needs'.	BSI, 1987
'Quality: degree to which a set of inherent characteristics of an object fulfills requirements'.	ISO, 2015
'Quality is the degree to which a set of inherent characteristics of a product, service, or result fulfills the requirements'.	PMI, 2017
'Quality can have two meanings: (1) the characteristics of a product or service that bear on its ability to satisfy stated or implied needs; (2) a product or service free of deficiencies'.	ASQ

As per 'the transcendent approach,' quality is 'innate excellence' (Garvin, 1988). It is a symbol of high achievement and meticulous standards that are flawless and accepted universally. It can only be felt through experience, cannot be precisely defined, and is occasionally associated with fine craftsmanship. The product-based definition presents quality as an accurate and measurable variable. The user-based definition revolves around the notion that quality 'lies in the eyes of the beholder.' Quality is evaluated purely on the wants and needs of individual consumers. The manufacturing-based definition is based on the motto of 'conformance to requirements.' 'Meeting specifications' and 'doing it right the first time' is what matters in the manufacturing industry. Value-based approach to defining quality is concerned with excellence at an affordable price or cost.

Though there are several definitions, for a user, quality is contentment with the performance, appearance, reliability, and durability of the project for a given price range (Jha, 2006). Most of the time, this term is associated with expensive products, but it does not mean that low-priced products are of poor quality. A product is called a quality product if it meets the requirements of the customer (stated and unstated). A lot of research on quality has been done in the manufacturing sector, and only a few have been reported from the construction sector.

1.3 EVOLUTION OF QUALITY CONTROL

The evolution of 'quality control' spans more than a century. It has been in use in the manufacturing industry as well as the service sector. It started in the manufacturing industry when goods started to be produced in bulk. In the period prior to the 1900s, the production of goods was carried out by individuals or small groups of people. During those periods, workers had the responsibility of ensuring quality, and hence Feigenbaum (1983) labelled it as the *operator quality control period*. The workers took pride in their workmanship, motivating them to move to better heights. The workmanship of those workers is evident from some ancient monuments and sculptures.

The next stage in quality evolution started in the early 1900s and continued till around 1920, which Feigenbaum (1983) termed the *foreman quality control period*. It was the start of mass production, with the dawn of the Second Industrial Revolution or the Technological Revolution. This gave rise to the standardisation of labour, and each worker was entrusted with a portion of the entire task. The workers became skilled only in their specific operations. Many workers were reporting to a foreman, due to which the accountability of labour started reducing, and it became the duty of the foreman or supervisor to ensure the quality of operations.

In the period between 1920 and 1940, post-World War I, the production processes became more complicated, and there was a tremendous surge in the production volume, making it impossible for the foremen to supervise all activities. Inspectors were employed to ensure quality at each stage of operations. As the level of responsibility increased, there was a need for the standards to be set against which quality could be compared. Defective and non-conforming products were discarded or repaired. This period was called the *inspection quality control period* by Feigenbaum (1983).

The period after the 1920s witnessed a lot of development in statistical quality control. It was then the control charts were developed by Walter A. Shewhart. And AOQL (Average Outgoing Quality Limit), a sampling plan for inspection was developed by Harold. F. Dodge and Harry. G Romig. During World War II and later, in the period from 1940 to 1960, production volume started seeing new heights, and it became impossible to check the quality of all items. Then, 100% inspections were substituted by inspection of samples using the sampling plans. This phase of quality evolution was termed the *statistical quality control phase* by Feigenbaum (1983). This development was initially embraced by Japan (which was completely set back after World War II) under the leadership of W. Edward Deming. During this time, the United States focused its emphasis on the area of sampling for quality, and the United States Department of Defence came up with the Quality Control and Reliability Handbook.

During the 1960s, the concept of quality started assuming new interpretations. The responsibility for quality, which was primarily entrusted to operators, foremen, and then the quality control department, had begun to involve several departments and the management. This phase came to be known as the *total quality control period* (Feigenbaum, 1983). The concept of zero defect started to get noticed after Philip Crosby started the zero-defect program to get things done right the first time. In the 1970s, quality started to get associated with all the members of an organisation, from top management to the operator and this phase came to be known as total quality control, which was implemented organisation-wide. The Ishikawa diagram, commonly known as the cause-and-effect diagram or the fishbone diagram due to the shape it resembles, began to be widely used in Japan in the 1970s. This graphical cause and effect tool aided in detecting the probable reasons when processes go out of control. The impact of total quality control on management and engineering practices paved the way for the development of organisation-wide total quality control, total quality system, total quality management, and quality as a major new business strategy from the 1980s and beyond (Feigenbaum, 1983).

In the 1980s with the explosion of computer usage, various quality control software programs started to be in use in organisations. Many companies started using quality control tools, and they insisted their vendors implement them as well. Ford Motor Company and General Motor Corporation were a few among them (Mitra, 2016). The quality concept became strategically important with the introduction of the Malcolm Baldrige National Award in 1987.

The focus on quality started shifting from products to customer satisfaction. Customer has become the driving force for setting the level of quality. The requirements or specifications change with the needs of the customer. It led to a need for continuous quality improvement to ensure customer satisfaction, and for that, standards and guidelines were required. The International Organization for Standardization developed the guidelines for quality management, which could be modified to make it applicable to all kinds of organisations. Various standards were developed in line with ISO, like ANSI (American National Standards Institute), ASQC (American Society for Quality Control), etc.

With the third Industrial Revolution or Digital revolution, towards the end of the twentieth century, information technology advanced and helped deliver quality data, problem-solving, and decision-making. Measuring quality and customer satisfaction has become much easier with the developed technology. In 2016, Klaus Schwab coined the term 'Fourth Industrial Revolution' (Lavopa & Delera, 2021). This term refers to the convergence of various technologies, including artificial intelligence, blockchain technology, robotics, Internet of Things, big data analytics, additive manufacturing, and cloud computing. It helps a lot in standardising operations as everything can be automated, thus helping to improve quality in manufacturing and service industries.

The effect of the Fourth Industrial Revolution, 4IR, or Industry 4.0, is very much evident in the construction industry with the application of Building Information Modelling, Blockchain Technology, 3D printing, robots, sensors, drones, etc. being used in construction projects. Advanced technologies can be utilised in the construction industry, too, to improve quality. Building information modelling and other technologies help address the challenges faced in the construction industry. BIM can improve the quality of the built environment.

Even with the tremendous advances in technology and quality ideas, many building projects still use conventional methods. Many failures occur in the construction sector due to design defects, faulty construction, poor workmanship, and poor management attention, among others. There are also instances where mistakes result in fatalities. The availability of faultless design and drawings, precise specifications, well-defined quality plans, high-quality materials, competent labour, functional equipment, sound construction methodology, and numerous other supporting management elements such as coordination, leadership and communication all contribute to the quality of construction.

1.4 QUALITY IN CONSTRUCTION

Quality is a major part of the construction sector. In ancient Babylon, King Hammurabi's code specified that if a building constructed by a builder was not strong and led to the death of the house owner, the builder would be put to death. The ancient Romans used to make the builders stand under the bridge they had constructed while a Legion would march over it after the construction was done. These laws of the land created a high sense of accountability and responsibility among constructors and led to high quality in construction, and that is possibly the reason why some of those structures still exist. Such harsh penalties cannot be executed in the current days, even if the consequences of poor quality are alarming. Poor quality leads to loss in productivity, additional expenses for repair and rework, re-inspection and retest, loss of reputation, loss of business, heartaches, frustrations, depression, claims and lawsuits. If the majority of companies are reluctant to consider quality in construction, it can tarnish the image of the country.

Various studies reveal that the cost of poor quality may go up to twice to thrice the construction cost in the early stages of work in some cases. It does not only incur costs but also drains limited resources. Once the defects are identified, the contractors are instructed to rectify them, but in some circumstances, they are not repairable, and the occupants have to use the structure with no other option than to accept it as a *fait accompli*. It is the owner who suffers in such situations as he has to keep attending to the defects from time to time until the life of the structure and sacrifice his comforts even after paying additional costs than what would be actually required to do it right the first time.

Quality in construction is attained when the end user's requirements are fulfilled. It should be in terms of both workmanship and the materials used. The definition of quality is extended to accomplishing the project on time, safely, without disputes, and within budget, and it is not just about supplying the right materials (Schexnayder, 2004), as it covers conformance to contract conditions and keeping the client apprised of changes and developments, and seeking to work with a positive and constructive attitude. Quality can be attained by sticking to specifications and delivering according to contractual obligations. The requirements of clients are presented in the form of specifications, drawings, bills of quantities, and conditions of contract (general and special). To achieve quality, construction should be done in accordance with specifications and drawings. Hence, these documents have to be unambiguous, free of errors, and clearly represent all the needs of the customer. The documents must be designed to clearly specify the materials to be used, approved sources, work method, test methods, codes for reference, sequence of work, tools, and plants, and every other information related to construction or the delivery method. The standards governing materials and workmanship must also be specified clearly, if the delivery method warrants these to be specified. It is advisable to avoid qualitative terms in contract documents so that disputes, which may arise due to a lack of understanding owing to subjectivity, can be avoided. Ultimately, the aim of quality in construction is to construct a facility that performs its intended function. Achieving quality requires continuous quality improvement based on customer needs and expectations and commitment and involvement from all stakeholders such as the owners, architects, engineers, contractors, suppliers, subcontractors and others (Deffenbaugh, 1993).

In quality management, customer satisfaction is highly important, as it relates to life cycle cost, which includes service after sales or cost incurred to users. Unfortunately, the accountability of a constructor is valid only up to the defect liability period, which may be six to twelve months after the completion of construction. Earlier, there was no legislation to hold the constructor responsible for defects, and the home buyers had to bear the cost of repair. However, the Real Estate (Regulation and Development) Act 2016 has norms to protect home buyers. As per RERA (GOI, 2016), Section 14, Clause 3,

> 'In case any structural defect or any other defect in workmanship, quality, or provision of services or any other obligations of the promoter as per the agreement for sale relating to such development is brought to the notice of the promoter within a period of five years by the allottee from the date of handing over possession, it shall be the duty of the promoter to rectify such defects without further charge, within thirty days, and in the event of promoter's failure to rectify such defects within such time, the aggrieved allottees shall be entitled to receive appropriate compensation in the manner as provided under this Act.'

In the construction sector, especially in public projects, the quality aspect has not gained much attention as the method of contractor selection is mostly based on the lowest bid system. It is assumed that all the contractors, including the lowest bidder, would construct with the same quality if a set of drawings and specifications were given. However, the lowest bidder would try to make a profit or try to avoid making a loss by compromising the quality. Very frequently, it is observed that such contractors produce bad-quality work and ignore customer complaints. The growth of such contractors will be short-lived. At the same time, there are builders and contractors who consistently attempt to produce good quality work. Though they may not be able to make a profit in the initial stages, gradually, they will turn out to be successful. Customers are ready to pay extra money for good quality work, especially in the private building sector. Good quality helps in improving the market share and thus leads to increased profitability. It also leads to improved customer satisfaction and customer loyalty. Therefore, it supports an organisation in its survival, growth, and profitability.

1.5 ORGANISATION OF THE BOOK

The objective of this book is to give an insight into the various aspects of quality and how it has been used in the construction industry. Though quality is an inevitable requirement in the construction sector, considering the cost, sustainability, and durability of structures, it has not been well incorporated into the industry.

This book consists of twelve chapters. Chapters 1 through 8 present management aspects of quality delivery. The first chapter introduces the reader to the significance of quality in construction. It describes how the concept of quality has evolved over the last two hundred years. The definitions given by various researchers and organisations have been discussed, which gives the reader an idea about the vastness of the topic. The second chapter aims to enable the reader to comprehend about the contribution of various pioneers, some of them who were popularly known as Quality Gurus. Their teachings and methodologies led to the evolution of quality as what we see today. In Chapters 3 and 4, different quality concepts like Total Quality Management and ISO Standards have been discussed. Total Quality Management is a philosophy that intends to achieve quality with support from all levels of management to satisfy a customer. Chapter 4 is on ISO standards for quality management and its guidelines for implementing Quality Management Systems in organisations. This chapter also introduces the reader to the various quality assessment tools used by various countries to evaluate the quality of their construction. In Chapter 5 the cost of quality (COQ) is discussed. COQ is about the cost of poor performance of a project. It deals with the complications and losses incurred due to the lack of importance given to quality by an organisation. It enlightens the reader about how money can be saved by investing in preventive and appraisal costs. Chapter 6 is on preparing the project quality plan. With the norms provided by ISO, a project quality plan can be prepared and used to improve quality in the construction industry. Chapter 7 deals with quality audit, which is an indispensable practice to achieve and sustain quality. Chapter 8 is regarding quality control, quality assurance and inspection in the construction industry. This chapter discusses the differences between quality control and quality assurance and how quality can be achieved by inspection and other techniques.

Chapters 9 to 12 focus on statistical aspects of quality delivery. Chapter 9 discusses the Six Sigma process that aims to reduce variations and thus improve quality. Chapter 9 also presents the operating characteristic curve (OCC) which is the quantitative part of acceptance sampling. The OCC helps to establish whether or not production is proceeding within permissible defects. Chapter 10 deals with quality control tools such as cause and effect diagram, control chart, process capability, Pareto chart, force field analysis and brainstorming. Chapter 11 focuses on the concept of failure rate, reliability analysis and availability of equipment and plant. Chapter 12 presents a specific application in applying statistical quality control to the evaluation of concrete strength results with the purpose of ensuring that concrete with acceptable strength is produced and used. The fundamentals in this chapter can potentially be used to improve IS 456 or related codes for producing concrete mixes for adoption in the industry.

SUMMARY AND CONCLUDING REMARKS

Chapter 1 gives the definitions of quality, its evolution, and its significance in the construction industry. The concept of quality is significant and sensitive and can be applied in all industries. Since the construction sector is very vast and diverse and consists of multiple stakeholders, implementing quality management in the construction field is different from the way it is done in the manufacturing industry, where statistical quality control tools were first applied. Another important factor is that quality is a concept that has diverse implications for different people. Though the need to achieve and improve quality is highly evident, there are few universal standards or regulations for accomplishing quality in construction. It is thus quite challenging for construction professionals to achieve and sustain quality, but necessary to do so, nevertheless.

WORKS CITED

ASQ. (2024), *Quality Glossary*, Retrieved January 10, 2024, from ASQ: https://asq.org/quality-resources/quality-glossary.

Broh, R. (1982), *Managing Quality for Higher Profits: A Guide for Business Executives and Quality Managers* (Hungary: McGraw-Hill).

BSI. (1987), *Quality Systems: Guide to the Application of BS 4778: Part 1 (BS 4778:1987)* (United Kingdom: British Standards Institution).

Burati, J. L., Matthews, M. F. and Kalidindi, S. N. (1991), 'Quality management in construction industry', *Journal of Construction Engineering and Management,* 117(2), 341–359.

Collins, J. F. (1996), *Quality: The Ball in Your Court* (New Delhi: Tata McGraw-Hill).

Crosby, P. B. (1979), *Quality is Free: The Art of Making Quality Certain* (United Kingdom: McGraw-Hill).

Deffenbaugh, R. (1993), 'Total quality management at construction job sites', *Journal of Management in Engineering*, 9(4), 382–389.

Deming, W. E. (1986), *Out of the Crisis* (Cambridge: Massachusetts Institute of Technology Press).

Feigenbaum, A. (1961), *Total Quality Control: Engineering and Management* (United Kingdom: McGraw-Hill).

Feigenbaum, A. V. (1983), *Total Quality Control* (New York: McGraw-Hill Book Company).

Garvin, D. (1988), *Managing Quality: The Strategic and Competitive Edge* (New York: The Free Press).

Gilmore, H. L. (1974), 'Product conformance cost', *Quality Progress*, 16.

Gitlow, H. O. (1989), *Tools and Methods for the Improvement of Quality* (USA: Irwin).

GOI. (2016), *The Real Estate (Regulation and Development) Act, 2016* (Ministry of Law and Justice, India: The Gazette of India).

ISO. (2015), *ISO 9000:2015(en) Quality Management Systems – Fundamentals and Vocabulary* (Geneva: International Organization for Standardization).

Jha, K. N. (2015), *Construction Project Management: Theory and Practice* (New Delhi: Pearson).

Jha, K. N., and Iyer, K. C. (2006), 'Critical factors affecting quality performance in construction projects', *Total Quality Management, 17*(9), 1155–1170.

Joseph M. Juran, A. B. (1988), *Juran's Quality Control Handbook* (United Kingdom: McGraw-Hill).

Kanji, G. K. (1990), 'Total quality management: the second industrial revolution', *Total Quality Management*, 1(1), 3–12.

Kuehn, A. A., and Day, R. L. (1962), 'Strategy of product quality', *Harvard Business Review*, 40(6), 100–110.

Lavopa, A., and Delera, M. (2021), *What is the Fourth Industrial Revolution?* Retrieved January 10, 2024, from iap.unido.org: https://iap.unido.org/articles/what-fourth-industrial-revolution

Love, C. G. (1995), 'Acceptable quality level versus zero-defects: Some empirical evidence', *Computers and Operations Research, 22*(4), 403–417.

Mitra, A. (2016), *Fundamentals of Quality Control and Improvement* (United States of America: Wiley).

Oakland, J. S. (2003), *Total Quality Management: Text with Cases* (United Kingdom: Elsevier Science and Technology).

PMI. (2017), *A Guide to the Project Management Body of Knowledge (PMBOK Guide)* (Newton Square, PA: Project Management Institute).

Schexnayder, C. J., and Mayo, R. E. (2004), *Construction Management Fundamentals* (Singapore: McGraw-Hill).

REVIEW QUESTIONS

Multiple Choice Questions

1. According to the Oxford Dictionary, quality is defined as:
   (a) The degree of perfection of something
   (b) The standard of something as measured against other things of a similar kind
   (c) The cost-effectiveness of a product
   (d) The inherent value of a product
2. Who is credited with reviving the Japanese economy after World War II through quality concepts?
   (a) Philip Crosby (b) W. Edwards Deming
   (c) Joseph Juran (d) Both (b) and (c)
3. What term did Feigenbaum use to describe the period prior to the 1900s regarding quality control?
   (a) Foreman quality control period
   (b) Inspection quality control period
   (c) Operator quality control period
   (d) Statistical quality control period
4. Which quality expert is associated with the statement 'Quality is fitness for use'?
   (a) Feigenbaum (b) Crosby
   (c) Juran (d) Deming
5. Which approach defines quality as 'innate excellence'?
   (a) User-based approach
   (b) Product-based approach
   (c) Transcendent approach
   (d) Manufacturing-based approach
6. What does ISO 9000:2015 define quality as?
   (a) Degree to which a product meets specifications
   (b) Degree to which a set of inherent characteristics fulfills requirements
   (c) Conformance to requirements
   (d) Fitness for use

7. Who developed the control charts in the evolution of statistical quality control?
   (a) W. Edwards Deming (b) Philip Crosby
   (c) Walter A. Shewhart (d) Joseph Juran
8. Which phase in the evolution of quality control involves the use of sampling plans instead of 100% inspections?
   (a) Operator quality control period
   (b) Inspection quality control period
   (c) Statistical quality control period
   (d) Total quality control period
9. What is the primary focus of total quality control as defined in the 1960s?
   (a) Operator involvement
   (b) Foreman supervision
   (c) Management and departmental involvement
   (d) Customer satisfaction
10. The concept of zero defects was introduced by:
    (a) Feigenbaum (b) Crosby
    (c) Deming (d) Juran
11. What historical period marked the beginning of mass production and standardisation of labour?
    (a) First Industrial Revolution (b) Second Industrial Revolution
    (c) Third Industrial Revolution (d) Fourth Industrial Revolution
12. What is the term used for the graphical cause and -and-effect tool widely used in Japan in the 1970s?
    (a) Control chart (b) Pareto chart
    (c) Fishbone diagram (d) Histogram
13. What does the acronym SQC stand for?
    (a) Standard Quality Control (b) Statistical Quality Control
    (c) Systematic Quality Control (d) Structured Quality Control
14. What is the key factor driving the focus on quality from products to customer satisfaction in recent times?
    (a) Technological advancements
    (b) Competitive market pressure
    (c) Customer needs and expectations
    (d) Regulatory requirements

15. Which quality expert emphasised 'doing it right the first time'?
    (a) Deming (b) Juran
    (c) Crosby (d) Feigenbaum
16. According to RERA 2016, how long is the defect liability period for a promoter to rectify defects without charge?
    (a) One year (b) Two years
    (c) Three years (d) Five years
17. The Malcolm Baldrige National Quality Award was introduced in:
    (a) 1980 (b) 1985
    (c) 1987 (d) 1990
18. Which term refers to the improvement of quality at a low cost by involving everyone's daily commitment?
    (a) Total Quality Management (b) Total Quality Control
    (c) Six Sigma (d) Lean Manufacturing
19. The term 'Fourth Industrial Revolution' was coined by:
    (a) Edward Deming (b) Klaus Schwab
    (c) Joseph Juran (d) Harold Dodge
20. Which model is associated with Japanese quality practices and involves continuous improvement?
    (a) Six Sigma (b) Lean Manufacturing
    (c) Kaizen (d) Balanced Scorecard

Short Answer Type Questions

1. What is the definition of quality according to the Oxford Dictionary?
2. What period did Feigenbaum term the 'foreman quality control period'?
3. What are control charts, and who developed them?
4. What does SQC stand for, and where is it commonly applied?
5. What is the significance of the Malcolm Baldrige National Quality Award?
6. What is the role of the Real Estate (Regulation and Development) Act 2016 in quality management?
7. What is the concept of zero defects, and who introduced it?
8. What is the focus of Total Quality Management (TQM)?
9. What is the primary objective of Building Information Modelling (BIM) in construction?
10. What are some consequences of poor quality in construction?

11. What does ISO 9000:2015 emphasise in its definition of quality?
12. What is the significance of continuous quality improvement in construction?
13. How did the concept of quality evolve during the 1960s?
14. What is the purpose of quality audit in construction?
15. Define the concept of 'Total Quality Control'.
16. What are some quality control tools mentioned in the document?
17. Who developed the Average Outgoing Quality Limit (AOQL) sampling plan?
18. What is the significance of the 'transcendent approach' to quality?
19. What is the role of customer satisfaction in quality management?
20. How has the Fourth Industrial Revolution impacted the construction industry?
21. What is the role of the International Organization for Standardization (ISO) in quality management?
22. How does the concept of value-based quality differ from other definitions?
23. Explain the term 'operator quality control period'.
24. What is the importance of specifying quality in construction contracts?

Long Answer Type Questions

1. Discuss the evolution of quality control from the early 1900s to the present day.
2. What are the different definitions of quality according to various experts, and how do they contribute to understanding the concept?
3. Explain the concept of Total Quality Management (TQM) and its importance in the construction industry.
4. Discuss the significance of customer satisfaction in quality management and how it influences quality standards.
5. What challenges are associated with implementing quality management in the construction industry, and how can they be addressed?
6. Explain the impact of the Fourth Industrial Revolution on quality management in the construction industry.
7. What are the key elements of a project quality plan in the construction industry?
8. How did the concept of quality change with the introduction of statistical quality control (SQC)?
9. Explain the role of quality management systems (QMS) in construction and how they contribute to project success.
10. What are the primary factors affecting quality performance in construction projects, and how can they be managed?

ANSWER KEYS

Multiple Choice Questions

1. (b)	**2.** (d)	**3.** (c)	**4.** (c)	**5.** (c)	**6.** (b)	**7.** (c)	**8.** (c)
9. (c)	**10.** (b)	**11.** (b)	**12.** (c)	**13.** (b)	**14.** (c)	**15.** (c)	**16.** (d)
17. (c)	**18.** (a)	**19.** (b)	**20.** (c)				

CHAPTER 2

Quality Management Scientists and their Teachings

2.1 INTRODUCTION

Continuous evolution and research are going on in every field of human endeavour. Researchers and practitioners come up with new ideas and approaches to solve the issues prevalent in their fields. Then, they become established as a part of theory and practice. In the specific area of quality, the researchers and practitioners whose original ideas form part of the body of acceptable knowledge, whose leadership and advice create a movement, have come to be known as 'quality gurus.'

In every field, quality is an important factor to be considered. Various tools, systems, and practices of quality continue to develop and they are all derivatives of the philosophies, tools, and methodologies developed by 'The Quality Gurus.' Some of the most well-known quality gurus are Deming, Juran, and Feigenbaum. There are many others who can be considered as gurus in this field. Each of them has developed unique views and ideas regarding quality. Some of the significant contributions in the field of quality have been brought about by the following quality management scientists and practitioners whose ideas and approaches have made a major impact and are everlasting:

1. Walter A. Shewhart
2. W. Edwards Deming
3. Joseph M. Juran
4. Kaoru Ishikawa
5. Armand V. Feigenbaum
6. Genichi Taguchi
7. Philip B. Crosby
8. David A. Garvin
9. Prasanta Chandra Mahalanobis
10. Harkirat Singh

2.2 WALTER A. SHEWHART

Walter A. Shewhart (1891–1967) is credited with creating statistical quality control. He was the one who challenged the inspection-based quality in his book 'Economic Control of Quality of Manufacturing' in 1931. It cleared the path for the contemporary era of quality management. Shewhart believed that in a production environment, control and management procedures were greatly affected by the lack of information. To assist a manager in making efficient decisions in a scientific and economical way, Shewhart developed **Statistical Process**

Control (SPC) methods. Nowadays, a control chart is the most widely used SPC tool. A control chart, also known as the Shewhart control chart, is a visual tool for tracking the progress of a process that has already started (Mitra, 2016). The horizontal axis indicates the samples from which the quality characteristic is taken, while the vertical axis shows the values of the quality characteristic. There is a central line in the control chart, which indicates the average value of the quality characteristic, and an upper line and a lower line representing the upper limit and lower limit of the quality characteristic, respectively (See Singh 2017, Chapter 12).

The control charts are used in production industries to show variations in processes or test results. The use of a control chart is illustrated with an example in Chapter 10.

Shewhart's approach to quality was finding the boundaries of variations that could be anticipated from a process running in a normal state. Basic statistical and graphical tools were created to analyse the processed data. When the charting of data indicates the occurrence of a special cause, analysis of the process should be done to identify the problem, and it has to be rectified. Then, the process can be restarted. Shewhart asserts that the quality control report should identify any assignable causes of variance in each quality characteristic, as well as the severity of the issue and the actions taken to resolve it (Shewhart, 1931). Shewhart's approach is called Statistical Process Control. This approach depends on sampling and not on 100 per cent inspection or sorting.

The **Plan-Do-Check-Act** cycle was developed by Shewhart for process improvement. The construction sector is an industry where continuous process improvements are taking place. The industry uses the PDCA cycle to continually improve construction processes and thus prevent rejections and defects during the inspection processes. In the planning process, architectural drawings and structural drawings are prepared. After they are approved, materials are chosen, and specifications are finalised. In the next stage, the planned projects are implemented as per approved drawings and specifications. In the third stage, inspections are done to check for non-conformities to specifications and approved drawings. In case of non-conformances, corrective actions are taken to rectify defects and prevent non-occurrences. The PDCA cycle is implemented in the construction sector as a measure to continually improve performance.

The interesting fact about the PDCA cycle is that larger cycles can have smaller PDCA cycles within them. Moreover, there is no activity in production or construction that is not ideally supposed to go through a PDCA cycle.

2.3 W. EDWARDS DEMING

The quality movement is credited to its founder, W. Edwards Deming (1900–1993). He modified the PDCA (plan, do, check, act) cycle which was originally created by Walter A. Shewhart. He called it the PDSA cycle (plan, do, study, act). Conceptually, the PDSA cycle is an approach to solving problems. In Figure 2.1, the PDSA cycle is depicted.

The Deming cycle, commonly known as the PDSA cycle, recommends creating a plan of what has to be done, which is followed by carrying it out (performing what has been planned). The plan's execution results are examined in the third step. In this step, it is reviewed to see if the execution went perfectly according to the plan or whether there were some variations. The fourth and last phase involves actually identifying what occurred as planned and what did not, which allows the results to be verified. The process is then repeated with a new and improved

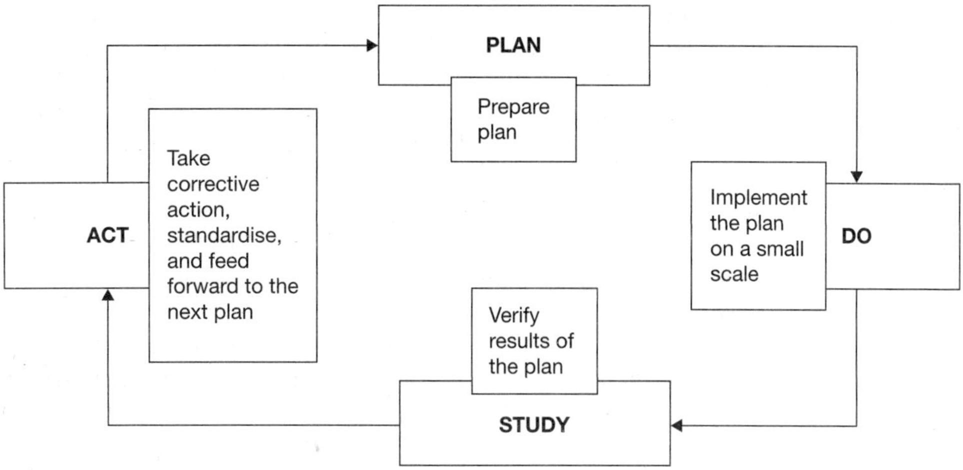

FIGURE 2.1 The PDSA cycle

plan developed using this knowledge. PDSA cycle is also used in the construction industry to improve the processes and standardise them for better results.

When a new technology or method is to be implemented in the construction sector, the PDSA cycle is usually followed. Initially, a plan has to be prepared for implementation, and then the plan will be executed. During its execution, it is further studied or checked to determine if it satisfies all the requirements. If the process is working as needed or produces the required results, it may be standardised. Otherwise, corrective actions are taken to rectify the problems. Once it is found to produce the needed results, standardisation of the processes can be done.

Over the decades, the construction industry has undergone a lot of changes. It has evolved to become a more industrialised and mechanised sector from a labour-intensive sector. Accordingly, construction technology has changed a lot. The adoption of these changes is possible by implementing the PDSA cycles.

Deming's 14 principles offer a management theory that can help organisations increase their quality, productivity, and competitiveness. Below is a concise summary of the 14 points that Deming made regarding achieving quality (Deming, 1986):

1. Maintain a constant focus on improving the products and services. Management must consistently show that it is dedicated to the stated aims and objectives. It is very important in the construction industry for the management to be dedicated to improving the quality of construction and to stick to the stated needs of the clients.
2. Everyone, even top management, must learn and implement the new mindset. The management needs to acknowledge the challenges of the new economic environment, comprehend their obligations, and take the lead in bringing about change.
3. Stop relying on inspection to attain quality. By integrating quality into the product from the start, the necessity for mass inspection can be eliminated. This is very significant in the construction industry as it is very difficult to rework and correct mistakes once they are discovered during the inspection process. Quality should be integrated right from the start of a project, as rework costs are quite high in the construction industry. This may be done by developing a project quality plan when a project is conceived.

4. Put a stop to the practice of contract awards determined only by cost. Choose to work with a single supplier to cut overall costs. In the construction industry, various studies have shown that most of the problems occur due to lowest price bidding. Alternate methods should be found that may consider the quality of construction and time taken for construction of previous projects by the contractor during the bidding process.
5. Each planning, production, and service procedure must be constantly and permanently improved. This should be applied in the construction industry as well. To use the knowledge of best practices from each project, new technologies, like blockchain and cloud data, must be utilised so that constant and continuous improvement is possible at each stage of the project.
6. Introduce on-the-job training at the institute level. Unlike other engineering sectors, the construction industry in India assigns highly significant tasks to newly graduated professionals. Hence, it is very important to equip the new graduates with sufficient knowledge by providing on-the-job training during the course of their professional education.
7. Establish and put leadership into practice. In the construction industry, personnel at each level should have sufficient leadership qualities as they might be required to make prompt decisions when contingencies occur.
8. Ensure that everyone can work productively for the firm by **eliminating fear** and fostering trust. The construction industry involves stakeholders from various sectors. It is required to inculcate trust among different stakeholders and provide a safe and healthy environment for everyone to work productively.
9. Remove obstacles between staff areas. Lack of coordination is often found to be the reason for rework in the construction industry. Hence, teamwork and collaboration are inevitable for the timely completion of the construction projects.
10. Eliminate target slogans and strongly urge the workforce to have higher productivity levels and zero defects.
11. Remove management's numerical targets as well as the workforce's numerical quotas.
12. a. Remove any barriers that prevent the employee from taking pride in their work. Supervisory responsibilities need to be reoriented from quantity to quality. Workmanship defects can be eliminated to an extent by allowing workers to take pride in their work.
    b. Eliminate obstacles that deny management and engineering staff their right to take pride in their work. This entails the elimination of management by objectives and the yearly or merit rating.
13. Provide everyone access to a comprehensive education and self-improvement programme. Training and development programs help in quality improvement in the construction industry. Workers and all other manpower resources must be trained and should be made aware of the consequences of poor quality.
14. Put all employees to work to complete the transformation. Everyone has to work on the transformation.

Deming asserts that loyal consumers, not just content customers, drive actual profits. Compared to businesses that simply rush products out of the door, those that cultivate loyal customers earn far more money. The idea that workers are to blame for American businesses' subpar quality and low productivity is false. The only group with the power to alter the system is the management (Stamatis, 1997). The findings of the study conducted by Tripathi & Jha (2018) indicate that the primary determinant of a construction organisation's performance is the competence of its top management.

2.4 JOSEPH M. JURAN

Joseph Juran stressed the significance of management's commitment to quality endeavour and active participation at all levels. In order to achieve ground-breaking achievements, Juran suggested project changes based on return on investment. The focus should not be just on the final customer but also on other internal and external clients. Quality is defined as 'fitness for use' (Juran & Godfrey, 1979).

In order to improve processes, Juran proposed using a quality trilogy (see Figure 2.2) and it consists of three components: quality planning, quality control, and quality improvement (Juran, 1986). The planning phase entails:

- Identifying the internal and external customers.
- Finding the demands of both external and internal customers.
- Developing deliverables that meet the customer's needs.
- Setting quality targets that satisfy supplier and customer expectations while maintaining the lowest possible total cost.
- Creating a procedure that can yield the attributes required for the final product.
- Demonstrating the processes' ability to achieve quality objectives while operating by demonstrating its ability to do so.

Credit: Skyline Graphics / stock.adobe.com

FIGURE 2.2 Juran's quality trilogy

The control part includes the following:

- Identifying the controllable variables and the methods for measuring them
- Deciding on the measuring units and the measurement.
- Specifying performance benchmarks.
- Assessing performance.

- Finding the differences from standards.
- Taking actions by considering differences.
- Acting in response to the variation between targeted performance and actual performance.

The improvement phase consists of the following:

- Show why improvements are needed.
- Specify the projects that need improvement.
- Plan to direct the projects.
- Prepare for diagnosing the causes of problems.
- Diagnose to identify the root reasons.
- Provide solutions.
- Show that the solutions work in real-world situations.
- Make provisions for maintaining control over the gains.

The procedure outlined above is repeated, beginning with the creation of a new goal.

As per Juran's quality trilogy, the first step is quality planning, which entails developing a procedure to achieve predetermined goals and do so under operational situations. Planning can be done for any process, including office processes for document production, engineering processes for product design, factory processes for manufacturing things, and service processes for handling customer demands.

After planning, the task is given to the operational forces. It is their duty to ensure that the process is operating as efficiently as possible. The errors in planning lead to wastage during operations. Management must make an effort to add a new managerial process—the quality improvement process—to the system of managerial duties. Quality improvement is an additional process to quality control, not a substitute for it.

Additionally, Juran is well-known for his 'triple role concept' (see Figure 2.3) of quality, which includes the supplier, processor, and customer. The 'triple role concept' states that every participant in the construction process, including those at the corporate, regional, branch, departmental, and individual levels, has three roles to play: supplier, processor, and customer. The architect/engineer, the owner, and the contractor are some of the project's stakeholders. The architect/engineer receives the owner's requirements and translates them into plans and specifications, which are then given to the contractor, who then turns them into a built facility. Each participant is a customer of someone and a supplier for another.

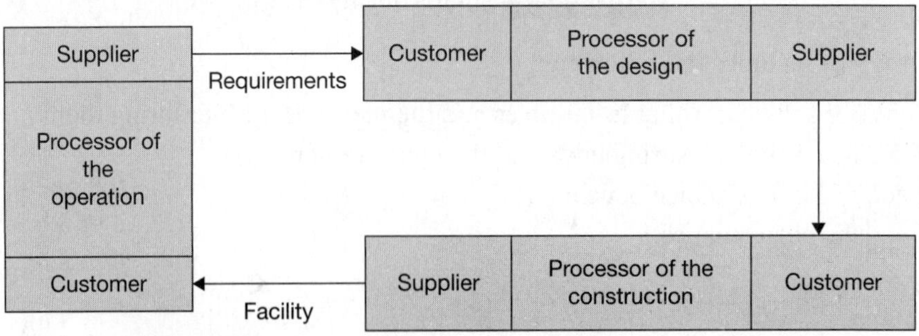

FIGURE 2.3 Triple role concept as applied in construction

According to the 'triple role' theory, the architect/engineer now fulfils the roles of a customer to the owner when he receives the owner's requirements, a processor when he analyses and designs the proposed facility, and a supplier when he gives the contractor the plan and specifications to make them a reality. When a contractor receives plans and specifications from an architect or engineer, he assumes the position of the customer, processes the construction, assumes the role of a processor, and then assumes the role of a supplier when he delivers the finished building to the owner. Better project quality would result from increased stakeholder satisfaction throughout the construction process.

2.5 KAORU ISHIKAWA

The concept of Quality Control Circles was developed by Kaoru Ishikawa (1915–1989). Quality Control Circles (QC) are helpful tools for resolving issues and raising quality. It consists of a group of volunteers (preferably 3 to 10) working in the same field who meet often to identify, select, and resolve problems. The person selected as leader would be taught about quality assurance and statistical methods like fishbone diagrams, Pareto charts, histograms, check sheets, and stratification principles. Leaders are responsible for teaching the members the knowledge they have acquired. QC Circle activities begin with the identification of problems, and then a problem is selected for studies. The group then analyses the selected problem based on data and facts. After discussion with group members, solutions are established, and the most feasible one will be presented to the management. After proper planning, the chosen solution will be implemented. The performance of QC Circle activities must be monitored and evaluated to track the benefits. This concept of empowering the workers also helps make them more responsible and productive. Ishikawa's QC Circle is a successful method for ensuring participation and sharing their expertise. Ishikawa lists the following ten ideas as helpful tips for leading QC Circle activities (Ishikawa, 1985):

1. Self-improvement
2. Voluntarism
3. Collective action
4. Participation of all staff
5. Application of QC methods
6. Activities that are closely related to the workplace
7. QC efforts must be active and ongoing.
8. Mutual improvement
9. Uniqueness and inventiveness
10. Understanding of quality, issues, and improvement.

Another very important contribution to the body of knowledge is Ishikawa's **fishbone diagram**. For process improvement, it is vital to take action whenever variation occurs. The fishbone diagram, otherwise known as the cause-and-effect diagram, is a simple tool to graphically display the knowledge a group has acquired regarding any given problem. Creating a fishbone diagram serves as a guide for discussion and brings in more ideas.

A fishbone diagram is used in the production industries to analyse the causes of problems. Further details are given in Chapter 10.

The companywide quality control movement that originated in Japan is also connected to Ishikawa. It is characterised by the participation of all employees from top management to lower-level employees from all divisions like engineering, design, manufacturing, sales, materials, accounting, human resources, and management departments. For problem-solving during the manufacturing process, material control, design control, policy making, and problem-solving at all functional levels and departments, statistical approaches and quality control concepts and procedures are utilised. The effects of companywide quality control, as claimed by Ishikawa, are listed below:

1. The consistency and quality of the product are increased. Defects are decreased.
2. Product reliability is increased.
3. Cost is decreased.
4. It is now feasible to create logical production schedules as production volume increases.
5. Rework and wasteful work are decreased.
6. The technique is developed and enhanced.
7. Inspection and testing costs are decreased.
8. Rationalisation of vendor-vendee contracts can be done.
9. A larger sales market is created.
10. Improvements are made in departmental relationships.
11. There is a reduction in false data and reports.
12. Conversations are conducted in a more open and democratic manner.
13. Meetings run more efficiently.
14. Equipment and facility installations and repairs are carried out more logically.
15. Relations between people are enhanced.

The company-wide quality control movement should also be implemented in the construction industry as the number of stakeholders involved in the construction industry is huge and of varying nature.

2.6 ARMAND V. FEIGENBAUM

Armand V. Feigenbaum (1920–2014) introduced the idea of **Total Quality Control**. *Total quality control is described by Feigenbaum as 'an efficient system for integrating the quality-development, quality-maintenance, and quality-improvement efforts of the various groups in an organisation so as to enable marketing, engineering, production, and service at the most economical levels which allow for full customer satisfaction'* (Feigenbaum, 1983). He said that quality is a fundamental way of managing an organisation. It should manage the business in terms of its customers. Total quality control helps improve basic business, management, and technical activities and thus achieves human resource effectiveness, lower cost, and customer satisfaction. The value of products and services must be improved with management innovation. He observed that in producing a new product, manufacturing was only one element in the long chain of activities. There are many other activities like design, raw materials procurement, storage, and delivery. Total quality control is achieved when all activities in a project play an equally important role in assuring the quality of a product. According to Feigenbaum, quality is everyone's duty. Quality control is to be implemented in a well-defined manner throughout the organisation as well as its supplier base. Feigenbaum presented detailed matrices showing the relationship between various functional areas and their appropriate quality control activity.

While working for General Electric Company, Armand V. Feigenbaum developed the concept of the cost of quality, based on dollars called 'quality cost'. Feigenbaum added up all the expenditures associated with creating the quality system, checking products, and paying for things that didn't live up to expectations. Dr Feigenbaum's quality cost idea has undergone numerous refinements to the point where it now offers an excellent management tool that can be utilised directly for quality improvement activities and for gauging the success of the entire quality system. Evaluation of the cost of quality is now an integral part of many quality standards today. The cost of quality, according to Feigenbaum, is the sum of prevention costs, appraisal costs, and failure costs.

Various experts have tried to determine the cost of quality in the construction industry. The cost of quality, which is the sum of appraisal cost, prevention cost, cost of internal failures, and cost of external failures, is quantified for various projects, and it has been found that a significant amount is lost in a project due to poor quality. This has led to higher investments in preventive and appraisal techniques so that failure costs can be reduced.

Feigenbaum is famous for the concept of the '**hidden plant**.' It states that in all factories, around 40 per cent of the capacity of the plant is wasted because of not doing things correctly the first time and that there exists a hidden plant within a factory that is into correcting these mistakes.

The nine M's, according to Feigenbaum, which affect the product and service quality are (Feigenbaum, 1983):

1. **Market:** Customers are looking for more products, and in response, the expanding market is providing them with more and better options. As a result, markets are expanding in size and diversifying further in terms of the goods and services they offer. Markets are expanding globally for a range of enterprises. As a result, companies need to be incredibly adaptable and quick to shift course.
2. **Money:** Due to increased competitiveness, it has become necessary to invest heavily in new procedures and equipment. Since the increased plant investment needs to be paid back through higher productivity, any sizable production losses from scrap and rework are now more critical. Costs for quality maintenance and enhancement have risen to previously unprecedented levels. Managers are paying close attention to the quality-cost sectors since they are one of the "soft spots" where operating costs and losses may be lowered to boost profits.
3. **Management:** The strain on management has increased as a result of the distribution of quality responsibility among several specialised groups, especially in light of the increased difficulty in determining who should be held accountable for resolving deviations from quality standards.
4. **Men:** Due to the rapid growth of technology and the rise of new businesses like electronics and computers, there is a great demand for competent workers. This situation has created a demand for a systems engineer who can integrate all these domains

of knowledge to design, create, and oversee several systems that would guarantee a desired result. Modern management has shifted its attention to the diverse components of business operating systems.

5. **Motivation:** The difficulty of introducing a high-quality product to the market has made each employee's quality contribution more significant. According to the human motivation study, employees require more than just monetary remuneration. They also require validation that they are making a meaningful contribution to the organisation's goals and that their work is appreciated. There is now a greater than ever need for high-quality education and more quality-conscious communication.
6. **Materials:** Engineers are working on exotic metals and alloys for unique applications to overcome constraints like high production costs and high-quality requirements. Consequently, there is a greater variety of materials available and stricter material requirements. There is a need to make measurements quickly, precisely, and conduct chemical and physical tests, as necessary.
7. **Machines and mechanisation:** In extremely competitive markets, businesses have been forced to use manufacturing equipment that is always becoming more sophisticated and dependent on the quality of the materials provided to it in order to save costs and boost output in order to satisfy consumers.
8. **Modern information methods:** The rapid advancement of computer technology has made it possible to gather, store, retrieve, and manipulate information on a scale that was previously unimaginable. Management now has access to more relevant, accurate, timely, and predictive data to help them make decisions that will impact the future of the firm.
9. **Mounting product requirements:** Product dependability and safety have become increasingly important due to increased product complexity and performance standards. Constant attention is needed to ensure that no known or unknown impacts reduce the reliability of components or systems during the process.

All of these factors are significant in improving the quality of the construction sector, too. Summarising the need for nine Ms in the construction industry as follows: With the expanding **market**, more options are available for improving the quality of construction. More **money** is required to invest in emerging technologies like automating and mechanising processes. **Management** is responsible for fulfilling the needs of the customers by sticking to the specifications. They have to assign tasks to all stakeholders accordingly and oversee that construction works do not depart from the required standards. The improvement in technologies has also led to the need for specialised **men** in the construction industry. **Motivation** and positive recognition of all personnel are required for the retention of employees in an organisation. The construction industry is a field where the experience and knowledge of workers are very important for good quality work. The problem with this industry is that there are not many provisions for knowledge backup and sharing due to the transient nature of the work. So, it is important that the good employees are retained. So, as per human motivational theories, they are to be retained not just with money but also with recognition and motivation.

In this era where sustainability has great significance, researchers are trying to find new **materials** for construction that are less polluting and more sustainable in nature. Accordingly, there is a need for new devices for its measurement and testing. Most countries are now switching their construction methodologies to **mechanised** and industrialised ones as it reduces the variations in constructed structures and increases the speed of construction. In the long run, it will prove to be cost-effective. The improvements in **modern information technologies** like blockchain and cloud computing are making it possible to collect, store, retrieve, and manipulate data in an unimaginable way. All these help management reduce defects and problems and make wise decisions for the growth of an organisation. Finally, there is a **mounting product requirement** of safety and reliability. The industry's growing complexity emphasises the need for safety and structural integrity.

2.7 GENICHI TAGUCHI

Genichi Taguchi (1924–2012) is known for his contributions to developing methods to enhance quality and reduce costs, which are known as the '**Taguchi Methods**.' The quality engineering aspects of Taguchi methods include (Oakland, 2014):

2.7.1 Total Loss Function

According to quality engineering, a product's downstream quality issues are signs of its functional instability (lack of robustness). 'Robustness is defined as the ability of a product or process to function consistently as the surrounding controllable or uncontrollable factors vary (Chowdhury & Taguchi, 2016)'. These issues are estimated by the total quality loss after shipping the product from the manufacturing plant. A product's overall quality loss is calculated as the sum of all financial losses and environmental impacts it causes over the course of its whole life. The quality loss function of a product is:

'Quality loss = Cost due to functional variation + operating cost
+ cost due to environmental factors' (Taguchi, 1995).

According to Taguchi, a product's quality can be evaluated by calculating the amount of loss it does to society from the moment it is shipped. When the quality is poor, the loss will be larger. Taguchi developed a quadratic loss function (QLF) to fit the quality loss cost considering the cost of a product that is within the limits of specifications. It is a novel approach to outlining investments in initiatives that aim to increase quality. According to Taguchi, deviations from the intended value of a process or product parameter result in losses for the client. Due to repair and rework, there may be a variety of losses, ranging from the inconvenience to the actual financial loss, which can result in a loss of goodwill and, ultimately, market share. The higher the variation from the target, the higher the loss. Taguchi's focus was on bringing down variations in products so that consistency and best-quality performance could be achieved.

Taguchi suggested a stricter interpretation of characteristic acceptability, stating that a higher quality measurement is one that will provide the least amount of variation from the goal value and that any departure from a characteristic's target value results in a loss. When the measurement of the characteristic equals the targeted value, there is no loss. The quadratic loss function is used in robust engineering to establish a product's specification limits. The QLF is applicable in the following three scenarios (Taguchi & Jugulam, 2002):

1. Nominal-the-best characteristic
2. Larger-the-better characteristic
3. Smaller-the-better characteristic

2.7.1.1 QLF: Nominal-the-best Characteristic

The equation for loss function for this scenario can be obtained using the following equation:

$$L(y) = \frac{A}{\Delta^2}\sigma^2 \tag{1}$$

where

$L(y)$ represents the quality level or the loss due to being farther from the target value m.

Δ is the tolerance

A is the loss due to a product falling below the standard

σ^2 is the average of square of the deviation from the target.

$$\sigma^2 = \frac{1}{n}\left[(y_1 - m)^2 + (y_2 - m)^2 + \ldots + (y_n - m)^2\right] \tag{2}$$

m is the target value specified in the document

$y_1, y_2, \ldots, y_n$ are the observed or obtained values of a process or product parameter.

Considering a single data, the quality loss is calculated as

$$L(y) = \frac{A}{\Delta^2}(y - m)^2 \tag{3}$$

$\frac{A}{\Delta^2}$ is referred to as the average loss coefficient, k. Hence, k is dependent on the loss in terms of cost and the tolerance allowed (width of specification limit).

For example, a company produces metallic washers whose target thickness is 10 mm. The accepted tolerance limit is ± 0.05 mm. Let us apply the Taguchi loss function to determine the cost of poor quality. The washer cost is ₹0.50 per piece. It is to be rejected when the thickness exceeds 10.05 mm and when the thickness is less than 9.95 mm.

In this case, A = ₹0.50, m = 10 mm and Δ = 0.05 mm

$$k = \frac{A}{\Delta^2} = \frac{0.5}{0.05^2} = 200$$

Now, we know that the loss coefficient is equal to 200. So, let us calculate the loss function due to variations from the target. When the thickness is 10.01 mm, the loss function can be calculated as

$$L(y) = 200 \times (10.01 - 10)^2 = 0.02$$

Hence, $L(y) = 0.02$.

When $y = 10.07$, $L(y) = 200 \times (10.07 - 10)^2 = 0.98$

Figure 2.4 shows the loss function for the variations from the target, and this is an example of the nominal-the-best characteristic. In this case, there is an increase in loss when the quality characteristic deviates from the target in both directions.

Consider another example to understand how the calculation will be done when a set of data is available. Steel sheets whose price is ₹100 have a dimensional tolerance of 1.00 mm. The difference between the measured thickness and the target value for sheets produced in a batch are 0.2, 0.6, –0.1, 0, –0.5, 0.8, 0.1, 0.3, 0.1, and –0.3. Let us compute the quality level or the loss due to variations.

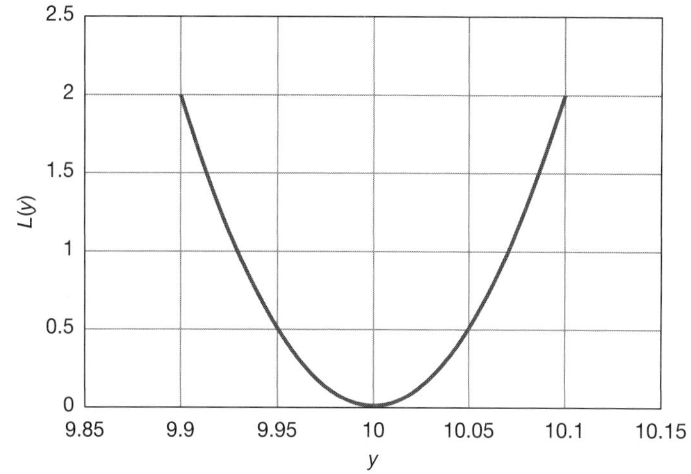

FIGURE 2.4 Nominal-the-best quadratic loss function

$$\sigma^2 = \frac{1}{n}\left[(y_1 - m)^2 + (y_2 - m)^2 + ... + (y_n - m)^2\right]$$

$$\sigma^2 = \frac{1}{10}\left[(0.2)^2 + (0.6)^2 + ... + (-0.3)^2\right] = 0.15$$

$$L(y) = \frac{A}{\Delta^2}\sigma^2 = \frac{100}{1} \times 0.15 = 15$$

Thus, the loss due to a variation from the target for the given values is ₹15.

2.7.1.2 QLF: Smaller the Better

Suppose the target is specified to be not more than a particular value; then it represents the case of smaller-the-better. The loss function equation for this scenario is given by equation.

$$L(y) = \frac{A}{\Delta^2}\sigma^2 \tag{4}$$

$$\sigma^2 = \frac{1}{n}\left[y_1^2 + y_2^2 + ... + y_n^2\right] \tag{5}$$

Let us consider the following example. Suppose the dimensional tolerance of roundness of the steel rod is specified to be less than 6 μm. It costs ₹5.00 if the product does not conform to the specifications. The measured values for a set of data in μm are 2, 0, 4, 3, 2, 1, 5, 6, 3, and 5.

Here, A = ₹5.00, and $\Delta = 6$ μm

$$\sigma^2 = \frac{1}{10}\left[2^2 + 0^2 + ... + 5^2\right] = 12.9\ \mu\text{m}$$

$$L(y) = \frac{A}{\Delta^2}\sigma^2 = \frac{5}{6^2} \times 12.9 = ₹1.80$$

Hence, the loss function is calculated as ₹1.80.

The graphical representation of the loss function for the variations from the target in the case of smaller the better is given in Figure 2.5.

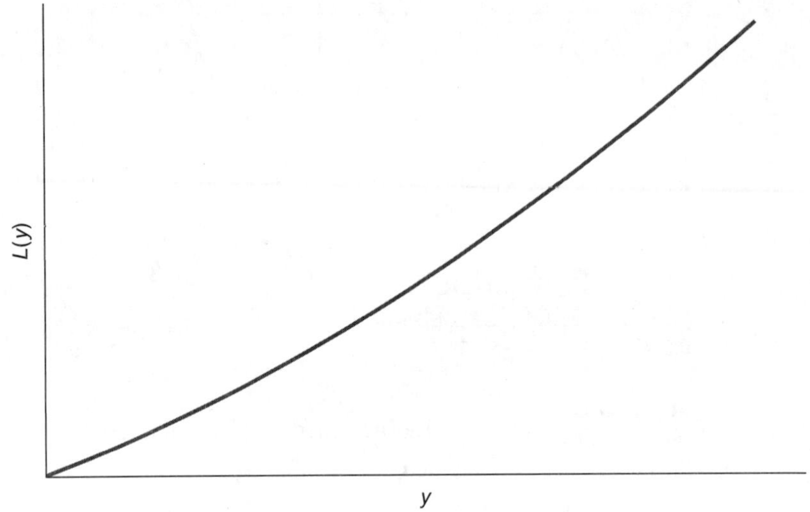

FIGURE 2.5 Smaller-the-better quadratic loss function

2.7.1.3 QLF: Higher the Better

In cases when the target is specified to be not less than a particular value, then it is called the higher-the-better loss function. The loss function equation is given by equation 6.

$$L(y) = A \cdot \Delta^2 \cdot \sigma^2 \tag{6}$$

$$\sigma^2 = \frac{1}{n}\left[\frac{1}{y_1^2} + \frac{1}{y_2^2} + \ldots + \frac{1}{y_n^2}\right] \tag{7}$$

For example, elongation is a critical quality characteristic for reinforcement bars. The lower tolerance limit for elongation of Fe 500 bar is 12 percent. The loss incurred for discarding the nonconforming material is ₹60 per kg. The elongation measured for ten specimens: 13%, 14%, 12%, 15%, 18%, 20%, 22%, 17%, 13%, and 14%.

Here, $A = ₹60.00$, and $\Delta = 12\ \%$

$$\sigma^2 = \frac{1}{n}\left[\frac{1}{y_1^2} + \frac{1}{y_2^2} + \ldots + \frac{1}{y_n^2}\right] = \frac{1}{10}\left[\frac{1}{13^2} + \frac{1}{14^2} + \ldots + \frac{1}{14^2}\right] = 0.0044$$

$$L(y) = A \cdot \Delta^2 \cdot \sigma^2 = 60 \times 12^2 \times 0.0044 = ₹38.48$$

Thus, the loss function for the given data is ₹38.48.

The graphical representation for quadratic loss function of higher the better scenario is shown in Figure 2.6.

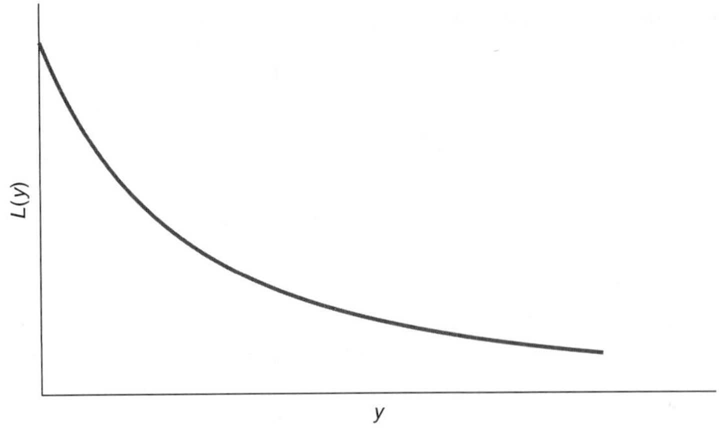

FIGURE 2.6 Higher-the-better quadratic loss function

2.7.2 Design of Products, Services, and Processes

Taguchi described control in two different ways: offline and online quality control methods. Quality control in this context includes control in quality planning, analysis, and improvement. Techniques for quality control online apply technology tools to manage quality and costs when producing goods or services, whereas offline techniques do so when designing items and processes.

2.7.3 Reduction of Variation

Taguchi introduced the three-step methodology to improve the functional robustness of a product or process technology, which is as follows (Taguchi, 1995):

(a) **System design**—choosing new technological concepts or systems;

(b) **Parameter design**—choosing the proper control factor settings to maximise the functional resilience of the recently chosen technology systems or concepts;

(c) **Tolerance design**—choosing the right tolerance settings while taking total cost, environmental effects, production capacity, etc.

2.7.4 Statistically Planned Experiments

In order to determine the settings of the product and process characteristics that will limit variance in performance, Taguchi advocated the use of statistically planned experiments. Design parameters and sources of 'noise' are the two categories impacting performance. Design parameters are those parameters that specify the requirements for the process or product. All the factors that lead to performance characteristics deviating from the intended values are considered sources of noise. Recognising the important noise components that are the main source of unpredictability is crucial. In order to minimise the impact on performance, Taguchi insisted on incorporating them into the experiments. For a constructed facility, the various sources of noise may be as follows (Chowdhury & Taguchi, 2016):

- **The environment in which it has been put to use:** The buildings will show variations according to the environment in which it is situated. For example, the metallic parts of a building located in a coastal region start to corrode much earlier than the ones away from the coastal region.
- **Ageing:** As the constructed facility ages, it starts to show more signs of deterioration and wear and tear.
- **Construction variation:** There will be differences in performance according to the variation in construction.
- **Surrounding subsystems:** The surrounding subsystems have an impact on the constructed facilities. The presence of a water body very close to the constructed facility will have some impact on it especially when there are frequent fluctuations in the water level.
- **Misuse:** The destructive actions by antisocial elements may also lead to the deterioration of buildings.

2.8 PHILIP CROSBY

'Do it right the first time' and 'zero defects' are two of Philip Crosby's most famous ideas. Philip Crosby (1926–2001) held the opinion that it is less expensive to do something correctly the first time than to find and fix a non-conformity. Quality, according to him, is the ability of a company to produce its goods in accordance with the standards that it has set for itself based on the needs of its customers. In every situation, he placed emphasis on prevention management.

Doing things rightly the first time is very significant in the construction industry as the rework costs are generally too high. When defects occur, it requires a lot of money to rectify and eliminate defects, and it also leads to higher costs of internal failures and external failures. The zero defects concept must be incorporated in all phases of construction, starting from translating client requirements to proper specifications and producing the required deliverables.

Philip Crosby lists the following as the **top five absolutes** for quality management (Crosby, 2005):

- 'Quality means conformance, not elegance.
- There is no such thing as a quality problem.
- There is no such thing as the economics of quality; it is always cheaper to do the job right the first time.
- The only performance standard is zero defects.
- The only performance measurement is the cost of quality.'

Crosby prescribed the '**Quality Vaccine**,' which is a medicine to prevent poor quality. Determination, education, and implementation are the actions required from management to continually administer the vaccine. The ingredients needed to prepare the vaccine are (Crosby, 1984):

- **Integrity:** Dedication from the entire team of employees from top to bottom to make the customer satisfied by giving them what they expect.
- **Systems:** Existence of appropriate systems for measuring conformance to requirements, providing quality education, review of performance of processes, corrective actions for improvement, defect prevention and thus customer satisfaction.
- **Communication:** It is necessary to keep all personnel informed of the status of quality improvement and achievement actions. Each employee should communicate with the top management on all matters related to error, waste, opportunity, or any other concerns they have.
- **Operations:** Support and training to suppliers to ensure that products are dependable and delivered on time. Examining and qualifying procedures, products, and systems prior to implementation and modifying them when there are opportunities for improvement.
- **Policies:** Quality policies must be clear. External communication and advertisements must be in compliance with the process capability.

Crosby also developed a Quality Management Maturity Grid (QMMG) (Crosby, 1979). This paradigm outlines the five phases of organisational maturity: ambiguity, awakening, enlightenment, wisdom, and certainty. This model identifies six characteristics of an organisation that can be measured: understanding and attitude of management, organisational quality status, problem-solving, cost of quality in terms of percentage of sales, quality improvement initiatives, and summation of corporate quality posture. QMMG is used as a quality improvement tool. It serves to assess the degree of maturity of the various quality management processes in an organisation, as well as how well they have been incorporated into the organisation's culture and shows the areas where improvement is required. The use of this model led to a decline in the cost of quality from 25 % to 2.5 %.

2.8.1 The Fourteen Steps to Quality Improvement

The fourteen steps advocated by Crosby for improving quality are given below (Crosby, 1979):

1. **Management Commitment:** Management has to participate wholeheartedly in quality management for the best results.
2. **Quality Improvement Team:** Quality improvement teams are to be formed from across organisational boundaries and give orientation to team members regarding the content and purpose of the program.
3. **Quality Measurement:** Establish procedures to measure and record quality and correct it whenever required so as to track improvement.
4. **Cost of Quality (CoQ) Evaluation:** Measure CoQ so that it will indicate corrective actions that would be profitable to the organisation.
5. **Quality Awareness:** Increase the quality awareness among employees, service, and administrative staff by giving training so that it will assist in the process of change.
6. **Corrective Action:** Encouraging people to identify problems and opportunities and communicate them to higher levels so that they can be corrected at the beginning.

7. **For the Zero Defects Program, create an Ad Hoc Committee:** Select an ad hoc committee to implement the zero-defect program and transmit the idea of doing it right the first time to all members.
8. **Supervisor Training:** Formal orientation is to be given to all levels of management before the implementation of the program.
9. **Day for Zero Defects:** Conduct a Zero Defects Day to emphasise the concept, and the supervisors should explain the significance to its people to reaffirm it in their minds.
10. **Goal Setting:** Motivate employees to establish goals and focus on achieving them as a team.
11. **Removal of Error Cause:** Encourage employees to disclose the problems they face in meeting their objectives. This enables trust to be built among employees so that their problems will be heard and solved.
12. **Recognition:** Recognise and appreciate the outstanding performance of employees.
13. **Quality Councils:** Establish quality councils comprising quality professionals and team chairpersons and communicate regularly to discuss upgrading and improving quality programs.
14. **Do it Over Again:** Repeat programmes like Zero Defect Day and frequent training so as to keep the quality concepts afresh in the minds of employees.

2.8.2 Application of Crosby's Quality Improvement Steps in Construction Industry

The above fourteen steps of quality management are highly applicable in the construction industry. The success of a construction organisation is possible only with management commitment. Since the construction participants are from diverse sectors, quality teams are to be formed of members from each sector. The team members are to be given proper orientation regarding the vision and mission of the organisation. It is very important in the construction sector to devise procedures for inspection, quality measurement and quality tracking. Measuring the cost of quality helps improve quality by pointing out the areas that require additional quality assurance and control. Whenever a problem is encountered, determine the actions that would be profitable for the organisation. Conducting frequent quality awareness training for all employees, administrative staff, and others aids in creating awareness of the new processes and the significance of quality. Management has to encourage the employees to detect defects and communicate them to higher levels in order to rectify them. Doing this will help them build trust that management will support them in times of need. When mistakes are rectified as soon as possible, it will be better; otherwise, it can lead to a higher cost of quality. The significance of zero defects and doing it right the first time has to be thoroughly taught to the employees. Sufficient training has to be given to supervisors at all levels of management before starting new projects. Employee motivation and recognition are very important in producing a defect-free construction.

The 14-step strategy by Crosby focuses on long-term employee engagement rather than short-term incentive techniques to help quality managers get their organisations on track. There appear to be three essential beliefs in Crosby's quality perspective: quantification of quality, leadership by management, and prevention instead of cure.

2.9 DAVID A. GARVIN

David A. Garvin (1952–2017) identified eight attributes that define quality (Garvin, 1984). These dimensions make a product or service valuable and outstanding from its competitors in the marketplace.

1. **Performance** → the product's main functional properties.
2. **Features** → the ancillary qualities that support a product's fundamental functionality.
3. **Reliability** → the likelihood that a product may fail within a certain time frame.
4. **Conformance** → the degree to which a product matches the predefined standards in its design and operational characteristics.
5. **Durability** → implies the duration of use that can be made before the physical deterioration of a product.
6. **Serviceability** → the speed and competence of repair.
7. **Aesthetics** → these are the looks, sound, smell, or taste of a product, which is dependent on personal judgment and preferences.
8. **Perceived quality** → the customers' judgment about a product, which may be based on their experience compared to their needs and expectations.

These dimensions are key to organisations using quality as a competitive tool. Organisations must choose the dimensions of quality to focus on and work on them to improve market share and gain profits at lower costs.

Different researchers gave different definitions for quality based on how it applied to their fields (philosophy, economics, marketing, and operations management). Garvin identified five major approaches to the definition of quality given by various researchers. They are as follows:

1. Transcendent approach
2. Product-based approach
3. User-based approach
4. Manufacturing-based approach
5. Value-based approach

Each of them has different advantages. While philosophy focused on the definitional issue, economics gave importance to profit maximisation and market equilibrium. Operations management was concerned with technical procedures and factory control, whereas marketing was focused on the factors that influence consumer behaviour and customer satisfaction. By adopting these approaches, it is possible to achieve cost savings, market share, and improvements in profits.

All the quality dimensions defined by Garvin are applicable in construction works, too. The performance dimension of the quality is concerned with the degree to which client specifications and requirements are met and whether the constructed facility meets the functional requirements. For example, a residential building performs the function of providing space for healthy and safe living. Features refer to the additional facilities that may be available in a constructed facility. Ample space, energy-efficient construction, good ventilation, and proper daylight may be considered as features that lead to customer delight. The third dimension of quality is reliability, which refers to the likelihood of the constructed facility serving the purpose for the designated life. Basically, it indicates the absence of defects for a specific period. Conformance refers to compliance with drawings and specifications as demanded by the clients. The buildings should be constructed in conformance with the standards and regulations. The durability aspect refers to the useful life period of the building. When it starts showing signs of deterioration or defects, the building should be serviceable. The defects in the building during its designed life period should be repairable and should not affect the safety and health of the occupants. Aesthetics refers to the appearance of the building. It includes arrangements of rooms, utilisation of space, and external and internal finishing of the building. The last dimension is perceived quality. It refers to how the customer perceives the constructed facility. Even if the construction is as per the client's requirements, how well it can satisfy the client is referred to as perceived quality. This is usually obtained from customer feedback.

2.10 PRASANTA CHANDRA MAHALANOBIS

Professor P. C. Mahalanobis is popularly known as the father of statistics in India. His contributions to the development of statistics include founding the Indian Statistical Institute, the Central Statistical Organisation, and the National Sample Survey. He was the President of the Mathematics and Statistics section of the Indian Science Congress. Mahalanobis gave importance to both theory and application of statistics in different scientific areas. He focussed on the application of statistics in various sectors like education, medicine, anthropometry, agriculture, meteorology, and, most importantly, the economic development of the nation. Most of his studies were connected to real-life problems related to the social, cultural, scientific, and economic development of society.

The sampling theory developed by Mahalanobis was based on the need to conduct large-scale sample surveys. He believed that the best way to capture the information about the society and the economy was through random sampling. Various concepts in sampling, such as pilot survey, the inter-penetrating network of sub-samples, cost function, optimum design of surveys, and variance function, were developed by Mahalanobis. His keen interest in anthropology led to the innovation of D^2 statistics in multivariate analysis. D^2 statistic was named the Mahalanobis Distance by Sir Ronald Aylmer Fisher (Rudra, 1996).

It was Mahalanobis who first tabulated the 5 and 1 per cent points of the distribution of the variance ratio. Other tables published by him in the periodical named *Sankhya* were 'Tables for L-tests' and 'Tables for Random Samples from a Normal Population'. Sankhya: The Indian Journal of Statistics was launched by Mahalanobis to overcome the prejudice faced by Indians (Rudra, 1996). This further promoted extensive research on statistics in India. Mahalanobis considered statistics a technology as it uses scientific knowledge to fulfil specific needs. Mahalanobis asserted that clarity about the purpose of statistics in a particular situation enables the construction of suitable concepts, definitions and standards. By beginning to collect and utilise information, it becomes easier to make improvements in methods of data collection and effectively utilise the information.

The extensive statistical research undertaken by Mahalanobis during the floods in 1922 and 1926 in North Bengal and Orissa, respectively, by studying the rainfall and flood data of over sixty years helped in supplying basic and relevant information for the construction of irrigation projects in Damodar Valley and Hirakud (Mahalanobis A. , 1983).

The statistical developments under Mahalanobis had a great impact on India's economic development. He used statistics and operational research to plan for long-term economic development. Surveys were conducted to collect data, and various programmes and policies were designed based on their analysis. During the programme execution, progress was measured, and the results were assessed to verify that they were as per the expectations (Mahalanobis, 1986). He was involved in the national development planning from the initial phase. He emphasised working at full capacity to increase production in small and large-scale industries. Mahalanobis was the principal architect in the framing of the Second Five-Year Plan. He used simple mathematical models to detect the problems related to planning (Mahalanobis, 1985). He was the first to bring quality control to India (Rudra, 1996). He wrote to the Government in 1942 about the advantages of implementing Statistical Quality Control in industries after his meeting with Walter Shewhart (Mahalanobis, 1983). Training in statistical quality control was arranged at the Indian Statistical Institute during 1945–1946 for the first time in India. Shewhart was invited to India in 1947 to attend a conference on standardisation and quality control, where he gave lectures on quality control, design and specifications, and inspection. Slowly, quality control started to be implemented in the Indian industries by 1953 under the guidance of the Indian Statistical Institute.

2.11 MAJOR GENERAL HARKIRAT SINGH

In the Indian context, Harkirat Singh, Major General and former E-in-C in the Indian army, 1960–65, was an early promoter of quality management, and strongly advanced quality practices in India in civil engineering. He was a King Commissioned Indian Officer who earned a Tripos in Mechanical Sciences from Cambridge University, in 1933. As Advisor (Construction, Urban Planning, and Water Supply) in the Planning Commission, 1965–68, he was the author of *Report on Economies in Construction Costs,* published by the Planning Commission in March 1968, which advanced construction management, construction planning, and quality control, especially in light of the 4th Five-Year Plan. For the preparation of this report, Major General Harkirat Singh led a high-level technical panel of Senior Chief Engineers of state governments, Chairmen of public sector organisations, Directors of IITs and Central Research Institutes, Vice-Chancellors, Presidents of professional societies, and Chairmen of relevant private sector corporations who represented the top talent in the science, practice and business of construction in the country. The full list of the panellists is given in the above-cited reference (Planning Commission, 1968).

The preface of the above report carried the following incentive in regard to construction, which carry meaning even today after 56 years, and are the motivation for new research even today:

> 'Some of the prevailing methods are outmoded, some designs are overburdened with safety factors and there are other design criteria which in the light of newer techniques and methodologies could be rationalised. There is scope for higher productivity in the manufacture of building materials and also for the introduction and promotion of some new materials. There is also considerable room for improvement in the organisational and administrative side dealing with the whole

> field of construction finance, credit systems, organisation and administrative procedures of public works departments, types of contracts and methods of accounting and payment'.

The aim of that panel and report was to realise savings in construction costs for the Fourth five-year plan to relieve the strain on the nation's resources and thereby release funds for large development projects. It was realised then that 50% of the total outlay of all five-year plans was given to construction projects that included infrastructure development and buildings. Hence, the Planning Commission decided after the Third Five-year Plan that the 'whole gamut of construction operations, including but not limited to administrative, organisational, financial, and technical aspects be studied in depth'. This is when the high-level panel was appointed in 1965 which led to the above-cited report in 1968 after three years of study and investigation. It should be noted that this panel recruited the most informed technocrats of the time under the singular leadership of Major General Harkirat Singh.

To improve the quality of constructed work in India, it was further realised in the Planning Commission that …("National Building Code", 1970)

> '…[b]uilding handbooks of public works departments and other agencies, building bylaws and regulations of municipal bodies which largely regulate the building activity in the country wherever they exist, were outdated. They did not cater to the use of new building materials and the latest developments in building designs and construction techniques. It also became clear that these codes and bylaws lacked uniformity and they were more often than not 'specification oriented' and not 'performance oriented'.'

Thus, the studies in the Planning Commission resulted in a top-level recommendation that …

> 'National Building Code be prepared to unify the building regulations throughout the country for use by government departments, municipal bodies and other construction agencies. The Indian standards institution was entrusted by the Planning Commission with the preparation of the national building code. This task was readily accepted by the Indian standards institution and a guiding committee for the preparation of the code with Major General Harkirat Singh as chairman was set up by the civil engineering division council of ISI in 1967. This committee, in turn, set up 18 specialist panels to prepare the various parts of the code. The specialist panels completed their work by the end of 1969 and in February 1970, a final draft of the code was approved by the guiding committee for publication.'

This national effort and report galvanised the country into advancing the cause of a unified National Building Code (NBC), such that the first NBC was released in 1970 under the aegis of the Indian Standards Institution (ISI). For his services to ISI and the nation, Major General Harkirat Singh was awarded the K S Moudgill Prize in 1971 for the pioneering work of developing the National Building Code. Thereafter, the Guiding Committee of ISI, again under the chairmanship of Major General Harkirat Singh, directly undertook the first revision of the NBC, which was released in 1983, at which time many diverse ISI codes of India in civil engineering were brought under the umbrella of the NBC. By all accounts, the development of the NBC was a monumental work.

Major General Harkirat Singh continued his work for improving the quality of construction in India for the Fifth Five-Year Plan through the Ministry of Science and Technology ('Handbook,' 1982):

> 'In 1972, the Department of Science and Technology set up an expert group on housing and construction technology under the chairmanship of Major General Harkirat Singh. This group carried out in depth studies in various areas of civil engineering and construction practices. During the preparation of the fifth five-year plan in 1975, the group was assigned the task of producing a science and technology plan for research, development and extension work in the sector of housing and construction technology. One of the items of this plan was the production of design handbooks, explanatory handbooks and design aids based on the National Building Code and various Indian standards and other activities in the promotion of the National Building Code. The expert group gave high priority to this item and on the recommendation of the Department of Science and Technology the Planning Commission approved the following projects which were assigned to the Indian Standards Institution:
>
> a) development program on code implementation for building and civil engineering construction, and
>
> b) typification for industrial buildings.
>
> A Special Committee for Implementation of Science and Technology Projects (SCIP) consisting of experts connected with different aspects was set up in 1974 to advise the ISI Directorate General for identifying and guiding the development of the work done under the chairmanship of Major General Harkirat Singh. The committee identified subjects for several explanatory handbooks covering appropriate Indian standards / codes / specifications which included the following:
>
> - 'Functional requirements of buildings
> - Functional requirements of industrial buildings
> - Summaries of Indian standards for building materials
> - Building construction practices
> - Foundations of buildings
> - Explanatory handbook on codes for earthquake engineering
> - Design aids for reinforced concrete to IS 456-1978
> - Explanatory handbook on masonry code
> - Explanatory handbook on Indian standard code for plain and reinforced concrete IS 456-1978
> - Handbook on concrete mixes
> - Concrete reinforcement detailing
> - Formwork
> - Timber engineering

- Steel code IS 800
- Causes and prevention of cracks in buildings
- Plumbing services
- Loading code
- Fire safety
- Prefabrication
- Tall buildings
- Design of industrial steel structures
- Inspection of different items of building work
- Bulk storage structures and steel
- Liquid retaining structures'

The Handbook on Concrete Mixes was planned for being 'useful to designers of concrete structures, field engineers, quality control engineers and laboratories engaged in design, research and testing of concrete mixes.'

To underscore the importance of these handbooks and efforts, it must be noted that the effort and resources of the entire country, represented by top experts at high levels were put into the preparation of these handbooks and the National Building Code. Thus, all major central civil engineering research, design, and construction departments; major private design consultants; and major construction companies participated in the creation and adoption of the NBC. As such, the National Building Code was a unified effort by all of India in the interests of advancing quality control and standardisation in India.

Speaking at the 7th Major General Harkirat Singh Memorial Lecture at the Institution of Engineers, Delhi State Centre, 1991, Lt General (retd.) Tilak Nanda, former Master General Ordnance (MGO), lamented the issue of quality in Indian construction and recognised the intense devotion of Major General Harkirat Singh to standards, codes, and ethics (Nanda, 1991).

Major General Harkirat Singh created the Institute of Work Study in the Army Corps' of Engineers and oversaw the structuring and expansion of the Border Roads Organisation in the aftermath of the Sino-Indian Conflict, an effort that is paying off now, 64 years later. He was a visionary, who, as Founding Chairman, Bharat Earth Movers Ltd, organised one of the first public sector undertakings to create an R&D wing in the undertaking. While serving as Chairman, Central Roads Research Institute (CRRI), he experimented with the first stretches of concrete road on the Faridabad Highway.

More importantly, he designed and constructed housing in WWII for Gen William Slim's army on the Burma border in a short time using prefabricated techniques at a time when the concept of prefabrication was just emerging, thus enabling the Allied forces to fight the Japanese successfully and defeat them in Imphal. It was his planning and vision that enabled the Leh airfield to be constructed in only the summer of 1963 after the 1962 conflict, when such speed of work may well be impossible even today. Earlier, he commenced the construction of Cochin Naval Base in 1948. He had much too many construction projects to his credit, much too many to recount here, and was involved in more construction around the country, with all due respect, than the respectable M. Visvesaraya, often known as one of the foremost nation-builders, who was focused only in Mysore.

Major General Harkirat Singh is revered as a legendary General and 'Father' of the Indian Army Corps of Engineers, being the first Indian E-in-C of the Corps. He was also the first permanent Indian Director of the Corps of Electrical and Mechanical Engineers (EME), 1957–60. Thus, he is the only person in the entire army to have been the head of two technical arms – the Corps of EME and the Corps of Engineers. He was also the Commandant of the College of Military Engineering (CME), Kirkee, 1954–56. At a time when India was emerging from independence, Major General Harkirat Singh was a tall figure and pioneer in matters of quality and technological advancement. He served twice as the President of Institution of Engineers (India), 1960–62[1], and then as President of the Association of Consulting Engineers (India) (1976–83), recognised nationally for his acumen and leadership.

CONCLUSION

This chapter contains the key themes of the works of a few illustrious quality management scientists, whose concepts served as the foundation stones for the creation of numerous quality management concepts. Walter A. Shewhart is the father of statistical quality control. He challenged the inspection-based quality and developed the statistical process control. It was Shewhart who first developed the PDCA cycle. Edward Deming, founding Father of the quality movement, developed the PDSA cycle for quality improvement and advocated fourteen principles that can help organisations increase their quality, productivity, and competitiveness. Joseph Juran created the quality trilogy, which consists of three components: quality planning, quality control, and quality improvement. Juran defined quality as fitness for purpose and also proposed the triple role concept. Kaoru Ishikawa is known as the Father of Quality Control circles and listed ten ideas for leading QC activities. Ishikawa developed the fishbone diagram to find out process variations. Armand V. Feigenbaum introduced the idea of 'Total Quality Control.' He described the nine M's that affect the quality of products and services and also introduced the concept of 'hidden plant.' Genichi Taguchi is known for his contributions to developing methods to improve quality and reduce costs, known as the 'Taguchi Methods,' which include total loss function, design of products, processes, and services, reduction of variation, and statistically planned experiments. Doing things correctly the first time and Zero defects are two of Philip Crosby's most famous ideas. He is also known for the Quality Vaccine, Quality Management Maturity Grid, the top five absolutes of quality, and fourteen steps to quality improvement. David A. Garvin discussed the eight attributes that define quality and identified five major approaches based on the quality definition given by various researchers. Prasanta Chandra Mahalanobis was a great Indian statistician who developed the D^2 statistics and used statistics for the economic development of the nation. Finally, Major General Harkirat Singh is recognised as the early pioneer in India to advance quality, codes, and standards, starting in the 1960s. India is following in its footsteps with the National Building Code.

The teachings and methods adopted by the above quality management scientists paved the way for lots of transformation in the way people work, manufacture products, and provide services. With each new quality concept, products and services started getting better.

---

[1] He was preceded as the President, Institution of Engineers (India) by Union Minister for Electricity and Power, Dr. K L Rao, and succeeded by Union Minister for Education, Dr. Triguna Sen.

Organisations started becoming more successful by finding out the processes that make them better and thus earn more profit. Quality concepts like statistical tools are used in the construction industry as quality determinants. For example, in construction, most tests used for quality evaluation, such as the strength of materials, density of compaction, use statistical evaluations.

The concept of quality, which started with inspection during the Industrial Revolution, saw significant developments with the work of quality gurus. Researchers realised that quality was a collective task, as advocated by the idea of total quality control. In the meantime, many other concepts were added to the body of knowledge, like QC circles, zero defects, total quality management, and Six Sigma. And the quest for improving the quality of products and services continues.

WORKS CITED

Chowdhury, S. and Taguchi, S. (2016), *Robust Optimisation* (United Kingdom: Wiley).

Crosby, P. B. (1979), *Quality is Free: The Art of Making Quality Certain* (New York: McGraw-Hill).

Crosby, P. B. (1984), *Quality Without Tears: The Art of Hassle-Free Management* (New York: McGraw-Hill).

Crosby, P. B. (2005), 'Crosby's 14 steps to improvement', *Quality Progress,* 60–64.

Deming, W. E. (1986), *Out of the Crisis* (Cambridge: Cambridge University Press).

Feigenbaum, A. V. (1983), *Total Quality Control* (New York: McGraw-Hill).

Garvin, D. A. (1984). 'What does "Product Quality" really mean?', *Sloan Management Review*, 25–43.

Ishikawa, K. (1985), *What is Total Quality Control? The Japanese Way* (Japan: Prentice-Hall).

Juran, J. M. (1986), 'The quality trilogy: A universal approach to managing for quality', *ASQC 40th Annual Quality Congress in Anaheim, California.*

Juran, J. M., and Godfrey, B. A. (1979), *Juran's Quality Handbook* (New York: McGraw-Hill).

ISI. (1970), *National Building Code of India* (New Delhi: Indian Standards Institution).

Mahalanobis, A. (1983), *Prasanta Chandra Mahalanobis* (New Delhi: National Book Trust, India).

Mahalanobis, P. (1985), 'Papers on Planning' in P. Bose, & M. Mukherjee (eds.) (Calcutta: Statistical Publishing Society).

Mahalanobis, P. (1986), 'Why Statistics and Other Essays', P. Bose, (eds.) (Calcutta: Statistical Publishing Society).

Mitra, A. (2016), *Fundamentals of Quality Control and Improvement* (United States of America: Wiley).

Oakland, J. S. (2014), *Total Quality Management and Operational Excellence* (London: Routledge).

Rudra, A. (1996), *Prasanta Chandra Mahalanobis* (Delhi: Oxford University Press).

Shewhart, W. (1931), *Economic Control of Quality of Manufactured Product* (New York: D. Van Nostrand Company).

Singh, A. (2017), *Quantitative Risk Management and Decision Making in Construction* (VA, USA: ASCE Press).

Stamatis, D. H. (1997), *TQM Engineering Handbook* (New York: Marcel Dekker, Inc.).

Taguchi, G. (1995), 'Quality engineering (Taguchi methods) for the development of electronic circuit technology', *IEEE Transactions on Reliability,* 44(2).

Taguchi, G., & Jugulam, R. (2002), *The Mahalanobis-Taguchi Strategy* (New York: John Wiley & Sons).

Tripathi, K. K., & Jha, K. N. (2018), 'Determining success factors for a construction organization: A structural equation modeling approach', *Journal of Management in Engineering,* 34(1).

REVIEW QUESTIONS

Multiple Choice Questions

1. According to Juran, what is quality defined as?

(a) zero defects (b) fitness for use

(c) conformance to specification (d) customer satisfaction

2. How many members typically make up a quality circle?

(a) 3–10 (b) 10–20

(c) 1–3 (d) all staff

3. Who developed the concept of quality control circles?

(a) Philip Crosby (b) P.C. Mahalanobis

(c) Kaoru Ishikawa (d) Shewhart

4. Fishbone diagram is also known as

(a) Cause and effect diagram (b) Ishikawa diagram

(c) None of these (d) Both (a) and (b)

5. Who is known as the Father of statistical quality control?

(a) Jospeh Juran (b) Kaoru Ishikawa

(c) Walter A. Shewhart (d) P.C. Mahalanobis

6. Who held a pioneering role in developing the National Building Code of India?

(a) Major General Harkirat Singh

(b) P.C. Mahalanobis

(c) M. Visvesvaraya

(d) Lt General Tilak Nanda

7. Who is known as the Father of statistics in India?
   (a) Major General Harkirat Singh (b) P.C. Mahalanobis
   (c) M. Visvesvaraya (d) Lt General Tilak Nanda
8. What are two of Philip Crosby's most famous ideas regarding quality management?
   (a) zero defects and do it right the first time
   (b) quality control circle and statistical quality control
   (c) fitness for use and cost of quality
   (d) hidden plant and total quality control
9. What is the primary determinant of a construction organisation's performance, according to the study by Tripathi & Jha (2018)?
   (a) competence of the workforce (b) motivation
   (c) competence of top management (d) good supervision
10. Who is the author of the book 'Economic Control of Quality of Manufacturing'?
   (a) Jospeh Juran (b) Kaoru Ishikawa
   (c) Walter A. Shewhart (d) P.C. Mahalanobis

Short Answer Type Questions

1. Who are some of the well-known quality gurus mentioned in the text?
2. What is Statistical Process Control (SPC)?
3. How are control charts utilised in the construction industry?
4. How does the construction industry implement the Plan-Do-Check-Act (PDCA) cycle?
5. Why is sampling done for quality control in the construction industry?
6. What modification did W. Edwards Deming make to the PDCA cycle originally created by Walter A. Shewhart?
7. In what way does the PDSA cycle help the construction industry?
8. What is Deming's first principle regarding achieving quality, and why is it significant in the construction industry?
9. What does Taguchi's quadratic loss function (QLF) aim to address?
10. Why does Deming advise against relying solely on inspection to attain quality in construction projects?
11. What are the steps involved in the planning phase of Juran's quality trilogy?
12. In the control phase, what are the actions taken in response to variations between targeted and actual performance?
13. What is the purpose of the improvement phase in Juran's quality trilogy?
14. How does Juran's 'triple role concept' apply to stakeholders in the construction process?

15. What kind of training does the leader of a quality control circle receive?
16. What is the leader's responsibility in a quality control circle?
17. What is the first step in the quality control circle activities?
18. What is the purpose of Ishikawa's fishbone diagram in process improvement?
19. What are the effects of company-wide quality control, according to Ishikawa?
20. How does Armand V. Feigenbaum define Total Quality Control, and what does he emphasise about its integration within an organisation?
21. How does motivation impact the quality of work in the construction sector?
22. According to Feigenbaum, what is the significance of quality in managing an organisation, and how does Total Quality Control contribute to achieving business objectives?
23. What was the reporting system developed by Armand V. Feigenbaum during his time at General Electric, and what concept did it lead to?
24. Explain the components of the cost of quality according to Feigenbaum and how this concept has evolved over time.
25. What is the concept of the "hidden plant" proposed by Feigenbaum, and how does it relate to manufacturing inefficiencies?
26. Why is the role of management crucial in maintaining quality standards in the construction industry?
27. What are the key technological advancements driving quality improvements in the construction industry?
28. What is robustness in the context of Taguchi Methods?
29. How is a product's overall quality loss calculated, according to Taguchi?
30. What are the three scenarios where the quadratic loss function is applicable?
31. According to Taguchi, what results in a loss for the client?
32. How is the loss function for the nominal-the-best characteristic represented, and what do the variables in the equation signify?
33. Using the example of metallic washers with a target thickness of 1 mm and an accepted tolerance limit of ±0.05 mm, how is the loss coefficient (k) calculated and applied to determine the loss function when the thickness is 1.01 mm. Suppose the product is to be rejected if it falls outside the tolerance limit and costs ₹ 2.00 per piece to the company when rejected?
34. What are the equations for the loss functions in the cases of smaller-the-better and larger-the-better characteristics, and how is the average quality loss (A) related to the loss coefficient (k) in these scenarios?
35. What are the two types of quality control methods described by Taguchi, and how do they differ?
36. What are the three steps in Taguchi's methodology to improve the functional robustness of a product or process, and what does each step entail?

37. What is the 'Quality Vaccine' proposed by Crosby, and what are the actions required from management to administer it continually?
38. Describe the Quality Management Maturity Grid (QMMG) developed by Crosby.
39. How are Crosby's principles of quality management applicable in the construction industry?
40. Why is doing things right the first time significant in the construction industry?
41. What actions are required from management to administer the "Quality Vaccine" continuously, according to Crosby?
42. Explain the performance dimension of quality and its relevance in construction works.
43. What does the reliability dimension of quality refer to, and why is it important in construction?
44. Describe the concept of conformance in quality, and how it applies to construction projects?
45. What is the significance of durability in the context of quality, and how is it relevant to construction?
46. Explain the concept of serviceability in quality management, and why is it important for constructed facilities.
47. What does the aesthetics dimension of quality encompass, and how does it impact construction projects?
48. Define perceived quality in the context of quality management, and how can it be measured in construction projects?
49. What were the major positions held by Major General Harkirat Singh?
50. What does Shewhart's approach to quality emphasise?

Long Answer Type Questions

1. Shortly explain Deming's 14 principles for enhancing quality.
2. What are the Fourteen Steps to Quality Improvement proposed by Crosby, and why are they important in quality management?
3. How are the quality dimensions defined by Garvin applicable in the construction industry, and what benefits do they offer to construction projects?
4. What are the five major approaches to the definition of quality identified by Garvin, and what advantages does each approach offer?
5. What are the top five absolutes for quality management according to Philip Crosby, and how does he define quality?
6. How do the factors identified by Feigenbaum as the nine M's impact quality in the construction sector?
7. How can a fishbone diagram be applied in the construction industry?

8. What are the ten ideas listed by Ishikawa as helpful tips for leading quality control circle activities?
9. What are the contributions of P.C. Mahalanobis in the field of statistics?
10. How does Joseph Juran's quality trilogy, encompassing quality planning, quality control, and quality improvement, offer a comprehensive framework for achieving and maintaining high standards of quality in various industries, particularly in the context of construction projects? Provide examples to illustrate each phase of the trilogy and explain how it contributes to enhancing overall project quality and stakeholder satisfaction throughout the construction process.
11. What are the contributions of Major General Harkirat Singh to the quality management in civil engineering in India?
12. Explain briefly the works done by any five quality management scientists and how can they be applied to improve quality in construction.

ANSWER KEYS

Multiple Choice Questions

1. (b) **2.** (a) **3.** (c) **4.** (d) **5.** (c) **6.** (a) **7.** (b) **8.** (a)
9. (c) **10.** (b)

CHAPTER 3 Total Quality Management

3.1 INTRODUCTION

Quality provided Japan with the competitive edge over the rest of the world in the early 1980s, when their manufacturing sector began to dominate the market. Knowledge gained from renowned quality gurus such as Deming and Juran played an important role in establishing superior brand image for Japanese products. This was the period when the concept of quality underwent a paradigm change: satisfying the customer's needs took precedence over following specifications to achieve quality. Taking care of the requirements and expectations of the client became the central idea of the new Total Quality Management philosophy. As per this concept, it became necessary for all employees to collaborate, cooperate, and coordinate at every interface to increase quality and improve the organisation's effectiveness. Only with upper management's commitment could all of this take place. It needed a change in the organisational culture[1] to adapt to the new changes in quality. Consequently, it was understood that culture is shaped by the norms, policies, practises, attitudes and managerial leadership of an organisation.

Stamatis (1997) stated, 'Total Quality Management is a philosophy, and its fruits will materialise through major changes in the organisation that will implement this philosophy'. However, TQM is a practical management implementation system for application in manufacturing and construction to meet the end and ongoing expectations of the client and customer. Substantial changes are required in the thought processes, such as how things are perceived, the organisational culture, how the customers and employees are being treated, attitudes towards the community, or relationships between shareholders. In improving total quality, one has to be focused on quality as the main variable. This includes the quality of the product, its functionality, durability, price, and performance. In effect, TQM is successful and effective only when it achieves functional improvement. The aim at every step, on a daily basis, has to be the creation of a new quality measure in the product or system.

According to Oakland (1995), Total Quality Management is a method for organising, planning, and comprehending each task that depends on each person at each level. It is an all-inclusive strategy to raise the organisation's overall competitiveness, adaptability, and effectiveness. Consequently, it helps to maximise the competitiveness of a nation and improve its economy. The techniques and methods used in TQM can be used in all types

[1] Organisational culture is defined as the set of attitudes, beliefs, and behaviour in an organisation.

of manufacturing and service industries, including the defence industry. TQM is thus a strategic interconnected management system that involves all levels of managers and uses quantitative methods for continuous improvement of an organisation's processes to fulfil the customers' demands, needs, requirements, and expectations. The Total Quality Management (TQM) philosophy considers all facets of an organisation and views quality as a strategic issue. TQM requires a strong drive for quality and a dedication to leadership and has to be supported by top managers. However, it can be implemented only through participation from personnel at all levels of the company. Thus, customer satisfaction can be increased by continuous improvement of current performance. To enable continuous improvement, all the people in the organisation must be empowered by giving them the required training and skill enhancement.

In a nutshell, Total Quality Management (TQM) is a way in which business can be done, and it functions by evaluating every aspect and operation of an organisation (Bates, 1993). All processes which may be operational, administrative, interdepartmental, and interpersonal should be continually refined and improved so that they can meet the changing needs of the clients. The different components that are seemingly independent but interdependent in reality and whose integration is important for a successful quality environment within any organisation or organisational unit are (Bates, 1993):

1. Strategy and structure of an organisation, which indicates the way in which an organisation does business.
2. The technical component, which includes organisation's practices, skills, tools, and methodology used within the organisation for the development of products and processes.
3. Organisational culture that represents the norms and behavioural expectations that the organisation has set for itself and its people.

3.2 THE FRAMEWORK FOR TQM

It is to be noted that planning, processes, and people, alongside commitment, culture, communication, and customers, which are necessary for managerial performance, are also essential for delivering leadership excellence (Oakland, 2011). Figure 3.1 represents Oakland's TQM model. These are espoused below in bullet form.

3.2.1 Planning

- This is to create the vision necessary for long-term success and constancy of purpose. Every organisation trying to improve its quality must have a clear vision. They should be consistent about the intention of the organisation. A construction company trying to improve should initially create a vision, which may be enhancing customer satisfaction, meeting global standards, etc.
- The creation, implementation, and updating of strategy and policy. After the vision is created, planning is done to implement the vision.
- Orienting organisation structure to support the implementation of strategy and policy.

FIGURE 1 TQM model (modified from Oakland 2014)

3.2.2 Processes

- This ensures the creation and implementation of a process management system.
- Make sure the management system is created, put into place, and continually upgraded by getting personally involved.
- Set priorities for improvement initiatives and ensure they are planned across the organisation.

3.2.3 People

- The 'people' function is necessary to improve team leaders' and managers' leadership and problem-solving abilities at every level.
- Encourage teamwork and empowerment to foster innovation and creativity.
- Support training, education, and learning efforts, and encourage others to do the same.
- Individuals and teams inside the organisation are to be inspired, supported, and appreciated.
- Aiding and abetting individuals in achieving plans, goals, objectives, and targets.
- Encourage people to take part in improvement initiatives by listening to them.

3.2.4 Performance

- It is of fundamental importance to identify the performance areas that are crucial.
- Create metrics that show levels of current performance.

- Establish objectives and track the progress in achieving them.
- People at all levels should be given feedback on how they performed in relation to the predetermined goals.

3.2.5 Commitment

- All involved personnel must actively engage in activities relevant to quality and improvement on a personal level.
- Review and improve personal leadership performance.

3.2.6 Culture

- Upper management must create the morals and values that will enable the supply chain to adopt a holistic quality culture.
- Integrate ethics and ideals into all activities and behaviour.
- Assure the development and implementation of learning, innovation, and creativity-related activities.

3.2.7 Communications

- Upper management and employees must encourage each other and stimulate communication and cooperation.
- Personalise the vision, beliefs, mission, rules, and strategies.
- Be available and listen attentively.

3.2.8 Customers

- Engage with clients and other stakeholders.
- Ensure that client (internal and external) demands are recognised and met.
- Make partnerships and participate in them because a consumer insists on constant improvement in all areas.

The three Ps—Planning, People, and Processes—are essential for providing customers with goods and services as well as for enhancing overall 'Performance.' These are the "hard management necessities" for a TQM model, whereas the "soft outcomes" of the model in a successful organisation are provided by the three Cs: culture, commitment, and communication.

3.3 TQM IN THE CONSTRUCTION SECTOR

TQM is a management-led strategy that can be applied to all company operations, and it is every responsible person's job in the company to make sure that quality is maintained. The TQM philosophy relies on prevention rather than defect detection. Thus, TQM is a method of thinking about organisations, goals, procedures, and individuals to ensure that proper tasks are carried out precisely the first time (Pheng & Teo, 2004). The bedrock of TQM is the combined behaviour of the individuals in the organisation. The leadership sets the vision that the customer is the king, and the employees are provided with support, tools, and rewards for doing their part to satisfy the needs of the customer. A satisfied customer becomes ready to pay a competitive price, besides becoming a repeat customer, which in turn adds to the profit of the organisation.

The use of TQM in the construction industry is meant to increase market share, customer happiness, and the quality of the constructed facility. Contrary to the conventional bureaucratic mentality of top management, in which staff passively follow orders, the adoption of TQM necessitates a total change in the business culture and management strategy.

The main criteria for defining quality in a building project are the client's demands. TQM starts with understanding the client's requirements. Thus, planning and designing, construction, and maintenance, and operation are the primary phases of a construction project. Figure 3.2 shows the elements of TQM and other factors affecting quality in a construction-specific industry.

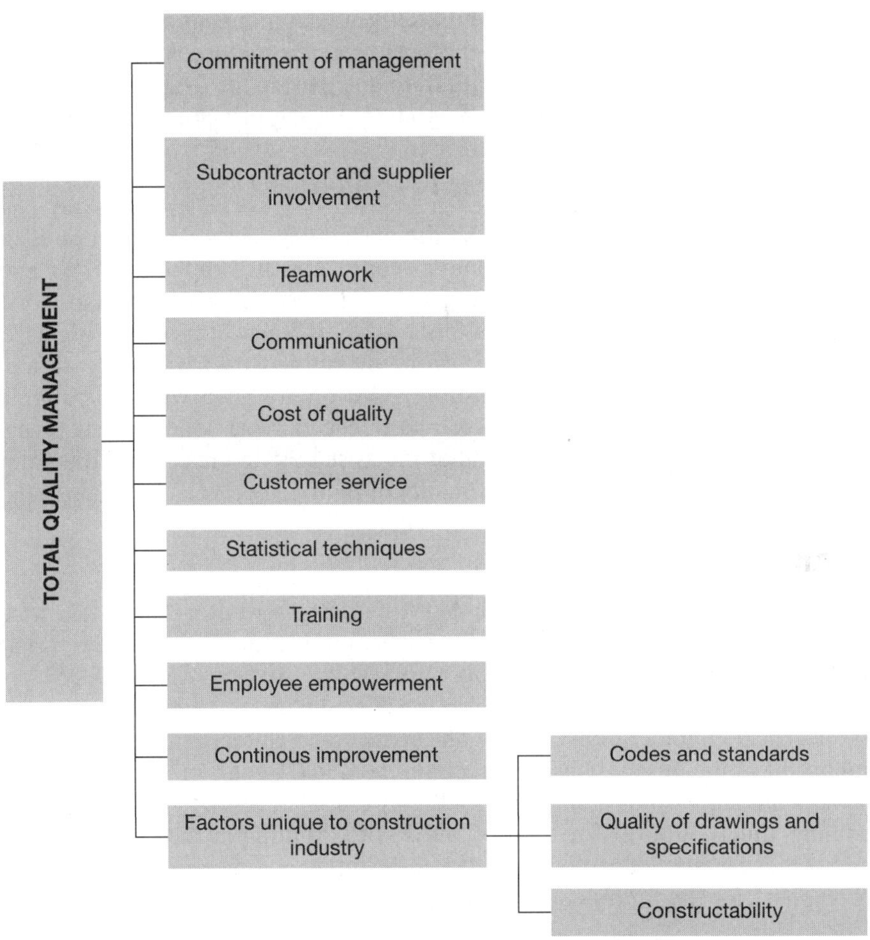

FIGURE 3.2 Elements of TQM in the construction process

3.3.1 Commitment of Management

TQM is initiated in an organisation with the decisions taken by top management. They have to be committed to executing quality in their organisation. The middle-level managers are responsible for imparting knowledge about TQM to their subordinate or low-level managers. It is required to change the attitude of the top management for the proper implementation of the TQM. There should be interaction between the various departments and at all levels. The success of TQM implementation depends on the level of commitment of management at all levels.

Poor management practices lead to a reduction in construction productivity, directly or indirectly. Generally, management by control, not participation, is generally the norm in the construction sector. In management by control, organisations look inwards instead of looking outward at the customers and satisfying their needs. The goals are established within the conventional triple constraints of cost, schedule, and quality. Rewards and incentives are given to project managers for achieving goals, which in turn increases competition among employees, leading to internal conflicts, poor relationships, reduced communication, accusations for not achieving goals, and fabricated reports of conformity. It affects the overall productivity and quality of work. Therefore, to avoid such a situation that exist in the organisation, the management must incorporate TQM by understanding its underlying principles and elements.

3.3.2 Subcontractor and Supplier Involvement

A project's quality is decided by the merit of the market, the designer's plans and specifications, the quality of the materials and equipment supplied by the suppliers, and the excellence of the work carried out by the subcontractors. Hence, it is very important to choose competent suppliers and subcontractors[2]. In successful organisations, long-term partnering agreements are formed with suppliers to ensure the best economy and quality. In consideration of future project work, some owners insist on establishing TQM programmes with their suppliers and contractors. Consequently, a construction company can partner long-term with particular reputed cement and steel producing companies for its supply and may insist they implement TQM in their organisation. In this way, the quality of their projects can be enhanced.

3.3.3 Teamwork

Continuous improvement is carried out in TQM by using a well-organised team structure coupled with the TQM methodology. Since construction includes stakeholders from various sectors, it is important in the TQM approach to involve everyone in the TQM processes. In construction, the various parties involved in the design phase are civil engineers, structural engineers, electrical engineers, environmental engineers, architects, and owners. Teamwork is very important in the design phase in reaching the quality goals of construction. This can reduce clashes among various stakeholders. Teamwork is necessary for finalising planning and scheduling, timely supply of resources, and so on, resulting in the smooth execution of activities to achieve goals. Secondly, teamwork is essential among various participants in the construction phase for the timely completion of the project within the estimated budget.

2 A detailed prequalification method is often used to select competitive vendors and contractors.

3.3.4 Communication

Communication is another vital factor in achieving good quality, especially in the construction sector. Construction usually happens in diverse locations with a transient workforce. It involves the participation of various stakeholders and mostly different workforce teams for each project. Construction includes personnel from various disciplines who must be regularly updated regarding the progress, changes, and other requirements. Hence, it is very important that they maintain good communication among each participant to enable completion of the project on time according to the client's requirements. There should be a mechanism for everyone to express their problems, views, and ideas and convey them to higher management. In many cases, it has been found that poor quality is due to a lack of proper coordination and communication among stakeholders. Hence, there should be good human resource management procedures to make operations successful. TQM gives high priority to good communication.

3.3.5 Cost of Quality

Cost of quality is a key instrument for gauging quality and assessing how well the TQM process is working. The sum of the costs for failure, appraisal, and prevention gives the cost of quality. It can persuade management and other stakeholders of the need for quality improvement by integrating the inspection, testing, costs of review, scrap, and rework.

Contractors are usually selected on a competitive basis in the construction industry, mostly for private constructions. It is crucial to take into account the contractors' equipment capabilities, technical assistance, safety record, and, most significantly, their reputation for producing high-quality work. Contractors with a poor reputation are less likely to receive orders in this competitive market. Therefore, to win contracts and survive in the competitive market, contractors must make investments in quality improvement techniques.

3.3.6 Customer Service

To achieve quality in construction, all the stakeholders should be actively involved in the TQM processes. Both internal and external customer participation is necessary for TQM to be successful. The satisfaction of all the customers must be maximised. According to Juran's 'triple role' theory, each party plays the role of supplier, processor, and customer in any process. It is also applicable to the construction sector. The designer is in the role of customer to the owner as the owner has to give the project requirements. The designer supplies a feasible design to the contractor. The contractor, who is now the designer's client, carries out the construction process using the designer's drawings and specifications. The owner is the client of the builder who gives the owner the finished structure. The quality of each phase is influenced by how well the preceding stages are performed. Therefore, the overall quality of the process must satisfy both internal and external consumers' needs. In essence, the customer is the next group, person, or entity to whom your services are transferred. If the quality of your work is not good, the customer will not be able to build on it without error, dispute, contention, and lost time. Figure 3.3 shows how the various stakeholders in construction are related to each other.

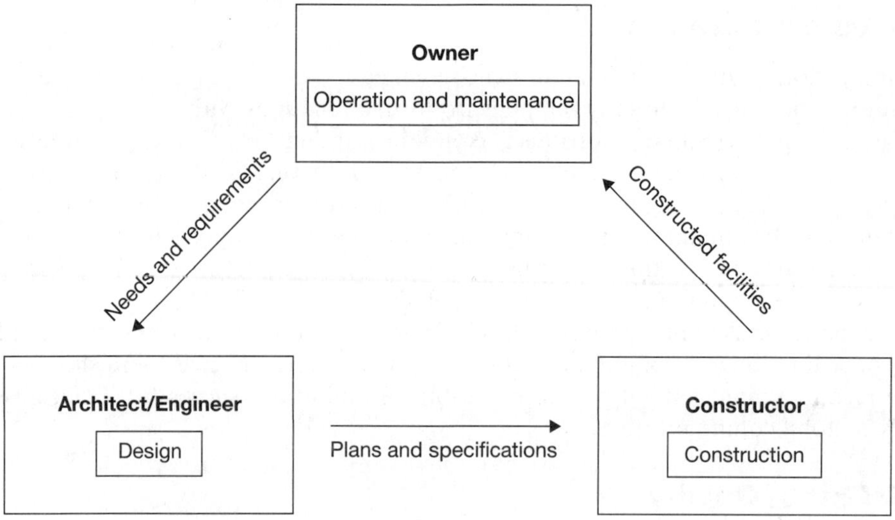

FIGURE 3.3 Relationship between stakeholders in construction

3.3.7 Statistical Methods for Quality Control

Various teams involved in construction can enhance processes using statistical methods because they can utilise them to find the root causes of quality issues. It facilitates clear communication in a common language among all team members. It makes it simple to validate, replicate, and duplicate data-based measures. Decision-making can be done based on precise data. Histograms, Pareto diagrams, graphs, control charts, fishbone diagrams, check sheets, and scatter diagrams are the most important statistical tools used in TQM. The use of statistical methods in quality improvement is also emphasised by ISO 9001. However, its role is presently very low in the construction industry. This is perhaps due to the lack of knowledge and lack of awareness in the construction industry, not to mention that cost and profit may be the driving objectives everywhere.

3.3.8 Training

As already mentioned, quality is everyone's responsibility in the organisation. Therefore, training should be given at all levels of management. The training programmes ought to be specially created to meet the requirements of managers, engineers, administrative and field office staff, technicians, support personnel, and workers. Quality teams must be formed and training programs must be conducted. The programmes should include instruction in quality awareness, leadership, meeting management, process improvement, and problem-solving (Chase, 1993). The training classes should also cover the fundamentals of TQM, cause-and-effect analysis, simple statistical techniques, and cost of quality measurement. Due to the transient nature of the construction workforce, the training process is a difficult endeavour. Even then, training must be given regarding quality awareness in the workplace.

3.3.9 Employee Empowerment

Another very important factor in TQM is the focus on employees. TQM emphasises the potential of every employee to make improvements in not just their areas but also in other areas as well. Hence, to tap the potential of employees, it is essential to motivate them, train them, and orient them towards the concept of TQM. Employees are to be provided with a safe, clean, and satisfying work environment. They should be trained in processes like planning, problem-solving, and decision-making, which is actually an elaborate process. They should be encouraged to take pride in their contribution. And, employees should be given recognition for their participation in quality improvement. Feedback should be taken to improve employee satisfaction as only a satisfied employee can contribute towards TQM in an organisation.

3.3.10 Continuous Improvement

TQM focuses on achieving client satisfaction through continuous improvement. The Plan-Do-Check-Act (PDCA) cycles are of great value for achieving continuous improvement. It is essential to measure and record data during all processes of execution. When any deviations occur from the required specifications, analyses should be done to identify the cause. After the cause-and-effect analysis is done, rectification measures should be taken. Organisations should strive for continuous improvement at all phases of construction. With continuous value addition, processes should be improved to enhance quality and raise productivity.

3.3.11 Focus On Customer Satisfaction

Organisations focussing on customer satisfaction should initially find out the customers' needs and expectations. The whole team has to work to fulfil the client's needs. There are various dimensions of quality that can make customers satisfied. But, customers should be satisfied with all stages of the project, from its operation to its maintenance. Also, it is required to note the changes or suggestions given by the customer during the construction phase and accommodate them, if possible.

3.3.12 Vision and Mission

Each organisation should have a clearly defined vision, mission, goals, and guiding principles that take the organisation towards improved quality, safety, customer satisfaction, business growth, worker satisfaction, etc. The vision of construction companies may be reaching global standards, delighting customers, setting a benchmark in the construction industry, creating an ideal work culture, and so on. With a vision, the organisation should set its mission, values, and guiding principles on which it should work.

3.3.13 Codes and Standards

Codes and standards are created to protect public safety in relation to structural adequacy, fire concerns, and health considerations (BIS, 2016). Verifying code and standard compliance should happen throughout the design and construction phases. The design professional must be competent enough and should be aware of all the important and relevant clauses in standards and codes. The quality of the final product depends on the initial design and specification. Initial design mistakes might result in significant errors and high costs and delays from rework plans and specifications.

3.3.14 Drawings and Specifications

Drawings and specifications are provided to the builder as a reference for the construction operations. While drawings indicate the architectural idea, dimensions and scope of the project, number of parts, and how they are combined into the finished project, specifications include information regarding materials and quality requirements. Drawings and specifications form a fundamental part of contract documents. They should be clear, precise, and complete and should not lead to any confusion during the construction phase, as they significantly impact the building's quality. Errors in the blueprints and specifications, or a poor comprehension of them, result in construction errors that necessitate rework and raise the expense of the project.

3.3.15 Constructability

The quality of design is affected by the constructability. Construction techniques and constructability depend on the geographical area where the construction is to be done. During the design process, the design expert must consider these elements. The design needs to be assessed considering the location's requirements, accessibility, the initial construction, and the subsequent operations. The design must be clearly and adequately communicated to the constructor by means of plans and specifications.

3.4 FACTORS UNIQUE TO THE CONSTRUCTION SECTOR

Although the development of quality control mechanisms in the construction sector followed that of the manufacturing sector, there are some aspects of the construction sector that are unique and should be considered when implementing quality programmes in construction. They are as follows (Rounds & Chi, 1985).

- Most construction projects are unique. Almost all products are produced only once for a single order.[3]
- Contrary to other businesses that have identical and repeated conditions for production, the construction industry does not have identical or repeated working conditions for its projects. Each construction project is different from the other in many ways.
- Construction projects have a much longer life cycle than most manufactured products, lasting hundreds of years in operation. Some structures, such as the pyramids, have lasted more than three thousand years.
- Considering that construction projects are single-order design projects, the owner generally has direct influence over production.
- Each construction project will more often than not have a different set of participants, including the owner, designer, contractor, subcontractor, material supplier, etc.

[3] This is also similar to airplane and ship manufacturing.

Due to the aforementioned reasons, quality in construction processes differs significantly from other industries. For instance, in manufacturing, the quality control for the manufacture of a nail checks how well the carbon steel is machined and made to exact dimensions. Before that, during the metallurgical process, the ratios of elements and impurities in the carbon steel are checked. In construction, the quality control for hammering a nail is governed by where it is hammered, the angle at which it is hammered, and whether it goes into the wood or drywall without getting bent; add to this how well the nail is stored, without acquiring rust over time. Therefore, the procedures for quality control that work well with the manufacturing industry are different to those of the construction industry, but the philosophy is the same in that a product is desired that will serve its user well, be durable, and fit the purpose. The only difference is that quality control in the construction sector has to be thought of differently from that in the manufacturing or metallurgy sector.

In the construction industry, the design and planning of projects are based on relevant codes, the requirements of owners, and the organisation's standard practices. Construction procedures are carried out in accordance with all applicable standards' requirements as well as the constructor's interpretation of them. Quality assurance normally happens after completion and in some situations, after receiving compensation from the authority concerned.[4] This process results in the following trends (Arditi & Gunaydin, 1997):

- Each project's quality is planned for and continually assessed. With the exception of some specialised types of construction such as nuclear power facilities, tunnel construction, metro construction, and interstate road construction that have to strictly follow the quality plan prepared by the regulatory authority, neither the whole industry nor key sections of the industry are covered by a comprehensive quality policy.
- Since repairing defects due to poor work after completion of construction is detrimental to the reputation of the company or individual's reputation, construction defects are often rectified or covered up before they get noticed by high-level management or the owner. The dearth of data regarding those defects prevents methods from being changed, which permits the defect to recur on the following projects.

Thus, it is probably meaningful to change the definition of quality control from 'controlling quality' to 'controlling management for quality' (Kubal, 1994). This would lead to utilising an integrated quality standard to develop rules and organisational structures for managing quality based on current industry-wide experience. A quality flow chart as depicted in Figure 3.4, illustrates the traits of an appropriately designed quality control programme for the construction sector and is explained below (Arditi & Gunaydin, 1997):

- The **quality standard** is created based on an up-to-date database with input from previous projects, providing a more thorough and consistent norm.
- **Quality management** is applied to the quality standards in various phases, such as planning and design, construction, operation, and maintenance, and its integration through the **construction management** project delivery system.
- Early detection and correction of defects is undertaken during the **assessment** phase.
- Collecting feedback is vital to improve the database's quality and to aid in preventing the recurrence of defects that have been detected.

---

[4] However, quality specification, as in all production industries, is done earlier.

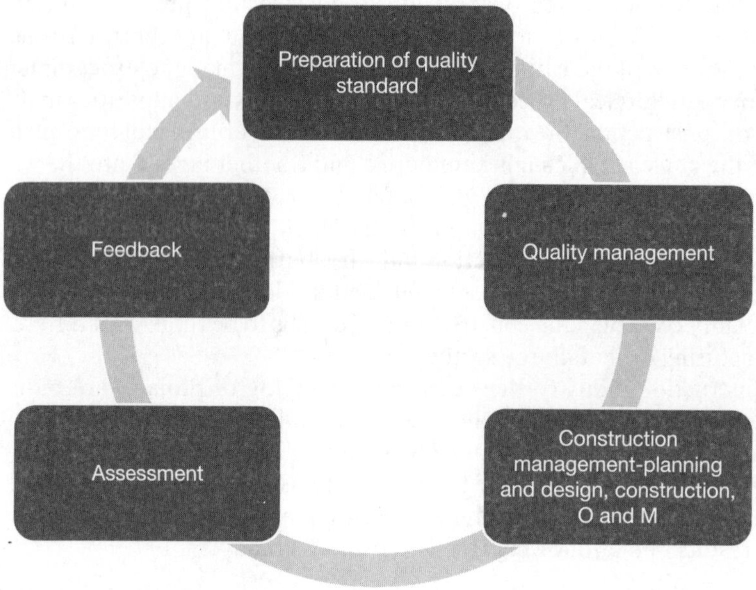

FIGURE 3.4 Total quality control flowchart

3.5 CONTINUOUS IMPROVEMENT

Continuous improvement is of fundamental import for quality enhancement, and it must be linked to organisational strategy. Thus, construction organisations may implement an eight-stage general continuous improvement framework, which includes (Oakland, 2014):

i. Top-down directives and effective leadership
ii. Supportive infrastructure
iii. A pragmatic, fact-based approach that produces quick results (e.g., Six Sigma)
iv. Improvers of skill (those educated, skilled, and residing within the organisation)
v. Widely accepted continuous improvement mindset
vi. Transfer/sharing of talent
vii. Improvements that can be measured in the service and delivery areas
viii. Continuous improvement

Oakland and his colleagues created a fully closed-loop methodology known as 'DRIVER' for continuous process improvement that combines the best elements of Lean, Six Sigma, and Cost of Quality methodologies.

The various stages include the following:

- **D**efine—the process's scope and objectives will be enhanced by taking customer needs into account.
- **R**eview—knowing the current processes, evaluating their effectiveness, and appreciating the value additions and waste.

- **I**nvestigate—identify the performance gap between the existing and desired levels and examine the underlying causes of any issues.
- **V**erify—provide solutions for improvement and prevent recurrence of problems.
- **E**xecute—implement the process improvements.
- **R**einforce—establish a method for re-evaluation to ensure continual improvement while concentrating on the improvement.

3.6 STEPS FOR IMPLEMENTING TQM

A framework recommended for the implementation of TQM in an organisation is explained in Figure 3.5. According to this framework, in order to apply Total Quality Management (TQM) in an organisation, all members of the organisation's team must know the components and prerequisites of TQM, which include a system for collecting customer feedback, continuous improvement, teamwork, fewer suppliers, training, process management and improvement through productivity studies, an effective system of communication within the organisation, a proper project structure, and most importantly top management's commitment. After comprehending these requirements, the top management has to decide whether to implement TQM. They should conduct a strategic analysis of the same either with their own resources or may employ experts from outside. Once the decision is taken to execute TQM in the organisation, a strategic implementation plan has to be made. The most important requirement in its implementation is to review the existing organisational culture. Teams are then formed to communicate the new philosophy to the entire organisation. Budgets and required resources are allocated for its execution. Once these prerequisites are ready, goals and targets are specified for different departments. Then, training programmes and monitoring methods are planned. Feedback is taken from employees to identify the training requirements. Training plans are prepared based on the areas where shortfalls are found. After setting all these, TQM is implemented and continuously monitored against the established goals and targets. Feedback is taken constantly to review the TQM implementation.

3.7 BARRIERS TO THE ADOPTION OF TQM IN THE CONSTRUCTION INDUSTRY

Being distinct from manufacturing and other industries, construction industry faces a number of issues that make the adoption of TQM difficult. The following are some significant issues that have been identified:

a. Lack of management commitment.

b. Resistance to change the culture.

c. Inadequate planning and scheduling.

d. Lack of standardisation.

e. Lack of teamwork.

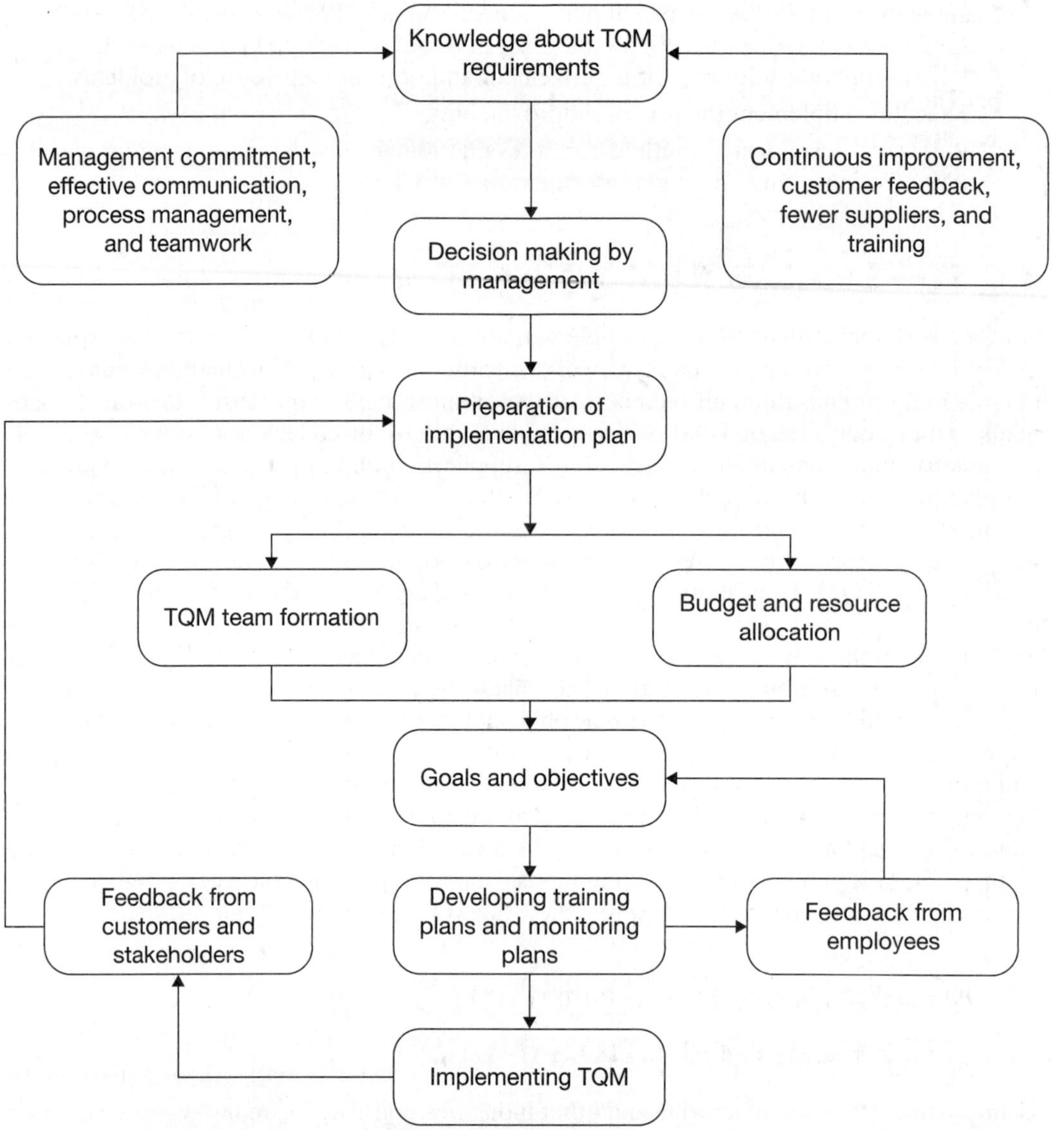

FIGURE 3.5 Framework for implementing Total Quality Management (modified from Pheng & Teo, 2004)

f. Poor change management.
g. Ineffective measurement technique and process control.
h. Fragmented nature of the construction industry.
i. Risks involved.
j. Conflicts of interest among different stakeholders.

The causes of the problems are as follows:

- **a.** Failure to understand the concept of TQM.
- **b.** There are no team-building activities at the beginning of projects.
- **c.** No initial training prior to the start of work.
- **d.** Failure to comprehend the demands of the team.
- **e.** There is little to no team-oriented scheduling and planning.
- **f.** Lack of training to update technology.
- **g.** Lack of coordination and communication.
- **h.** Uniqueness of each project.
- **i.** Unlike manufacturing, the team constitution will be different for each project whose requirements will be different.
- **j.** The inclination of contractors towards profit and desire to cut costs for quality implementation.
- **k.** Lack of perseverance and commitment.
- **l.** Lack of knowledgeable staff.
- **m.** Increased paperwork.
- **n.** Contractor selection based on lowest bids.

CONCLUSION

The construction industry has a lot of room for quality improvement. In the current scenario, sustainability is given prime importance as there is a shortage of resources and there are not many resources to waste for repair and rework. Hence, it is important to adopt practices like total quality management. TQM principles can be applied to the construction industry with necessary modifications considering its unique features. Good leadership and appropriate organisation culture can overcome all obstacles in the path of implementing TQM. The management team should become all-inclusive and delegate responsibilities to its staff after training them. By adopting TQM in the construction industry, customer satisfaction can also be enhanced.

WORKS CITED

Arditi, D. and Gunaydin, H. M. (1997), 'Total quality management in the construction process', *International Journal of Project Management*, 15(4), 235–243.

Bates, G. D. (1993), 'An organisational development process to prepare for total quality management', *Journal of Management in Engineering*, 9(4), 291–294.

BIS. (2016), *National Building Code of India* (New Delhi: Bureau of Indian Standards).

Burati, J. L. and Oswald, T. H. (1993), 'Implementing TQM in engineering and construction', *Journal of Management in Engineering*, 9(4), 456–470.

Chase, G. W. (1993), 'Effective total quality management (TQM) process for construction', *Journal of Management in Engineering*, 9(4), 433–443.

Kubal, M. T. (1994), *Engineered Quality in Construction* (New York: McGraw-Hill).

Oakland, J. S. (1995), *Total Quality Management Text with Cases* (Oxford: Butterworth Heinemann).

Oakland, J. (2011), 'Leadership and policy deployment: the backbone of TQM', *Total Quality Management*, 22(5), 517–534.

Oakland, J. S. (2014), *Total Quality Management and Operational Excellence* (London: Routledge).

Pheng, L. S. and Teo, J. A. (2004), 'Implementing total quality management in construction firms', *Journal of Management in Engineering*, 20(1), 8–15.

Rounds, J. L. and Chi, N. Y. (1985), 'Total quality management for construction', *Journal of Construction Engineering and Management*, 111(2), 117–128.

Stamatis, D. H. (1997), *TQM Engineering Handbook* (New York: Marcel Dekker, Inc).

REVIEW QUESTIONS

Multiple Choice Questions

1. What was identified as the most competitive weapon after Japan began to dominate the market in the 1980s?

(a) Innovation (b) Cost reduction
(c) Quality (d) Marketing

2. What became the central idea of the new Total Quality Management (TQM) philosophy?

(a) Reducing production costs (b) Satisfying the customer's needs
(c) Increasing sales (d) Following specifications strictly

3. Whose commitment is essential for the implementation of TQM according to the text?

(a) Middle management (b) Upper management
(c) Frontline employees (d) Customers

4. How does TQM view quality according to the text?

(a) As a secondary issue (b) As a strategic issue
(c) As a marketing tool (d) As a cost-saving measure

5. What role do top managers play in TQM?

(a) They should focus on marketing strategies
(b) They must support TQM
(c) They need to reduce operational costs
(d) They should only supervise the process

6. In TQM, what role does the organisational culture represent?
   (a) It focuses on financial performance
   (b) It represents the norms and behavioural expectations of the organisation
   (c) It determines the technological tools to be used
   (d) It dictates the marketing strategies to be employed
7. What are the four Ps essential for delivering leadership excellence according to Oakland (2011)?
   (a) Planning, Processes, People, Performance
   (b) Planning, Policies, People, Performance
   (c) Processes, Policies, Performance, People
   (d) Planning, Performance, People, Procedures
8. What are the three Cs essential for delivering leadership excellence according to Oakland (2011)?
   (a) Commitment, Culture, Communication
   (b) Communication, Coordination, Collaboration
   (c) Culture, Coordination, Customer-focus
   (d) Commitment, Cooperation, Customer-focus
9. What is the fourth C mentioned in Oakland's TQM model?
   (a) Coordination (b) Collaboration
   (c) Customers (d) Cooperation
10. What is the purpose of the 'Planning' function in Oakland's TQM model?
    (a) To reduce costs
    (b) To create the vision necessary for long-term success and constancy of purpose
    (c) To enhance marketing strategies
    (d) To streamline production processes
11. Which components are considered the "hard management necessities" in Oakland's TQM model?
    (a) Planning, People, Processes (b) Commitment, Culture, Communication
    (c) Performance, Planning, People (d) Culture, Communication, Customers
12. Which components are considered the 'soft outcomes' in Oakland's TQM model?
    (a) Planning, People, Processes
    (b) Commitment, Culture, Communication
    (c) Performance, Planning, People
    (d) Culture, Communication, Customers

13. What is the significance of continuous improvement in TQM?
    (a) It focuses solely on cost reduction
    (b) It aims to achieve client satisfaction through continuous improvement of processes
    (c) It emphasises marketing strategies
    (d) It reduces the need for training
14. What is the importance of employee empowerment in TQM?
    (a) To increase marketing reach
    (b) To tap the potential of employees for making improvements in various areas
    (c) To reduce the number of employees
    (d) To increase financial performance
15. What are the key statistical tools used in TQM?
    (a) Bar charts and pie charts
    (b) Histograms, Pareto diagrams, graphs, control charts, fishbone diagrams, check sheets, and scatter diagrams.
    (c) Line charts and area charts
    (d) Financial graphs and charts
16. How does Juran's 'triple role' theory apply to the construction sector?
    (a) It emphasises cost reduction
    (b) Each party plays the role of supplier, processor, and customer
    (c) It focuses on speed of execution
    (d) It reduces the number of employees required
17. What is the primary purpose of codes and standards in construction according to BIS (2016)?
    (a) Reducing project costs
    (b) Protecting public safety in relation to structural adequacy, fire concerns, and health considerations
    (c) Enhancing architectural design
    (d) Increasing construction speed
18. When should compliance with codes and standards be verified during a construction project?
    (a) During the construction phase
    (b) During the design phase
    (c) After project completion
    (d) During the design and construction phases

19. Which of the following is NOT a stage in the continuous improvement framework according to Oakland (2014)?

(a) Define (b) Reinvent

(c) Investigate (d) Verify

20. What methodology combines the best elements of Lean, Six Sigma, and Cost of Quality methodologies according to Oakland and his colleagues?

(a) DMAIC (b) DRIVER

(c) Kaizen (d) PDCA

Short Answer Type Questions

1. What is TQM? What are the key components of a successful quality environment?
2. What are the four P's and three C's in TQM?
3. What is TQM in the construction industry and its aims?
4. How does incorporating TQM solve poor management in construction?
5. Explain the relationship between planning, people, and processes in achieving overall performance in a TQM model.
6. What should be done to encourage teamwork and empowerment within an organisation?
7. What is the initial step a construction company should take to improve its quality, according to the planning section?
8. What is the role of processes in Total Quality Management (TQM)?
9. How does TQM differ from conventional management practices in the construction industry?
10. What role does top management play in the initiation and implementation of TQM in an organisation?
11. What are the consequences of poor management practices in the construction sector?
12. Why is communication vital for achieving good quality in construction projects?
13. Which statistical methods are commonly used in TQM for quality improvement?
14. What is the significance of PDCA cycles in achieving continuous improvement in TQM?
15. How do drawings and specifications impact the quality of a construction project?
16. How does the concept of Juran's 'triple role' theory apply to the construction sector?
17. What is unique about most construction projects compared to other industries?
18. What is the role of an up-to-date database in creating quality standards for construction?
19. Why is collecting feedback crucial in the construction industry's quality control process?

20. How is quality management applied in various phases of construction projects?
21. What does the DRIVER methodology stand for in continuous process improvement and what steps are included?
22. What are some significant barriers to the adoption of TQM in the construction industry?
23. What role does training play in the successful implementation of TQM?
24. How does the uniqueness of each project present a challenge to TQM adoption in construction?
25. What is a common issue with communication and coordination in the construction industry?

Long Answer Type Questions

1. Explain the framework for TQM in detail with the role of each component.
2. Mention the elements of TQM in the construction industry and explain five of them in detail.
3. What is the impact of poor management practices in the construction industry and what could be the solution to be incorporated?
4. Why is the coordination between stakeholders important in achieving quality? Explain with a suitable figure.
5. Illustrate Juran's triple role theory in construction by giving a suitable example.
6. What are the differences and similarities in the construction and manufacturing industries?
7. Explain the DRIVER methodology for continuous improvement.
8. What are the various causes of problems in the construction industry?
9. Write about the steps used in implementing TQM in the construction industry.
10. What are the various barriers to adopting the TQM in the construction industry?

ANSWER KEYS

Multiple Choice Questions

1. (c)	**2.** (b)	**3.** (b)	**4.** (b)	**5.** (b)	**6.** (b)	**7.** (a)	**8.** (a)
9. (c)	**10.** (b)	**11.** (a)	**12.** (b)	**13.** (b)	**14.** (b)	**15.** (b)	**16.** (b)
17. (b)	**18.** (d)	**19.** (b)	**20.** (b)				

CHAPTER 4

ISO Standards and Quality Assessment Systems

4.1 INTRODUCTION TO ISO STANDARDS

The development and advancement of technology has influenced humanity in nearly all aspects, not only in general engineering but also in social engineering. It further led to the evolution of various concepts related to quality as products began to be manufactured that had to be fit for the purpose. A widely accepted definition of quality is the 'conformance to specifications' for which standards were necessary. Also, large-scale manufacturing and globalisation led to a growing need for the adoption of generalised standards across the world for various processes, their management, inspection, safety, tests, specification, and security. This was as much to protect the consumer as it was to protect the manufacturer. This led to the creation of the International Organization for Standardization[1] in 1946, with its Central Secretariat in Geneva, Switzerland, where experts from various fields gathered to formulate the best ways of doing things. Standards are the refined wisdom of knowledgeable people who are experts in particular fields and know the technical requirements needed. Standards specify the guidelines, norms and the technical requirements of a process or a product and state the degree of quality to be attained.

ISO is a voluntary organisation with representatives from 172 nations (ISO, 2024). The committee has so far produced a large number of standards covering many topics, such as management of quality, environment, health and safety, energy, food safety, information technology security, and so on, after taking into consideration the national standards of various nations. ISO 9000–Quality Management Systems Standards, developed in 1987 (ASQ, 2023), attained global attention and respect during the early 1990s, and with them, ISO standards became an inevitable part of the industry worldwide. There are currently 841 technical groups and subcommittees focused on standards development, and there are 25,614 international standards in use. With the help of experts from various nations that make up its membership, ISO creates relevant, innovative solutions to global challenges, and therefore helps the end goal of having a mutually-respectable society and an improved quality of life.

---

[1] ISA (International Federation of the National Standardizing Associations), founded in New York in 1926 and run from Switzerland; and UNSCC (United Nations Standards Coordinating Committee), founded in 1944 and run from London, were combined to form ISO (ISO, 1997).

4.2 THE ADVANTAGES OF ISO STANDARDS

The ISO standards can be used by both parties, involving clients and contractors in contractual scenarios, because of their generic nature. The most often adopted standard, ISO 9000, can be used by organisations of various shapes and sizes. It helps a company satisfy its customers through continuous improvement of the product or service. Accredited agencies certify companies that follow ISO standards and they will conduct audits at regular intervals. ISO 9000 is much more than a certificate due to the following benefits of implementing ISO standards:

- It has become an inevitable requirement for participation in global tenders and exports in hundreds of thousands of organisations.
- It provides an edge for differentiating among players in an increasingly competitive global market.
- It helps in building customer confidence by meeting their requirements and regulations through dependable processes.
- It reduces the cost of activities and reduces the risk of failure and wastage of time, effort, and materials. It can thus lead to improved productivity and profit.
- It provides specifications of the products and services and ensures that they work as per the customer's requirement.
- It helps in the continuous improvement of organisations through efficient documentation of processes and regular audits.
- It makes the replication of processes within an expanding organisation easier through the adoption of set standards.

4.3 FAMILY OF ISO 9000 STANDARDS

The standards in the ISO 9000 family give guidelines for executing quality management systems in organisations. ISO standards enable organisations to improve their processes. Processes consist of activities that are linked to each other and require resources to produce an output. In some cases, the input for one process may be the output of the other.[2] ISO 9001 is the most widely known guideline for quality management, but there are other standards as well that enable an organisation to get fully benefitted by the quality management system and focus on customer satisfaction. A few of them are listed below:

1. 'ISO 9000, Quality Management Systems—Fundamentals and Vocabulary' (ISO, 2015a), contains explanations of the quality management principles and gives definitions of fundamental terminologies used in other QMS-related ISO standards.
2. 'ISO 9001, Quality Management Systems—Requirements' (ISO, 2015b), gives guidelines for establishing Quality Management Systems (QMS) in an organisation, and it provides confidence to customers that the organisation can provide products and

[2] This concept also becomes the basis of defining the customer, where the finished product of one party becomes the input of work of another party, such that the second party is defined as the customer of the first party.

services that meet their needs and expectations. ISO 9001 certification of companies by external bodies is done based on the criteria laid down in ISO 9001.

3. 'ISO 9004, Quality of an organisation—Guidance to achieve sustained success' (ISO, 2018c)— gives guidelines that are useful for the long-term success of the organisation by considering a wider range of objectives. It serves as a guide for those organisations whose top management is in pursuit of continuous and systematic improvement of their overall performance through ISO 9001. Though it is not designed for certification purposes, it can be used to prioritise areas for improvement and gauge the maturity of the systems.
4. 'ISO 19011, Guidelines for Auditing Management Systems' (ISO, 2018a), provides directions for performing internal and external audits of ISO 9001-certified organisations. It gives an overview of how to operate an audit programme and what the requirements of the audit team are. Auditing is done to ensure that the organisations implementing QMS are meeting the requirements specified in ISO 9001.
5. 'ISO 10005, Quality Management—Guidelines for quality plans' (ISO, 2018b) gives guidelines on setting and using quality plans that integrate the demands of the process, product, project, or contract-to-work methods and practices that support product realisation. Creating a quality plan enhances the confidence that requirements will be satisfied and that processes are in control, thus motivating the people involved.
6. 'ISO 10006, Quality Management Systems—Guidelines for quality management in projects' (ISO, 2017) may be modified and utilised for any type of project, no matter how big or small, straightforward or complex, one-off or a portfolio of projects. The project manager uses this standard to certify that their organisation is following the procedures outlined in the ISO quality management system standards.

4.4 PRINCIPLES GOVERNING QUALITY MANAGEMENT SYSTEMS

Since the ISO 9000 series of standards are general in nature, it is simple to modify them to adapt to the requirements of any organisation. The purpose of these standards is to prepare a guideline incorporating details of what an organisation has to do to ensure quality, then work according to it, and record and document what has been done as per the guideline. ISO 9000, ISO 9001, and other standards for quality management are established from the seven quality management principles given below (ISO, 2015c).

1. **Customer focus:** For any organisation to be successful, it is very important to retain the loyalty of customers. To do that, the organisation should consider customers' present and future needs and focus on delivering them.
2. **Leadership:** The success of an organisation depends on leaders who can unite the purpose and direction and engage people in such a way that their resources, strategies, processes, and policies are aligned to achieve the organisation's objectives.
3. **Involvement of people:** For effective and efficient management of an organisation, the involvement of people at all levels is essential, and it is important to respect them as

individuals. All people in the organisation should be given recognition and empowerment for achieving the quality objectives of an organisation.

4. **Process approach:** An organisation can improve efficiency in its operation and achieve consistent results by understanding and managing its activities as interrelated processes.
5. **Improvement:** It is essential to continually improve in order to sustain performance levels and react to changing internal and external circumstances that create new opportunities.
6. **Decision-making based on evidence:** Making decisions is a complicated process since it requires a variety of inputs, facts, data, and interpretations. Hence, decision-making should be done after careful analysis and interpretation of evidence and facts.
7. **Relationship management:** Maintaining good relationships with interested parties like suppliers and partners influences the success of the organisation. Therefore, a good relationship should be kept to optimise their effect on performance.

4.5 QUALITY SYSTEMS TRIANGLE

Figure 4.1 depicts a quality systems triangle. The various functional departments contributing to the quality management of a construction organisation, in general, are tendering, design,

FIGURE 4.1 Quality systems triangle

construction method and planning, contract procurement, material purchasing, budgeting, work execution, quality assurance, commissioning, and operation and maintenance departments, and come at the base of the triangle on which the triangle is built. These give data and information on the quality to be achieved, which is maintained in a record for quality, Tier I. The quality records to be maintained by the quality assurance department are present in Tier I. It records the actual performance of the activities in comparison to the requirements of standards.

Tier II has work method statements for execution by supervisors and operators. Tier II gives detailed descriptions of how each activity is to be performed.

Tier III is the quality plan and quality specification. It describes how quality management can be applied to a particular project to produce a required deliverable. Quality specifications specify the activities of individual functional units. Therefore, the associated people are the project head and staff.

Finally, at the apex of the quality triangle is the quality manual of an organisation, Tier IV. Upper management guides the development of the quality manual, which is a framework of how the quality management system of an organisation works. It directs the organisation to work towards its stated vision and mission. This quality manual is then used throughout the organisation.

Thus, the integrated nature of quality management and enforcement is not to be underestimated but must be emphasised repeatedly, as it takes the entire organisation to make quality successful.

4.6 ABSTRACT OF ISO 9001-2015

The abstracts of various sections of 'ISO 9001-2015, Quality Management Systems—Requirements' are presented in Table 4.1. The contents of this standard include scope, normative reference, words and definitions, organisational context, leadership, planning, support, implementation, performance evaluation, and improvement. Table 4.1 contains summaries of the major sections and the subsections of ISO 9001-2015.

TABLE 4.1 ISO 9001:2015 sections and subsections (ISO, 2015b)

Sections	Sub-sections	Description
1. Scope		The scope defines the requirements for a QMS that may be used by any organisation, regardless of the nature, scale, or services or goods it offers. For example, in a construction company, the scope specifies the type of work, which may be construction, procurement, inspection, testing, and commissioning undertaken to meet the needs of the client, satisfying the regulatory requirements.
2. Normative Reference		Normative references for all concepts and definitions are provided in this document.

(Continued)

TABLE 4.1 (*Continued*)

Sections	Sub-sections	Description
3. Terms and Definitions		Definitions of terms used in this document are given in ISO 9000:2015.
4. Context of the Organisation	4.1 Understanding the organisation and its context.	Identification of problems within and outside the organisation pertinent to an organisation's goals and strategy and that have an effect on its capability to produce the outcomes demanded by its quality management system.
	4.2 Understanding the needs and expectations of interested parties	Determining the stakeholders associated with QMS and finding out their needs related to QMS, and reviewing and monitoring this information.
	4.3 Determining the scope of quality management systems	Establishing the scope of QMS by taking into account factors within and outside the organisation, the requirements of participants, and the nature of services and products.
	4.4 Quality management system and its processes	The establishment, execution, upkeep and ongoing improvement of a quality management system, as well as the necessary processes, their interactions and the upkeep and preservation of process documentation.
5. Leadership	5.1 Leadership and Commitment	By prioritising the requirements of the customer, top management may demonstrate commitment to QMS.
	5.2 Policy	A quality policy is established and communicated.
	5.3 Organisational roles, responsibilities, and authorities	The top executives of the organisation must delegate, explain, and guarantee that everyone in the organisation understands the tasks and powers.
6. Planning	6.1 Actions to address risks and opportunities	Considering the demands of the stakeholders and also the problems within and outside the organisation, understand the risks and opportunities to be handled. Then, plan and carry out the necessary measures. Finally, assess the success of the activity.
	6.2 Quality objectives and planning to achieve them	Defining a plan for the QMS's execution and establishing quality goals for various functions, levels and processes.
	6.3 Planning of changes	If a need for changes occurs, the changes shall be made considering the purpose, consequences, integrity of QMS, resource availability, and delegation of responsibility and authority.
7. Support	7.1 Resources	Identifying the organisational resources and expertise necessary for the setting up, execution, upkeep, and continuing betterment of a QMS; and delivering those resources and expertise. People, buildings, the environment in which processes can operate, and tools for measuring and monitoring resources are all examples of resources.

Sections	Sub-sections	Description
	7.2 Competence	Determine and ensure competency of personnel, and take actions for acquiring competency if needed, and further, assess its effectiveness. Document all pieces of evidence.
	7.3 Awareness	Ensuring that all employees are knowledgeable about the organisation's quality objectives, policies, and rewards for increased performance, as well as the implications of non-conformance.
	7.4 Communication	Determination of relevant external and internal communications considering the content, time, persons involved, and method.
	7.5 Documented information	Recording the information needed for QMS, including its creation, updation, and control.
8. Operation	8.1 Operational planning and control	Planning, executing, and controlling of processes necessary for the products and services.
	8.2 Requirements for products and services	Communicating the information connected with products and services to customers, identifying the requirements, reviewing the organisation's ability to meet requirements, and modifying it if required.
	8.3 Design and development of products and services	Establishing a design and development process to provide appropriate products and services. Implementing it and maintaining it.
	8.4 Control of externally provided processes, products, and services	Ensuring the compliance of procedures, goods, and services provided by a third party.
	8.5 Production and service provision	Implementing product and service provision according to documented information, using suitable monitoring and measuring resources.
	8.6 Release of products and services	Releasing goods and services after ensuring that their specifications have been satisfied.
	8.7 Control of non-conforming outputs	Ensuring that non-conforming outputs are identified and prevented from delivery or use.
9. Performance Evaluation	9.1 Monitoring, measurement, analysis, and evaluation	Determining various aspects like what to monitor, when to monitor, methods of monitoring, and its analysis and assessment.
	9.2 Internal audit	Conducting an internal audit to check if the QMS conforms to the organisation's requirements and ISO standards and evaluate the effectiveness of QMS implementation.

TABLE 4.1 (*Continued*)

Sections	Sub-sections	Description
	9.3 Management review	Checking the QMS for appropriateness, sufficiency, effectiveness, and alignment with the strategic intention of the organisation.
10. Improvement	10.1 General	Meeting customer needs and raising customer satisfaction, and also identifying areas for improvement and taking the appropriate steps.
	10.2 Nonconformity and corrective action	In case of nonconformance, take necessary action, implement it and review its effectiveness.
	10.3 Continual improvement	Continue to address new demands and opportunities to increase the effectiveness, appropriateness, and efficiency of QMS.

4.7 CONSTRUCTION QUALITY IMPROVEMENT STRATEGIES

Quality is a concept that took shape and is evolving since the dawn of history. Though it has been successfully implemented in the manufacturing sector in its modern versions, it has not been as remarkably successful in the construction sector, especially in developing nations. The realisation is simply absent. Or if the importance of quality is perceived, there are too many other pressing issues, such as social justice, to pay attention to engineering quality. Hence, the construction industry is facing challenges and barriers in the successful implementation of various techniques, in addition to its unique nature. But the lack of quality in new construction is an issue faced by everyone around the world. Many developed countries have come up with different strategies for quality management. It is said that something measurable can alone be improved. Hence, many countries like Singapore, Malaysia, Hong Kong, and so on, have developed construction quality assessment techniques that are based on measuring the quality of work done the first time. It has been found beneficial to promote doing things right the first time, by reducing rework costs and increasing sustainability. Among others around the world, some of these are the CONQUAS in Singapore, PASS in Hong Kong, and QLASSIC in Malaysia.

4.8 CONQUAS: CONSTRUCTION QUALITY ASSESSMENT SYSTEM

Construction Quality Assessment System, which is commonly referred to as CONQUAS, is a national standard for building quality assessment in Singapore, introduced by the Construction Industry Development Board (CIDB) in 1989 (BCA, 2022; Pheng *et al.*, 1999). Major public sector organisations in Singapore, such as the Public Works Department, Housing and Development Board, and Public Utilities Board, were consulted during the development of this system (Pheng *et al.*, 1999).

The buildings are assessed to evaluate the workmanship against the standards and specifications in an objective manner. Building assessment is done by site inspection. To assess the project's quality, a sampling strategy is employed to reflect the entire project. The samples selected for assessment should be representative of the whole project and the number of sampling units will depend on the area of the building. The weights assigned to various components vary according to the types of buildings: commercial, industrial, academic, and other entities; private housing; public housing; and land-based housing (BCA, 2022). After evaluating the various components stipulated in the CONQUAS manual, scoring is done out of 100 for each assessed building. The main intention of this system is to reduce rework by not considering re-scoring after initial evaluation and assigning scores. The buildings must be one to three years old to qualify for assessment. The one-year lower limit aids in finding defects and the three-year upper limit ensures that the building is still recognised as a new development (Pheng *et al.*, 1999).

The main goals of CONQUAS are to improve building construction quality by implementing a system for evaluating quality in construction projects, to set quality evaluation goals by comparing completed works to specifications and standards of workmanship, and to make systematic evaluations possible within reasonable time and cost constraints (BCA, 2022). According to Balakrishnan (2002), CONQUAS has established itself as the *de facto* national quality benchmark for the construction sector since its founding in 1989. Hence, this is a major step and accomplishment made in improving quality. During the bidding process, it helps to evaluate the contractor's quality performance of previous works (Smith, 1999).

The evaluation standards are modified to keep up with the pace of technological advancement and societal quality expectations. Initially, CONQUAS started with the assessment of structural, architectural, mechanical and electrical works. In the eleventh edition launched in 2022, CONQUAS® 2022, the assessment framework has been simplified, and the structural, mechanical, electrical and plumbing (MEP) works assessment has been removed. It includes only the evaluation of external and internal finishes and verification of installation and functional tests.

The CONQUAS system has now become a benchmarking tool that is being used in various countries like Malaysia, China, Hong Kong SAR, the United Kingdom, Australia, and South Africa. There are some Indian construction companies, such as the Brigade Group, which have deployed CONQUAS to attain better quality by following the principle of doing it right the first time (Das, 2019). It helps them improve quality as each activity is inspected during construction, thus minimising defects and reducing the completion time. According to a study by Ooi *et al.* (2014), selling price and appreciation rate are strongly correlated with the quality of new building construction. They suggested that higher-quality products would bring in more money for developers and produce better capital gains for investors and homeowners.

The sixth edition of CONQUAS covers most of the components of building such as structural components, architectural works, and mechanical and electrical works. The works like piling, heavy foundation, and sub-structure works which are heavily equipment-based and come under separate contracts or sub-contracts are not included in this assessment. Workmanship is assessed through site inspection and field testing. Structural works and mechanical and electrical works are assessed throughout the construction process and the architectural works are assessed on the completion of building construction. Structural integrity is a highly important parameter, as the cost of quality is high for structural components.

The elements assessed under structural works during the construction stage include site inspection of formwork, steel reinforcement, and prefabricated components. Assessment of prestressed concrete and structural steel is done if it accounts for more than 20% of the total structural cost. Laboratory testing is done to assess compressive strength of concrete and tensile strength of steel reinforcement. Evaluation of the uniformity and cover of hardened concrete is done using non-destructive testing.

Workmanship is mostly assessed from architectural works, and it mainly deals with finishes and components. Site inspections of internal finishes, roofs, external walls, and external works at completion of building construction are done for assessment of architectural works. Floors, internal walls, ceilings, doors, windows, and components are included in internal finishes. Material tests and functional tests such as wet area water tightness, window water tightness, and adhesion of internal wall tiles are also done as a part of functionality evaluation. Testing of waterproofing of internal wet areas is done during its installation.

Mechanical and electrical (M&E) works are very significant as they affect the performance of the building and incur high costs. Elements assessed under M&E works are electrical works, air conditioning and mechanical ventilation works (ACMV), fire protection works, sanitary and plumbing works, and the basic M&E fittings. For ACMV ductworks, electrical conduits and concealed pipes, inspection is done onsite before embedding or concealing them. Site inspection is done after installation of the air handling unit (AHU), cooling tower, fire alarm control panel, etc. Performance tests are done to evaluate water pressure, earthing, etc.

Table 4.2 shows the scoring criteria for different editions of CONQUAS. In the sixth edition, the structural components were given 25% weightage. Subsequently, it was reduced to 10% in the ninth edition. It has not been considered at all in the eleventh edition. At the same time, the importance of architectural components increased from 55 % to 100% from the sixth to eleventh edition. When an assessed item complies with the CONQUAS standard, '√' mark will be given and when it does not comply, 'X' is given. Items not applicable for assessment are given '–'. The CONQUAS score is calculated by adding the number of compliances of the items assessed. Scoring is done only once and there is no re-scoring after rectification has been done. This is how it encourages the contractors to do things rightly the first time.

The weightages provided are a compromise between the cost proportions of the various components in a building and their aesthetic consideration. Private housing is very expensive in Singapore. Hence most of the residential buildings are built by the government and are sold to the residents (public residential–sold flats). Rental buildings are those allotted to low-income people. Hence, it may not be required to have more aesthetics as compared to publicly sold flats and private residential buildings. So, there is a difference in the weightage of structural works and architectural works in CONQUAS scoring for the different groups of residential buildings. Architectural features are comparatively more visible to the users than the structural components. Hence, by considering the feedback from the homeowner surveys, more weightage has been given to the architectural components in the subsequent editions of CONQUAS.

TABLE 4.2 CONQUAS scoring criteria (taken from various editions of CONQUAS)

Edition	Components	Category A	Category B		Category C		Category D
		Commercial, Industrial, Institution, Mixed Development & others – having central cooling system (%)	Commercial, Industrial, Institution, Mixed Development & others – not having central cooling system (%)	Private housing (%)	Public housing (Sold flats)(%)	Public Housing (Rental flats) (%)	Landed housing (%)
6th 2005	Structural works	25	30	25	35		30
	Architectural works	55	60	65	60		65
	M&E works	20	10	10	5		5
	CONQUAS Score	100	100	100	100		100
9th 2017	Structural works	10	15	10	15	20	10
	Architectural works	75	80	85	80	75	85
	M&E works	15	5	5	5	5	5
	CONQUAS Score	100	100	100	100	100	100
11th 2022	Internal finishes	50		60	55		
	Installation methods verification and functional tests	30		20	25		
	External finishes	20		20	20		
	Bonus points	7		8	7		
	CONQUAS score	107		108	107		

4.9 PASS: PERFORMANCE ASSESSMENT SCORING SCHEME

Hong Kong's construction industry initiated a quality assessment system under the aegis of the Housing Authority of Hong Kong. Performance Assessment Scoring Scheme (PASS) is a yardstick to measure the quality of work executed by contractors. The assessments of the contractor's performance with regard to the compliance of user requirements are done through site visits, desktop assessments, and inspection of records. These are done by members of the PASS Assessment Team (PAT) and Project Team. They conduct work assessments (comprising engineering works and architectural works assessments), general assessments (which include assessment of management input, programme, progress, environmental and safety assessments), and maintenance period assessments (HKHA, 2022).

Structural works and site formation works are evaluated under the assessment of engineering works. For assessing structural works, sites are inspected during various activities like reinforcement, formwork and falsework, and concreting. Inspections of site records of these works are also done to assess the construction quality. In site formation work assessment, geotechnical jobs and related records are inspected. It includes inspection of excavation and provision of lateral support, retaining wall construction, slope formation, backfilling and compacting, and other geotechnical activities.

The architectural works are evaluated twice, an interim assessment during the construction phase and a final assessment after the project completion. In the interim evaluation, material quality and workmanship of the various factors such as floor, wall finishes—internal and external, ceiling, window, plumbing, precast components, waterproofing, cladding, front elevation, and other components are assessed along with inspection of the quality records. In the final assessment, a detailed site inspection is done to assess workmanship and the finishing quality. Assessment is done for 14 factors: floor, wall finishes—internal and external, ceiling, windows, plumbing, precast components, signages, elevation, external works—roads, emergency access, footpath, pedestrian area, and others. Cleanliness and care taken in maintaining finishing works are also noted, along with the final inspection of records.

Management input assessment of PASS evaluates the site management capabilities of the contractor. The performance of different contractors is compared using it. The factors considered under this head include: the way the contractor manages and organises the work, the resources under possession, coordination and control strategies followed and how they respond to instructions, and how well documentation has been done.

Programme and progress assessment verifies the completeness and inclusion of newer technology in the contractor's programme. Progress of work is gauged at all stages, including site formation, structural works, architectural works and building services, until completion. Environmental and other obligations assessment include assessment of factors related to environment and health. It also evaluates the provision of site security, access to the site and material storage. Safety assessment verifies the safety aspects on site. In the maintenance period assessment, functional aspects of buildings are assessed during the occupation.

Each of these factors is verified for conformance to the pre-defined standards. Upon qualifying the input, output, and maintenance criteria, PASS scores are awarded to the contractors. For each compliance, "√" is given, and for non-compliance, 'X' is given. Weightage is applied differently to different categories based on their importance, the more being for output characteristics. The location for assessment is chosen randomly by the computer based on the instructions in the PASS manual. Better scores earn the contractors higher chances of winning tenders. The contractors are also provided with feedback for improvement.

4.10 QLASSIC: QUALITY ASSESSMENT SYSTEM IN CONSTRUCTION

The Construction Industry Development Board (CIDB) of Malaysia developed the Quality Assessment System in Construction (QLASSIC) as a yardstick to measure quality (CIDB, 2023). This was introduced to assure quality in construction and thus enhance customer satisfaction by reducing quality-related issues in products and workmanship. It verifies the performance of work by contractors by referring to approved standards and procedures, specifications and drawings as mentioned in contractual requirements.

The QLASSIC was developed with a view to achieve the objectives as follows:

- **a.** For the betterment of construction quality in Malaysia
- **b.** For developing a system for assessing workmanship quality
- **c.** For evaluating workmanship quality of construction activities
- **d.** To assess the contractor's performance
- **e.** To collect and store data for analysis.

The various aspects covered in QLASSIC are the assessment of structural, architectural, external, mechanical, and electrical works. Marks are awarded after assessing the quality of workmanship and conformance to standards based on field testing and site inspection. Tests are conducted to ascertain the functional performance of building services and installations thus ensuring comfort, safety, and aesthetics. Inspection of structural works and mechanical and electrical works starts from the beginning of the work till its completion, whereas assessment of architectural works, M&E works and external works are done only after the projects are completed. Selecting locations for assessment from floor plans and site plans is done by sampling.

To promote the objective of doing things right the first time, scoring will be done only once, i.e., after the initial inspection. There will not be re-scoring after rectification of defects detected during the initial inspection. For the items that comply with approved quality standards, "√" is awarded, and for non-compliance, 'X' is given. The score will be based on the count of the number of complying items. The assessment is done by accredited assessors and is under CIDB regulations.

The factors assessed in structural works consist of the quality of reinforcement, concrete, and prestressed concrete structures. Site inspection, field tests for strength, and non-destructive testing for examining cover and uniformity are included in the assessment of structural works. Assessment of architectural works comprises evaluating finishing works as these are the activities that showcase the quality of materials and workmanship. The M & E works are significant because of their high-cost component and their influence on building performance. It includes electrical and mechanical fittings, heating ventilation and air-conditioning (HVAC), fire and safety, plumbing, and other building services. While assessing external works, various components considered are pathways, roads, car parks, drains, turf, gates, playgrounds, security cabins, substations, fences, swimming pools, and waste collection centres.

The weightages are allocated considering the cost proportions, cost of quality, and aesthetics. The weightage given to various components varies according to the types of buildings. The buildings are categorised into four types; residential buildings like landed housing and stratified housing fall under Category A and Category B, respectively, and non-residential buildings include public buildings, commercial buildings, and industrial buildings without centralised cooling under Category C and with centralised cooling system under Category D. By adding the marks awarded to each component, the total score can be calculated.

The assessment will be completed before delivering the project to the client. The QLASSIC scores assure a guarantee to the buyers regarding the quality of the work. This system creates a sense of need among contractors to strive for better quality. As it is associated with the reputation of the contractors and hence affects their marketing, contractors often work to improve on the weak areas identified through this scoring system.

Table 4.3 shows the weightage allocation in different evaluation frameworks like the CONQUAS, QLASSIC, and PASS. The CONQUAS scoring criteria is based on the ninth edition of the CONQUAS manual, and QLASSIC evaluation criteria is based on CIS-7:2014. The PASS criteria has been obtained from the journal paper 'Quest for continuous quality improvement for public housing construction in Hong Kong' by Tam *et al.* (2000). The PASS assessment consists of works assessment, general assessment, architectural works, and maintenance period assessment. The ninth edition of CONQUAS is chosen for comparison because of its similarity with the other two evaluation methods.

TABLE 4.3 Comparison of weightage allocation in different evaluation frameworks for residential buildings

Component	CONQUAS - 9th edition, 2017			QLASSIC - 2014		PASS
	Private housing	Public housing-sold flats	Public housing-rental flats	Landed housing	Stratified housing	Public housing
Structural works	10	15	20	15	20	35
Architectural works	85	80	75	70	60	35
M&E works	5	5	5	5	10	10
External works	-	-	-	10	10	-
General obligations like safety and other factors	-	-	-	-	-	20
TOTAL	100	100	100	100	100	100

The concept of evaluating the quality score started after Singapore developed the CONQUAS. The other two nations developed their scoring systems based on CONQUAS. Hence, there is a similarity in the weightage given for various components. However, there are differences in weightages because of the difference in priority that the respective construction industry gives to various components. As construction technology progressed, BCA Singapore started to include more norms to increase productivity and reduce the workforce by introducing prefabrication and precast technologies. Buildability and constructability scores were thus introduced to raise the standards of construction. Henceforth, those scores took care of the structural aspects, and more weightage has been given to architectural elements in the recent version of CONQUAS. Not much revision has happened in QLASSIC since 2014. In PASS, management aspects and safety have also been considered when assessing the quality of construction.

4.11 AGREEMENT CERTIFICATES BY BRITISH BOARD OF AGREEMENT (BBA)–QUALITY APPRAISAL SCHEME IN UK

The motive of the BBA Agrément[3] Scheme is to issue fitness for construction products and systems after it has been assessed by BBA in detail. The BBA is an accredited product certification body of UKAS (United Kingdom Accreditation Service) (Agrément, n.d.). The assessment of the product is done against many key factors and supplementary information applicable to a particular product or system based on the characteristics and intended use of the product or system under assessment. The Agrément Certificate, which is the output of assessment, is used by others in the supply chain to develop specifications. BBA Agrément Certificate denotes excellence, and it is based on national and European standards. It demonstrates a construction product's competency, distinctiveness, and specialist formulation.

Construction products in the following product areas are included in the certification scheme (Agrément, B. B., n.d.):

1. 'Building systems and kits
2. Ceiling products
3. Concrete and plaster products
4. Heating and ventilation products and systems
5. Finishings
6. Floor products
7. Highway works, products, and systems.
8. Jointing products, components, and materials
9. Masonry products
10. Roof and roofing products and systems
11. Draining and plumbing products and systems
12. Wall and cladding products and systems
13. Window, door, and opening products and systems'.

The key factors considered for assessment are strength and stability, fire protection, health and hygiene environment conservation, safety and availability, protection from noise, energy saving and heat retainment, sustainability in using natural resources, durability, design, installation, workmanship, and maintenance.

[3] *Agrément* means 'approval'.

The assessment is done in various stages as listed below:

1. Based on the type of product and its intended use, a detailed assessment specification is prepared.
2. Information like test data, calculations, technical documentation, installation manuals, etc., are requested from the client.
3. After receiving the information, BBA will carry out the following jobs: evaluation of calculations, test data, assessment of the product for key factors, conducting factory visits and audits, carrying out testing at BBA, assessing fitness using professional judgment, completing an evaluation report, drafting a certificate and providing a recommendation for the statement on the product's fitness.
4. The client will be informed of the progress throughout the process and will be contacted in case additional information is required.

After reviewing the technical file and considering the recommendation, the decision is taken to award the BBA Agreement certificate. If the product is non-conforming to requirements, BBA informs the client. A certificate is awarded to confirm that the specifications have been met. BBA certification is a trusted way to enhance the market credibility of the products. The assessment activities are coordinated by the Product Approvals and Certification Department. The internal policies and procedures support the requirements in the Scheme Manual.

CONCLUSION

This chapter gives an overview of the relevance of ISO standards in aiding organisations to attain quality management. Various standards associated with quality management are ISO 9000, ISO 9001, ISO 9004, ISO 10005, ISO 10006, and ISO 19011. Those organisations following QMS as per ISO standards are ISO 9001 certified. ISO certification provides confidence to the customers regarding the quality of the products and services offered by the certified organisations. A summary abstract of the ISO 9001 is also included in this chapter. ISO 9001 provides general guidelines for following quality management in different types of organisations. It can be modified as per the requirement and the type of organisation.

Apart from ISO certification, another strategy followed in the construction sector to enhance quality is the application of quality assessment systems. Countries like Singapore, Hong Kong, and Malaysia have introduced systems, namely CONQUAS, PASS, and QLASSIC, to assess the quality of construction of newly constructed buildings. In these systems, the quality assessment is done during and after construction, and a score is evaluated. The peculiarity of these systems is that scoring is done only once after the construction, and no re-scoring will be done after rework or rectification. In this way, it urges the contractor to do things right the first time. These systems have thus helped enhance the quality of construction in these countries. Another scheme in use in the U.K. is the BBA Agrément Scheme, which certifies the quality of construction products. By following various strategies, countries are trying to improve the quality of the construction sector.

WORKS CITED

Agrément, B. B. (n.d.), BBA *AgrémentCertificate*, Retrieved from British Board of Agrément: https://www.bbacerts.co.uk/bba-agrement-certificate/

ASQ. (2023), *What is ISO 9001:2015 - Quality Management Systems?* Retrieved from asq.org/quality-resources/iso-9001: https://asq.org/quality-resources/iso-9001

Balakrishnan, V. (2002, April 25), *At the BCA Award Ceremony,* Singapore Government Press Release. https://www.nas.gov.sg/archivesonline/data/pdfdoc/2002042505.htm

BCA. (2022), *CONQUAS*, Retrieved from Building and Construction Authority: https://www1.bca.gov.sg/buildsg/quality/conquas

CIDB. (2023), *Quality Assessment System for Building Construction Works,* Retrieved from cidb.gov.my: https://www.cidb.gov.my/eng/qlassic-quality-assessment-system-for-building-construction-works/

Das, A. (2019), 'Bengaluru: What makes Bengaluru's developers best in country', *The Times of India*, 2 May.

HKHA. (2022), *Building PASS*, Retrieved from housingauthority.gov.hk: https://www.housingauthority.gov.hk/en/business-partnerships/resources/performance-assessment/building-pass/index.html

ISO. (1997), *Friendship Among Equals,* Retrieved from Friendship among equals: https://www.iso.org/files/live/sites/isoorg/files/about%20ISO/docs/en/Friendship_among_equals.pdf

ISO. (2015a). *ISO 9000:2015(en) Quality Management Systems - Fundamentals and Vocabulary* (Geneva: International Organization for Standardization).

ISO. (2015b). *ISO 9001 - Quality Management Systems - Requirements* (Geneva: International Organization for Standardization).

ISO. (2015c), *Quality Management Principles,* Retrieved from iso.org: https://www.iso.org/files/live/sites/isoorg/files/store/en/PUB100080.pdf

ISO. (2017), *ISO 10006 - Quality Management - Guidelines for Quality Management in Projects* (Geneva: International Organization for Standardization).

ISO. (2018a), *ISO 19011 - Guidelines for Auditing Management Systems* (Geneva: International Organization for Standardization).

ISO. (2018b), *ISO 10005 - Quality Management - Guidelines for Quality Plans* (Geneva: International Organization for Standardization).

ISO. (2018c), *ISO 9004 - Quality Management- Quality of an Organisation - Guidance to Achieve Sustained Success* (Geneva: International Organization for Standardization).

ISO. (2024). *ISO About us*, Retrieved October 23, 2024, from iso.org: https://www.iso.org/about-us.html

Ooi, J. T., Le, T. T. and Lee, N. J. (2014), 'The impact of construction quality on house prices', *Journal of Housing Economics*, 26, 126-138.

Pheng, L. S., Kee, T. B. and Leng, A. A. (1999), 'Effectiveness of ISO 9000 in raising construction quality standards: Some empirical evidence using CONQUAS scores', *Structural Survey,* 17(2), 89–108.

Smith, G. M. (1999), 'Contractor qualification methods focusing on quality', *Proceedings, Annual Conference - Canadian Society for Civil Engineering*, 217–226.

Tam, C. M., Deng, Z. M., Zeng, S. X. and Ho, C. S. (2000), 'Quest for continuous quality improvement for public housing construction in Hong Kong', *Construction Management and Economics*, 18(4), 437–446.

REVIEW QUESTIONS

Multiple Choice Questions

1. When was the International Organization for Standardization (ISO) created?
   (a) 1940 (b) 1946
   (c) 1950 (d) 1960
2. Which ISO standard is most commonly adopted by organisations worldwide?
   (a) ISO 14000 (b) ISO 9000
   (c) ISO 26000 (d) ISO 45000
3. What is a significant benefit of implementing ISO standards?
   (a) Reduced marketing costs
   (b) Increased product complexity
   (c) Improved customer confidence
   (d) Higher production volume
4. Which ISO standard focuses on quality management systems requirements?
   (a) ISO 9000 (b) ISO 9001
   (c) ISO 9004 (d) ISO 10005
5. Which ISO standard provides guidelines for auditing management systems?
   (a) ISO 9000 (b) ISO 9001
   (c) ISO 9004 (d) ISO 19011
6. Which principle is not part of the seven quality management principles?
   (a) Customer focus (b) Leadership
   (c) Profit maximisation (d) Process approach
7. What is the purpose of the ISO quality system triangle?
   (a) To manage product design
   (b) To define quality procedures
   (c) To describe the quality system levels
   (d) To audit financial performance
8. What does ISO 10006 focus on?
   (a) Quality management systems requirements
   (b) Guidelines for quality plans

(c) Quality management in projects
(d) Auditing management systems

9. Which ISO standard provides guidelines on setting and using quality plans?
(a) ISO 10005 (b) ISO 9001
(c) ISO 9004 (d) ISO 19011

10. What is the main goal of the Construction Quality Assessment System (CONQUAS)?
(a) To increase project costs
(b) To improve building construction quality
(c) To simplify construction processes
(d) To reduce construction duration

11. Which country introduced the CONQUAS system?
(a) Malaysia (b) China
(c) Singapore (d) Hong Kong

12. What does PASS stand for in the context of construction quality assessment in Hong Kong?
(a) Performance Assessment Scoring Scheme
(b) Project Audit Scoring System
(c) Professional Assessment Standards System
(d) Performance and Safety Scoring

13. What is the main purpose of QLASSIC in Malaysia?
(a) To certify international standards
(b) To measure quality of construction
(c) To reduce construction costs
(d) To improve labour efficiency

14. What does the BBA Agreement Certificate represent?
(a) Environmental compliance (b) Market credibility
(c) Safety standards (d) Construction product quality

15. Which factor is not considered in the BBA assessment?
(a) Fire protection (b) Noise protection
(c) Financial profitability (d) Durability

16. What does ISO 9004 provide guidelines for?
(a) Certification processes (b) Sustained organisational success
(c) Financial audits (d) Risk management

17. What is the key benefit of CONQUAS?
(a) Lower construction costs
(b) Improved quality through reduced rework
(c) Faster project completion
(d) Increased use of manual labour

18. Which section of ISO 9001:2015 includes 'Actions to address risks and opportunities'?
    (a) Leadership (b) Support
    (c) Planning (d) Improvement
19. What is the goal of the 'Customer focus' principle in quality management?
    (a) To reduce production costs
    (b) To meet customer needs and expectations
    (c) To increase employee satisfaction
    (d) To streamline internal processes
20. Which ISO standard includes guidelines for quality management in projects?
    (a) ISO 9000 (b) ISO 10006
    (c) ISO 9004 (d) ISO 19011

Short Answer Type Questions

1. What led to the creation of the International Organization for Standardization (ISO)?
2. In which year was the ISO founded?
3. Where is the Central Secretariat of ISO located?
4. What is the widely accepted definition of quality according to ISO standards?
5. Name one of the most widely adopted ISO standards.
6. What does ISO 9000 focus on?
7. Why are ISO standards considered beneficial in global tenders and exports?
8. What is the purpose of ISO 9001?
9. Which ISO standard provides guidelines for the long-term success of an organisation?
10. What does ISO 19011 provide guidelines for?
11. List one principle governing Quality Management Systems (QMS) according to ISO 9000 series.
12. What is the primary purpose of a quality manual in the ISO quality system triangle?
13. What is included in the 'Scope' section of ISO 9001:2015?
14. What does the 'Normative Reference' section of ISO 9001:2015 provide?
15. What is assessed under 'Management review' in ISO 9001:2015?
16. What is the main objective of CONQUAS in the construction industry?
17. Which country developed the CONQUAS system?
18. What is PASS in the context of construction quality assessment?
19. What does QLASSIC aim to achieve in Malaysia?
20. What is the significance of the BBA agreement Certificate in the UK?
21. List one key factor considered in the BBA assessment.

22. Which ISO standard focuses on guidelines for quality management in projects?
23. What is the importance of the 'Customer focus' principle in ISO quality management?
24. What is the role of leadership in ISO quality management principles?
25. What is assessed in the 'Performance Evaluation' section of ISO 9001:2015?

Long Answer Type Questions

1. Describe the history and purpose of the International Organization for Standardization (ISO). Include its formation, main objectives, and its role in global standardisation.
2. Explain the concept of quality as defined by ISO and why it is important for global trade and manufacturing.
3. Discuss the advantages of implementing ISO standards in organisations. How do these standards benefit both clients and contractors?
4. Detail the family of ISO 9000 standards and their specific focus areas. How do these standards collectively contribute to effective quality management?
5. What are the seven quality management principles established by ISO? Discuss each principle and its significance in quality management systems.
6. Describe the ISO quality system triangle and its components. How does this structure help in implementing a quality management system within an organisation?
7. Summarise the key sections and subsections of ISO 9001:2015. What are the main requirements for an organisation to achieve ISO 9001 certification?
8. Discuss the Construction Quality Assessment System (CONQUAS). What are its main goals and how is it implemented in the construction industry?
9. Explain the Performance Assessment Scoring Scheme (PASS) used in Hong Kong's construction industry. What factors are assessed and how are scores awarded to contractors?
10. How can quality in construction be improved in India, in your opinion?

ANSWER KEYS

Multiple Choice Questions

1. (b)	**2.** (b)	**3.** (c)	**4.** (b)	**5.** (d)	**6.** (c)	**7.** (c)	**8.** (c)
9. (a)	**10.** (b)	**11.** (c)	**12.** (a)	**13.** (b)	**14.** (d)	**15.** (c)	**16.** (b)
17. (b)	**18.** (c)	**19.** (b)	**20.** (b)				

CHAPTER 5 Cost of Quality

5.1 INTRODUCTION

Quality is the most fundamental attribute a customer expects from a product or service. It was believed that the better the quality, the higher would be the cost. However, it was later realised that cost does not increase with improved quality. Here comes the significance of the cost of quality. The cost of quality (COQ) or the quality cost is the sum of the cost incurred for ensuring quality and, at the same time, includes the cost expended due to poor quality. Higher qualities are attained when the resources are fully utilised, thus reducing the cost. Substandard quality results in higher costs due to poor resource utilisation, leading to various costs such as repair, rework, recall, lost revenues, and lost customers.

Evaluating the cost of quality dates to the 1950s, when Armand V. Feigenbaum, who was then working at General Electric Company, came up with a 'dollar-based reporting system named - quality cost' (Harrington, 1987). It is the combination of costs connected with the development of a system for quality, inspection of products, and the money expended when there is non-conformance to the requirements. The cost of quality is a concept that evolved over the years through continuous refinement to become a highly sought-after management tool that may be utilised for quality improvement activities and for gauging the quality management system. The accounting and reporting of the quality cost is an inevitable part of many quality standards today.

Joseph M. Juran introduced the term cost of poor quality (COPQ) and used it in the Quality Handbook instead of the term 'quality cost' (Juran & Godfrey, 1999). He explained COPQ as the cost that would not occur if the product or process was perfect and free of error and non-conformances, not requiring rework, and so on. COPQ, otherwise known as Cost of poorly performing processes (COPPP), is the aggregate of the costs due to poor quality products or services and their poor performance, costs due to their inability to meet customer requirements, and costs due to not providing products or services on time, and cost incurred for repairing them to meet customer needs. He also explained the cost of quality in terms of the economics of quality conformance. COPQ is an effective cost-control method for converting deficiencies into money. Though it is not possible to calculate COPQ accurately, the goal of quality improvement is reducing the cost of poor quality. COPQ includes investments for making the product saleable (preventive and appraisal costs) and waste of money due to deficiencies (failure costs).

Numerous ideas and principles related to COQ were put forth by many quality experts, including Philip Crosby, Burati, Juran, Feigenbaum, and Dobbins. Philip Crosby stresses the significance of COQ in his book 'Quality is Free.' Crosby points out that 'what costs money are the "unquality" things, i.e., the cost incurred due to not doing the job right the first time' (Crosby, 1979). COQ is the sum of the price of conformance and the price of non-conformance. The cost of prevention and appraisal falls under conformance cost, and the cost of internal/external failure belongs to non-conformance costs. Crosby's approach emphasises that quality is free, i.e., it does not incur cost. When a job is done correctly the first time, there will not be any mistakes; hence, there will not be any need to track and correct them, thus making it more cost-effective.

The accounting technique known as 'cost of quality' (COQ) assists an organisation in determining the amount of resources allotted to activities that enhance the company's goods and services, avoid poor quality, and deal with internal and external failures (ASQ, 2023). All expenses to prevent non-conformance with requirements, enhance a product or service to comply with requirements, and costs incurred because of requirements not being met constitute quality costs. Hence, the cost of quality is the difference between a product or service's actual cost and the cost incurred when there is no poor service, defective products, or manufacturing defects (Wood, 2013).

Without understanding this knowledge, organisations needlessly waste money by performing substandard work. The cost of quality is a strategically important factor that an organisation must not ignore while performing management accounting (Shank & Govindarajan, 1993). Though there are a few variations in methods and viewpoints about the cost of quality, in a broad sense, all of them are in consensus that ensuring a continuous improvement process for achieving customer satisfaction is the central tenet of quality.

5.2 SOME REAL-LIFE CASES FROM THE CONSTRUCTION INDUSTRY TO ILLUSTRATE COST OF QUALITY

In this section, we present a few real-life cases taken from the Indian construction industry. It is very typical to witness instances of poor quality even during a casual visit to any construction site. The honeycombing in concrete, poor construction joints and subsequent patchwork, uneven concrete surfaces, unsafe construction, etc., are some commonly observed visuals at a construction project.

Achieving quality in cast in situ concrete construction is dependent on many factors, starting with the selection of good quality aggregates, cement, other additives, and water. In a number of cases, it has been found that water used for concrete construction is not of adequate quality. Sometimes, the water used for construction is drawn from the ground using a bore well, and the water has not even been tested for use, since only fresh drinking water is best for concrete. Most of this water contains chlorides, which are harmful. After a few years of construction, the occupants start to face problems such as peeling off plasters and corrosion in rebar. There are plenty of housing societies in Dwarka and Mayur Vihar in Delhi, where the residents face problems due to the poor quality of water used for construction. In some cases, it has been found that builders use recycled water without proper testing and purification. This results in the corrosion of rebars within a few years, leading to the failure of RC slabs.

In a recent incident in Gurugram, a few residents lost their lives during the collapse of a few slabs in a leading housing society. In another instance in Gurugram, a number of multi-storied residential towers were ordered to be demolished after a few years of construction because they were not found to be safe due to the high level of corrosion of rebars used in RC Slab construction.

The proverb 'A stitch in time saves nine' fits aptly in the above two cases. The cost of providing good quality water for construction would not have cost much to the builder. But the consequences of cutting corners here have resulted in a thousand times more cost and a loss of reputation to the builder, besides facing legal issues.

5.2.1 Case 1: High-Rise Residential Apartment in Gurugram

The Incident

ABC Construction Limited (actual name withheld), a private company registered as a home builder, started the construction of a multi-storeyed residential building in 2013. The project consisted of the construction of ten residential building blocks. The project was headed by the Vice President of the firm. There were two Project managers under him and several project engineers and supervisors coordinating the work. The construction work progressed well and was completed on time as scheduled. The apartments were handed over to the clients in 2017.

Life went well for the homeowners for the initial few years. After three years of occupancy, many apartments in the buildings started showing signs of deterioration in some of the blocks. Cracks started to be formed on the slab, beam, and other structural members. The homeowners started getting frustrated due to the presence of defects. They demanded that repairs be undertaken. However, the builder refused to take any action in this regard as the defect liability period, as per the contract with the clients, was for two years.

In another two years, the defects aggravated. There was a spalling of concrete cover from the ceiling, and the flooring tiles started to break. A few tiles debonded from the base material. The distressed homebuyers demanded the repair again. The builder now had no other choice than to repair. They engaged a few labourers for the repair work. The repair work started in an apartment on the sixth floor of block A. The workers removed the tiles, and they also removed the concrete cover that had broken. Then, it was observed that the reinforcement had corroded very severely. The engineers who visited the site realised that additional reinforcement needed to be provided to support the slab as the existing reinforcement had corroded badly. The next day, labourers started demolishing concrete to retrofit the slabs structurally. Sometime after the work started, the entire slab of the hall detached from the beam, collapsed, and fell to the floor below. This accident led to the collapse of the subsequent few floors to the ground floor. Unfortunately, as the slab collapsed on the other floors, it took the lives of two residents.

The police visited the site and prepared the First Information Report (FIR). The district administration inspected the site and requested that a premier technical institute closest to the location investigate the case. The Professors from the institute visited the site and studied the problem. It was found that the reinforcement of the entire building complex had degraded due to corrosion. As the report was submitted to the district administration, they ordered the immediate evacuation of the residents so that the deteriorated buildings could be demolished. The investigation report studied the causes of corrosion, where it was discovered there was inadmissibly high chloride content in the concrete. It was found that the water used for construction purposes had high quantities of chloride, which led to early-age corrosion of the rebar. After further investigations, the builder learned about the mistake they had made during construction.

The construction industry consumes a large quantity of water. Urbanisation results in high amounts of water consumption, and this rising demand results in groundwater depletion. Since water scarcity is a major problem faced by many Indian cities, the State Government drafted a bill in 2012 mandating the use of treated sewage water for construction purposes. The building construction by ABC Construction Limited was done utilising the water processed in a Sewage Treatment Plant (STP).

The type of treatment done in this particular case was insufficient to make water suitable for construction purposes. IS 456, Indian Standard for Plain and Reinforced Concrete, stipulates the quality of water to be used for construction activities. The builder did not test the water to check its suitability for construction purposes, for which he had a responsibility and a duty. The high chloride content went unchecked and thus was responsible for the early-age degradation of the concrete.

The Costs Incurred

Let us now try to understand the various costs incurred and how they can be accounted for under different components of the cost of quality. As we know, the cost of quality is the sum of prevention, appraisal, and internal and external failure costs.

In the case discussed above, the builder had not invested in the prevention cost, which is the reason for the subsequent higher internal and external failure costs. Prevention costs are those costs incurred in equipping the system to prevent quality problems. The cost of treating water to the required standards is a preventive cost. However, the builder did not spend money on treating the water to the required standards. The appraisal costs are connected with the determination of compliance with requirements. However, the builder did not conduct the mandated tests to confirm compliance of materials with specifications. Next, the quality of the treated water was not tested before being used for construction purposes. And, the builder did not spend sufficient money to prevent poor-quality construction or inspect for quality, which constitutes the conformance cost.

Internal costs are the costs incurred for repair before handing over the building to the occupants. In this case, no internal failure cost was incurred as corrosion was not detected before the handover. However, the extent of external failure cost is quite widespread, and it may not be possible to determine it completely. External costs are the costs incurred after the client has received the product and detected the defects. It includes the cost for the following activities.

- Cost of inspection.
- Cost of repair—which is the cost of labour, cost of repairing materials, and cost of design for repair.
- Compensation for the workers who met with the accident.
- Compensation to the bereaved families.
- Cost of demolition of the buildings.
- Compensation to the homeowners of the buildings who had been evacuated for demolition purposes.

- Compensation to the homeowners of the buildings who had been evacuated for repair purposes.
- Compensation to the loss of rent to homeowners of the buildings evacuated for repair purposes.
- Payment of rent to families who opted for the reconstruction of flats
- Lost revenue from unsold apartments.
- Loss of goodwill and reputation.
- Arbitration or litigation charges.
- Lost productivity hours.

The meagre savings on the preventive and appraisal costs or the negligence in adhering to regulations resulted in high external failure costs. The cost of prevention is a meagre amount in this case. That cost would have only been towards providing an RO (Reverse Osmosis) Plant for making the water fit for the construction process, some expense on laboratory testing, and some money towards supervision charges. Moreover, this would have saved the lives of those who got killed in the collapse of slabs in that multi-storeyed tower, subsequent costs incurred in legal proceedings, compensation to the affected families, and the cost of reconstruction. The incident attracted a lot of media attention, and it brought a lot of bad press to the company, as well as a loss of customers and clientele. In this case, the amount of external failure is so extensive that it cannot be adequately measured. Often, builders ignore the need to adhere to specifications mandated by the codes and rules. They look forward to saving money and time for performing preventive and appraisal measures. But this often results in huge losses to the builders and the community.

5.2.2 Case 2: Cooperative Society in Noida

In a recent case in Noida, the residents of a large cooperative society fought a prolonged legal battle with the contractor. The court decided in favour of the residents and ordered the contractor to repair all the defects in the structure at his cost and risk. This is the case of the construction of about 600 flats for a group housing society for leading lawyers and judges of the country. The society entrusted the job of construction to a contractor. During the construction, the quality of construction work was apparently compromised, and the flats, after a few years of occupation, started showing signs of distress. The members of the society took the contractor to court. The court decided that a distress mapping of all flats be carried out and all expenses toward this be absorbed by the contractor. The distress mapping showed poor conditions of RC members, plenty of instances of corrosion, peeling off of plaster, leakages in the basement, and instances of dilapidated balconies, some of them on the verge of collapse.

A consultant was hired to suggest the repair methodology for each RC member, and thus, a repair methodology was suggested to the contractor, all at the expense of the contractor. To supervise the repair work, a Project Management Consultant (PMC) was also hired at the expense of the contractor. At the time of writing this book, the said repair works are still going on. The contractor has employed about 150 workers, a separate test laboratory for checking the quality of repair materials is established at the site, and the work is expected to be completed in another two years. The readers can imagine the cost of maintaining such a large workforce, the cost of repair materials, and supervisory staff. Besides, the cost of hiring the PMC agency is also going to be substantial. Had the work been done with proper quality at the very beginning, this situation and the extra cost would not have been incurred by the contractor.

5.2.3 Case 3: Construction of a Government Building

In another instance in Noida itself, the construction of a government building was awarded to a contractor. It appears that the contractor had won this bid at a very low price. During the construction, the quality of work was compromised. The supervision officials from the government side did not supervise the construction process and nor did they inspect the construction materials used in construction. The schedule of work was also not being followed by the contractor. After a few notices, the contractor was blacklisted. When the structure of the building was nearly complete, the instances of poor quality came to the notice of higher officials. An enquiry was initiated, and an agency was hired to ascertain the strength of the in-situ concrete. As expected, the strengths of columns, beams, and slabs were much below the design strength. Based on the reduced strength, the structural models were reviewed and strengthening measures were suggested. The government has to now spend a lot of money to repair the structure of this building.

5.3 COST OF QUALITY MODELS

Many researchers have worked on framing the cost of quality models. Some of the major models are mentioned and discussed below:

- **Quality cost model (Feigenbaum, 1983)**

$$\text{Quality cost} = \text{Cost of control} + \text{Cost of failure of control}$$

$$\text{Where, Cost of control} = \text{Prevention costs} + \text{Appraisal costs, and}$$

$$\text{Cost of failure of control} = \text{Internal failure cost} + \text{External failure cost}$$

- **Juran's cost of poor quality (Juran & Godfrey, 1999)**

$$\begin{aligned}\text{Cost of poor quality} = {} & \text{Cost of nonconformities} \\ & + \text{Cost of inefficient processes} \\ & + \text{Cost of lost opportunities for sales revenue}\end{aligned}$$

- **Crosby's model (Crosby, 1979)**

$$\text{COQ} = \text{Prevention cost} + \text{Appraisal cost} + \text{Failure cost}$$

- **Poor quality cost (PQC) model (Harrington, 1987)**

$$\text{PQC} = \text{Direct poor-quality costs} + \text{Indirect poor-quality costs}$$

$$\begin{aligned}\text{Direct poor-quality costs} = {} & \text{Controllable poor-quality cost} \\ & + \text{Resultant poor-quality cost}\end{aligned}$$

$$\text{Controllable poor-quality cost} = \text{Prevention cost} + \text{Appraisal cost}$$

$$\text{Resultant poor-quality cost} = \text{Internal error cost} + \text{External error cost}$$

Indirect poor-quality cost = Customer-incurred cost
+ Customer-dissatisfaction cost
+ Loss-of-reputation cost

- **Opportunity or intangible cost model (Sandoval-Chavez & Beruvides, 1998)**

$$C_T = C_P + C_A + C_F + C_O$$

Where,
'C_T = Total COQ in terms of revenue lost and profit not earned
C_P = Total cost incurred for prevention of non-conformance
C_A = Total cost incurred for appraisal
C_F = Total cost in failure items
C_O = Losses due to opportunity factors.'

- **Process cost model (BSI, 1992)**

COQ = (Cost of conformance + Cost of non-conformance) for individual cost elements (people, equipment, material, environment) in a process

Cost of conformance is the price of carrying out the process as specified with 100% efficiency. This doesn't mean that the process is inefficient or even required; it only means that it can't be done for less money when carried out according to the specifications. This represents the process's bare minimum cost.

Cost of non-conformance (CONC) is the price of incapability within the given process, i.e., excessive costs of personnel, supplies, and equipment resulting from substandard inputs, mistakes committed, refused products, and other forms of waste. All of them are viewed as expenses due to unwanted processes.

5.4 CATEGORIES OF COST IN QUALITY COST

The quality cost can be classified as per BS 6143-2:1990 and most other COQ models into four types as follows:

- Costs of appraisal
- Costs of prevention
- Costs of internal failure
- Costs of external failure

From Figure 5.1, which depicts the quality cost breakdown, it is evident that,

Cost of Quality = Cost of Quality Control + Cost of Failure

Where Cost of Quality Control = Prevention costs + Appraisal costs

And Cost of Failure = Internal failure costs + External failure costs

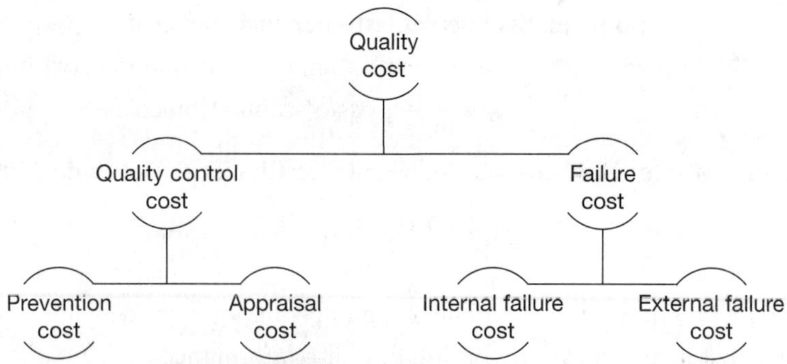

FIGURE 5.1 Quality cost breakdown

5.4.1 Prevention Cost

Prevention costs are the expenses incurred for the activities undertaken to prevent or avoid quality problems in products or services. The costs associated with creating, putting into practice, and maintaining a quality management system are included in the term 'preventive cost'. Investments made in defect prevention programmes for operations involving the quality of products or services are known as prevention costs. All these expenses occur prior to actual operation and they consist of the following:

- New product review.
- Creation of specifications for inputs, procedures, completed goods, and services.
- Preparation of quality plan.
- Establishing strategies and procedures for dependable production, operation, and inspection.
- Establishing and maintaining the quality assurance system.
- Quality education and training programs.
- Equipping the entire system to ensure quality.

In the construction industry, prevention costs are incurred for planning, training staff and workers, preparing a quality management system, ISO certification, and other activities that need to be specially designed to deliver quality work when the workers are not aware of how to do so. Preventive costs are incurred mostly during the starting phase of the project when it is required to equip the organisation to execute the project with high quality.

5.4.2 Appraisal Costs

Costs connected with appraisals are incurred to determine compliance of performance with quality criteria. Inspection, measurement, and monitoring of quality-related operations come under appraisal costs as they are done to ensure that products, and other materials are in compliance with the specifications, thus eliminating defects before they impact the customers. A few of them are:

- **Verification:** Inspection of raw materials, manufacturing processes, and finished goods to ensure that they meet the standards.

- **Quality audits:** Conduct audits to ensure the quality system is properly functioning.
- **Document review:** Review documents and correct errors before forwarding them to the next level.
- **Peer review:** Proofreading of reports and vetting of documents.
- **Supplier rating:** Evaluation, approval, and rating of supplier's products and services.
- **Calibration:** Calibrating equipment used for testing and measurement.

Examples of appraisal and inspection costs in the construction industry include testing the quality of construction materials like steel, cement, bricks, tiles and others using various tests, site inspection during construction, third-party audits, etc. If the deficiencies are discovered at the initial stage, it can avoid severe failure costs later. Developing additional and redundant inspection methods that are effective and efficient will reduce failure costs. Thus, the costs incurred at this stage ensure consistent performance.

5.4.3 Internal Failure Costs

Internal failure costs are expenses needed for repair, replacement, or disposal of defective work discovered before the consumer receives the goods or service. It is the amount required to rectify the non-conformances before delivering the product or service to the customer. These expenses result from the product or process failing to fulfil design quality standards and customer expectations and are discovered before the customer makes a purchase. They include the following:

- Wastage of time and money in performing repair work or holding of stock resulting from errors, poor organisation, or communication.
- Scrapping the faulty material or product that cannot be fixed, used, or sold and items that do not adhere to requirements.
- Rework of defective material or errors.
- Retesting.
- Repainting of scratches.
- Failure analysis to identify the root causes of internal product or service failure.

Costs incurred for rectification and rework of faulty construction before handing over to the client fall under the internal failure cost. In the construction industry, the detection of leakage or failure in pressure tests in the pipeline before commissioning and the cost associated with its detection and correction will fall under internal failure costs. Another example of internal failure cost is the expense of snagging and correcting defects prior to handover.

5.4.4 External Failure Costs

Costs of external failure are the costs related to defects found after the client's receipt of the product or service. External failure costs are related to the rectification of the defects identified by customers. These costs are incurred because of the failure of the products or services to meet design quality standards as required by the customer. These defects remain undetected until the project is handed over to the customer. The costs incurred for the correction of defects identified by the customers are the most expensive failure costs. A company loses its goodwill and reputation in addition to replacement or repair costs. Expenses due to external failure costs also intend to regain customer satisfaction and lost sales. The cost will increase further if the poor quality leads to litigation. The following costs fall under external failure cost:

- Service and repairs of returned and in-use damaged products.
- Claiming a warranty by replacing or repairing failed products.
- Handling, processing, and investigating customer complaints.
- Cost of rejected or recalled products.
- Cost of transporting defective products.
- Lost sales and profit.

For example, when a defect is identified in a vehicle, and it has been detected only after sales of the vehicle, the manufacturer has the responsibility to recall the product and correct that issue for all the vehicles in stock and for those that had been sold to the customers at their own risk and expenses. They must identify sold vehicles, recall their product, transport, repair, and send them back to the customer. All the costs associated with it fall under external failure cost.

The cost incurred in demolishing and reconstructing defective components or structures during their designed life or defect liability period comes under external failure cost.

The list of activities in a construction project that belong to different categories of cost of quality has been summarised in Table 5.1 in the light of descriptions given by various quality experts.

TABLE 5.1 Cost of quality in the construction industry

Type of cost	Impacted areas in the construction industry	Participant involved
Preventive cost	Preparation of PQP (Project Quality Plan), Contract review, specification review, vetting of drawings	Client, contractor, QC team,
	Review of architectural drawing and structural design, MEP clash detection, setting up standard operating procedures (SOP)	Design team
	Vendor evaluation, subcontractor evaluation, supplier review and evaluation, approving sources	Purchase team
	Method statement preparation, training labour to follow the correct construction procedure, quality planning, QMS planning, equipment maintenance	Planning team
	Approval from authorities concerned, implementation of PQP and SOP, training, inspection, periodic audit, toolbox meeting, hike in site staff salaries, selection of eligible contractors, the appointment of a quality team, quality control equipment, monitoring of suppliers and subcontractors	Administration and execution team

(Continued)

Type of cost	Impacted areas in the construction industry	Participant involved
Appraisal cost	Testing of purchased construction materials prior to use	Purchase team and QC team
	Establishing testing labs on site, quality checks at site, identification of defects, site inspection, calibration of testing equipment	Quality control team
	Inspection of works, third-party audit, certification	QC team
	Review meetings	QC team
Internal failure costs	Defect identification and analysis to find the corrective action	QC team
	Scrap cost and rework cost before sales	Purchase team, QC team
	Snagging, defect rectification, retesting, and re-inspection, demolition costs, demolition waste disposal, reconstruction, retrofitting costs	QC team
	Internal audit	Audit team
External failure costs	Rework on defects identified after handover, user complaints, arbitration and litigation, warranty claims, lost sales, compensation, fines and time spent.	Operations and maintenance team, administration

5.5 OPTIMUM COST OF QUALITY

The goal of measuring quality cost is to reduce costs and increase profit to the possible extent. The schematic graph shows that the cost of failure declines as the quality improves towards perfection, whereas there will be an increase in appraisal costs and prevention costs. It indicates that when more money is spent on prevention and appraisal, the quality will improve; hence, the failure cost will be reduced and vice versa. Efforts should be taken to enhance the quality to an 'optimum quality level' where the total costs of prevention, appraisal, and failure are minimal. The total quality cost will rise if efforts are made to improve quality beyond the optimal level. Figure 5.2 depicts the relationship between cost and level of quality. However, this graph is not precise and only illustrates the concept. For instance, the slope and trajectory of the cost lines are likely to be unique for each project.

Quality costs can be reduced by identifying the root causes of quality issues and taking the required steps to eradicate them. Continuous improvement approaches like re-engineering, KAIZEN, Six Sigma, Lean Six Sigma, and statistical quality control will be useful in this endeavour. Many construction projects apply various technologies to improve quality and reduce wastage. This helps them to reduce the cost of quality.

Quality cost measurement aims to give guidance to management for decision-making and taking action. It may not be possible to estimate the reduction in revenue due to lost goodwill and damage to the company's reputation. External failure costs can be calculated using

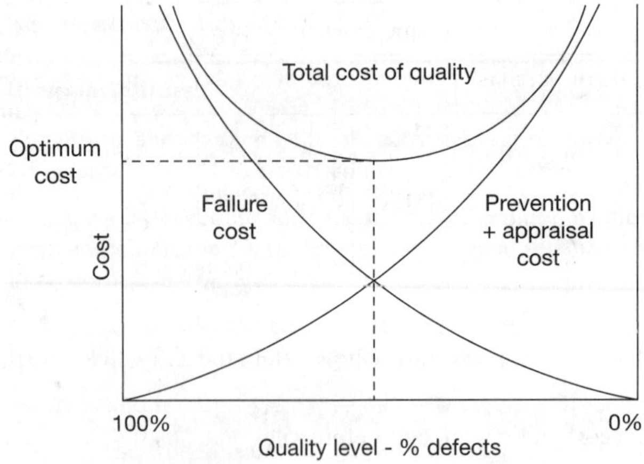

FIGURE 5.2 Cost versus quality level

specialised audits, statistical sampling, and market analysis. Personnel from all departments, like quality, marketing, and accounting, have to collaborate on these tasks.

The annual studies on the cost of quality help the organisation prioritise corrective action. With these data, the allocation of resources can be done in a better way to improve the return on investment. To supplement these techniques, the root causes of problems can be identified with the help of Pareto analysis, control charts, and cause-and-effect diagrams (Refer to Singh, 2017). Pareto analysis is used to identify the 'vital few' causes of poor quality while analysing the failure cost. Hence, resource allocation can be done judiciously rather than uniformly for all activities.

5.6 SIGNIFICANCE OF COST OF QUALITY

In many organisations, quality costs are hidden costs. Cost due to additional time for engineering, management, shop and site downtime, increased inventory, reduced sales, delivery issues, and lost orders would fall under hidden cost. As a result of this, unmeasured quality costs tend to increase. When the quality is poor, it results in higher quality costs and poor customer satisfaction and, hence, results in a reduction in revenue. This situation can pose a threat to the survival of an organisation. To prevent the occurrence of such a crisis, it is important to do rigorous cost-of-quality analysis.

Figure 5.3 illustrates the costs associated with failure in quality. The cost of quality includes charges for scrap, rework, inspection, returns under warranty, and quality assurance as the cost incurred towards the cost of quality. A company can reap the benefits only when the quality costs are calculated, controlled, and eliminated.

Since preventing a mistake is significantly less expensive than rectifying one, preventive expenses should be prioritised among all other costs. The 1-10-100 rule shown in Figure 5.4 illustrates the relationship between various costs. Thus, a rupee invested in preventive action can potentially save ₹10 in appraisal expenses and ₹100 in failure-related costs. Errors become more expensive as they proceed through the sequence of events from design to delivery.

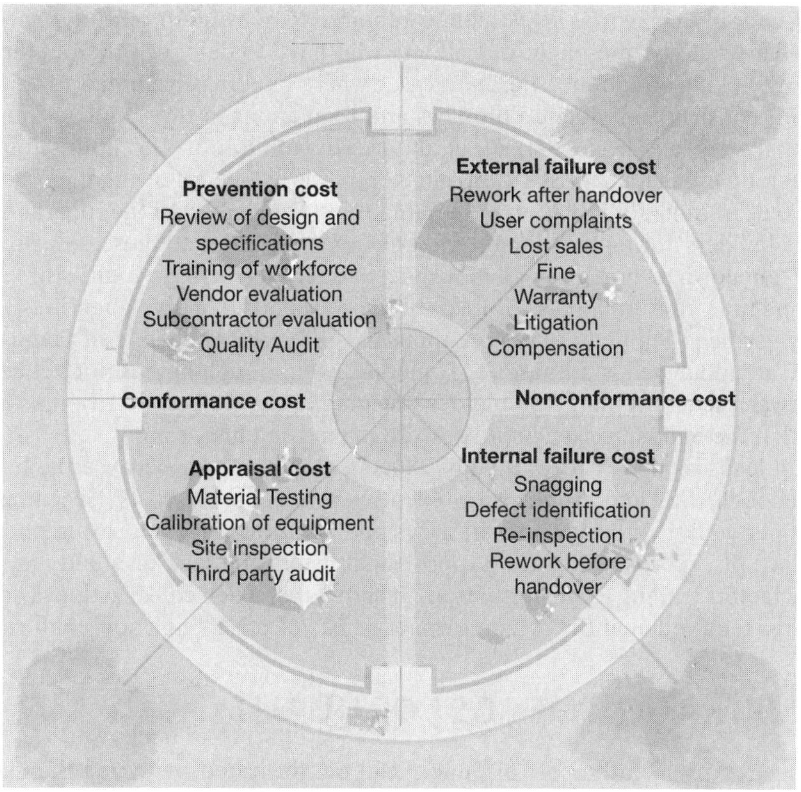

Credit: AI Image © Pearson Education

FIGURE 5.3 Costs of quality

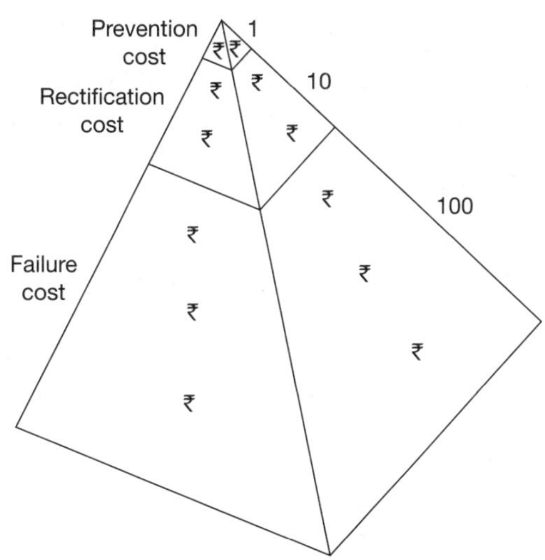

FIGURE 5.4 The 1-10-100 rule (modified from Omanachu & Ross, 2004)

Overall, a lot of managerial investment is required to deliver a project in the construction industry. What would be the plight of builders who have to demolish the buildings because of poor quality of construction? There are cases where buildings have had to be demolished because their construction violated the laws and regulations in the country. The demolition of the Twin Towers in Noida (SCI, 2021) and the demolition of four multi-storeyed apartments in Maradu municipality (SCI, 2019) in Kerala were done following the orders from the Supreme Court of India for violation of building rules. The neglect of the rules and laws of the place by the builders during the planning stage of the project led to these unfortunate events, leaving the homeowners homeless. Demolishing and reconstructing a multi-storeyed building is a costly and time-consuming task. It leads to the wastage of massive quantities of resources. But quality has been implied in laws for thousands of years. The Code of Hammurabi #233 says that 'If a builder builds a house for someone, even though he has not yet completed it; if then the walls seem toppling, the builder must make the walls solid from his own means' indicating that the builder must expend costs to make good his wrongs.[1]

But what leads to high costs of quality? Such situations occur because the builders have not spent enough time and money on preventive and appraisal costs. Executing the work without proper vetting of design and drawings and administrative approvals, poor quality of materials, lack of expertise of workers, poor supervision, and lack of quality inspection are some of the factors leading to such situations. It shows that when construction is done without expending the required quantity on conformance cost, it leads to high non-conformance costs.

5.7 ILLUSTRATION OF COST OF QUALITY

In a construction project, the cost of quality can be illustrated by taking the example of a leaking slab. The components of the cost of quality are divided as follows:

5.7.1 Conformance Cost

Prevention Cost

This would include the cost of numerous actions that aid in defect prevention, such as the structural design of the slab, the creation of specifications and work procedures for the preparation of building joints, designing the concrete mix, calculating the time required to remove formwork, approving the sources and suppliers, and staff and worker training.

Appraisal Cost

This covers the cost of all verification activities to see if what has been done is correct. It involves testing the materials used for concrete-making and comparing them with the specifications, inspecting the area before pouring concrete, calibrating and maintaining the test equipment, and site inspection during concreting.

5.7.2 Nonconformance Cost

Internal and external failure costs constitute the failure cost; combined, they represent the cost of making a mistake.

[1] The Code of Hammurabi, Translated by L W King, Yale Law School, The Avalon Project, https://avalon.law.yale.edu/ancient/hamframe.asp, accessed Mar 15, 2024.

Internal Failure Cost

This covers expenses resulting from material waste, labour charges for rework, the cost of grouting the roof slab with waterproof materials, reexamining corrected work, and related items.

External Failure Cost

This comprises the cost of repair after handover and covers the cost of replacing the flooring components, which includes the expenses for transportation, the expenses for dealing with customer complaints and repairing defects, and the effect on reputation and image, which has a direct impact on sales prospects.

In the construction sector, the magnitude of the cost incurred for prevention and appraisal is much less than the total project cost. Further, in a construction project, if any sort of failure or defect occurs, it would not just include the defect correction cost but also involve a lot of time and resources, ultimately affecting the timely completion as scheduled. This further adds to the indirect cost of the project. By taking proper prevention and appraisal measures, the failure or non-conformance cost can be reduced. It can be concluded that conformance costs are controllable variables, whereas non-conformance costs are resultant variables and can be substantively high.

5.8 THE BASE FOR CALCULATING THE COST OF QUALITY

A suitable base is required for analysing quality costs to represent quality cost as a percentage of an appropriate base. Several bases are often used depending on the area where quality cost measurements are applied. Some commonly used bases recommended by the British Standards Institution are provided in Table 5.2 (BSI, 1990).

TABLE 5.2 Commonly used bases for calculating the cost of quality

S. No.	Cost of quality in terms of	Example	Remarks
1	Labour base	$\frac{\text{Total failure cost}}{\text{Total labour cost}}$	Costs in terms of direct labour, indirect labour or total labour
2	Cost base	$\frac{\text{Total quality cost}}{\text{Total material cost}}$	Costs in terms of manufacturing cost, material cost, labour cost or total cost
3	Sales base	$\frac{\text{Total quality cost}}{\text{Sales revenue}}$	Cost in terms of sales revenue, value of finished items, billed items
4	Unit base	$\frac{\text{Appraisal cost}}{\text{Units produced}}$	Cost in terms of quantity generated or the output
5	Value base	$\frac{\text{Total quality cost}}{\text{Value added}}$	Cost in terms of manufacturing activity unaffected by changes in sales and the price of goods and services purchased.

The costs in the numerator can be any of the following: prevention cost, appraisal cost, internal failure cost, external failure cost, total quality cost, or a combination of any of these. When the quality cost is expressed as a percentage of production cost, net sales or selling cost or any other relevant data, it generates an index that can be analysed using statistical techniques. This helps in the comparison of the processes, which would be beneficial in assessing the continuous improvement programs of the organisation. It would also help benchmark the performance with other organisations.

5.9 COST OF QUALITY AND ORGANISATIONAL OBJECTIVES

Cost of quality is a very important means of measurement of quality. Philip Crosby demonstrated its power in his book 'Quality is Free', which increases understanding of the value of quality. He referred to the cost of quality as the 'price of non-conformance' and is of the opinion that some businesses deliberately opt to pay more for subpar quality.

All organisations should set the objective to reduce the cost of quality. They should manage costs for survival and growth by doing a quality job. They should conduct quality improvement programmes and achieve their goals. The quality cost must be thoroughly analysed as it validly indicates the quality effort. They provide a method to assess the QMS's effectiveness, identify problem areas, opportunities, and savings, and prioritise activities.

Quality-related expenses range from 15 to 20 per cent of sales revenue for many organisations. It can reach up to 40% of total operations in some cases (ASQ, 2023). However, these costs are usually not measured and accounted for separately. In the construction industry, the direct rework cost varies from 5 to 23% of the total contract value (Love & Edwards, 2004). This figure can be reduced substantially by effectively applying quality improvement programs, thus contributing to the organisation's profit. Otherwise, it will be difficult for organisations to survive, grow, and make a profit in the competitive market.

The study conducted by Garg & Mishra (2022) found that the prevention-appraisal-failure model is suitable for calculating the cost of quality in the construction of buildings. As per this study, the overall COQ for building projects in India varies from 3.5 to 10.01 per cent of the project cost, whereas the prevention, appraisal, conformance cost (CC) and failure cost vary between 0.19 and 8 per cent, 0.05 and 5 per cent, 0.3 and 10 per cent, and 0.01 and 5 per cent, respectively.

5.10 REDUCTION OF QUALITY COSTS BY TOTAL QUALITY CONTROL

Since it is impossible to generalise the relative share of quality cost segments throughout the industry, Feigenbaum assumes that internal and external failure costs may constitute 65–70 per cent, appraisal costs around 20–25 per cent, while prevention costs do not exceed 5 to 10 per cent of the total quality cost (Feigenbaum, 1983). As the number of defects or nonconformities increases, the failure cost increases. In order to reduce the defects or nonconformities, it is required to increase inspection, which is an appraisal cost. However, it is not possible to improve quality by increasing appraisal costs. It only helps in identifying the defects. Hence, it is to be noted that without taking proper preventive measures it is futile to spend more money on appraisal costs. Only with successful prevention activity can appraisal and failure costs be reduced. A total quality control approach (preventive action) can only reverse this cycle.

When preventive costs are increased to improve the processes, it reduces the defects and hence reduces the failure costs. When non-conformities are reduced, the need for routine inspection reduces, thus reducing appraisal costs. Upgrading quality control equipment, personnel and practices leads to an additional reduction in appraisal costs. The final output is a substantial reduction in the cost of quality and an improvement in the level of quality. This, in turn, leads to the profitability of the organisation. Lower quality costs are strongly related to the quality system of an organisation. A good quality system is among the most attractive returns on investment opportunities. Three stages necessary for establishing a quality cost program for total quality control are (Feigenbaum, 1983):

- **i.** To identify quality cost items
- **ii.** To structure the quality cost reporting (includes analysis and control)
- **iii.** To improve the quality program to ensure that higher-quality business objectives are being met at lower cost.

5.11 WHY USE COQ?

The concept of quality cost has proved to be a very effective technique for changing management and employee attitudes toward defects. It helps in the following ways:

- **i.** To get management's attention, awaken the quality awareness of management by talking in terms of money and providing information to them that they can easily relate to. It makes quality a reality that competes with the cost and schedule constraints.
- **ii.** To utilise resource allocation as a strategic management tool for the development and execution of strategies.
- **iii.** To change the thought process of the employees about defects—employees are to be made aware of the cost of the defects they create and make them accountable for it.
- **iv.** To obtain a higher return on problem-solving efforts.
- **v.** To find possibilities for improvement, prioritise them, create goals, and track development.
- **vi.** To improve decision-making regarding major investments.
- **vii.** To gauge the results of corrective action and process improvement changes.
- **viii.** To determine the potential for financial gain.
- **ix.** To reduce expenses associated with procurement and suppliers.
- **x.** To find overhead that is being wasted on tasks that the client is not requesting.
- **xi.** To determine systems that are redundant.
- **xii.** To compare the quality improvement programs based on the results gained.
- **xiii.** To assess if quality costs are distributed fairly. The total cost of quality should be optimum.

xiv. To set objectives for financial planning and budgeting.

xv. To assess issues in quality planning.

xvi. To separate the 'trivial many' from the 'important few'.

xvii. To analyse the problem areas.

xviii. To measure the impact of poor quality.

xix. To objectively evaluate performance.

Thus, it is seen that the effects of COQ are quite pervasive, spanning the length and breadth of company organisation and personnel, and entering into every activity undertaken for the project. This is not a small matter, which is why quality is often spoken of as a new philosophy and 'religion'. Without the management – especially upper management – buying into quality concepts, the implementation of quality is difficult and the benefits cannot be easily attained.

5.12 APPLICATIONS OF QUALITY COST

Quality cost is a basic tool for quality control managers to make decisions in areas that affect the costs in various segments to obtain minimum operating quality costs to deliver the desired quality level. They are used as follows (Feigenbaum, 1983):

i. As a **measurement tool**—since quality cost is comprised of various costs in various segments, it is possible to obtain a cost measurement of each activity. It thus helps in comparing measurements of the values of quality programs versus the value of results achieved.

ii. As a **process-quality analysis tool**—quality costs are broken down into various segments of process flow to help identify the major problem areas and serve as an efficient analysis tool.

iii. As a **programming tool**—actions can only be performed based on analysis. To carry out these courses of action, a programme must be established. It requires resources to execute a programme. The segment-wise quality cost helps to identify high-priority areas and judiciously select those actions which provide the highest potential payoff. Resource allocation should be based on this, as resources are limited and expensive.

iv. As a **budgeting tool**—executing all programmes may not be feasible immediately in view of constraint resources. So, it has to be scheduled by setting priority. This would help ensure realistic budgets and attain specific quality goals.

v. As a **predictive tool**—quality cost data helps to evaluate and ensure the performance of the programmes with respect to the goals and objectives of the company.

5.13 LIMITATIONS OF QUALITY COST

Quality problems cannot be resolved, or the determination of the cost of quality cannot mathematically optimise quality systems. It is just a mechanism that helps management identify the intensity of the quality problem, take remedial measures, and make improvements. It throws light on the opportunities and scope for betterment and assesses the growth being made by the actions taken for improvement.

It is difficult to accurately measure the cost of quality as most construction firms do not record the expenses under the various heads of prevention, appraisal, and failure costs. Moreover, it is difficult to separate the cost of quality from the basic tasks required for project delivery, which undoubtedly must be delivered with quality. Also, the costs incurred due to defects and their rectification during construction are frequently not recorded separately as internal failure costs, though these can be assigned a separate work account.

5.14 MEASURES TO REDUCE QUALITY COSTS IN THE CONSTRUCTION INDUSTRY

By referring to the guidelines for Quality Management System (QMS) in ISO 10006 (ISO, 2017), it is prudent on the part of any organisation to carry out the following processes to reduce the quality cost and hence improve the quality aspects to enhance potential profit.

- **Management responsibility**
  a. **Management commitment:** Management should take the initiative to establish and implement QMS on the construction site.
  b. **Customer focus:** Management should try to understand customers' needs through continuous interaction with them and try to enhance their satisfaction by meeting their needs.
  c. **Quality policy:** Management should prepare project-specific Standard Operating Procedures and Quality Manual.
  d. **Quality planning:** There must be proper planning to implement QMS on site.
  e. **Responsibility, authority, and communication:** Management has to identify the duties of key personnel and empower them to take action to ensure quality. There should be proper transmission of information to all required levels through effective Management Information Systems (MIS).[2]

- **Resource management**
  a. **Resource management:** Management of resources by timely supply of resources, training of personnel to educate them about the importance of the project activities in achieving the project objectives and the quality and conducting toolbox meetings[3].
  b. **Infrastructure:** Management must provide necessary infrastructure facilities for the employees and labour and keep them motivated and enthusiastic. It includes a good work culture, salary, facilities, and a lot more.[4]
  c. **Work environment:** Proper housekeeping, protection, and safety in workplaces.

---

2 MIS is itself a full subject area, and, in some universities, a whole degree program. Thus, there is a lot of depth and breadth in MIS.

3 Short meetings conducted before starting of a work to discuss the work plan for the day and to promote safety awareness at work site.

4 Motivation is another very large subject area, with many nuances and intricacies. It is heavily influenced by human psychology, with many theories and techniques available.

- **Product/process realisation**
  a. **Planning of product realisation:** Before starting a project, there should be proper planning and scheduling, considering all the resources, risks, and constraints associated with the work. Implementation should be done as per Standard Operating Procedures during the entire life cycle of the project. Timely monitoring and reviewing should be done as planned in the project quality plan.
  b. **Customer-related processes:** Management should try to accommodate the changes in design as per customer requirements.
  c. **Design and Development:** Review contract documents, specifications, and drawings, prepare a list of inadequacies to meet construction practices/codes and get it corrected and approved by the client before the start of construction.
  d. **Purchasing:** The purchasing team has to do vendor evaluation and inspection of materials required for the construction activities.
  e. **Production and service provision:** Prepare the method statements for the activities meeting the appropriate design specifications, safety norms, and codes of practice as per contractual requirements and use them after obtaining approval from the client.
  f. **Control of monitoring and measuring devices:** Measuring equipment must be calibrated on time. There should be timely inspection and maintenance of equipment to keep it in working condition.
- **Measurement, analysis, and improvement**
  a. **Measurement and analysis:** Audits and inspections should be conducted as scheduled. Proper technology must be adopted for measuring non-conformity in processes. Collate information relating to customer satisfaction, conformity of the product, trends of process and products, and perform preventive action and thus reduce customer complaints.
  b. **Improvement:** Take corrective actions and preventive measures as required, train workmen and supervisors to meet specifications, encourage them to do things right first, and make continuous contact with customers for feedback.

SUMMARY

Quality control and quality economics should be two of the core components of strategic planning since there is a strong correlation between an organisation's growth and the cost of quality. This is necessary for an organisation's survival in the competitive national and international markets. Though the cost of quality has been defined differently by various experts, it intends to quantify the cost incurred due to poor product or service quality and the cost spent to ensure quality. The major categories of quality cost are appraisal, preventive, and internal and external failure costs. Investing more in preventive costs can drastically reduce the cost of quality. It has been established that profit can be increased even without increasing sales but by reducing quality costs. Now, it has become a most sought-after management tool for quality improvement. The construction sector must identify the costs incurred for various activities related to quality and determine the cost of quality for each project. This will enable the industry to track the loss due to poor quality and help promote technological advances to prevent poor quality.

WORKS CITED

ASQ, (2023), *Cost of Quality*, Retrieved from asq.org: https://asq.org/quality-resources/cost-of-quality.

BSI. (1990), *BS 6143-2:1990 Guide to the Economics of Quality - Part 2: Prevention, Appraisal and Failure Model.* (London: British Standards Institution).

BSI. (1992), *BS 6143-1:1992 Guide to the Economics of Quality - Part 1: Process Cost Model.* (London: British Standards Institution).

Crosby, P. B. (1979), *Quality is Free : The Art of Making Quality Certain.* (United Kingdom: McGraw-Hill).

Feigenbaum, A. V. (1983), *Total Quality Control.* (New York: McGraw-Hill).

Garg, S., & Mishra, S. (2022), 'Understanding the components and magnitude of the cost of quality in building construction'. *Engineering, Construction and Architectural Management*, 26-48.

Harrington, H. J. (1987), *Poor-Quality Cost.* (New York: Marcel Dekker, Inc.) and (Milwaukee: ASQC Quality Press).

ISO. (2017), *ISO 10006- Quality Management — Guidelines for Quality Management in Projects.* (Switzerland: International Organization for Standardization).

Juran, J. M. (1986), 'The quality trilogy: A universal approach to managing for quality'. *ASQC 40th Annual Quality Congress in Anaheim, California.*

Juran, J. M., & Godfrey, B. A. (1979), *Juran's Quality Handbook.* (New York: McGraw-Hill).

Love, P. E., & Edwards, D. J. (2004), 'Determinants of rework in building construction projects'. *Engineering, Construction and Architectural Management, 11*(4), 259-274.

Omanachu, V. K., & Ross, J. E. (2004), *Principles of Total Quality.* (Florida: CRC Press).

Sandoval Chavez, D. A., & Beruvides, M. G. (1998, Winter), 'Using opportunity costs to determine the cost of quality: A case study in a continuous process industry'. *The Engineering Economist, 43*(2), 107-124.

SCI, (2019, May 8)., *The Kerala State Coastal Zone ... vs The State of Kerala Maradu Municipality ... on 8 May, 2019.* Retrieved March 22, 2024, from indiankanoon: https://indiankanoon.org/doc/162357936/

SCI, (2021, August 31), *Supertech Ltd vs Emerald Court Owner Resident Welfare ... on 31 August, 2021.* Retrieved March 22, 2024, from Indiankanoon: https://indiankanoon.org/doc/199986312/

Shank, J. K., & Govindarajan, V. (1993), *Strategic Cost Management: The New Tool for Competitive Advantage.* (New York: The Free Press).

Singh, A. (2017). *Quantitative Risk Management and Decision Making in Construction.* (VA: ASCE Press).

Wood, D. C. (2013). *Principles of Quality Costs: Financial Measures for Strategic Implementation of Quality Management.* (Milwaukee: American Society for Quality, Quality Press).

REVIEW QUESTIONS

Multiple Choice Questions

1. Who came up with the concept of quality cost initially?
   (a) Armand V. Feigenbaum (b) Joseph M. Juran
   (c) Philip Crosby (d) Sandoval Chavez
2. What was the term introduced by Joseph M. Juran for quality cost?
   (a) Cost of quality (b) Cost of poor quality
   (c) Appraisal cost (d) None of the above
3. Who is the author of the book 'Quality is Free'?
   (a) Armand V. Feigenbaum (b) Joseph M. Juran
   (c) Philip Crosby (d) Sandoval Chavez
4. Cost of quality is the sum of ___________.
   (a) conformance cost and nonconformance cost
   (b) appraisal cost and preventive cost
   (c) internal and external failure costs
   (d) None of these
5. The cost incurred for the activities undertaken to prevent or avoid quality problems in products or services is called:
   (a) Preventive cost (b) Appraisal cost
   (c) Internal failure cost (d) External failure cost
6. Cost for new product review is a _______.
   (a) Preventive cost (b) Appraisal cost
   (c) Internal failure cost (d) External failure cost
7. Inspection, measurement, and monitoring of quality-related operations come under _______.
   (a) Preventive cost (b) Appraisal cost
   (c) Internal failure cost (d) External failure cost
8. _______ are expenses needed for repair, replacement, or disposal of defective work discovered before the consumer receives the goods or service.
   (a) Preventive cost (b) Appraisal cost
   (c) Internal failure cost (d) External failure cost

9. _______ are the costs related to defects found after the client's receipt of the product or service.
   (a) Preventive cost (b) Appraisal cost
   (c) Internal failure cost (d) External failure cost
10. Which of the following is not a preventive cost?
    (a) Vendor evaluation (b) Preparation of PQP
    (c) Training (d) Third-party audit
11. The cost of snagging comes under ________ cost.
    (a) Preventive cost (b) Appraisal cost
    (c) Internal failure cost (d) External failure cost
12. What is the ideal requirement to reduce quality costs?
    (a) Increase preventive cost (b) Increase appraisal cost
    (c) Increase inspections (d) Reduce failure cost
13. Which cost should be prioritised among all other quality costs?
    (a) Preventive cost (b) Appraisal cost
    (c) Internal failure cost (d) External failure cost
14. What leads to a high cost of quality?
    (a) Investing less on preventive measures
    (b) Reduced appraisal cost
    (c) Reduced inspections
    (d) None of these
15. Under which quality cost can quality auditing be considered?
    (a) Preventive cost (b) Appraisal cost
    (c) Internal failure cost (d) External failure cost
16. Feigenbaum assumes that internal and external failure costs may constitute _____ per cent, appraisal costs around _____ per cent, while prevention costs do not exceed _____ per cent of the total quality cost.
    (a) 65–70 per cent, 20–25 per cent, 5–10 per cent
    (b) 5–10 percent, 20–25 per cent, 65–70 per cent
    (c) 70 per cent, 15 per cent, 15 per cent
    (d) None of these

17. What are the benefits of determining the cost of quality?
    (a) Get management's attention
    (b) Determine the potential for financial gain
    (c) Compare the quality improvement programs
    (d) All of these
18. What are the applications of cost of quality?
    (a) As a measurement tool (b) As a process-quality analysis tool
    (c) As a programming tool (d) All of these
19. Which chart is associated with vital few and trivial many?
    (a) Control chart (b) Fishbone diagram
    (c) Run chart (d) Pareto chart
20. To which cost does the cost due to project rework after handover belong?
    (a) Preventive cost (b) Appraisal cost
    (c) Internal failure cost (d) External failure cost

Short Answer Type Questions

1. What is the cost of poor quality?
2. Discuss briefly preventive costs.
3. Explain appraisal cost.
4. What is internal failure cost?
5. Write about external failure cost.
6. What are the examples of internal failure costs?
7. Distinguish between conformance cost and nonconformance cost.
8. Which component of quality cost should be prioritised and why?
9. Is it possible to increase profit without increasing sales? How?
10. Why is it not possible to measure accurately the cost of quality in the construction industry?

Long Answer Type Questions

1. Describe how the determination of quality cost was developed and what its significance is in management.
2. Is quality free? How do you substantiate your view?
3. Explain the various models of the cost of quality.
4. How to make quality free? Explain.

5. Explain the cost of quality and its components with examples from the construction industry.
6. Why does the cost increase when quality is poor?
7. Give examples of nonconformance costs in the construction industry.
8. Explain with a figure the optimum cost of quality.
9. Why is it important to increase preventive costs?
10. What are the commonly used bases for measuring the cost of quality?
11. Why is it important to measure the cost of quality?
12. What are the applications of quality cost?
13. What are the limitations of the cost of quality?
14. How do we reduce quality costs?
15. How is quality control related to quality economics?

ANSWER KEYS

Multiple Choice Questions

1. (a)	**2.** (b)	**3.** (c)	**4.** (a)	**5.** (a)	**6.** (a)	**7.** (b)	**8.** (c)
9. (d)	**10.** (d)	**11.** (a)	**12.** (a)	**13.** (a)	**14.** (a)	**15.** (b)	**16.** (a)
17. (d)	**18.** (d)	**19.** (d)	**20.** (d)				

CHAPTER

6 Planning for Project Quality

6.1 INTRODUCTION

According to PMI, 2021, 'a project is a temporary endeavour undertaken to create a unique product, service, or result'. The outputs of projects are generally called deliverables. The common deliverables in the construction industry are buildings, roads, bridges, tunnels, dams, and canals. The quality of a construction project is measured by evaluating the deliverable's conformance to acceptance criteria and fitness for use. It is necessary that the construction project meets the client's requirements and follow the standards and regulations. To attain quality in a project, it is thus essential to satisfy stakeholders' expectations and fulfil product and project requirements. The 'requirement' may be a condition or capability that should be present in a deliverable to meet an intended purpose. Project quality can be achieved by balancing the three factors namely, scope, time, and cost.

A company that prioritises quality would cultivate a culture that leads to behaviours, attitudes, actions, and procedures that generate value by satisfying the expectations of customers and stakeholders. To improve the overall performance of an organisation, it is essential to implement a Quality Management System that adds to the competitive advantage. As a result, QMS provides solutions to several issues that exist in the industry, such as a framework for various stages of the project—beginning from planning and going on to implementing, monitoring, and controlling—to improve the quality performance of activities. An organisation's quality management system sets its goals before determining the procedures and materials needed to achieve the intended outcomes. Thus, the QMS oversees the interconnected processes and best uses of the resources to add value to their goods and services. Project traits, quality management concepts, project quality management procedures, and a Project Quality Plan(PQP) are all included in the QMS. Being as important as it is, directions for implementing quality management in projects are provided by ISO 10006: 2017, prepared based on quality management principles.

6.2 QUALITY MANAGEMENT PRINCIPLES

There are seven basic quality management principles upon which the ISO 9000, ISO 9001 and other quality management standards are established. 'Quality management principles are a set of fundamental beliefs, norms, rules, and values that are accepted as true and can be used as a basis for quality management' (ISO, 2015).

The quality management principles given by ISO are as follows:

- **QMP 1:** Customer focus—every organisation has to strive to meet customer needs and exceed customer expectations to achieve sustained success.
- **QMP 2:** Leadership—leadership ought to create unity of purpose and align it with the organisation's strategies, policies, and processes.
- **QMP 3:** Involvement of people—involving people at all strata, empowering them, and enhancing their competence to achieve the organisation's quality objective.
- **QMP 4:** Process approach— understanding the interrelationship between the processes to assist in optimising the system and its performance.
- **QMP 5:** Improvement—focus on improvement, essential to create new opportunities and react to external and internal conditions.
- **QMP 6:** Rational decision-making—decisions are to be made based on the evidence and interpretation of data.
- **QMP 7:** Relationship management—managing good relationships with all interested parties or stakeholders is vital for sustained success.

The relative significance of each principle varies with the type of organisation and is dynamic, i.e., it changes with time. All these principles are significant in the construction industry. For effectively implementing a QMS that incorporates the seven quality management principles, an organisation will need to undergo operational changes. For each project that the organisation may undertake there has to be a specific quality plan.

6.3 PROJECT QUALITY PLAN

Without an integrated set of quality plans, the quality effort can be misdirected. Hence, a PQP is a management plan that is particular to a project, and it lists the standards, practices, tools, and activities required to ensure quality in the project. Quality plans are a means to relate the product, process, service, project, or service requirements to actual work methodology and practices. It is an assurance to the stakeholders that the requirements will be met. Thus, a quality plan is a description of how an organisation is going to provide the required deliverable(s). Guidelines for creating, evaluating, adopting, implementing, and modifying quality plans are included in ISO 10005: 2018(E) and these are a fundamental source of having high quality on a project. Consequently, the PQP aims to provide deliverables to the client based on their specifications and needs. For construction projects, the clients' requirements are contained in contract documents such as the contract conditions, drawings, and specifications.

In terms of quality, all procedures and activities are obliged to follow established quality standards put out by regulatory bodies: it is not just the final product's quality that counts because the final quality could be below established standards, such as those of the ISI (Indian Standards Institution). Hence, all the activities and processes are required to be monitored and well-documented for improvement, otherwise it can become hard to attain the desired output. Usually, defects or nonconformance to standards mainly occur due to a lack of knowledge about procedures and standards. So, if there is a well-documented PQP, it would help improve the project's overall quality.

It thus follows that every organisation has a proper quality plan specific to each project to meet the customer's requirements and ensure quality at every stage of the work. The roles of PQP are as follows:

- **(a)** Set out organisational policies and their application in the project.
- **(b)** Determine the customer's expectations for quality, then explain the project's nature to the employees based on those expectations.
- **(c)** Identify all activities, processes, subprocesses and their sequence and interaction with each other for effective functioning of the system.
- **(d)** Determine the quality criteria and standards required for the realisation of customer requirements.
- **(e)** Describe the procedures for implementation, measurement, monitoring, and controlling activities.
- **(f)** Manage human resources and staff training.
- **(g)** Assign roles and responsibilities to staff at all levels.
- **(h)** Assist in procurement, testing, storing, and supply of materials.
- **(i)** Document all processes, subprocesses, and activities involved in a project.
- **(j)** Audit the activities, prepare nonconformance reports, and take corrective and preventive actions when required.
- **(k)** Schedule the tools that will be used in the project.
- **(l)** Help in continuous improvement.
- **(m)** List out the reference materials.

A project needs to be divided into interdependent processes to achieve the desired quality plan. Planning, organising, staffing, monitoring, regulating, coordinating, and reporting all project procedures must be addressed. Project management also includes continuously taking corrective and improvement actions to achieve the project objective.

The PQP is a management practice that facilitates an organisation in achieving quality by providing directions to all the activities involved in a project. It requires documentation of all related records and monitoring activities at each stage to control deviations. Dedicated quality officers are dutybound to attend to these requirements at all times. It aids in continuous improvement by taking necessary actions, ensuring that the deliverable meets the customer's quality requirements. Finally, the benefits of PQP come from a concerted effort of all team members.

6.4 NEED FOR PROJECT QUALITY PLAN

A PQP serves the needs of an organisation, as given below:

- **(a)** To show how the organisation will apply its QMS in a particular project.
- **(b)** To meet stakeholders' specific requirements.
- **(c)** To organise and manage activities and resources.

(d) To reduce nonconformity.
(e) To minimise risk.
(f) To monitor and assess compliance with requirements.
(g) To demonstrate how criteria will be fulfilled internally and externally.
(h) To maximise resource utilisation to achieve quality goals.
(i) To manage the creation of a new or changed organisation, location, or partnership.

Needless to say, this is a full-time task for the quality officers.

6.5 DEVELOPING A QUALITY PLAN

The following guidelines for establishing the PQP are based on ISO 10005, which gives directions on the development of a quality plan. While developing PQP, it is advisable to identify risks and opportunities to be addressed. For that, it is useful to understand the setting of the quality plan and its expected results. The quality plan's context includes the following (ISO, 2018):

(a) currently implemented management plans or practices supporting the quality plan, whether or not they belong to a recognised management system,
(b) internal conditions that may impede the organisation from reaching the expected results, which may be resource constraints, gaps in communication of the quality plan to its consumers, and variations due to changes in locations,
(c) external elements that are relevant to the specific situation, such as market and competitive challenges, legal, and regulatory requirements,
(d) issues facing the firm both within and outside that apply to the specific situation, such as quality objectives and market goals.
(e) the requirements and goals of stakeholders like clients, staff, and outside suppliers.

It is necessary to recognise and manage risks to ensure that desired outcomes can be realised and negative repercussions can be avoided or mitigated. Consider areas where improvements can be made, such as satisfying customers or increasing the ability and usefulness of products or services. After the quality plan's context and targeted outcomes are studied, the quality plan's scope and goals may be determined. The quality plan's format and degree of accuracy can both be customised. A sample PQP is given in Appendix 2.

6.5.1 Inputs for the Quality Plan

The inputs to the quality plan are the requirements of customers, statutory and regulatory norms, industry standards, requirements specific to the project, risks, resources available, documentation, and communication requirements. The company has to decide on what needs to go into the quality plan. The following are a few examples of inputs to be considered while preparing the quality plan:

(a) **Client demands, legal, official, and industry standards:** Quality is an aspect that is not negotiable to users; hence, it is very important for construction organisations to meet customer requirements. It is useful to follow regulatory and statutory standards to stay competitive in the market. In India, for example, building constructors are obliged to follow the Indian Standards codes of practice, the National Building Code, local regulatory standards, and other national standards apart from considering client demands while constructing a building.

(b) **Data about the requirements of consumers:** While preparing the PQP, information about the users' needs, budget, scope, time, and material and inspection plans are to be considered.

(c) **Additional applicable quality plans:** The contractor has to consider quality plans of similar projects, if available while preparing a PQP.

(d) **All the requirements of the particular case must be considered:** Certain requirements may be specific to the project, such as the type of project, location of the site, types of materials available, access to the site, and climatic conditions.

(e) **Identify the opportunities and risks that may occur in a particular project**, especially with regard to health and safety. For example, if a road widening project is to be executed, various factors to be considered include shifting utilities, adequate safety measures to divert the traffic, and required permissions from authorities.

(f) **Consider each project's resource requirement and availability:** The resources include human resources, materials, and equipment. Assessment of the availability of resources according to the requirement, such as the number of competent and qualified project managers who can be deployed for a project per the client's need.

(g) **Organisational need for the management system:** There might be a need for systems like ERP, MIS and other software requirements for the successful management of a project.

(h) **Recorded data significant to the quality plan:** Considering data already documented by the organisation for other projects that may be relevant for a new project.

(i) **Reporting of the quality plan:** The organisation needs to consider the client's communication needs.

It is necessary to note down valid references concerning each input. A project outline or summary of the requirements may be supplied to users to assist them in understanding the background of their work. In other situations, a thorough list of specifications created using input documentation may be employed. It is necessary for the quality plan to identify its processes and quality characteristics and determine the resource requirements.

6.5.2 Defining the Scope of the Quality Plan

Putting in the inputs is one thing, but a clear definition of the scope ought to be included in the quality plan. It needs to have a description of the objectives and anticipated outcomes. It is indicated that it has the characteristics of the instance to which it will be applied, the constraints to its application, and the conditions of its application, such as exposure conditions, topography, proximity to the coastal region, or other notified regions. However, the scope depends on customer and stakeholder needs that vary with the nature of products and services. Hence, the contractor must work closely with the owner or owner's representative. It should be noted that the scope of work for the construction of a building might include all the works such as the construction of the building, MEP works, services, interior fittings and development of area if all these are to be done by a particular contractor.

6.5.3 Quality Objectives

The quality objectives of the organisation are also included in the quality plan. They need to be measurable in any specific way since there are different objectives and yardsticks for every product. It will contain the quality characteristics of the matters affecting customer satisfaction and opportunities for betterment. Consequently, a construction project may include the following objectives in the quality plan:

- Executing the project as per the contractual requirements.
- Implementing the activities in the correct procedure.
- Using the materials as per the specifications.
- Achieving the workmanship as per the client's requirements.
- Maintaining quality records.
- Ensuring proper communication and coordination with the client and various departments like engineering, design, procurement, and execution.
- Conducting the audits as scheduled.
- Analysing the nonconformance reports and taking actions for correction and prevention.
- Monitoring and reviewing the implementation of QMS.
- Preventing damage to executed work.
- Ensuring that the contractual requirements are met through QMS.
- Improving teamwork and leadership, creating a better work environment and better coordination and communication among team members.

6.5.4 Responsibilities of Managers

PQP shows the organisation structure[1] and defines the responsibility and authority of each function. Large construction projects will have critical project management functions assigned to the project manager, construction manager, planning manager, contracts manager, quality manager, and health and safety manager. The quality plan specifies the personnel in charge of the following:

(a) Organising, managing, executing, and delivering projects on time.
(b) Tracking and storing the resources and monitoring progress.
(c) Examining the inputs for the quality plan, documenting these evaluations, and solving disputes and uncertainties.
(d) Conveying needs to all involved departments, functions, customers, and outside suppliers, as well as fixing issues that appear at their interfaces.

---

1 'Organisational structures are any arrangement of or relation between the elements of project work and organisational processes. These structures can be based on roles, functions, or authority' (PMI, 2021).

(e) Examining the findings of any conducted audits.
(f) Carrying out safety inspections, conducting fire drills, and organising campaigns for fire safety.
(g) Examining and approving modifications or changes from the quality plan.
(h) Operating, maintaining and repairing the plant and machinery at the site.

An organisational chart[2] may be used to show the lines of reporting for personnel responsible for carrying out the quality plan.

6.5.5 Documentation Control

Documentation control ensures that relevant information is available and shows the location of its availability. Documents to be maintained are decided at the beginning of the project, and responsibilities are assigned to the person concerned at the site. It also is an assurance that documents are protected. Regarding documentation, the quality plan specifies the following:

(a) The method to identify the relevant information from the documentation.
(b) The person who will examine and approve the material that is documented.
(c) The method of sharing the information and restrictions to access the data.
(d) The methods used to preserve and safeguard recorded information.
(e) The type of information to be documented.

To give proof of compliance with regulations, the quality plan specifies the kind of documentation to be maintained. Examples of such documented information are listed below:

(i) Quality plan inputs,
(ii) Reviews of design and development,
(iii) Drawings and related documents,
(iv) Findings of inspection and tests,
(v) Outputs of process monitoring and measurement,
(vi) Work orders,
(vii) Meeting minutes,
(viii) Assessment and audit reports.

Certain factors are to be considered during documentation, and they are as follows:

(a) The method of documentation, place of storage, and duration for which these documents are to be retained.
(b) The nature and scope of the customer and legal and regulatory requirements.
(c) The procedures to be followed to guarantee the information recorded as proof of conformity, its protection against unauthorised change, and making it available upon request.

2 An organisation chart is a graphical representation of the internal structure of the organisation used to display the various roles, positions, and the responsibilities of the officials in a hierarchical manner.

(d) The kind of information to be provided to the consumer in writing and when and how to provide it.
(e) The language, format, and media in which the documentation has to be available.
(f) Procedure for recording all outgoing and incoming correspondences, mail, faxes, and registers. These may be recorded by mentioning the subject and date of receipt that are to be kept in site offices and home offices as required.
(g) List of codes used to be maintained. The ones validated for the latest issue are to be maintained at the site.
(h) Formats of registers for receipt of materials, storage, and issue.
(i) Format of registers to control the movement of files outside the office.
(j) Records that are stored in electronic media and backup details of important files that are to be maintained.

A PQP shall include prescribed formats for documenting each process and the responsibilities assigned. The various types of documents in a PQP include controlled and uncontrolled documents. Controlled documents include policies and strategies and reference documents like contract documents, IS standards, and public data. It also includes the derived documents like specifications, plans and drawings, schedules, and project quality plans. The documents that are included in PQP are work methods, various formats, and inspection and test plans. Proposals, brochures, and records like minutes of meetings, test results, reports, and certificates are other derived documents. Uncontrolled documents include correspondences like letters, memos, and emails.

6.5.6 List of Resources

PQP contains the list of types and quantity of resources required for the quality plan's successful implementation. The types of resources include people, internal and external processes, products or services, infrastructure, and facilities for the operation of processes, monitoring and measuring resources, and specialised knowledge and experience. The criteria or standards these resources adhere to should be expressed or mentioned in the quality plan when there are special requirements for goods and services. The competence required for the various roles have also to be specified in the quality plan. Any particular organisational knowledge, training, or other actions that are necessary for staff members can be specified in the quality plan. Requirements for training new employees and teaching new or updated operational procedures to current employees may be included. Details of workmanship requirements for each task have to be specified in the quality plan. Human resources and plant and machinery requirements for each construction site are to be mentioned. PQP is used to outline a system for acquiring resources, monitoring and controlling resources, and tracking target achievement.

The quality plan needs to describe the needs of specific cases, which may be structures and utilities, workplace, equipment and tools, information and communication technologies, support services, and transportation. When operational conditions directly affect the quality of deliverables, the quality plan has to mention the necessary environmental factors to be considered. The methods to control monitoring and measuring resources also have to be specified in the quality plan, together with requirements for calibration or verification or references to particular written information.

6.5.7 Communication Between Clients and Other Interested Parties

Communication with clients and other stakeholders is essential in an organisation. The PQP mentions the personnel in charge of maintaining contact with clients and other stakeholders. Without this contact, essential information can be lost or go unseen. In most construction organisations, Customer Relationship Managers are generally employed to communicate and interact with clients and potential customers, to help in improving relationships. PQP specifies the various communications modes that may be used such as emails, letters, and faxes. Documents are also used for communicating among team members, different levels of management, and the customer. At all times, the customer is necessary to be treated with the utmost respect. PQP gives instructions on the procedure to be followed after receiving customer feedback. It also specifies the type of written information and complaints received from clients and other interested parties that need to be retained. A Management Information System (MIS)[3] may be used to communicate within the organisation, enabling interested parties to make decisions based on accurate information. PQP specifies the conditions and instances when communication is required. There has to be a mechanism to communicate the action plans prepared to correct nonconformities to the department concerned.

6.5.8 Steps in Preparation of the Quality Plan

The steps followed in the preparation of the quality plan are discussed hereunder.

Initiation

The organisation defines the roles, responsibilities, and authority of people within and outside the organisation. Employees and stakeholders connected to a particular project have to participate in preparing the quality plan. Suppose the scope of building construction includes MEP works and interior design; the PQP includes quality plans for MEP works and interior design in addition to the building construction activities. Hence, the participation of all stakeholders is essential. The PQP outlines the method for meeting resource requirements when a specific resource has a limited supply.

Establishing the Quality Plan

The steps for execution of all activities are specified in the quality plan along with the detailed inspection test plan. It also stipulates the acceptance criteria for the workmanship of various tasks directly or by referring to the applicable documents such as method statements, checklists, and related software. When an organisation has a formal QMS, it may choose, modify, or add to the existing documents to suit the current project. If there is a need to deviate from the existing QMS, it is advantageous to consider the associated risks and opportunities, which are then justified and approved by all stakeholders. It specifies the resources to be used at different stages and by whom. Essentially, creating and implementing a PQP and QMS are an enormous task. Usually, a dedicated department would be assigned to this big and important task.

Ensuring Consistency with Scope

The scope, inputs for the quality plan, user needs, and the quality plan's intended outcomes should be considered while creating the content and format for the quality plan. The amount

[3] But MIS is a massive subject area and degree program in its own right.

of specificity in the quality plan has to be in accordance with any requirements that have been agreed upon, the organisational ways of operation, and the difficulty of the activities that need to be carried out. The requirement for interoperability with other management plans relevant to the case has to be taken into account. An organisation may create a quality plan that complies with the relevant ISO 9001 requirements, IS codes of practice, and other applicable regulations.

Presentation of the Quality Plan

The methods used to define and present a quality plan formally are graphical representations (such as process maps, Gantt charts, images supported by texts, workflow charts), written work instructions (such as detailed texts, texts with images, tables, document matrices, checklists, and manuals), videos, visual means and electronic media, software applications, and a mix of techniques. These techniques should suit the quality plan's application and consumer needs. Various other plans, such as those for particular aspects, procedures, or functions, may be included in the quality plan. Essentially, anything that works can be used. Hence, creativity is encouraged and permitted.

The processes covered under the quality management system, their order, and interaction with various processes for effective maintenance of the system are to be depicted in the Process Flow chart, which gives a briefing of the processes, subprocesses, activities within them, their outputs, process owners, and process controllers. None of these tasks should be underestimated or under-emphasised. The sub-processes included in the process mapping for site operations in the construction industry are as follows:

- **(a)** Organisation's vision and mission.
- **(b)** The objective setting of the project in alignment with the organisation's vision and mission.
- **(c)** Planning and scheduling.
- **(d)** PQP preparation.
- **(e)** Mobilisation of resources.
- **(f)** Execution.
- **(g)** Management Information System, MIS.
- **(h)** Monitoring and review.
- **(i)** Preventive measures.
- **(j)** Corrective action.
- **(k)** Training.
- **(l)** Commissioning.
- **(m)** Demobilisation.
- **(n)** Operation and maintenance.

6.5.9 Inclusion of Design and Development Plan

The appropriate design and development plan(s) are laid down in the PQP. The PQP considers applicable specifications, codes, industry standards, quality traits, and legal and regulatory requirements. There are different codes of standards to be followed for different types of work. In some cases, it requires following the norms specified by regulatory bodies like the Ministry of Environment and Forests. The criteria to approve the inputs and outputs of design and development, the stage(s) when they are to be reviewed, confirmed, and validated and by whom are outlined in the PQP. Note that design and development can be complicated in some situations which demand help from the experts. Others with a lower level of complexity will need a structured approach to guarantee that risks will be managed arising from the design and development outputs. Hence, adequate strategic planning is needed to minimise the consequence of undesirable outputs.

The procedure to control the requests for modifications of design and development outputs is also included in the PQP, as it costs a lot to modify anything once the project has commenced. It specifies the persons who have the authority to submit a modification request and the process by which the effects of modification will be evaluated. PQP specifies the person who has the power to accept or reject modifications and how to verify the execution of changes. This requires an extensive matrix of tasks and responsibilities, even if all combinations and circumstances cannot be thought of beforehand. To regulate modifications to the intended design and development outputs, the organisation may need to control certain matters, such as authorising the use of alternative materials, adapting service outputs to meet particular client needs, or reacting to changes in the resources that are available.

6.5.10 Details on Outsourcing Products and Services

It is quite normal for construction projects to outsource services and products because of the lack of expertise within the organisation. The quality plan ought to include the following details regarding the external services and products it might receive:

- **(a)** the essential characteristics of outsourced procedures, items, and services that can impact a particular situation;
- **(b)** how to convey those attributes to the external service providers;
- **(c)** the procedures to be followed for the assessment and management of external providers;
- **(d)** need and references for additional PQP or external provider PQP;
- **(e)** the procedures to be followed to fulfil the needs, such as statutory and regulatory requirements, that are relevant to goods and services provided by third parties;
- **(f)** the company's plan for ensuring that the goods and services it receives from outside sources meet its standards.

The fundamental idea in doing this is to cover all bases to assure quality because important things such as this cannot be left to chance.

6.5.11 Execution and Delivery of the Project

The primary purposes of the quality plan are execution and timely delivery, along with the technical monitoring and measuring methods applicable to it. Creating Gantt charts, process maps, or flow charts can effectively convey the relationships between processes. The inputs, procedures, and outputs necessary to carry out the execution of the project are to be specified in the quality plan. Consequently, the organisation uses risk-based thinking when incorporating the following aspects in the quality plan:

(a) the steps involved in construction activities;
(b) relevant documentation;
(c) the resources and procedures used to meet the needs, along with any information on materials, products, services, processes, software applications, certification, or validation that may be required;
(d) conditions necessary to fulfil predetermined plans and techniques for confirming compliance with requirements;
(e) prerequisites for qualification and competence of contractors;
(f) acceptability standards for goods, services, and other outputs;
(g) legislative and statutory needs that apply;
(h) industry standards and procedures;
(i) application of measures to avoid mistakes by people; and
(j) make plans for delivery, commissioning, and maintenance.

Where installation or commissioning is necessary, the PQP specifies how it is to be done and which attributes are inspected and validated. The PQP contains details of how the organisation plans to ensure conformance with rules and legislation, industry standards, and practices. It also contains details regarding the competency of staff and trainees and the accessibility to technical support, especially when post-delivery activities like maintenance and training services are involved.

6.5.12 Procedures for Traceability

The PQP outlines the procedures to be followed where output identification is necessary to guarantee that the needs are met. The quality plan describes the scope and application of traceability where it is needed and ensures that outputs that are affected will be recognised. Traceability gives customers the confidence that the products come from a known and traceable supply chain. The PQP specifies:

(a) the contractual requirements or other traceability requirements that are to be included in recorded information;
(b) type of records needed to be kept showing that traceability requirements have been met, and how will they be managed; and
(c) guidelines and techniques for determining the outputs' inspection and testing status.

6.5.13 Property Owned by Clients or Other Parties

For some construction projects, the client supplies some services and materials. In such scenarios, the PQP has to specify the following factors:

(a) the methods used to identify and regulate goods and services offered by clients or other providers;
(b) the ways to check that these goods and services adhere to the required standards;
(c) the measures that will be taken to control nonconforming goods and services; and
(d) storage of goods.

6.5.14 Process for Identifying Nonconforming Activities

The PQP needs to outline the process for identifying nonconforming activities and correcting them, as well as specifying the formats of nonconformance reports. The PQP may need to include restrictions, such as the scope or kind of rework or repair permitted and the process for authorising such rework or repair. The appropriate actions and communications relevant to the outcomes or prospective repercussions of such nonconformities need to be stated or mentioned in the quality plan.

6.5.15 Monitoring and Measurement Processes and Compliance

Processes for monitoring and measuring compliance need to outline the methods for gathering verifiable proof of compliance. Clients may ask for monitoring and measurement plans (also known as "inspection and test plans") without any other quality plan details to monitor compliance with predetermined requirements. The following points are mentioned in the quality plan:

- **(a)** monitoring and measuring of materials and activities;
- **(b)** the phases at which they are to be used;
- **(c)** the properties to be checked and measured at each level;
- **(d)** the criteria for acceptance of material and workmanship;
- **(e)** statistical techniques that may be used;
- **(f)** when tests or inspections are to be conducted or supervised by the client;
- **(g)** when, where, and how to engage external agencies to conduct testing or inspections; and
- **(h)** the standards to which goods, services, or other outputs are delivered.

In a quality management system, defined procedures are established for monitoring, measuring, and analysing the processes as well as for taking the necessary steps to attain the desired results. It is also used in the continual development of these procedures. Additionally, it keeps track of the processes that are outsourced and takes the necessary control over them.

6.5.16 Conducting Audits

The kind of audits to be conducted for a particular project, their scope and character, and the purpose of the audit data should be specified in the quality plan. There are several uses of audits, including the following:

- **(a)** monitoring the effectiveness of PQP as they are implemented;
- **(b)** monitoring and verifying compliance with the criteria;
- **(c)** monitoring the suppliers and external agencies; and
- **(d)** to offer an unbiased, independent review necessary to satisfy the needs of clients or other interested parties.

6.5.17 Controlling and Operating the Quality Plan

This phase has its own unique set of action plans, as described hereunder.

Examining and Approving the Quality Plan

It is essential that the PQP prepared is approved by the client. If any revisions are necessary, they can be incorporated because meeting the requirements of the client and other interested parties is crucial to the project's success.

An authorised person or group that includes representatives from relevant organisational functions assesses the quality plan for sufficiency and effectiveness before giving it their formal approval. When a project is carried out in phases, the organisation could be required to give the client a PQP for each stage before it begins.

Executing and Monitoring the Quality Plan

The organisation takes the following factors into account while putting the quality strategy into practice and monitoring it:

(a) distribution of the quality plan to everyone who is required to know about it;

(b) training the staff on the use of PQP, especially in the case of distinct projects; and

(c) check for compliance with PQP by supervising the setup, reviewing milestones, and conducting audits.

In most cases, audits are conducted on a sampling basis. When PQP is presented to clients or stakeholders, they may set up rules to ensure that the plans are followed. Such monitoring can help with the following:

- Evaluating the management's commitment to the efficient execution of the quality plan.
- Assessing the quality plan's effective execution.
- Identifying potential risk areas associated with particular activities.
- Taking corrective and preventive actions.
- Identifying areas where the quality plan and its related actions can be improved.
- Documenting the nonconformities and the corrective actions taken will enable continuous improvement.

6.5.18 Revising the Quality Plan

Certain circumstances in the project execution demand changes from the approved plan. Those changes are to be incorporated in the PQP also. The company has to update its quality plan for effective implementation. As such, the company needs to:

(a) consider any risks or modifications to the quality plan's inputs, including:

- the particular project for which the quality plan is created;
- the procedures for providing goods and services;
- the management system of the organisation; and
- requirements set forth by statute or regulation.

(b) include a quality plan improvement mutually agreed upon by the client and the contractor.

(c) include the missing details in the PQP.

The requirement for document changes is reviewed by management, approved after discussion with the customer, and added to the existing PQP. Only the Master copy has to be maintained at the site.

The organisation has to define the circumstances when deviations can be accommodated. It mentions the details of the person authorised to request changes, the procedure for change requests, and the form of request. It must also identify the persons responsible for and authorised to accept or reject changes. A qualified person will be allocated to review the effectiveness, sufficiency, and impact of the changes made to the quality plan. There are prescribed procedures to inform the clients, customers, stakeholders, and external suppliers regarding the changes made in the quality plan. It is required to update the documents that are affected by the modifications made to the quality plan.

6.5.19 Assessing Feedback and Improvement

It is useful to examine and assess the experience obtained from implementing a quality plan. Organisations can evaluate how the quality plan has been implemented after consulting with clients, suppliers, and other interested parties. The organisation's PQP and corresponding management system can be improved using the lessons learned from the evaluation.

Review meetings are conducted at various levels to evaluate the effectiveness of QMS. Communication of the minutes of the meeting to all stakeholders of the project will help ensure transparency and effectiveness.

6.6 QUALITY MANAGEMENT IN PROJECTS

A quality management system consists of activities by which an organisation defines its goals and ascertains the procedures and materials needed to reach those goals (ISO, 2015). The QMS manages the interdependent procedures and resources needed to provide the desired outcomes. The project quality management system corresponds as closely as possible with the quality management system (QMS) of the originating organisation where the project organisation functions.

Quality management of a project includes (ISO, 2017):

- **(i)** a project's quality management system;
- **(ii)** project management's responsibility;
- **(iii)** project resource management;
- **(iv)** realisation of goods and services in projects; and
- **(v)** project measurement, analysis, and improvement.

6.6.1 Quality Management System of the Project

The context in which a project quality management system functions has to be considered by both the project organisation and the originating organisation and the client and the contractor. Some internal and external problems may make it more difficult for the project to produce the expected results. As a result of taking into account both internal and external factors that may affect the project quality management system, both organisations can (ISO, 2017):

(a) be aware of the demands and objectives of all parties involved.
(b) establish or apply project quality management procedures to achieve the desired project results.
(c) assess the risks and possibilities associated with the project's procedures and anticipated results.

6.6.2 Management Responsibilities and Duties

Management responsibility is a big topic and is probably of the foremost importance in the success of the quality plan. The various aspects of responsibility are outlined below:

Management Commitment

Commitment is probably of the first order. If there is no commitment, there is no interest or motivation, and without those, the workers cannot be inspired. Hence, the client and contractor's top management must have commitment and active involvement in the project to develop an efficient and effective quality management system. Thus, a culture of quality will serve an excellent purpose in the organisation, which can help existing and future projects to be improved continuously.

Dedicated leadership ensures interactions among team members. Managers learn to empower leaders at the site level with decision-making power as they have to interact with customers, law regulators, and society. In addition, policies and strategies of the organisation are discussed and developed collectively by team members. Complex problems can be solved by constant interactions. The staff is regularly updated through training to expand their capabilities in response to changes in the industry.

QMS is effectively implemented by the management by establishing quality objectives for all processes of the organisation in line with the organisation's quality policy and strategy. To ensure the effectiveness and adequacy of QMS, periodic management review meetings shall be conducted at various levels per the established procedure and timetable. Quality improvement can be made through learning from corrective and preventive actions. The management can try to designate a representative to prepare the QMS and ensure the implementation of quality on-site. Thus, it is essential that the organisation's structure be well defined; quality professionals are to be positioned accordingly, and the proper mobilisation of competent resources is undertaken to understand and satisfy the project's criteria.

Customer Interaction and Satisfaction

With the aim of enhancing customer satisfaction, customer interaction is done on a continuous basis. Feedback is taken to identify areas of dissatisfaction/ improvements, and suggestions are invited during the execution of the project. The company could aim to have well-established processes for communicating with the customers and informing them of the status of the work. Discussions will thus be conducted at various levels, and corrective actions will be taken based on the inputs. As the success of a project depends on the satisfaction of the customers, an effort is required to understand all requirements, while the processes focus on attaining them.

Policies for Quality Implementation

Quality Policy is articulated by top management in concurrence with the organisation's vision. It helps meet customer expectations and continuously enhances the efficiency of the QMS. The quality policy of an organisation provides a structure to establish and review quality objectives. The quality manual is used to spread awareness of the policy, and it is issued to all sections and disseminated among all department personnel. The quality policy of an organisation has to be displayed in places of strategic importance.

Planning for Quality

The quality objectives derived from the quality policy for various units/departments for operations applicable at the project site are to be defined at the time of project commencement. The quality objectives are set based on the quality management principles applicable to the specific project.

To fulfil customer expectations, regulatory requirements, and organisational goals based on contractual requirements, QMS Planning has established a procedure to plan, monitor, and achieve quality systems. Strategies are prepared to ensure product quality, safety on site, and timely delivery. Process and product performance are evaluated through audits.

Improvements are made to the processes following the management review meeting. System integrity can be maintained while changing the PQP for improvement. Documentation of all processes and tracking of planned versus actual ought to be done.

Responsibility, Authority, and Communication

The organisation chart with critical positions will be marked for implementing/managing the quality system at the project level. It helps to identify and state roles and responsibilities at the corporate and site levels. Experienced personnel are to be nominated at the site for effective administration of the quality management systems. They have to ensure the preparation of a PQP and get approval from management and customers if contractually required. They prepare and incorporate all the work methods, the corresponding inspection and test plans, and the formats stated in the contract. Suitable methods are employed to measure the adequacy/effectiveness of the QMS and coordinate the data collection. Internal audits and product quality ratings, with the coordination of all concerned, are arranged for the timely disposal of nonconformity reports. They organise and conduct meetings and communicate notes to all participants.

Table 6.1 displays the roles and responsibilities of a few of the vital site staff.

Management Review

The project head conducts periodic reviews to assess the effectiveness of the quality management system. The process of conducting management review meetings is as follows:

- Plan and conduct review meetings for the site at frequent intervals.
- Inform the concerned attendees the date and time of the meeting well in advance.
- The points discussed during the review meetings might be as follows:
    - Progress of work and quality objectives.
    - Future resources requirements.
    - Audit reports.

TABLE 6.1 Roles and responsibilities

Position	Responsibilities
Project Manager	Organising and managing the site activities and resources to ensure the timely completion of work to satisfy contractual requirements.
Planning Manager	Preparing the schedule and monitoring the project, arranging the materials on time, communicating with the top management regarding the work progress, and coordinating with all departments.
Billing Engineer	Preparation of bills, tracking progress based on the cost incurred, and reconciliation of materials with work progress.
Planning Engineer	Monitor and track progress, update the project, and reconcile materials.
Site Engineer	Execute the work as per the method statement, arrange and manage the site activities, inspect the work, and coordinate the site activities,
Stores Manager	Receive and store supplies and materials, track the supply of materials to the site, and inspect incoming materials.

- Corrective action reports.
- Preventive action reports.
- Report of customer satisfaction.
- Rating of quality.
- Customer feedback and complaints.
- Suggestions for improvement.
- Appreciation of best practices.
- Pending points of the last meeting.

The output of the meetings results in ideas for improvement of the QMS, processes, quality, customer satisfaction, requirement of resources, and best practices that can be adopted. After the meeting, actions are to be implemented as decided in the review meeting within the selected time frame.

6.6.3 Managing Resources

Planning Resource Requirements

Resource management is done to plan resource requirements of staff, materials, labour, plant and machinery, and specialised agencies meet contractual requirements as per the contract documents. Resource management helps identify any potential resource-related problems and prevents delays. Resource plans, including estimates, allotments, and constraints, ought to be outlined and incorporated in the PQP. Reviews are performed to ensure the availability of resources. Personnel required to manage the quality based on discipline, functional experience, and skills are also selected. After acquiring resources, they are organised as per PQP. If any gaps are found in human resources performance, appropriate training is to be given. The organisational structure shall suit the construction methods, project scope, team size, and local circumstances. Job descriptions and the division of authority and responsibility are to be prepared and documented.

Specifying the qualifications, training, and experience required for staff working on a project is essential. PQP also includes the list of QMS training that prepares every employee individually and collectively to contribute their complete expertise and achieve goals according to priority and availability. Training is also provided to sub-contractors and workers after identifying their shortcomings. Evaluation of training is done to find the adequacy and effectiveness of training. Toolbox meetings are conducted on work procedures for highly skilled workers like drillers, blasters, masons, carpenters, fitters, and others at the site to enhance their knowledge and competence in their respective trades and execute the work safely. The quality of end products is evaluated to assess their effectiveness.

All these come from the basic philosophy of management.

Infrastructure Requirements for Personnel

It is essential that the organisations provide the infrastructure conducive for personnel to achieve product quality requirements at offices and project sites. The infrastructure requirements include the following:

- Site office building.
- Staff quarters/housing.
- Drinking water.
- Electrical facilities.
- Labour camp.
- Communication facilities.
- Emergency medical facilities.
- Transport facilities.
- Firefighting equipment.
- Storage spaces for different materials.
- Steel fabrication yard.
- Software requirements.
- Equipment, plant, and machinery.

Nothing related to project fulfilment must ever be missed here, as inordinate delays and additional expenses can result.

Proper Work Environment

As mentioned in the work method, a proper work environment is indispensable to ensure and monitor for effectiveness through internal audits. The following environmental factors affecting product conformity are identified and included in the work method as applicable:

- Conditions of approach roads, access ways.
- Housekeeping.
- Security services.
- Protection of sheds.

- Lighting arrangements.
- Safety devices.
- Storage facilities.
- Statutory and contract requirements.

6.6.4 Product Realisation

The process of creating a product, known as 'product realisation', involves a number of steps from inception to completion. It covers every phase, including design, implementation, and maintenance.

Planning and Procedures for Product Realisation

Planning is done to establish and maintain a procedure for implementing and controlling construction activities at the site. This helps in the effective realisation of the product as per the contract in accordance with the approved plans and methods to satisfy the needs of the project stakeholders.

The interconnected processes that make up a project include project initiation, project management plan formulation, interaction management, change management, and process and project closing.

The processes or activities include the following:

(A) Planning and scheduling
- (a) Budgeting.
- (b) Preparation of schedules.
- (c) Preparation of estimate.
- (d) Statutory and regulatory requirements.
- (e) Prepare Project Specific Quality Plan.

(B) Monitoring and Reviewing
- (a) Updating construction activities.
- (b) Monitor and improve quality objectives as per PQP.
- (c) Review of materials in stock.
- (d) Prepare a monthly performance report.
- (e) Prepare action taken report.
- (f) Invoicing.
- (g) Bills certification.
- (h) Utilisation of plant and machinery.
- (i) Quality audits.
- (j) Statements of cash, purchase of materials, stock, and so on.

(C) Project completion
- (a) Checklist for defect liability period.
- (b) Project completion report.

Review and Communication with the Customer

The customer requirements related to the product are determined through contract review by the tendering department and will be communicated to the site. With the progress of work, the client may come up with changes in requirements. Such changes are to be reviewed and approved. The procedure for review and communication with the customer regarding the product and related processes are as follows:

(a) Review contract for customer requirements.
(b) The change orders from customers are received and assessed for cost implications, considering the changes that have occurred after the tendering stage.
(c) After making necessary changes, approval is sought from customers for acceptance.
(d) Maintain register for change management.
(e) Project status reports are communicated to customers – daily, weekly, and monthly.
(f) Handling customer complaints.

Review of Contract Documents for Design and Development

The contract documents are to be reviewed for design and development and to check for inadequacies. If any deviations are found from construction codes or practices, the customer has to be informed. Accordingly, modifications may be made, further cost implications and schedules may be prepared, and the same have to be approved by the customer. Method statements are to be prepared in compliance with codes and regulations.

Material and Subcontractor Management

For procurement of materials, a materials schedule is needed. After obtaining approval from the organisation and customer, vendors are identified based on the supply source and their capability to supply. Capable vendors are selected after preparing comparative statements. Price approval is to be taken from top management for materials procured at the site. The quality of materials is to be inspected on delivery.

A well-defined procedure for proper identification and easy traceability of materials received and maintained at the site is to be laid down. Registers are to be maintained to track materials from the time of raising indent, purchase approval, material collection, and material issue to track the movement of materials.

Screening and selection of subcontractors are done as per procedures. Potential agencies are identified based on previous performance. Assessment and selection are made based on their technical and financial competence. Their performance is evaluated periodically based on the safety record, ability to mobilise, labour productivity, control over wastage of materials, control over workers, judicious and efficient utilisation of resources, cooperation with other agencies, and compliance with labour regulations.

Method Statements

Method statements are prepared for all the activities required to be executed to meet the project requirements. The database of the method statement, standard procedures, inspection and test plan, formats for data collection at the site, and checklists for all the activities are also to be developed. This database may be stored electronically for easy access to the users. While the procedures are prepared, existing quality documents in the organisation can be used as a reference and tailored to suit the project's requirements. Qualified personnel are responsible for preparing the method statements for the activities, meeting the design specifications, health and safety norms, and relevant codes of practice as per contractual requirements.

Inspecting Machines, Instruments, and Equipment

To ensure that the equipment performs tests to the required accuracy, they are to be calibrated and inspected regularly. Appropriate action is to be taken when nonconformity is found during inspections. A list of instruments requiring calibration has to be prepared and the calibration dates should be documented.

6.6.5 Measurement, Analysis, and Improvement

The last part of any QMS deals with monitoring, measurement, analysis, and improvement of processes of all activities to ensure product quality and QMS effectiveness. Method statements to execute work inspection and testing plan and relevant records are checked for adequacy. In this, only those items necessary to deliver the results should go into the QMS. There is no scope for research activities to be included in the QMS because the QMS is a very practical document for direct implementation that need to be understood by project foremen.

Audits have got to be performed to determine the efficacy and applicability of the Quality Management System. Audits help to measure adherence to quality standards and relevant codes. An audit calendar has to be prepared, and notification be given to the department concerned. After preparing checklist points, auditing is not to be missed at the scheduled time. Corrective and preventive actions should be taken at the appropriate time. Nonconformance reports are verified for action taken and results obtained. Audit findings are discussed during management review meetings to improve process and product quality and implement the action as decided.

Thus, an action plan should be prepared to remove nonconformity. Implement corrective action and if possible, remove the underlying cause of the nonconformity, and confirm that the product complies with the standards. Reject those products where correction is not possible. If the deviation is minor and will not affect the performance, a concession can be taken from the customer for its use. Preventive action should be taken to prevent the potential causes of nonconformities. The team members may conduct necessary brainstorming sessions to improve the processes, and required actions may be implemented. Recording all the measured results and achievements, stages of detection, and disposition of non-conformance are essential as they support learning and provide data for analysis and improvement of activities for the upcoming activities and projects.

An inspection and test plan has to be prepared for monitoring and measuring the activities, listing when and where monitoring and auditing are to be done, how many samples are to be tested, criteria for acceptance, list of reference documents, and the people responsible. Depending upon the type of activity, several tests are to be conducted. It may be soil testing, aggregate testing, concrete testing, rebar strength testing, or non-destructive testing. Only accredited/certified lab facilities should be utilised for testing and calibration purposes. For continual improvement of processes, the project performance should be reviewed with regard to the quality objectives.

A leading Indian construction company Larsen & Toubro Ltd. uses the following approach laid out in their operation manual for measuring quality ('Project Quality Plan', n.d.).

- A sampling approach is adopted and a 'Product Quality Check matrix' is prepared to measure the conformance of various civil, mechanical, and electrical works to specification and workmanship standards.
- The rating for composite projects is determined by calculating the rating for individual components such as foundation and steel and then determining a final rating.
- The final rating is determined by using the equation below:

$$\text{Final rating} = \sum_{i=1}^{n}\left(\frac{\text{Individual rating of the component}_i \times \text{Sales value of the component}_i}{\text{Contract value}}\right)$$

Construction organisations follow different quality management strategies to ensure that they deliver projects that meet the client's requirements. They take the help of the ISO guidelines to prepare their own QMS. Project quality plans are then prepared based on the QMS for each project to meet the specific needs of the project.

6.7 SUMMARY OF ISO 10006:2017

ISO 10006:2017 provides a framework for the implementation of quality management in projects as shown in Table 6.2.

TABLE 6.2 Overview of processes for quality management in projects with reference to ISO 10006:2017

Clause	Subclause	Process	Process description
Management responsibility in projects	Strategic process	Strategic	A method for creating goals that involve organising the creation and implementation of the quality management system using the quality management principles.
Resource management in projects	Resource related processes	Resource planning	Identifying, calculating, planning, and allocating appropriate resources.
		Resource control	Assessing resource plans versus actual utilisation and taking appropriate action.
	Personnel related processes	Establishment of project organisational structure	Establishing a project organisational structure that is adapted to the needs of the project, figuring out what roles need to be played, and defining authority and accountability.
		Allocation of personnel	Choosing and assigning enough qualified workers to the project to meet its requirements.
		Team development	Enhancing project performance through enhancing individual and team skills.

(Continued)

TABLE 6.2 *(Continued)*

Clause	Subclause	Process	Process description
Product/ service realisation in projects	Interdependent processes	Project initiation and project management plan development	Analysing client demands and those of other interested parties, creating a project management strategy, and initiating other procedures.
		Interaction management	Coordinating communications throughout the project.
		Change management	Preparing for and managing change throughout all processes.
		Process and project closure	Completing tasks and getting feedback.
	Scope related processes	Concept development	Describing the general parameters of a product's features.
		Scope development and control	Identifying and controlling the project product's measurable features.
		Definition of activities	Determining and recording the tasks and procedures necessary to accomplish the project's goals.
		Control of activities	Exercising control over the project's actual work.
	Time-related processes	Planning of activity dependencies	Recognising relationships, logical connections, and dependencies between project tasks.
		Estimation of duration	Calculating the time needed to complete each task considering the unique conditions and the available resources.
		Schedule development	Finding the project time based on objectives and verifying the proposed schedule for taking necessary actions for recovering from delays.
	Cost related processes	Cost estimation	Creating project cost estimates.
		Budgeting	Preparation of budget using a cost estimate.
		Cost control	Controlling project costs and budgetary discrepancies.

Clause	Subclause	Process	Process description
	Communication-related processes	Communication planning	Planning the project's information and communication system.
		Information management	Supplying members and stakeholders with the information they need.
	Risk related processes	Communication control	Regulating communication to follow the established communication system.
		Risk identification	Identifying project-related risks.
		Risk assessment	Assessing the impact of risk occurrences on the project and the likelihood of occurrence.
		Risk treatment	Creating strategies for handling risks.
		Risk Control	Putting the risk plans into action and revising them.
	Procurement processes	Procurement planning and control	Determining and regulating what must be bought and when.
		Documentation of procurement requirements	Combining the technical and commercial requirements.
		External provider management and development	Choosing subcontractors and other providers to supply items.
		Contracting	Invitations to tender, review of tenders, negotiations, planning, and placement of subcontractors.
		Contract control	Ensuring that the work of the subcontractor complies with the terms of the contract.
Measurement, analysis, and improvement in projects	General	Improvement	Providing direction on how the originating and project organisations should learn from projects.
	Measurement and analysis	Measurement and analysis	Providing direction on data measurement, collection, and validation for continuous improvement.

(Continued)

TABLE 6.2 *(Continued)*

Clause	Subclause	Process	Process description
	Improvement	Improvement by the originating organisation	Originating organisations should take steps for continuous improvement of the projects.
		Improvement by the project organisation	Project organisation should provide complete and accurate information to the originating organisation so as to enable them continuous improvement.

CONCLUSION

In reality, the Project Quality Plan (PQP) is a living document that evolves over the project lifecycle, adding details at each stage. The PQP tries to ensure that quality is maintained with project progress milestones. All procedures and actions should follow the standards for quality if the company wishes to stay out of trouble. In implementing the PQP, the problems identified during execution are analysed to find root causes. Improvements are made based on thorough analysis, and an action plan is taken to eliminate defects. There exist well-defined processes for collecting data for every activity, and communication plays a major role in PQP. This is the PQP protocol. However, it is important to document all activities in offices and backed up electronically. This helps in the retrieval of data at any time and aids in decision-making for continuous improvement of the processes. Thus, PQP ensures that customer requirements are satisfied and quality is maintained through following proper protocol. It is essential that PQP be made mandatory for all projects to ensure the quality of deliverables.

WORKS CITED

ISO. (2015), *Quality Management Principles* (Geneva: International Organization for Standardization).

ISO. (2017), *ISO 10006- Quality Management – Guidelines for Quality Management in Projects* (Geneva: International Organization for Standardization).

ISO. (2018), *ISO 10005 Quality Management – Guidelines for Quality Plans* (Geneva: International Organization for Standardization).

PMI. (2021), *The Standard for Project Management and A Guide to the Project Management Body of Knowledge (PMBOK Guide) (Seventh Edition)* (Newtown Square, PA: Project Management Institute).

__________'Project Quality Plan', Manual of Larsen & Toubro Ltd, Chennai, India, n.d.

REVIEW QUESTIONS

Multiple Choice Questions

1. __________ is a temporary endeavour undertaken to create a unique product, service, or result.
   (a) Process (b) Portfolio
   (c) Project (d) Programme
2. What are deliverables?
   (a) Product (b) Service
   (c) Results (d) All of the above
3. Project quality can be achieved by balancing the three factors and they are:
   (a) Scope (b) Time
   (c) Cost (d) All of the above
4. Which among the following is not a quality management principle?
   (a) Customer focus (b) Leadership
   (c) Process approach (d) Profit maximisation
5. Guidelines for creating, evaluating, adopting, implementing, and modifying quality plans are included in:
   (a) ISO 10005: 2018(E) (b) ISO 10006: 2018(E)
   (c) ISO 9001: 2018(E) (d) ISO 19011: 2018(E)
6. The PQP is a management practice that facilitates an organisation in achieving quality by providing _________ to all the activities involved in a project.
   (a) directions (b) control
   (c) improvement (d) compliance
7. _________ is a management plan that is particular to a project, and it lists the standards, practices, tools, and activities required to ensure quality in the project.
   (a) Quality management system (b) Project Quality Plan
   (c) Quality Audit (d) Contract document
8. Which of the following factors are considered while developing a PQP?
   (a) Internal conditions (b) External conditions
   (c) Stakeholder requirements (d) All of the above
9. Which of the following is not an input while developing a PQP?
   (a) National standards (b) Client budget
   (c) Location of the site (d) Employee satisfaction

10. __________is a graphical representation of the internal structure of the organisation used to display the various roles, positions, and responsibilities of the officials in a hierarchical manner.

(a) Organisation chart (b) Organisation structure
(c) Quality plan (d) Bar chart

11. ______ is used to communicate within the organisation, enabling interested parties to make decisions based on accurate information.

(a) MIS (b) PQP
(c) QMS (d) MEP

12. Methods to present quality plans graphically include:

(a) process maps (b) Gantt chart
(c) workflow chart (d) All of the above

13. The processes covered under the quality management system, their order, and interaction with various processes for effective maintenance of the system are to be depicted in the _______.

(a) Gantt chart
(b) Management Information System
(c) Process flow chart
(d) Organisation chart

14. The process of creating a product, which involves a number of steps from inception to completion, is known as ________.

(a) product realisation (b) process analysis
(c) planning (d) process design

15. __________ is performed to determine the efficacy and applicability of the Quality Management System.

(a) Process analysis (b) ISO certification
(c) Audit (d) Brainstorming

16. ________ is (are) prepared for monitoring and measuring the activities, listing when and where monitoring and auditing are to be done, how many samples are to be tested, criteria for acceptance, list of reference documents, and the people responsible.

(a) Work instructions (b) Method statement
(c) Project quality plan (d) Inspection and test plan

17. _________ are conducted on work procedures for highly skilled workers like drillers, blasters, masons, carpenters, fitters, and others at the site to enhance their knowledge and competence in their respective trades and execute the work safely.

(a) Toolbox meetings (b) Review meetings
(c) QMS training and seminars (d) Quality audits

18. _______ receives and stores supplies and materials, tracks the supply of materials to the site and inspects incoming materials.

(a) Site engineer (b) Store manager
(c) Billing engineer (d) Cost auditor

19. According to ISO, _______consists of activities by which an organisation defines its goals and ascertains the procedures and materials needed to reach those goals.

(a) Project quality plan (b) Quality policy
(c) Quality management system (d) External failure cost

20. _______ gives customers confidence that the products come from a known and traceable supply chain.

(a) Vendor evaluation (b) MIS
(c) Mobilisation (d) Traceability

Short Answer Type Questions

1. What is a project?
2. What are deliverables?
3. How to measure the quality of a deliverable?
4. How to attain quality in a project?
5. Why is traceability significant?
6. What are the several uses of audits?
7. Under what circumstances is PQP revised?
8. Why is assessing feedback important?
9. What is the difference between a PQP and QMS?
10. What are the factors discussed during a review meeting?
11. List the infrastructure requirements in a construction project site.
12. What facilities are required to create a conducive environment for better productivity?
13. Write a short note on the inspection and test plan.
14. Why is PQP considered a living document?
15. What is change management?

Long Answer Type Questions

1. Discuss about the ISO quality management principles and how they are relevant to the construction industry.
2. Why is a project quality plan required?
3. What inputs are required to develop a PQP?

4. What are the important factors to be considered during documentation?
5. Describe the steps in the preparation of a PQP.
6. Explain the major factors included in a QMS.
7. Enumerate the roles and responsibilities of vital staff in a construction project site.
8. Discuss the various activities and processes required for product realisation in the construction industry.

ANSWER KEYS

Multiple Choice Questions

1. (c)	**2.** (d)	**3.** (d)	**4.** (d)	**5.** (a)	**6.** (a)	**7.** (b)	**8.** (d)
9. (d)	**10.** (a)	**11.** (a)	**12.** (d)	**13.** (c)	**14.** (a)	**15.** (c)	**16.** (d)
17. (a)	**18.** (b)	**19.** (c)	**20.** (d)				

CHAPTER 7 Quality Audit

7.1 INTRODUCTION

Every customer wants satisfaction or delight for the money invested, whether for a service or a product. But how does the organisation meet the requirements of their clients? The answer is that it is done through continuous and sustainable quality improvement, by ensuring quality in the services rendered and in the goods manufactured. In the construction industry, satisfying the client/customer is possible by fulfilling their needs specified in the contract.

ISO (the International Organization for Standardization) 9001 lays the framework for developing a quality management system that helps organisations meet regulatory requirements, increase customer satisfaction, and continuously improve the organisation. ISO certification is an assurance to users regarding the quality of goods or services provided by the organisation. Every organisation ought to have a quality policy, which will be a guideline for setting quality objectives. Management and quality audits ensure that the quality management system is suitable to accomplish the specified goals. It has been an established practice for major companies to audit their suppliers, sub-contractors, and their own quality management systems.

Audits are the physical verification and inspection of items of interest. The idea of a quality audit first emerged during the Industrial Revolution when inspectors evaluated the quality of goods produced in large quantities in factories. The practice of auditing became popular with the introduction of BS 5750 and ISO 9000 series of standards (Wealleans, 2000). The American Society for Quality (ASQ), founded in 1946, includes audits as part of its quality philosophy.

The origin of the word 'audit' is from the Latin word '*auditus*' which means hearing. The dictionary meaning of audit is 'a methodical examination and review' (Dictionary, 2023). Quality audit is 'a systematic, independent, and documented process for obtaining objective evidence and evaluating it objectively to determine the extent to which the audit criteria are fulfilled' (ISO, 2018). It is done by comparing the actual activities, processes, or products with the documented requirements.

An impartial assessment of several facets of quality performance is known as a quality audit, and it aims to inform those who require assurance about that performance (Juran & Godfrey, 1999). Numerous applications have been made to the manufacturing industry, including audits of both product and activity (product audit and systems audit). Compliance with governmental requirements is frequently a focus of audits for products such as those in the medical and financial sectors.

A quality audit investigates the organisational system to determine whether contractual obligations are met. Quality audits ensure that the processes are designed and operated to meet the client's agreed requirements. Whereas the company can undertake auditing internally or externally by a hired consultant, the audit results shall be used to evaluate the performance of an organisation's activities to enhance quality. Audit results form the basis for improvement in the system, processes, activities, or any other element that has been audited.

For effective auditing, all the interested parties have to use the same rule book, the audit standards, which are the guidelines that both the auditor and auditee need to adopt. The audit of project execution is done by comparing the documented quality policies, procedures, and requirements with the observed practices. It is rather a check whether they have been properly executed and whether they achieve the established objectives. Thus, quality audits play a significant role in reporting the status of a process. It must be understood that the cost incurred for quality auditing is a preventive cost (BSI, 1990), such as an insurance policy, to save potentially greater losses down the line.

7.2 GOALS AND OBJECTIVES OF AUDIT

A quality management system is a framework for managing quality in an organisation. The QMS addresses the quality of an organisation's products, services, processes, and operations, where customer satisfaction depends on the quality of products, services, processes, and procedures, which are further predicated on the quality system prevalent in the organisation. The adequacy and effectiveness of a product or service can be assessed by compliance with specified and relevant standards. In this context, standards refer to those documents that define acceptable product conditions, features, and performance. It also ensures that a product has desirable attributes like quality, reasonable pricing, environmental fitness, safety, efficiency, and reliability. In this regard, ISO has developed more than 1,100 standards and documents for the construction industry (ISO, 2017). Many other organisations produce standards pertaining to rules and regulations to be followed in the construction sector that are specific to each nation. The Bureau of Indian Standards develops the standards to be followed in India.

Audit plays an essential role in implementing organisational performance evaluation and improvement actions. It is an application of the 'check' and 'act' of the PDCA cycle (Plan-Do-Check-Act). The quality audit ensures the compliance of the QMS in an organisation with the standards applicable to the nature of their work. The quality audit must be handled based on predefined objectives of the audit, scope, and criteria that align with the purposes of the overall audit programme. Hence, the audit objectives essentially include the following:

- **(a)** Determine whether the management system complies with the audit criteria.
- **(b)** Evaluate how well the management system supports the organisation to satisfy its commitments, rules, and statutory regulations.
- **(c)** Evaluate the management system's effectiveness in satisfying the quality objective.
- **(d)** Identify the areas where improvement is required in the management system.
- **(e)** Evaluate the management system for its adequacy and suitability to the auditee's setting and strategic goals.

(f) Evaluate the management system's capacity to create and accomplish goals, address risks and opportunities effectively in a dynamic environment, and implement the required actions.

The scope of the audit covers factors such as activities, processes, and functions to be audited, as well as the location and time of the audit. It has to be in compliance with the audit programme and audit objective. The audit criteria may include policies, rules, guidelines, and performance standards, including goals, regulatory and statutory requirements, information related to risks and opportunities, codes of conduct, management system requirements, or any other planned arrangements. Lastly, the audit programme must be modified and communicated for approval whenever there is a change in the audit objective, scope, and criteria.

7.3 QUALITY AUDIT IN THE CONSTRUCTION INDUSTRY

Quality in construction plays a vital role in ensuring the durability and safety of a structure, the satisfaction of the customer and the long-term prospects of the organisation. Periodic quality audits at different project stages covering various elements are essential in attaining quality. Construction audit systems provide a framework for evaluating the performance at various phases, such as design, execution, operation, and maintenance. Audit assesses the quality of design, materials, workmanship, and performance of the constructed structures with reference to the approved quality standards and quality needs of the client as per the contract. Quality audits will also evaluate the management approaches, leadership, and organisational structure that is most conducive to a good quality program. Audits are carried out at various stages of construction to ensure that all the quality needs of the client as per the contract are fulfilled.

The design team performs the quality audit to verify if the design satisfies the strength requirements of the structure and fulfils the requirements as per relevant codes and standards. In certain countries, designs are audited by regulatory bodies, especially in nations where earthquakes are prevalent. The reviewing agency verifies the compliance with the statutory requirements. The approved design is sent to the owner for approval if required. After approval from the regulatory bodies and owner, the design is used for construction purposes.

During the construction stage, the contractor checks the executed works prior to auditing by the quality control engineer appointed by the owner. External auditing in construction is performed by a quality engineer appointed by the owner for important works. There are independent accredited agencies for auditing activities like geotechnical investigation, designing the concrete mix, and testing of materials such as concrete, rebar, timber, etc. Regulatory bodies can undertake quality compliance audits at any time, by surprise, or as they deem fit.

The uniqueness of the construction industry lies in the fact that a contractor may be working simultaneously on several projects of a diverse nature. Each project will likely have its own unique contract document, which requires the contractor to prepare a separate project quality plan for each project to ensure that the project's quality requirements are met according to the client's requirements. So, the list of manuals and documents, reports and forms depends on the nature of the work; hence, the nature of the audit may also vary accordingly.

Each organisation establishes a procedure for internal auditing to assess the QMS effectiveness and implementation level. The planning and execution of internal audits are outlined in this procedure. Consultants, subcontractors, and sub-consultants will all be included in the audit scope. The scheduling of the audits is based on the importance of the work and the risks involved.

Examining the actual construction is the main goal of the construction quality audit. The quality of components being built either on-site or in the prefabrication yard will naturally be compared against the project specifications by the engineers. Construction audits are done to verify the conformance of the quality of components and structures, that are either built at the site or in a prefabrication yard, with the project specifications. Normally, the quality audit is carried out in real-time as the construction is being done. The audit has to be carried out before the work is covered up or hidden. Since construction quality audits are carried out during construction, they provide the chance for defects or ongoing work to be corrected, ultimately improving the finished structure. They are to be carried out in a constructive way to support the auditee in learning and improving as opposed to a harsh one. Compared to financial audits, construction quality audits have the potential to save significantly more money. A facility of poor quality could need extremely expensive rectification and maintenance, might not offer the required service, or might even fail catastrophically leading to loss of time, resources, and money.

Instead of concentrating on day-to-day control, the audit's main goals are system improvement and comprehensive control. Some recommendations, however, might be project-specific or pertain to works-in-progress and can be implemented immediately. Corrections are done when the audit finds major project-specific non-conformities or defects. Training field staff as a direct or indirect outcome of the audit is another advantage of the audit. Audits are an inevitable component of quality and safety management in the construction industry.

The summary of the objectives of construction facilities audits is as follows (Samuels, 1994):

- **(i)** Improve the effectiveness of the quality system.
- **(ii)** Monitor the suitability of organisational planning.
- **(iii)** Track the success of applying policies and procedures.
- **(iv)** Improve the system as suggested and put it into practice.
- **(v)** Ensure uniformity among projects and inspectors.
- **(vi)** Examine the performance of standardised designs and standards.
- **(vii)** Improve the constructability of project documents through analysis.
- **(viii)** Obtain information on life-cycle facility management.
- **(ix)** Identify training requirements.

7.4 PRINCIPLES OF AUDITING

Auditing is based on certain principles, making it useful and trustworthy in controlling and supporting management policies. It provides information that can be utilised to improve the performance of an organisation. It is essential to adhere to these principles to provide relevant and sufficient audit conclusions and to ensure that similar conclusions are reached in similar situations, even when auditors work independently.

The seven principles upon which auditing is based are given in Sections 7.4.1 to 7.4.7 (ISO, 2018).

7.4.1 Integrity

Integrity is the strong adherence to honesty and moral values and is a virtue that every auditor must possess. It is a fundamental requirement of professionalism. An auditor needs to stand by his moral values even when there are disagreements and compulsions from the auditee side. They need to be fair, transparent, and impartial in all their dealings. While conducting an audit, they must avoid being influenced by conflicting interests. An auditor ought to be responsible and ensure that they perform the audit activities only in their areas of expertise.

7.4.2 Fair Presentation

Auditors are obliged to report the findings and conclusions faultlessly and honestly. Audit report has to be clear and complete in all respects. It has to report the obstacles encountered during the audit. The audit report has to include the differences in opinion between the auditee and the audit team. All the anomalies detected must be noted in the report. Since audits are a means to continuous improvement, the communication of audit findings and conclusions must be fair, honest, straight, well-timed, complete, and precise.

7.4.3 Due Professional Care

Auditors are obliged to exercise due care during an audit and make a reasonable judgment. Applying due professional care involves understanding the objectives and scope of the audit. Auditors need to have enough training to know the competencies required to execute the audit and the policies and procedures for the internal audit activity. An auditor is required to have sufficient field expertise and has to be updated through periodic training and continuous learning. They are trained to discern the significance of the task to be accomplished. However, the clients and the stakeholders need to have trust in the auditor to trust the audit.

7.4.4 Confidentiality: Security of Information

Auditors have the responsibility to protect and ensure the confidentiality of the information acquired during the audit process. They are not supposed to use it for personal interests in a way harmful to the auditee. It is very important to handle the sensitive and confidential information appropriately. It is not allowed to disclose the findings, any part of them, or any information gained during an audit to a third party unless permitted by the auditee and the audited organisation.

7.4.5 Independence

Another critical factor in the conduct of an audit is the independence of the auditor. Auditors are chosen in such a way that they are unrelated to the function and activity being audited. Since it is not always practical for internal auditors in small organisations to be independent of the activity under audit, it is essential to take measures to avoid partiality and promote objectivity. During the audit, an auditor is obliged to avoid all conflicts of interest and has to be impartial. The audit findings and conclusions must be based on audited evidence only. Maintaining objectivity is very important during an audit process.

7.4.6 Evidence-based Approach

The audit is a process conducted within a defined period using limited resources, so verifying all samples is impossible. Hence, information is collected from random samples for auditing. Sampling is done in a way that represents the population in a reasonably good way. All evidence collected needs to be verifiable. Audit conclusions are to be arrived at by following a rational method.

7.4.7 Risk-based Approach

Audits are very significant for the client. The goals of audit programmes are to be met by using a risk-based approach during the design, execution, and reporting of audits. Consider all the risks and opportunities while auditing.

7.5 TYPES OF AUDITS

There are mainly six types of audits based on the purpose served. They are (i) Systems audit, (ii) Process audit, (iii) Product audit, (iv) Adequacy audit, (v) Compliance audit, and (vi) Desk audit. These are discussed below.

7.5.1 Systems Audit

Quality system audits are the verification of an organisation's quality system. It will determine the capability of the organisation to meet its commitment to a quality system. It also checks the efficiency of the control mechanism of management in meeting the specific requirements of their products or services. System audits have a wide scope since systems represent the whole set of processes, including interaction among groups, and consist of interrelated and interdependent elements. System audits concentrate on the relationships between the various processes in the system. Since construction projects are complex and consist of various systems, processes, and activities, the quality audit concerns the quality of the system. It examines that activities are performed in conformance with the requirements mentioned in the standards, documented systems, and procedures.

7.5.2 Process Audit

Processes are organised activities that add value to the inputs and thus create a product or service. Process audits check if the actual operations are done according to the processes, as documented. Process audits mainly focus on processing or manufacturing activities. The process audit assesses the effectiveness of processes and the compliance of the process to standards. These audits examine how well employees and equipment meet the established requirements. Additionally, it examines if the process controls over the equipment operators are adequate, appropriate, and effective.

7.5.3 Product Audit

Product quality audits determine various aspects of product quality: quality owing to design, quality in consideration with conformance to the standards, quality of the product in meeting market requirements, performance of products, compliance with safety standards, and quality due to product support. Product audit results are compared with the customer requirements and the engineering requirements. They measure the level of conformity of the product to the regulatory standards, workmanship, performance, adequacy, effectiveness, and quality. Unlike inspection, only a few samples are collected and examined. Product audits are mostly conducted in the marketplace so that the auditor can evaluate the impact of other associated operations like transportation, packaging, handling, storage, etc. It is an indication that a customer is receiving quality service. This also enables the product to be compared with that of their competitors.

7.5.4 Adequacy Audit

Adequacy audit is an examination of the adequacy of criteria in quality manuals and quality plans. It establishes how thoroughly the system is documented concerning the relevant standards. The project quality plan or quality manuals are translations of requirements stipulated in ISO standards or any other applicable codes. Since the organisation will be operating based on these documents, it is a good idea to compare the requirements of standards with the processes that have been defined and point out differences, if any.

7.5.5 Compliance Audit

Compliance audit is done to determine the level of conformance of implementation with the documented system and to examine whether the organisation's personnel follow it. It is done by evaluating the system, examining documents, and supervising the various activities in operation. This makes it possible to determine whether the documented system is appropriate, sufficient, and efficient.

7.5.6 Desk Audit

Desk audit is the examination of the documentation system, and it takes place without a physical meeting between the auditor and the auditee. Both will be working at their respective organisations. The audit of documents conveys whether a quality system has been developed. The audit of documents verifies whether a quality system has been developed and is as per the standards, as per the auditor's requirement, or not. The auditee is informed of the shortcomings through a preliminary report. Documentation may be modified by taking necessary corrective action, or a new one can be developed. Once the auditor accepts the documentation, an on-site visit may be scheduled to examine the implementation.

7.6 AUDIT CLASSIFICATIONS

Audits can be both internal and external. First-party audit, also known as internal audit, is the assessment of the effectiveness of the quality system within the organisation by the members of the organisation. The external audit may be a second-party audit or a third-party audit. The second-party audits are audits by customers on their suppliers or suppliers on their subcontractors. A certifying body or statutory authority, usually unrelated to the supply chain or the project, conducts the third-party audit.

7.6.1 First-party Audit

An internal audit is performed by an organisation on its own, which helps it to assure compliance with the established company policy. It also allows them to follow appropriate procedures to safeguard the company's assets. Auditing is done by an internal staff or by a public accountant. It serves as a management control mechanism and facilitates the implementation of corrective measures for non-conformities. This offers the following advantages:

(i) The expense to the company would be mitigated.

(ii) The internal auditor is aware of the procedures, culture, and operations within the company.

(iii) The auditors may have a personal rapport with the members of the departments being audited that can help in obtaining information and identifying the major issues.

7.6.2 Second-party Audit

A company with a contract to purchase goods or services performs this audit on the supplier organisation or the service provider. This gives the purchasing organisation confidence in the supplier's ability to deliver goods or services that meet quality standards. This helps suppliers better understand customer requirements and improve quality systems. Additionally, it highlights the parts of the supplier's system that need improvement so that the client can implement better supervision. An organisation that purchases materials or an agent acting on its behalf conducts second-party audits. It is not a comprehensive audit as the audit focuses only on those business activities that directly affect the quality of supplied goods or services. This offers the following advantages:

(i) The audit is focused on the product.

(ii) The audit seeks to ensure compliance, thereby helping both the supplier and the customer.

(iii) The agenda is driven by the specifications, codes, and quality requirements alone, rather than process or organisational structure, though these can be secondary to the primary aim.

7.6.3 Third-party Audit

Third-party audits are performed for the purpose of certification. It is done by recognised certification agencies that do not directly control the organisation. It does not belong to its organisational structure nor has any interest in the audit's outcome. Auditing for ISO certification is an example of third-party audit. Certification provides assurance to the customers regarding the quality of products or services and confidence to the organisation about its performance concerning the successful implementation of the quality system standards. Statutory authorities also conduct an audit of the provider to determine whether all legal requirements are being met. This offers the following advantages:

(i) The audit is unbiased and professional.

(ii) Established auditing rules are followed.

(iii) There is credibility in the outcome report.

7.7 PERSONNEL CONDUCTING SYSTEM AUDITS – INTERNAL OR EXTERNAL

Systems audits may be assigned to the following types of personnel:

- **Production Management:** The audit of the production process in comparison to the quality plan is carried out by the middle or top operations managers. Skilled people can learn a lot from observations because most manufacturing operations are visible. Operations managers typically have these abilities and place high importance on direct observation.
- **Inspectors:** Certain inspections are carried out to monitor the process rather than to measure the product. These observations serve as an examination of how well the plan is being executed. It is possible to extend these patrol inspections to look at other execution details.
- **Independent auditors:** The auditing of critical work shall ideally be performed by individuals who are not members of the department being inspected. These auditors typically examine both production employees' and inspectors' methods of operation.

A combination of the above personnel is also possible, depending on the quality problems at hand.

7.8 ELEMENTS OF AUDITING

The different elements of auditing are explained in Sections 7.8.1. to 7.8.10.

7.8.1 Audit Scope

Auditors need to know what has to be examined. For this, they need to define the scope carefully, where the boundaries and extent of an audit are covered by the audit scope, which ought to be in line with the auditing programmes and goals. The scope outlines the physical and virtual locations, roles, tasks, procedures, and the duration of the assessment. The scope is further determined by the auditor in consultation with the auditee. Then, the lead auditor decides the number of members to be included in the audit team and the time required for the audit, for which the resources required are planned and procured before the audit. The audit framework is created by taking into account all aspects of an organisation's operations, including its administrative structure, operational processes, documentation, and level of quality performance. It is necessary to mention the limitations in the audit scope when an audit is limited only to a few functions of the organisation.

7.8.2 Audit Criteria

The set of requirements known as audit criteria is the benchmark for evaluating objective evidence. The information for developing the benchmark includes the following:

(i) Organisational policies.

(ii) Standard procedures.

(iii) Processes involved.

(iv) Work methods and instructions.
(v) Legal obligations.
(vi) Contractual requirements.
(vii) Performance criteria including objectives.
(viii) Management system requirements.
(ix) Information related to the risks and opportunities.
(x) Codes of conduct.
(xi) Criticality of the deliverables.
(xii) Other related matters.

The terms 'compliance' or 'non-compliance' are used in the audit results when the audit criteria are related to statutory, legal, regulatory, or contract obligations.

7.8.3 Audit Plan

It is impossible to investigate and inspect every activity in an organisation during an audit. The auditors must use their discretion in selecting the activities to be examined during the limited time available in the auditee's location. But, despite that, an audit reveals vital information. The description of the procedures and activities for an audit is contained in the audit plan. The extent and complexity of the audit determine how specific the quality plan needs to be, while audit planning aids in the scheduling and coordination of audit operations.

The first planning task is to define what constitutes the individual audit forms and decide what to look upon during each audit, to ensure that the whole system is covered. After deciding the frequency of audits, the schedule can be prepared. Then, the audit team is selected based on expertise required, experience, and availability. Proper coordination is required between the auditors and the auditee to avoid obstacles in the smooth conduct of the audit plan.

7.8.4 Depth and Duration

The depth and duration of a quality audit depends on audit objectives, scope, and criteria. It varies with the size of the organisational unit to be audited and its complexity, the audit scope and criteria, availability of human resources, finance involved, the time required, the expertise of auditors, and the criticality of the system or process or product being audited. Various factors to be considered to determine the duration of the audit are the following:

- Type and number of activities within an organisation.
- The location and layout of the organisation.
- Types of operation and their sophistication.
- Process complexity.
- Applicable regulatory and legislative controls.
- The extent of automation.
- Availability of auditors and auditee.
- Products or services offered.
- Types of projects executed.

- Task forces involved.
- Expertise and experience of the auditors.
- Location of off-site operations.
- Risks involved in auditing the items.
- Significance of the activities or projects undertaken by the organisation.

7.8.5 Frequency of Audit

Quality audits are conducted periodically to evaluate the effectiveness of the quality management system, to determine how efficiently the quality issues are being resolved and also to identify the possibilities for improvement. The frequency of audits is determined by considering the following factors:

- Functional areas representing high-risk involvement.
- Activities that are crucial to the success of the business.
- History of non-conformances.
- Corrective actions requiring frequent monitoring.
- Change in the system or organisation which impacts the effectiveness of the system.
- A new and unknown factor is introduced.
- Availability of resources for the audit.
- Organisational structure.
- Number, kind, and nature of the departments and sites involved.
- Time required by auditee for taking corrective actions between audits.
- The scope of the audit is large, and when the sample in an audit examines only a small proportion of the work.

The potential impact of activities is to be analysed to prioritise and design the audit to ensure that high-risk areas are audited more frequently.

7.8.6 Working Documents

The working documents required in an audit include the following:

- Contract documents, drawings (structural, architectural, and MEP drawing), and specifications
- Organisational chart including the roles and responsibilities of personnel.
- Project quality plan.
- Method statement.
- Quality assurance plan.
- Testing facilities.
- Test reports.
- Site documents.
- Checklists and test proformas.
- Housekeeping record.

- Health and safety records.
- Non-conformity reports of the previous audit.
- Action taken report.
- Records of revision.
- Complaint and feedback records.
- Training records.
- Store manual and related documents.
- Accidents report.
- Minutes of meeting.
- Evaluation of subcontractors and inspection of subcontracted work.
- Invoices.

The need for all the above documents also means that the company must have good record-keeping under the charge of responsible managers.

7.8.7 Work Instructions

Work instructions specify quantitative or qualitative ways to assess whether each operation has been completed successfully. The fact that work instructions are used by operational staff, supervisors, inspectors, managers, and even customers means these criteria must also be appropriate for use with associated inspections or tests. Work instructions should be concise and straightforward and written in language that is easy for the individual performing the work to understand. Note that instructional compliance is subject to assessment and audit. The following topics are covered in the work instructions to ensure that the work is executed successfully:

- The methods that specify how production, installation, or servicing will be done (prefabricated construction).
- The process by which the work will be completed.
- The tools needed to complete the task.
- The environment at work.
- Adherence to additional guidelines and documents.
- Process parameters that will be assessed and how they will be assessed.
- Product attributes to be tracked and the methodology for tracking them.
- Workmanship standards.
- Processes for maintenance.
- Verification procedures.
- Safety instructions to be followed.

7.8.8 Audit Team Assignments

The audit team consists of one or more persons who conduct the audit. One auditor will be selected as the audit team leader. If needed, they will be supported by technical experts who have expertise in the discipline to be audited. They will be provided with experts to deal with language or culture barriers. Each member of the audit team will be assigned specific tasks for examination based on their expertise. When choosing the audit team's size and composition, the following criteria are taken into account:

- The overall competence of the audit team, based on their qualification, skill, training, and experience is required to meet audit objectives, considering audit scope and criteria.
- Audit complexity level and processes that will be audited.
- The method chosen for the audit.
- Attributes like objectivity, confidentiality and impartiality of the auditors to avoid any clashes in the audit.
- The interaction of auditors with the relevant interested parties and representatives of the auditee to work effectively.
- Other major issues are the language barrier and the diversity in social and cultural characteristics. Auditors may handle these problems on their own or with the help of translators and a technical specialist.

The team is formed in consultation with the team leader. Sometimes, changes in the constitution of the audit team will be necessary in case of clashes or differences in opinion or competence issues. Appropriate resolution strategies must then be implemented to go beyond the conflicts.

7.8.9 Audit Method

There are several methods by which an audit can be conducted. The selection of the audit method depends on the audit objectives, scope and criteria, location of audit, and duration. The availability of a competent auditor and any other uncertainties associated with the audit method shall also be considered before choosing the audit method. To optimise the efficiency, different combinations of audit methods can be considered. Audits can be organised with or without human interaction both on-site and from remote locations. It is the audit team leader's responsibility to select the right audit method.

An interactive audit involves interaction between individuals from the organisation being audited and the auditor during the audit. The non-interactive audit is performed to examine equipment, facilities, and documentation where human interaction is not required. A summary of interactive and non-interactive audits is given in Table 7.2. If there are multiple participants, both on-site and remote approaches may be used at the same time. The audit performed at the location of the auditee is called an on-site audit, and at any location other than the auditee's location is the remote audit.

7.8.10 Audit Sampling

Quality auditing is a sampling exercise, and it is never a 100 per cent verification, as it may not be possible for the audit team to examine the information, records, and activities entirely during an audit. The auditor creates a sampling strategy to choose a sample that will accurately represent the auditing population. This will give confidence that the goals will be met through an audit. Sampling runs the risk of not adequately representing the population, which could result in biased audit findings. The following steps are involved in audit sampling:

TABLE 7.2 Audit methods (ISO, 2018)

Auditor and the auditee involvement level	Location of the auditor	
	On-site	**Remote**
Interactive audit	• Sampling. • Conduct interviews. • Complete checklists and questionnaires with auditee participation. • Conduct a review of the document.	• Conduct interviews by interactive communication remotely. • Observe work performance with the aid of a remote guide. • Complete checklists and questionnaires. • Conduct document review with auditee participation.
Non-interactive audit	• Conduct document review. • Observe work performed. • Conduct site visit. • Complete checklist. • Sampling.	• Conduct document review. Observe work being done through surveillance while taking into account social, legal, and regulatory considerations. • Analysis of data.

- defining the sampling objectives;
- determining the nature of the population from which sampling will be done;
- choosing a technique for sampling;
- figuring out the right sample size;
- executing the sampling procedure; and
- results gathering, assessment, reporting and documentation.

Auditing a false sample will not yield sufficient and accurate data and, hence, does not produce a beneficial outcome. Therefore, the quality of the data chosen must be considered. The selection of the sample may be using a statistical method or a judgment-based method.

7.9 ROLES OF AUDITORS AND AUDITEE

7.9.1 Role of Auditor

Audits are conducted by a single auditor or a team of auditors. Lead auditors lead the audit teams. They are bound to manage and control the audit process. The responsibilities of the lead auditors are as follows:

- Outline the scope of the audit in consultation with the client and review any known constraints.
- Review the audit criteria and audit objectives.
- Select the audit team based on their competence.
- Organise the audit activities.

- Coordinate and schedule the audit programme.
- Plan the audit and ensure the provision of all necessary resources.
- Delegate tasks to team members.
- Inform the audit requirements of the team members.
- Prepare and provide the checklists and forms required.
- Establish a communication system between auditors and auditee.
- Organise opening and closing meetings.
- Observe uniformity in the performance of all auditors.
- Motivate the team to accomplish the task.
- Manage disputes and handle complaints during the audit.
- Identify hurdles encountered and report it.
- Observe, evaluate, and enhance the auditing programme.
- Note and report all non-conformity.
- Support and guide members in report preparation.
- Present the report.

7.9.2 Role of Auditee

Auditee is the organisation, as a part or the whole, being audited. An organisation will be audited as a whole in some cases, such as ISO certification audits, whereas in other cases, only certain departments, projects, or offices at certain locations will be audited. Whatever be the type of audit, the auditee has the following responsibilities as follows:

- Appoint senior and competent personnel as a guide to accompany the audit team.
- Have a formal arrangement for communication with the audit team.
- Discuss the audit scope and objectives.
- Provide all necessary resources and documents needed for auditing.
- Cooperate and coordinate with auditors and ensure that they get support from the concerned department.
- Allow the auditors to access and review all required information, documents, and records.
- Attend and participate in opening and closing meetings.
- Assist the auditor in identifying participants to attend the interviews and confirm the timing and location.
- Arrange access to various locations of the organisation to be audited.
- Provide clarification and assistance in collecting information.
- Resolve conflicts between auditors and employees.
- Attend to the critical non-conformities immediately.
- Obtain and file the audit report and its conclusions.
- Perform an analysis of the problem and report the action taken to address the issue.

7.9.3 Competence and Evaluation of Auditors

Audits are performed in organisations to support management to improve its systems and processes. Audits help the management find the deviations in their functioning. During the audit, an auditor has a great role to play. It is the auditor who is responsible for pointing out the non-conformities and deviations from the standards. Hence, an auditor is required to have certain qualities as follows:

- Exhibit attributes like integrity, ethics, open-mindedness, diplomacy, observation, perceptiveness, adaptability, focus, rationalism, boldness, decisiveness, self-reliance, willingness to learn, sensitivity, tactfulness and collaboration, which are required in accordance with the principles of auditing.
- Possess knowledge and skills that are specific to the sector.
- Possess the expertise and abilities needed to ensure that the audits produce the intended results.
- Acknowledge the various opportunities and risks related to auditing.
- Effective planning and organisation of audit and its completion within the agreed schedule.
- Prioritise and concentrate on important issues.
- Effective verbal and written communication.
- Collect information effectively through interviews, observation, listening and document review, including records and data.
- Wisely use appropriate sampling techniques for auditing.
- Understand technical experts' opinions and give them due consideration.
- Audit a process thoroughly, taking into account the interrelationship between various processes and functions.
- Check the significance and correctness of the data gathered.
- Understand the importance of management system standards and other references.
- Understanding of business principles, management, procedures, and terminology, including planning, budgeting, and personnel management.
- Have a thorough understanding of all applicable laws, regulations and other audit-related information.

The auditors are to be evaluated qualitatively and quantitatively to assess their competence. The qualitative aspects include expected behaviour and skills, whereas quantitative aspects consist of qualification, experience, number of audits conducted, and training attended. Trainings are provided to auditors when certain criteria are not fulfilled and they are subsequently evaluated.

7.10 CONDUCTING AN AUDIT

The audits are conducted in a sequence of steps that suits the method chosen for the audit. Figure 7.1 depicts the steps in auditing that are followed, in general ((ISO, 2018). The audit steps may vary as per the changing situations.

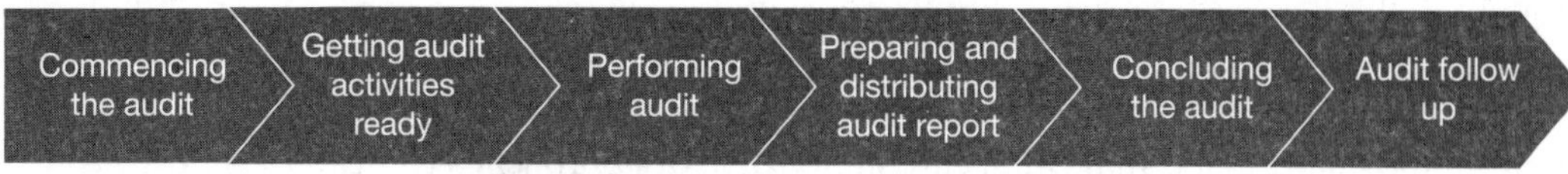

FIGURE 7.1 Sequence of audit activities

7.10.1 Commencing the Audit

Conducting the audit is the team leader's responsibility. The team leader contacts the auditee and conveys details about the audit's scope, objective, standards, procedures, and team makeup. Audits can be successfully completed when all audit objectives are satisfied with the help of auditee's cooperation and the availability of relevant information. If the audit cannot be completed, the auditee and the auditor have to agree on an alternative strategy.

7.10.2 Getting Audit Activities Ready

To comprehend the operations of the auditee and find the potential problems, it is necessary for an auditor to analyse the documentation of the QMS of the auditee. It enables the auditor to prepare for the audit's activities. The audit team leader uses a risk-based planning approach based on verified facts. Planning makes it possible to schedule and coordinate audit actions to effectively fulfil audit goals. The auditor chooses the appropriate sampling strategy and selects team members based on the competency needed during preparation. The team members are given roles and duties for the entire procedure. To create a checklist to assist auditing, details of the audit sample, and the information relevant to the audit assignments are gathered and examined.

7.10.3 Performing Audit Activities

An audit opening meeting is held to make sure everyone is on board with the audit plan and to make sure all scheduled tasks can be completed. The team leader introduces his team and their roles during the opening meeting. The method of audit varies with factors such as objective of audit, its scope, the criteria, location, and duration of audit. The location of the audit may be physical or virtual and it depends on where and how the information will be available to the audit team for auditing. Data related to the audit's criteria, scope, and objective involving relevant processes, activities, functions, and interfaces is one of the many types of information that are collected using appropriate sampling procedures and verified. Information may be collected by various means, like review of documents, interviews and observations made from the auditee's location. The audit team leader communicates the progress and significant findings to the auditee during the audit. The assessment of audit evidence against audit criteria yields the audit results. Audit results may show compliance or non-compliance with the audit criteria. The auditor gives recommendations for improvement and suggests good practices to the auditee based on the findings. Non-conformity based on supporting evidence can be graded quantitatively or qualitatively. Non-conformities are to be adequately reviewed with the auditee, and acknowledgements must be obtained from the auditee regarding its accuracy. The audit conclusion must address the degree of compliance with the audit criteria, the strength of the QMS, the efficacy of steps taken by the auditee to mitigate risks, and effectiveness of the application of the quality management system. Finally, it is recommended to hold a closing meeting to discuss the audit's findings and recommendations. Any disagreement between the auditee's and the audit team's perspectives ought to be addressed and resolved. The audit must follow established methods of fact-finding and questioning to the heart of the matter. (See Jha, Patel, and Singh 2022 for approaches to a safety audit).

7.10.4 Preparing and Distributing the Audit Report

The audit report is a thorough and accurate account of the audit, containing all relevant information, the audit's findings and conclusions, and the degree of compliance with the audit criteria. Within the stated time frame, the audit report shall be provided to the auditee and any interested parties. Ensure the confidentiality of the report by taking appropriate measures.

7.10.5 Concluding the Audit

When all the planned audit activities have been completed, the audit is deemed to be finished. The audit team is not supposed to disclose any information obtained during the audit to others unless required by law. Disclosing of information shall not be done without the consent of the auditee.

7.10.6 Audit Follow Up

In the case of audit findings of non-conformity, corrective actions are to be taken within the agreed time frame. Communicate the status of these actions to the audit team. Verification of corrective actions may be done in subsequent audits. The audit findings thus help to improve the performance of the organisation.

7.11 TECHNIQUES

In every job, we need to know the basic tools of the trade and the techniques to make it successful. Auditing is a complex skill that follows a set of rules, and the processes can be fitted into a standard audit framework. Time management is an important aspect of auditing. The proposed scope needs to be covered in the given time, and a report on what has been covered during an audit has to be provided to the auditee. The most powerful tool of an auditor that is easy to understand consists of open-ended questions. Interview candidates are chosen based on their managerial levels and tasks that fall under the audit's purview. By employing active listening techniques listen to the answers given by the auditee to the questions. Information can be gathered by observation as well as non-verbal communication. In the construction industry, audits are done mainly by examining the documents, conducting site inspections by experts, and reviewing customer complaints.

7.12 CONFORMITY AND NONCONFORMITY

The main objective of the audit is to find out the conforming and non-conforming products or processes, as the case may be. The benchmark against which conformance is assessed is the audit criteria. The audit criteria, audit evidence, declaration of non-conformity, and associated audit findings have to be taken into consideration when recording non-conformity. For best adoption, non-compliance statements need to be objective, unbiased, non-prescriptive, factual, complete, self-explanatory, traceable, verifiable, and without criticism.

Non-conformity may be graded qualitatively or quantitatively based on the risks involved, the procedure involved in their rectification, the cost incurred for rectification, additional expenses required for training, and other factors. In quantitative grading, the level of non-conformance may be ranked by category from 1 to 6, or qualitatively, it can be marked as minor, significant, or major. The non-conformity may be categorised as shown in Table 7.3 for six categories.

TABLE 7.3 Categories of non-conformity

Category	Non-Conformity
1	A non-conformance situation that: • can be readily fixed by the auditee, such as repeatedly failing to pay attention to detail or filling out forms incorrectly. • does not call for staff training. • can be easily fixed without putting the company at financial risk.
2	A non–conformance situation that: • is solvable by the auditee but might need manager approval. • might require staff training. • can be easily fixed without putting the business at financial risk.
3	A non-conformance situation that: • can be fixed only by publishing updated procedure text or content along with related documents. • might require staff training. • can be resolved at little or no expense to the organisation.
4	A non-conformance situation that: • can be fixed only by publishing updated procedure text or content along with related documents. • can be resolved by Site Manager, however doing so can have broader business effects. • require staff training. • the company must pay for corrective action.
5	A non-conformance situation that: • can only be resolved by developing the relevant procedure(s) and/or documentation. • can be resolved by the Site Manager, however doing so can have broader business effects. • needs to be resolved by purchasing more materials or resources. • requires staff training. • may incur large costs for remedial measures.
6	A very serious non-conformance situation that: • calls for rejection. • can have an impact on system integrity or business. • needs to be forwarded for further action to higher management.

The audit results are brought to the notice of higher management for taking necessary corrective actions. They are discussed in meetings for review and direction. Follow-up audits are conducted, as necessary, to verify the implementation of corrective actions. The audit findings of the follow-up audits are to be documented for quality improvement purposes.

7.13 PROCESSES INVOLVED IN CORRECTIVE ACTIONS

The processes involved in taking corrective actions are illustrated in Figure 7.2.

7.14 RISKS IN AUDITING

As much as there are benefits in quality auditing, the following risks must also be noted:

- **(i)** Lack of clarity in the scope and objective of audits.
- **(ii)** Lack of competency of auditors.
- **(iii)** Inability to check all the transactions that need to be audited and problems associated with sampling.
- **(iv)** The auditor fails to identify and assess the risk in the audited item.
- **(v)** The auditing procedure is insufficient in the extent of coverage of areas.
- **(vi)** Limitations in auditor's understanding of the organisation and the environment, including internal control systems in which it operates.
- **(vii)** Lacking the essential qualities required for an auditor.

To avoid the risks, it is usually suggested to go with external companies that have a track record of quality audits, or else create an internal quality audit department that understands the policies and procedures of the company.

SUMMARY

An audit is a comparison of the actual performance of activities, processes, or deliverables with the standards and the requirements that have been documented. The audit findings form the basis for improvement that is necessary to fulfil obligations. An effective quality audit helps prevent problems through timely corrections while they are still acceptable but might be tending toward an eventual crisis. Thus, the attention of management in making necessary corrections based on an audit report can often prevent future problems. To conclude, we can say that an audit allows a critical review of current practice and focuses on how performance can be improved. Quality audits are thus a quality assurance method and a quality improvement procedure that help in reducing the cost of quality.

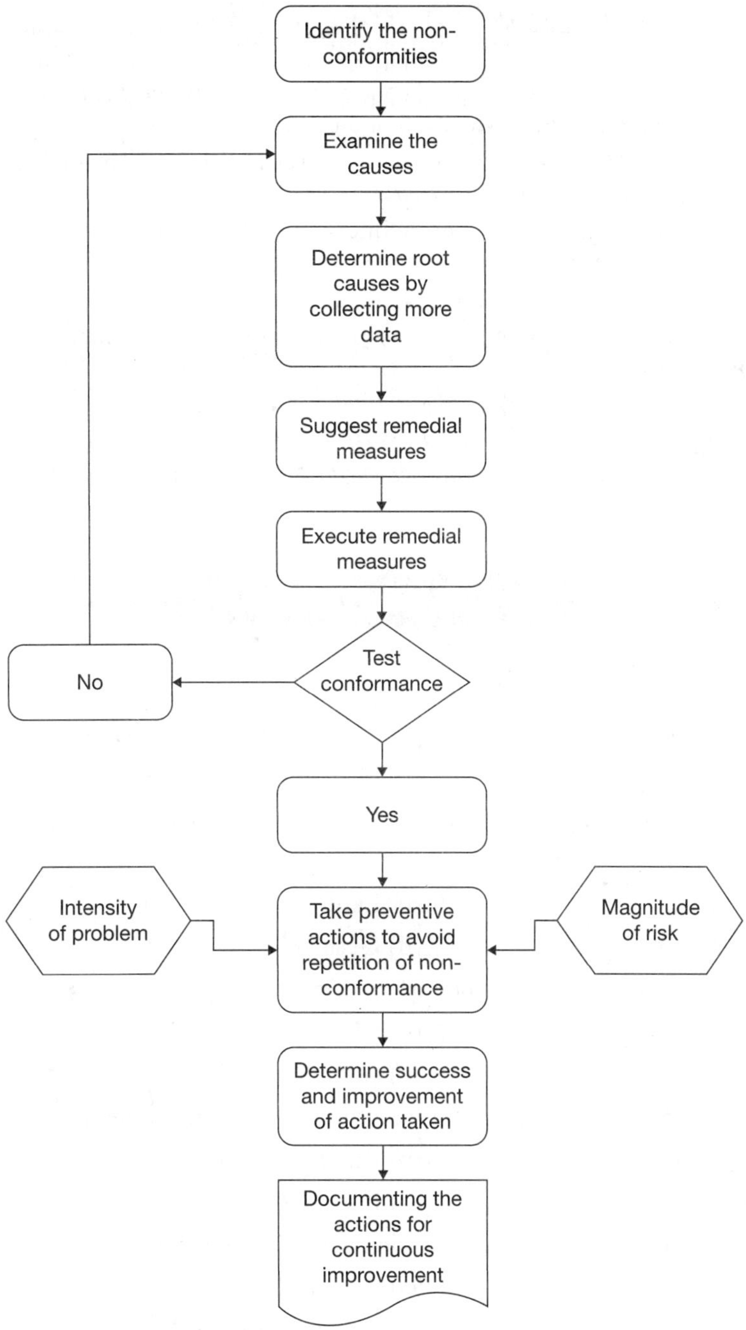

FIGURE 7.2 Corrective action process

WORKS CITED

BSI. (1990), *BS 6143-2:1990 Guide to the Economics of Quality- Part 2: Prevention, Appraisal and Failure Model* (London: British Standards Institution).

Dictionary, M. W. (2023). *'Definition of Audit'*, Retrieved 2024, from Merriam-Webster Dictionary: https://www.merriam-webster.com/dictionary/audit

ISO. (2017), *ISO and Construction* (Geneva: International Organization for Standardization).

ISO. (2018), *ISO 19011:2018 (E) Guidelines for Auditing Management Systems* (Geneva: International Organization for Standardization).

Juran, J. M., and Godfrey, A. B. (1999), *Juran's Quality Handbook* (United States of America: McGraw Hill).

Samuels, A. F. (1994), 'Construction facilities audit: Quality system performance control', *Journal of Management in Engineering, 10*(4), 60–65.

Wealleans, D. (2000), *The Quality Audit for ISO 9001:2000* (England: Gower Publishing Limited).

REVIEW QUESTIONS

Multiple Choice Questions

1. What is the primary objective of a quality audit in the construction industry?
   (a) Reduce costs (b) Meet contractual obligations
   (c) Improve marketing strategies (d) Increase workforce size
2. The term 'audit' originates from which language?
   (a) Greek (b) Latin
   (c) French (d) German
3. Which organisation has developed over 1,100 standards for the construction industry?
   (a) ANSI (b) BIS
   (c) ISO (d) ASQ
4. Which principle of auditing ensures auditors report findings clearly and honestly?
   (a) Integrity (b) Fair presentation
   (c) Confidentiality (d) Independence
5. What does the PDCA cycle stand for in quality management?
   (a) Plan-Do-Check-Act (b) Prepare-Design-Create-Analyse
   (c) Plan-Direct-Control-Audit (d) Prepare-Develop-Control-Act
6. What is the purpose of ISO 9001 certification?
   (a) Ensure profitability
   (b) Guarantee product innovation

(c) Develop a quality management system
(d) Increase market share

7. Which of the following is NOT one of the seven principles of auditing?
(a) Integrity (b) Risk-based approach
(c) Marketing strategy (d) Due professional care

8. Which organisation was founded in 1946 and includes audits as part of its quality philosophy?
(a) ISI (b) ASQ
(c) BSI (d) BIS

9. According to the text, what should audit results be used for?
(a) Marketing purposes (b) Feedback
(c) Financial audits (d) Quality improvement

10. What is the definition of a quality audit according to ISO (2018)?
(a) A random inspection process
(b) A systematic, independent, and documented process
(c) An informal review process
(d) A financial assessment method

11. What is the primary goal of a construction quality audit?
(a) To assess financial performance
(b) To verify the conformance of the quality of components and structures
(c) To improve marketing strategies
(d) To increase employee productivity

12. Which principle involves collecting information from random samples for auditing?
(a) Evidence-based approach (b) Risk-based approach
(c) Integrity (d) Confidentiality

13. Who is responsible for protecting the confidentiality of information during an audit?
(a) The client (b) The auditor
(c) The contractor (d) The regulatory body

14. Which principles require auditors to avoid being influenced by conflicting interests?
(a) Integrity (b) Fair presentation
(c) Due professional care (d) Independence

15. Under which quality cost can quality auditing be considered?
(a) Preventive cost (b) Appraisal cost
(c) None of these (d) Both (a) and (b)

16. What is the primary purpose of a systems audit?

(a) Verify financial records

(b) Verify an organisation's quality system

(c) Verify marketing strategies

(d) Verify employee satisfaction

17. What does a process audit mainly focus on?

(a) Financial transactions

(b) Employee satisfaction

(c) Compliance of processes to standards

(d) Customer feedback

18. Which audit checks the adequacy of criteria in quality manuals and quality plans?

(a) Systems audit (b) Process audit

(c) Product audit (d) Adequacy audit

19. What is the main focus of a compliance audit?

(a) Quality of products

(b) Financial performance

(c) Conformance of implementation with the documented system

(d) Employee performance

20. Which audit involves no physical meetings between the auditor and the auditee?

(a) Systems audit (b) Process audit

(c) Desk audit (d) Product audit

21. What type of audit is performed by an organisation on its own?

(a) First-party audit (b) Second-party audit

(c) Third-party audit (d) Desk audit

22. Who usually conducts third-party audits?

(a) Internal staff

(b) Suppliers

(c) Certifying bodies or statutory authorities

(d) Customers

23. Which personnel are involved in systems audits for the production process?

(a) Inspectors

(b) Independent auditors

(c) Production Management

(d) All of the above

24. What is defined by the audit scope?
    (a) Audit budget
    (b) Boundaries and extent of an audit
    (c) Auditor's salary
    (d) Audit frequency
25. Which of the following is not typically part of the audit criteria?
    (a) Organisational policies (b) Standard procedures
    (c) Marketing strategies (d) Legal obligations
26. What document outlines the procedures and activities for an audit?
    (a) Audit scope (b) Audit criteria
    (c) Audit plan (d) Audit frequency
27. What affects the depth and duration of a quality audit?
    (a) Audit objectives (b) Organisational size
    (c) Complexity of the audit (d) All of the above
28. How should work instructions be?
    (a) Complicated and lengthy (b) Concise and straightforward
    (c) Vague and brief (d) Only verbal
29. What does the audit team leader do?
    (a) Performs all the audit tasks alone
    (b) Selects the audit method
    (c) Approves financial transactions
    (d) Manages marketing campaigns
30. What is a remote audit?
    (a) Conducted without any tools
    (b) Conducted at the auditee's location
    (c) Conducted at a location other than the auditee's location
    (d) Conducted in the auditor's office
31. What is the risk of audit sampling?
    (a) High cost
    (b) Inadequately representing the population
    (c) Lengthy duration
    (d) Increased workload
32. Who is responsible for leading the audit team?
    (a) Client (b) Auditee
    (c) Lead Auditor (c) Quality Manager

33. Which of the following is not a responsibility of the lead auditor?
(a) Outline the scope of the audit
(b) Delegate tasks to team members
(c) Provide clarification and assistance in collecting information
(d) Present the audit report

34. What is the primary role of the auditee?
(a) Conduct the audit
(b) Assist in identifying non-conformities
(c) Provide resources and documents needed for auditing
(d) Evaluate the audit team

35. Which attribute is not required in accordance with the principles of auditing?
(a) Integrity (b) Confidentiality
(c) Creativity (d) Independence

36. What should the audit report not include?
(a) Audit findings and conclusions
(b) Degree of compliance with audit criteria
(c) Confidential matters
(b) Recommendations for improvement

37. What is the first step in conducting an audit?
(a) Getting audit activities ready
(b) Preparing and distributing the audit report
(c) Initiating audit
(d) Conducting audit follow up

38. Which of the following is an essential requirement in auditing?
(a) Time management (b) Risk management
(c) Conflict resolution (d) Project management

39. Non-conformity statements should be all except:
(a) Objective (b) Biased
(c) Factual (d) Self-explanatory

40. What is the main objective of the audit?
(a) To train employees
(b) To find non-conforming products or processes
(c) To develop new business strategies
(d) To manage resources efficiently

Short Answer Type Questions

1. What does ISO 9001 certification assure users regarding an organisation?
2. What are the main goals of a quality audit in the construction industry?
3. What does the term "audit" mean in Latin?
4. How does ISO 9001 help organisations?
5. What are the seven principles of auditing mentioned in the text?
6. What role do quality audits play in the PDCA cycle?
7. What is the main focus of a product audit?
8. How are internal audits different from external audits?
9. What is the importance of confidentiality in auditing?
10. What is the significance of the audit results?
11. Why is it essential for auditors to be independent?
12. What does the principle of 'Due professional care' entail for auditors?
13. What is the scope of a quality audit in the construction industry?
14. What is meant by a 'Risk-based approach' in auditing?
15. How can audit findings lead to system improvement?
16. What does a systems audit verify?
17. What is the focus of a process audit?
18. What aspects does a product audit determine?
19. What does an adequacy audit examine?
20. What is the purpose of a compliance audit?
21. What is unique about a desk audit?
22. What is a first-party audit?
23. Who conducts second-party audits?
24. What is the role of third-party audits?
25. What should auditors define in the audit scope?
26. What constitutes audit criteria?
27. What is included in the audit plan?
28. What factors influence the depth and duration of an audit?
29. Why are quality audits conducted periodically?
30. What types of documents are required in an audit?
31. What should work instructions specify?
32. Who can be included in an audit team?

33. What is the audit method?
34. What is audit sampling?
35. What is the final step in audit sampling?
36. What are the main responsibilities of a lead auditor in an audit process?
37. Describe the role of the auditee during an audit.
38. List three qualities an auditor must exhibit according to the principles of auditing.
39. What is the significance of the opening meeting in an audit process?
40. Why is time management important in auditing?
41. How should non-conformity statements be recorded?
42. What are the key steps involved in conducting an audit?
43. Mention two risks associated with auditing.
44. What should be included in an audit report?
45. How can an organisation ensure the competence of its auditors?

Long Answer Type Questions

1. Describe the historical development of quality audits and their significance in modern industries.
2. Explain the principles of auditing and their importance in ensuring effective audits.
3. Analyse the role of quality audits in the construction industry and how they contribute to project success.
4. Describe the process of conducting a quality audit in the construction industry, from planning to reporting.
5. Discuss the impact of quality audits on customer satisfaction in the construction industry.
6. Explain the significance of the 'Evidence-based approach' principle in the auditing process.
7. How can quality audits lead to cost savings in the construction industry?
8. Describe the relationship between quality audits and continuous improvement in an organisation.
9. What challenges might auditors face when conducting quality audits in the construction industry, and how can they overcome them?
10. Explain the role of regulatory bodies in the quality auditing process in the construction industry.
11. How do quality audits contribute to achieving long-term organisational goals in the construction industry?
12. Discuss the differences between a product audit and a process audit.

13. What are the key elements of an audit plan, and why are they important?
14. Describe the roles and responsibilities of the audit team leader.
15. How does an adequacy audit differ from a compliance audit?
16. Explain the significance of audit scope and how it is defined.
17. What factors should be considered when selecting an audit method?
18. Discuss the process and importance of audit sampling.
19. Explain the role of audit frequency in maintaining quality standards.
20. How does audit documentation support the audit process?
21. What are the potential risks associated with audit sampling, and how can they be mitigated?
22. Explain the comprehensive role of a lead auditor in managing an audit process from start to finish.
23. Discuss the responsibilities of an auditee in ensuring a smooth and effective audit process.
24. Describe the attributes and skills required for an auditor to be considered competent.
25. How should an audit team prepare for and execute an audit, considering both physical and virtual environments?
26. Explain the process of identifying, recording, and addressing non-conformities during an audit.
27. Discuss the importance of audit follow-up and the steps involved in this process.
28. What are the risks associated with auditing, and how can they be mitigated?
29. In what ways can an audit contribute to the overall improvement of an organisation's quality management system?
30. Evaluate the role of effective communication in the auditing process and its impact on audit outcomes.

ANSWER KEYS

Multiple Choice Questions

1. (b)	**2.** (b)	**3.** (c)	**4.** (b)	**5.** (a)	**6.** (c)	**7.** (c)	**8.** (b)
9. (d)	**10.** (b)	**11.** (b)	**12.** (a)	**13.** (b)	**14.** (a)	**15.** (b)	**16.** (b)
17. (c)	**18.** (d)	**19.** (c)	**20.** (c)	**21.** (a)	**22.** (c)	**23.** (d)	**24.** (b)
25. (c)	**26.** (c)	**27.** (d)	**28.** (b)	**29.** (b)	**30.** (c)	**31.** (b)	**32.** (c)
33. (c)	**34.** (c)	**35.** (c)	**36.** (c)	**37.** (c)	**38.** (a)	**39.** (b)	**40.** (b)

CHAPTER 8

Inspection and Quality Control

8.1 INTRODUCTION

The concept of quality checking through inspection has been with humankind since time immemorial. In construction, various measuring instruments such as the plumb bob, levels and Mason's square, have been in use since the dawn of civilisation. These were not just measuring tools but also tools used for quality inspection at different stages of construction. We can see many of the ancient structures, or at least their remains, mainly because of the good standards and quality of those constructions.

8.2 INSPECTION, QUALITY CONTROL, AND QUALITY ASSURANCE IN CONSTRUCTION

Construction projects consist of several activities involving multi-stakeholders during various project stages. As a result, there is a potential for disagreement in quality control concerning who has to be given responsibility and power for quality assurance. Earlier, designers who were owner's agents used to be responsible for ensuring that works were done as per design specifications. The clerk of works, who worked in the field for the designer, kept an eye on the contractor's performance. Though they were given the responsibility of supervising the work performance, they were not given the authority to ensure compliance. A linear responsibility chart (LRC) was then suggested to solve the responsibility and authority problem in quality control (QC) (Parsons, 1972). It included information about the individuals involved with the QC programme, their roles, levels of responsibility, and connections to QC. The quality control matrix that describes the QC procedures and requirements facilitates LRC. The development of the QC programme was based on these two charts. Thus, every project benefits from a precisely defined quality control programme and an explicitly laid out organisational structure.

Since quality has different meanings to different stakeholders, cooperation must be developed among the participants to reduce the adversities in relationships. The owner, designer, and contractor have to work closely to meet the project goals and objectives. The entire project team will be in charge of ensuring quality control. And, inspections are to be conducted to encourage and ensure good workmanship. However, the inspections are not to be done merely to penalise the contractors. To be successful, the contractors must be able to fulfil the specifications, for which the specification writers (designers) have to ensure that the specifications are achievable and consider the variations in workmanship. Though various factors influence quality control in construction, it is achievable with proper teamwork and sound policies. Incentive policies may be adopted to improve workmanship. Certain organisations have made it mandatory to display the contractor's name after completion of work, and others even display the worker's name for specific activities during the construction stage. This creates a sense of accountability among the persons involved and helps to improve workmanship and quality. Note that numerous standards, codes, and legislations have been developed to protect the public's health, safety, and welfare to guarantee higher quality in construction.

8.3 QUALITY ASSURANCE (QA)

Some sources define quality assurance as partly given in Table 8.1, being a sample representative of the other definitions out there:

TABLE 8.1 Definition of quality assurance

Definition	Source
'Planned and systematic actions established by the owner or its agent to establish a level of confidence that project design documents comply with applicable codes, standards, and criteria and that the resulting construction complies with the contract documents'.	The ASCE manual, Quality in the Constructed Project , (ASCE, 2012).
'Quality assurance is broadly the prevention of quality problems through planned and systematic activities (including documentation). These will include the establishment of a good quality management system, the assessment of its adequacy, the audit of the operation of the system, and the review of the system itself'.	Oakland (2003)
All those planned and systematic actions are necessary to provide adequate confidence that a product or service will satisfy the given requirements for quality.	British Standards 4778, (Ashford, 2003)
'Part of quality management focused on providing confidence that quality requirements will be fulfilled'.	ISO 9000–2015

Quality assurance is a preventive mechanism that helps to earn the confidence of managers and customers regarding the quality of the work. It has to be planned systematically before the start of a project. In a construction project, quality assurance consists of activities like planning for checks, monitoring, inspection, and control of processes. It merits notice that QA is a means to demonstrate quality requirements, which includes all administrative and surveillance functions proposed by the regulatory agencies and project client or owner to enforce and certify confidently the adherence to project quality requirements. This will ensure that the completed structure or any accomplished task will efficiently, effectively, and economically satisfy the desired outcomes. It gives an expectation of the level of quality to be achieved. The more complex the project, the more efficient the QA measures that are to be taken to ensure that they comply with the contract specifications.

The following steps are included in quality assurance programmes:

- Set up a procedure to define, develop, and establish quality standards for project design, construction, and operation. These quality standards will help check compliance and quality at various project stages.
- Set up a procedure to monitor, inspect, test, measure, and conduct a review of the activities to ensure compliance with established standards applicable to material, personnel, and processes.
- Define all the conditions, processes, roles, responsibilities, information flow patterns, and other management and administrative tasks necessary to carry out, record, and guarantee the achievement of quality standards. It will also include establishing the qualification requirements for various professionals like designers, architects, and engineers.

Already, these are tall orders, which makes quality management a dedicated task, ideally conducted by a whole department. Though QA and QC are two different functions, they are used interchangeably by engineers and contractors in the field. To be more precise, QA is the owner's responsibility and is a construction management process. The end users are the beneficiaries of quality assurance. By offering guidance to regulate variations from the standard, it focuses on preventing defects. Contrarily, quality control (QC) is a process focusing on defect detection while the construction is being undertaken. Error detection should not be done only after the product is produced, as that can be costly. Thus, error detection must be done alongside the construction or manufacturing process to catch errors at the source and nip them in the bud. This means that the costs incurred for quality assurance are to institute preventive measures that hopefully offset the costs of error. This is what brings about the adage that 'quality is free'.

8.4 QUALITY CONTROL (QC)

Quality Control consists of controlling and verifying materials, processes, or facility characteristics against the set standards. It includes observations, inspections, tests, calculations, and documentation to confirm the effectiveness of quality systems and processes in achieving quality. The definition of quality control given by various sources is given in Table 8.2.

The owner and the entire project team are responsible for quality control. Contractors, specialised consultants like consulting engineers, or testing laboratories perform quality control on the construction site. Inspection, testing, measuring, and recording are all part of quality control, which is used to improve the construction standard. It also includes techniques to be followed when there are deviations from the standard. Quality control helps create a secure, durable, and reliable construction that gives the owner the highest return on investment. However, the heterogeneity of construction works makes it difficult to apply a standard procedure to quality control in construction works.

Quality Control activities include the following:

- Checking the quality of materials and workmanship through various tests, observations, checks, computations, and documentation to verify the efficiency of quality systems and procedures in achieving quality.

TABLE 8.2 Definition of quality control

Definition	Source
'Plans, procedures, resources, and organisation performed by the design professional necessary to control the quality of the contract documents to ensure consistency with applicable codes, standards, and criteria, or by the construction professional necessary to control the quality of its construction to ensure compliance with the contract documents'.	The ASCE manual, Quality in the Constructed Project, (ASCE, 2012)
'"Quality control" is essentially the activities and techniques employed to achieve and maintain the quality of a product, process, or service. It involves monitoring activity, but also concerns finding and eliminating causes of quality problems so that the requirements of the customer are continuously met'.	Oakland (2003)
'The operational techniques and activities that are used to fulfil requirements for quality'.	British Standards 4778, (Ashford, 2003)
'Part of quality management focused on fulfilling quality requirements'.	ISO 9000–2015

- Execution of procedures to ascertain if the criteria have been met or not.
- Enforcing and maintaining the defined standards.

Correspondingly, the following quality control techniques are frequently used in construction projects to check on errors and conformance:

- Inspection
- Testing
- Sampling

The methods used for quality assessment vary with the products being produced. It may be a subjective evaluation or an objective assessment. The method depends on the construction work type, the systems being examined, and the level of assurance sought. But to avoid confusion, the contract terms might state the methodology to be used for each project, even if left to the contractor. In modern projects, the methods adopted are the privilege of the contractor. If the owner prescribes the methodology, the owner also takes responsibility for errors and the ensuing liability. Hence, owners prefer to refrain from prescribing the methods to be adopted. So long as the owners get the product they desire, it doesn't really matter what construction method was used. However, achieving complete conformity with specifications is not always feasible due to the unique nature of construction. Thus it's the quality inspection that aims to evaluate how closely the contract documents are followed. In order to accomplish that, first, a quality standard specifying criteria for acceptance and rejection is established. Secondly, using appropriate quality control methods, verify if the variations are within the tolerance limits. The best results can be obtained by using a disciplined technique with proper techniques and reliable quality control tools.

On construction sites, there are two types of control: quality *control of methods* and *control of end results* (CPWD, 2022). The methods followed by contractors have to be supervised, especially for activities like piling, concreting, waterproofing, and other highly critical works, for better quality control of methods. It needs to be verified that the method followed is as per the method statement[1]. Field and laboratory tests are done for end-result controls. They check if the required quality specification has been achieved after the completion of an activity and before the start of a subsequent activity. Inspecting the compaction of earthwork after filling the earth and before the start of the next activity is an example of checking for quality control of results. All works are monitored to detect variations that do not fall within tolerable limits. Acceptance testing is done to ensure compliance with the contract or any other standard documents. Thus, quality control guarantees that workmanship, quality of materials and equipment, and work execution are in conformance with the plan and specifications.

8.5 INSPECTION

Inspection involves comparing the characteristics of a product to the required specifications. It includes taking measurements, testing, examining, and gauging the characteristics of products or services and comparing them with requirements as given in the contract. The inspections are mainly of three types: visual inspection, laboratory testing, and field testing. Visual inspection is used to compare performance to standards; as a result, it is subjective. It is used to find out the physical condition of the structure and materials, such as the colour of a median barrier or the colour of painted wall. Not all defects in construction materials can be detected through visual inspection. If lumps are found in the cement bag during inspection, they are likely defective and the manager could opt to discard the affected bags. Defects like cracks, honeycombing, and sagging / bending are detected by visual inspection, though the width of cracks are measured by distance measuring devices.

Some inspections require gauges or tools to conduct measurements or examinations of materials and activities. These are called quality inspection tools. Measuring tape, level, plumb bob, thermometer, rebound hammer, rebar locator, and moisture meter are some quality inspection tools commonly used in construction sites. Also, inspection of machinery and equipment must be done before its acceptance. Measuring the slump of concrete using a slump cone and analysing its consistency is a method of inspecting the workability and quality of concrete. Quality tests will be done on project sites and some in laboratories.

The stages at which inspections are conducted are as follows:

1. **Upon receipt of the raw materials, components, assemblies, and other goods:** The raw materials may be cement, steel, tiles, bricks, and aggregates for building construction. Different types of materials are used in a construction project. Each item must be inspected before using it for construction because the cost of removing, repairing, and rectifying defective work is very high.
2. **After processing:** After every process is complete, an inspection is to be done.
3. **Final examination before accepting the product:** Inspection after completing all the construction activities and before handing over the constructed facility to the client is required to detect and repair the mistakes that have been made during construction.

[1] Method statements gives the description of the procedure to execute a project to achieve its stated objectives (Shen & Walker, 2001).

The final inspection done to find defects in buildings before handing it over to the client is sometimes known as 'snagging'.

The quality requirements, standards, criteria, and methods for inspecting and testing the project deliverables and outputs are described in a *quality inspection and test plan*. This is prepared before the start of the work. It is to be a part of the project quality plan. It includes the process for implementing the activities and the inspections to be conducted, modes of inspection, inspection frequencies, tools to be used, responsibility of personnel, acceptance criteria, and format of records. The results of the inspection are to be recorded properly and communicated to personnel concerned in case of deviations from standards.

Though the quality assurance team has specified the requirements and inspection processes, it is cumbersome for site staff to go through the QA plan every time to inspect different activities. Hence, checklists that are easy to understand and handy for site staff are prepared to be used for inspection purposes. A checklist makes it easier to compare what has been accomplished with the attributes or qualities that are needed from a process or product. A sample checklist for the inspection of reinforcement is given in Table 8.3.

TABLE 8.3 Sample checklist for inspection of reinforcement

S. No.	Items for inspection of reinforcement	Compliance		Remarks
		Yes	No	
1	Is the 'Good for Construction' drawing available?			
2	Are the reinforcement bars placed as per the approved drawing?			
3	Have the bars been tied at every intersection with annealed steel wires (two strands each having 0.9 to 1.6 mm thickness) wherever one bar crosses the other?			
4	Are spacers used when there is more than one reinforcement layer or when there is congestion?			
5	Are the bars cleaned of rust before placing?			
6	Are the splices staggered?			
7	Is the lap length provided as per the drawing?			

8.6 STAGES OF INSPECTION AND QUALITY CONTROL

When executing a building project, inspections must be performed at every stage and continuously. A competent person or a quality engineer has to take responsibility for inspection. They have to check that the work is completed as per the standards, specifications, and drawings. The defects or non-conformity, if found, are to be corrected immediately to avoid waste of effort and time. Inspections may be carried out at every stage, including for earthwork, masonry, concreting, plastering, painting, woodwork, finishing, plumbing, electrification for a building construction project, and all tasks and activities of all contractors and sub-contractors. The criteria for inspection for a few activities in building construction are discussed below.

8.6.1 Earthwork

Inspection during earthwork seeks to check that setting out (or layout) has been done in accordance with the drawings. After the proper layout, trenches/excavations are made according to the length, width, and depth criteria specified in the drawing. Inspection ensures safety during excavation. The sides of trenches ought to be protected, and excavated earth has to be stacked at a distance from the excavation for safety purposes. All these are to be ensured during the inspection. Checking of backfilling needs to be done for proper compaction of the respective layers.

8.6.2 Masonry

Masonry works are inspected for compliance with the specifications for the materials, bond, level, verticality, perpendicularity of corners, and alignment. The quality of the bricks needs to be verified before construction. Quality checks for bricks include compressive strength, dimension check, water absorption, uniformity in shape and size of bricks, efflorescence, and colour. Mortar mixing has to be done after inspection of the mortar proportion. The masonry work ought to be checked for the bond since the continuity of joints weakens the strength of the masonry. The plumb bob is used to check verticality; the spirit level is used to verify the levels, and the tri-square is used for checking the perpendicularity of corners. Further, it is also suggested that the masonry work must also be checked to ensure proper filling of joints with mortar. Defects, if found, ought to be corrected immediately. Curing has to be done with diligence.

8.6.3 Plain Cement Concrete

For good quality concrete, careful inspection and quality control are essential. The mix needs to be designed to standards, and a competent authority has to approve it. The materials used – primarily cement, sand, and stone – have to be tested for quality as per relevant IS standards before designing the mix. It is recommended that aggregates only be obtained from authorised sources. The designed mixes are also tested for compliance with specifications to achieve strength, durability, workability, and economy. Standard practices and specifications must be followed during each stage of concrete manufacturing, from batching, mixing, transporting, laying, compacting, to curing. The slump and air content have to be tested prior to concreting. Every stage ought to include a thorough inspection to ensure the following:

i. **Quality of materials:** Testing the materials like cement, fine and coarse aggregates, water, admixture, and any other supplementary cementitious materials, if any, is to be done per IS standards and accepted only if they conform to specifications.
ii. **Proper batching:** Correct quantities of materials, i.e., cement, fine and coarse aggregates, water, and admixture, are weighed and batched.
iii. **Proper mixing:** Mixing is to be done in mixers for a specified time to ensure uniformity and homogeneity of the mix.

iv. Careful transporting and handling to prevent segregation of ingredients.
v. Laying and compacting within the initial setting time.
vi. Proper consolidation will prevent honeycombing and voids in concrete, which is very important for its durability.
vii. Adequate curing of concrete is to be done so that hydration takes place completely without escape of moisture.
viii. Placing of conduits for electrification in designated locations prior to concreting.

8.6.4 Reinforced Cement Concrete

In RCC works, there are three stages when the inspection is required: formwork, reinforcement, and concreting. The checks are the same for concreting as those required for plain cement concreting.

8.6.5 Formwork

Inspect whether:

i. The formwork material is of approved quality.
ii. The shape of the formwork is as per the drawing.
iii. The placement of formwork is as per drawings.
iv. Braced and supported correctly to take the load of concrete as well as the live pressures during concreting.
v. Oiling has been done to lubricate the forms so that they may be removed easily after concreting.
vi. Alignment, levels, and verticality are correct.
vii. The surface is clean and devoid of dents and bends.
viii. It is watertight, and the gaps are sealed.

Inspection is also required during deshuttering. Check for the deshuttering time and the sequence of deshuttering and inspect if proper support has been provided after stripping of formwork.

8.6.6 Reinforcement

The following checks must be done for reinforcement:

i. Conformance of quality of steel to specifications or belonging to approved make list.
ii. Cleaned to be free of dirt, oil, and deleterious materials and protected from corrosion using epoxy coating or cement slurry.
iii. Cut and bent according to structural drawings and the bar bending schedule.
iv. Placement is done according to the positions shown on drawings.
v. The lap has been staggered and is as per the drawings.
vi. All joints are tied properly using binding wire of specified gauge or else adequately welded in place.

vii. Supports and chairs are provided at appropriate positions, and the assembly is rigid.
viii. Sufficient cover is given on all sides.
ix. Cover blocks are appropriately fixed.
x. Cover blocks are made of the same grade as the main concrete.

8.6.7 Plumbing and Electrification

Since pipes carrying water are mostly concealed in modern-day construction, it is important to check for leaks, slopes, and alignment after laying pipes before packing grooves. The same requirements apply to sewer pipes as well. The manholes and inspection chambers must be inspected, and their covers are to be checked for strength. Inspect the drainage facilities in the bathrooms, roof, and sunshade, as the stagnation of water may lead to dampness, lack of hygiene, and deterioration of structures. The as-built drawings ought to be prepared and recorded for future reference.

Inspections ensure that the electric cables, switches, panels, and meters are provided as per design and specifications. The earthing is to be tested for its effectiveness and functionality. The inspection of the electrical system ensures flawless service. Verify the locations of lights, fans, and switches with drawings and ensure that none of the electric lines or appliances come in contact with moisture. It is to be confirmed that the structural members are not cut to provide chases for electric lines, which is a common mistake seen in construction sites. Inspection during construction ensures safety at the construction site.

8.6.8 Inspection of Built Structures

The structural members are tested for their stability, safety, and soundness. The quality characteristics of concrete are usually assessed by conducting the test for compressive strength, which is the most direct method. However, conducting this test and assessing quality is not feasible for a built structure. So, the quality can be determined by non-destructive tests, full-scale load tests, leakproof, and dampness tests. Non-destructive tests are used to estimate the strength and quality of the finished works without endangering the structure. These tests also help to determine if load tests or core tests are required. The various tests done to determine the strength and soundness of concrete are the Schmidt rebound hammer test, Ultrasonic pulse velocity test, Gamma radiography, Electromagnetic cover meter test, Elastosonic test, and Core test.

Schmidt Rebound Hammer Test

The rebound hammer test can be used to assess the compressive strength of concrete. It is usually done in buildings to assess the strength of structural members. A rebound hammer comprises a mass controlled by a spring that moves along a plunger inside a tubular casing. The spring-controlled mass, which has constant energy, hits the surface when it is forced against it and bounces back. It operates under the principle that the elastic mass's rebound depends on how hard the material's surface is, and it utilises a graduated scale to evaluate hardness. The term 'Rebound Number' refers to this measurement. While excellent-quality concrete exhibits higher rebound values, poor-quality concrete absorbs more energy and produces lower rebound values. The compressive strength is associated with the rebound hammer index. In general, the rebound number rises as the compressive strength increases. IS 13311-2: covers the purpose, principles, tools, and steps of the rebound hammer test method (BIS, 2018a). Based on the average rebound number, Table 8.4 displays the rebound hammer number for different qualities of concrete.

TABLE 8.4 Average rebound number and quality of concrete.

Average Rebound Number	Quality of concrete
> 40	Very good hard layer
30–40	Good layer
20–30	Fair
< 20	Poor concrete
0	Delaminated

Ultrasonic Pulse Velocity Test

Another non-destructive test that is used to evaluate the quality of concrete is the ultrasonic pulse velocity test. It can determine the homogeneity of concrete, cracks, voids, and other imperfections. IS 516 (Part 5/Sec 1): 2018 covers the purpose, principles, tools, and steps of ultrasonic pulse velocity test method (BIS 2018b). When an electro-acoustical transducer's ultrasonic pulse is induced into concrete, it experiences numerous reflections at the boundaries of several material phases. Although a number of waves, including longitudinal (compressional), shear (transverse), and surface (Rayleigh) waves, emerge, the receiving transducer only notices the onset of the longitudinal waves since they are the fastest (BIS, 2018b).

The velocity of the pulses depends on the elastic properties of the materials through which they pass. When the concrete's density, homogeneity, and consistency are good, higher velocities are attained. When concrete quality is poor, or if it has cracks, voids, or defects, pulses pass around the discontinuity and, hence, take a longer time to reach the other end, lowering the velocity. Table 8.5 shows the relationship between velocity and concrete quality as per the IS code.

TABLE 8.5 Velocity criterion for concrete quality grading (BIS, 2018b)

Pulse velocity (km/s)	Quality of concrete
> 4.5	Excellent
3.5–4.5	Good
3.0-3.5	Medium
< 3.0	Doubtful

8.7 ELEMENTS OF QUALITY

The properties or characteristics which specify the nature of a product or service are called *quality characteristics*. In the case of products, they are the measurable variables used by the producer to assess if the product meets the specifications, whereas, for a service, they are those attributes required to satisfy the customers. These are required for quality control, too. The quality characteristics of a few commonly used construction materials are given in Table 8.6.

TABLE 8.6 Quality characteristics of construction materials

No.	Material	Quality characteristics
1	Concrete	Characteristic compressive strength, slump, water-cement ratio
2	Cement	Fineness, soundness, setting time, loss on ignition, compressive strength
3	Brick	Dimensions, compressive strength, water absorption
4	Reinforcement bar	Ultimate tensile strength, bend-rebend, percentage elongation, yield stress
5	Coarse aggregate	Particle size distribution, surface moisture, bulk density, aggregate crushing value, aggregate impact value, aggregate abrasion value

Every material will have certain characteristics that define it, and there will be a range of limits within which it has to remain to be used for a specific purpose. All materials to be used in construction must satisfy the quality characteristic within the limits of tolerances specified for the purpose as per the standards. When more than one quality characteristic is listed in the contract, the material can only be finally accepted if it meets all of the requirements.

The degree to which the actual construction work achieves the design standards is called *quality of conformance*. In a construction project, conformance quality depends on resources, workmanship, and construction methodology. The resources include workers, supervisors, managers, materials, machinery, tools, equipment, and funding.

8.8 FACTORS AFFECTING THE QUALITY OF CONSTRUCTION

As construction projects can be very complex and consist of several processes that are linked and involve various parties, the construction quality depends on a variety of factors. A few of them are presented below:

a. **Organisational culture:** The emphasis that management places on quality is the major driving force for ensuring quality in construction. The entire culture, when it revolves around creating quality, will lead to customer satisfaction.
b. **Management commitment and responsibility:** Management ought to be committed to improving the quality of an organisation. It is the responsibility of management to establish a quality management system within the organisation to work towards achieving quality.

c. **Teamwork:** As construction is an amalgam of various connected and parallel activities, it involves many resources. Hence, it is vital to have coordination and teamwork for good quality control.

d. **Leadership:** Leaders need to encourage everyone to ensure quality in their tasks.

e. **Systems and processes:** They have to be quality-oriented.

f. **Supplier management:** Ensure the quality of material supply by selecting suppliers judiciously, after vetting them.

g. **Design requirements:** The client's requirements shall be well documented in the form of design, specifications, and drawings, as these are the references for carrying out the construction activities. They have to be flawless to ensure the quality of work. The mistakes in any of these lead to rework and thus affect the quality of work.

h. **Planning:** Proper planning of work and scheduling of activities will result in the absence of resource clashes. All the quality assurance and control procedures have to be well-planned and established.

i. **Construction methods:** The construction methodology chosen also determines the quality of conformance. If more activities are automated, the chances of errors and defects can be minimised.

j. **Supervision and control:** All works are to be thoroughly inspected by qualified personnel at each stage for better quality control.

k. **Quality of materials:** For quality control, the materials used for construction must be tested for their conformance to specifications and collected from approved sources.

l. **High quality of tools, plants, and machineries:** The tools and plants, machinery, and all other equipment need to be of high quality to result in efficient and quality work.

m. **Training and skill enhancement of workers:** Workmanship depends on the skill of workers. Well-trained workers can execute the work with high quality in less time.

n. **Safe and stress-free working environment:** Skilled and trained workers can ensure a better quality of work if they work in a safe and stress-free environment.

o. **Managerial control:** Managerial control affects the quality of conformance.

p. **Knowledge of supervisor or inspector:** The person entrusted with supervision must have knowledge about the principles and methods involved in work implementation. They shall be competent enough to identify defects and faulty constructions.

q. **Authority to supervisor and inspector:** The supervisor or inspector ought to be given the power to stop any activity carried out in non-conformance with the plan and specifications.

r. **Communication:** Proper communication between officials at different levels is essential. If any non-conformity is detected, it has to be communicated to the person concerned so that it can be corrected as soon as possible.

8.9 IMPORTANCE OF QUALITY IN CONSTRUCTION

There are a lot of challenges and issues in the construction sector, especially in developing and underdeveloped countries. Most of these problems are related to a lack of quality, which leads to rework, and hence to delays and additional costs. Thus, conducting planned inspections and undertaking quality assurance and control measures are very important. It is well known that construction works are carried out based on drawings and specifications. So, when construction is done in compliance with drawings and specifications, it will result in good quality work at the estimated cost.

There are also national and international standards available for every process in construction. They specify the tolerance limits for varied characteristics of materials. Sufficient care is to be taken during project execution to conform to the standards and specifications. With proper inspection at each stage of construction, it is possible to make the processes defect-free. If defects are identified after the completion of entire processes, it is more expensive and difficult to correct those mistakes.

An organisation that is passionate about defect-free and safe construction will have policies to ensure that works are done as per standards and to the required quality. So, the procedures for QA and QC would be designed accordingly. In most cases, all these require expenses like appraisal and prevention costs. Though the quality of conformance is cost-incurring, it will reduce the chances of failure and thus lead to decreased quality cost. Quality in construction will enhance the durability of structures and lead to sustainability in construction.

The purpose of inspection, quality assurance, and quality control can be summarised as follows:

- **a.** Achieve good quality at a reasonable cost.
- **b.** Ensure defect-free construction.
- **c.** Eliminate the occurrence of rework.
- **d.** Reduce the cost of quality.
- **e.** Increase durability.
- **f.** Enhance customer satisfaction.
- **g.** Ensure the safety and health of the public.

CONCLUSION

Three facets of quality management are covered in this chapter: inspection, control, and assurance. First of all, every organisation needs to prepare a quality assurance plan prior to the commencement of any construction project. Then, it has to do the quality control as specified in the plan. Conducting inspections on time at all stages of work is important because as work progresses as scheduled, defective works could go unnoticed, and subsequent activities succeed them without correction of the previous activities and works. This may thus lead to the accumulation of defects, which can make the effort of correction laborious and costlier. One such example is that a lack of inspection during concreting may lead to insufficient concrete cover in the finished concrete. When this defect goes unnoticed, excessive plastering is done on it to patch up this mistake. But when the structure becomes operational, the lack of cover leads to corrosion and may lead to cracks, spalling, and consequent collapse.

Apart from quality management at each stage of work, inspecting the safety aspects at the construction sites is also important. SP 70: 2001 is a manual on safety practices that may be followed at every construction site (BIS 2001). Inspections may be done based on the recommendations in this handbook. It is also important to keep the construction sites neat and clean in the best possible way so as to prevent accidents and reduce the wastage of materials. Hence, apart from inspection at each stage, housekeeping and safety aspects shall be inspected. In the authors' experience, a clean and safe site is correlated with high-quality standards.

WORKS CITED

ASCE. (2012), *Quality in the Constructed Project: A Guide for Owners, Designers, and Constructors.* (USA: American Society of Civil Engineers).

Ashford, J. L. (2003), *The Management of Quality in Construction.* (London: E & FN SPON).

BIS.(2001)SP 70: 2001, *Handbook on Construction Safety Practices*. (New Delhi: Bureau of Indian Standards).

BIS. (2018a), *IS 13311 (Part 2): 1992 Reaffirmed 2013 Non-destructive Testing of Concrete-Methods of Test. Part 2 - Rebound Hammer.* (New Delhi: Bureau of Indian Standards).

BIS. (2018b), *IS 516 (Part 5/Sec 1): 2018 Hardened Concrete- Methods of Test Part 5 Non-destructive Testing of Concrete Section 1 Ultrasonic Pulse Velocity Testing.* (New Delhi: Bureau of Indian Standards).

CPWD. (2022), *Quality Assurance Manual for Building Works.* (New Delhi: Central Public Works Department).

ISO. (2015), *ISO 9000:2015(en) Quality Management Systems — Fundamentals and Vocabulary*. (Switzerland: International Organization for Standardization).

Oakland, S. J. (2003), *Total Quality Management Text with Cases*. (Oxford: Butterworth Heinemann).

Parsons, R. M. (1972), 'System for control of construction quality', *Journal of the Construction Division, 98*(1), 21–36.

Shen, Y., and Walker, D. (2001), 'Integrating OHS, EMS, and QM with constructability principles when construction planning - a design and construct project case study', *The TQM Magazine, 13*(4), 247–259.

REVIEW QUESTIONS

Multiple Choice Questions

1. What is the primary purpose of quality inspection in construction?

(a) To increase project costs

(b) To penalise contractors

(c) To ensure compliance with standards

(d) To delay project timelines

2. Who is traditionally responsible for ensuring that construction works are done as per design specifications?

(a) Contractor (b) Clerk of works

(c) Owner (d) Designer

3. What does the Linear Responsibility Chart (LRC) solve?
   (a) Project scheduling issues
   (b) Budget overruns
   (c) Responsibility and authority problems in quality control
   (d) Worker performance issues
4. Which of the following quality control techniques are used in the construction sites for quality control?
   (a) Inspection (b) Testing
   (c) Sampling (d) All of the above
5. What is quality assurance primarily focused on?
   (a) Detecting defects after construction
   (b) Preventing quality problems through systematic activities
   (c) Increasing construction costs
   (d) Delaying project timelines
6. What is the primary function of the rebound hammer test?
   (a) To measure the moisture content in concrete
   (b) To assess the compressive strength of concrete
   (c) To check the alignment of structures
   (d) To measure the temperature of concrete
7. What is the pulse velocity range indicating 'Excellent' concrete quality as per IS 516 (Part 5/Sec 1): 2018?
   (a) > 4.5 km/s (b) 3.5–4.5 km/s
   (c) 3.0–3.5 km/s (d) < 3.0 km/s
8. Which quality characteristic is not typically associated with concrete?
   (a) Compressive strength (b) Slump
   (c) Water absorption (d) Bend-rebend
9. What does the term 'snagging' refer to in construction?
   (a) Initial inspection
   (b) Final examination before accepting the product
   (c) Routine maintenance
   (d) Cost estimation
10. Which document outlines the quality requirements, standards, criteria, and inspection methods for project deliverables?
   (a) Project charter (b) Quality inspection and test plan
   (c) Budget plan (d) Risk management plan

11. What is the typical method to ensure proper placement and alignment of formwork in RCC works?
    (a) Visual inspection
    (b) Using measuring tape
    (c) Using spirit level and plumb bob
    (d) Slump test
12. Which non-destructive test is used to evaluate the homogeneity and detect imperfections in concrete?
    (a) Rebound hammer test
    (b) Schmidt hammer test
    (c) Ultrasonic pulse velocity test
    (d) Gamma radiography
13. What does the acronym 'CPWD' stand for?
    (a) Central Public Works Department
    (b) Construction Project Workers Division
    (c) Civil Public Works Directorate
    (d) Central Project Works Department
14. In construction, what is the primary goal of using checklists during inspections?
    (a) To increase project costs
    (b) To ensure proper documentation of defects
    (c) To simplify and ensure thorough inspection processes
    (d) To delay project completion
15. Which of the following is a key characteristic of a 'Good' concrete layer based on rebound hammer values?
    (a) > 40 (b) 30–40
    (c) 20–30 (d) < 20
16. Which method is not typically used for quality assessment in construction projects?
    (a) Inspection (b) Sampling
    (c) Testing (d) Budgeting
17. What is the primary role of the quality assurance team in construction?
    (a) To detect and fix defects
    (b) To establish procedures and ensure compliance with standards
    (c) To delay project timelines
    (d) To increase project costs

18. What is the main purpose of the slump test in concrete inspection?
    (a) To measure the moisture content
    (b) To assess the workability and consistency of concrete
    (c) To test compressive strength
    (d) To measure the air content

19. What type of inspection tool is used to measure the slump of concrete?
    (a) Rebound hammer
    (b) Ultrasonic pulse velocity tester
    (c) Slump cone
    (d) Plumb bob

20. Which characteristic is not a quality characteristic of bricks used in construction?
    (a) Compressive strength
    (b) Water absorption
    (c) Slump
    (d) Dimensions

21. Which of the following statement/statements is/are true?
    Statement (A) Quality assurance is a preventive mechanism.
    Statement (B) Quality control focuses on defect detection.
    (a) Both statements are false
    (b) Statement (A) is true and Statement (B) is false
    (c) Statement (A) is false and Statement (B) is true
    (d) Both statements are true

22. Which test is used to assess the compressive strength of concrete in existing structures?
    (a) Slump test
    (b) Schmidt rebound hammer test
    (c) Ultrasonic pulse velocity test
    (d) Core test

23. What is the role of a quality inspection and test plan in a construction project?
    (a) To increase project costs
    (b) To outline quality requirements and inspection methods
    (c) To delay project timelines
    (d) To reduce project quality

24. Which factor is crucial for achieving quality conformance in construction projects?
    (a) Poor planning
    (b) Lack of supervision
    (c) Good coordination and teamwork
    (d) Ignoring quality standards

25. What is the key benefit of conducting non-destructive tests on concrete structures?
    (a) Reduces construction costs
    (b) Estimates strength and quality without damaging the structure
    (c) Delays project timelines
    (d) Increases project costs

Short Answer Type Questions

1. What is the primary purpose of quality inspection in construction?
2. What is the Linear Responsibility Chart (LRC) used for in quality control?
3. Define quality assurance (QA) in the context of construction.
4. What does the rebound hammer test measure?
5. What pulse velocity indicates 'Excellent' quality concrete according to IS standards?
6. What are the three types of inspections commonly conducted in construction?
7. What is the main focus of Quality Control (QC) in construction?
8. What is 'snagging' in construction?
9. Why are checklists important during inspections in construction?
10. What is the primary role of the quality assurance team in construction?
11. What does the slump test in concrete inspection assess?
12. What tool is used to measure the slump of concrete?
13. Name a key quality characteristic of bricks used in construction.
14. Why is maintaining a safe and stress-free working environment important in construction?
15. What is the purpose of a quality inspection and test plan in a construction project?
16. List a few common tools used for visual inspection in a construction project.
17. What is the effect of proper curing on concrete?
18. What non-destructive tests are used for testing concrete structures?
19. What is the role of the owner in quality assurance in construction?
20. What does the term 'quality characteristics' refer to in construction?
21. What is the importance of proper planning in achieving quality construction?
22. Why are non-destructive tests preferred for built structures?
23. What does the Schmidt rebound hammer test measure?
24. What are the common quality control techniques used in construction, and how do they contribute to project quality?

Long Answer Type Questions

1. Explain the historical importance of quality inspection in construction and how it has evolved over time.
2. Describe the Quality Control (QC) and Quality Assurance (QA) in construction.
3. What is the Linear Responsibility Chart (LRC) and how does it help in resolving quality control issues?
4. Discuss the importance of cooperation among owners, designers, and contractors in achieving quality construction.
5. What are some key components of a quality assurance program in construction?
6. Explain the difference between visual inspection, laboratory testing, and field testing in construction.
7. Describe the Schmidt rebound hammer test and its application in assessing concrete quality.
8. What is the ultrasonic pulse velocity test, and how does it help in the quality assessment of concrete?
9. What are the essential quality characteristics of commonly used construction materials like concrete, cement and bricks?
10. Discuss the factors that affect the quality of construction projects and how they can be managed.
11. What is the significance of conducting non-destructive tests (NDT) on concrete structures?
12. Explain the process and importance of quality control (QC) in construction projects.
13. What are the benefits of implementing a comprehensive quality management system in construction projects?
14. Discuss the challenges and issues related to quality in construction, particularly in developing and underdeveloped countries, and suggest potential solutions.

ANSWER KEYS

Multiple Choice Questions

1. (c)	**2.** (d)	**3.** (c)	**4.** (d)	**5.** (b)	**6.** (b)	**7.** (a)	**8.** (d)
9. (b)	**10.** (b)	**11.** (c)	**12.** (c)	**13.** (a)	**14.** (c)	**15.** (b)	**16.** (d)
17. (b)	**18.** (b)	**19.** (c)	**20.** (c)	**21.** (d)	**22.** (b)	**23.** (b)	**24.** (c)
25. (b)							

CHAPTER

9

Acceptance Sampling and Six Sigma Applications

9.1 INTRODUCTION

Quality programs are designed to ensure that the deliverables produced by the organisation meet customer specifications. Since 100% conformance to the targeted values is not always possible due to natural variations that happen within the system, the limits for specifications must be defined for every product. Those products which do not conform to the specifications are considered defective. It is not possible to check the quality of every process or deliverable. Hence, acceptance sampling is adopted to verify conformance to requirements by inspecting samples from each lot or population. Operating characteristic curves are used to determine the probability of acceptance of lots after sampling.

Six Sigma is a quality improvement strategy that focuses on meeting customer requirements and minimising the occurrence of defects. Six Sigma was developed at Motorola's Communication Division in the early 1980s to improve the quality of their products under the leadership of their -CEO (Bertels, 2003). This concept evolved from philosophies of *Total Quality Management and Statistical Process Control* (Stewart & Spencer, 2006). It is now widely used in various industries irrespective of the type of product or process, degree of complexities, and dissimilarities. It gained wide popularity after its successful implementation in General Electric and Allied Signals. It is to be noted that the fundamental statistical knowledge applied in Six Sigma has been around long before the early 1980s, going back to the late 19th century.

9.2 WHAT IS SIGMA?

9.2.1 Mean, Deviation and Variance

When there is a set of values, the **mean,** $\bar{x}$, is the average of those values, i.e., the value obtained by dividing the algebraic sum of all values by the number/count of values.

Suppose $x_1, x_2, x_3, \ldots, x_n$ are the n values.

$$\text{Mean } \bar{x} = \frac{(x_1 + x_2 + x_3 + x_4 \ldots\ldots + x_n}{n}$$

$$\bar{x} = \frac{\sum_{i=1}^{n} x_i}{n}$$

The **deviation,** δ_i, is the difference between the value considered and their mean value.

$$\delta_i = x_i - \bar{x}$$

And, the **variance,** ν, is the mean of the squared deviations, or also known as the square of the standard deviation, σ. Hence,

$$\nu = \sigma^2 = \frac{\sum_{i=1}^{n} \delta_i^2}{n} = \frac{\sum_{i=1}^{n} (x_i - \bar{x})^2}{n}$$

In statistics, the **standard deviation,** σ (sigma), measures how far a random variable deviates from the mean. The lower the value of standard deviation, the lesser the deviation from the mean, which means that most values are closer to the mean, indicating low risk. Whereas if the value of standard deviation is high, it indicates the wide dispersion of values from the mean, indicating a larger spread and higher risk. For a population, *n*, the standard deviation is given by

$$\sigma = \sqrt{\frac{\sum_{i=1}^{n} (x_i - \bar{x})^2}{n}}$$

However, the standard deviation of a sample is measured somewhat differently. Because the standard deviation of a small sample is usually lesser than that of a whole population, the standard deviation of the sample has a lower number in the denominator to inflate the standard deviation so as to be better representative of the population. This is done in statistics by having $n - 1$ in the denominator of the above equation instead of only *n*. Thus, the standard deviation of a sample, *s*, is

$$s = \sqrt{\frac{\sum_{i=1}^{n} (x_i - \bar{x})^2}{n-1}}$$

Let us consider the following example of a sample to understand this concept.

The failure loads of ten concrete solid block samples are 45 t, 55 t, 65 t, 75 t, 70 t, 80 t, 65 t, 75 t, 55 t and 70 t. Table 9.1 shows the calculation of mean, deviation, variance, and standard deviation for the given values.

9.2.2 Sampling Distribution of Mean

The two types of statistical analysis are descriptive statistics and inferential statistics. In descriptive statistics, we study the characteristics of data under observation/study, whereas in inferential statistics, conclusions are derived about the totality of the dataset by analysing a part of the total dataset. The totality of the dataset is known as the population and the subset is called the population sample. Population measures are known as parameters and the sample measures are called statistics. Population mean (μ) and population variance (σ^2) are parameters, while sample mean ($\bar{x}$), sample standard deviation (s), and sample variance (s^2) are statistics. The size of the population may be infinite, and very often, any sample size greater than 30 can be treated as an infinite sample. As it is difficult to study the entire population, it

TABLE 9.1 Calculation of standard deviation (for sample)

Values x	Mean $\bar{x}$	Deviation $x_i - \bar{x}$	$(x_i - \bar{x})^2$	Variance $\sigma^2 = \frac{\sum_{i=1}^{n}(x_i - \bar{x})^2}{n-1}$	Standard deviation $\sigma = \sqrt{\frac{\sum_{i=1}^{n}(x_i - \bar{x})^2}{n-1}}$
45	65.5	20.50	420.25	119.17	$\sqrt{119.17} = 10.9$
55		10.50	110.25		
65		0.50	0.25		
75		–9.50	90.25		
70		–4.50	20.25		
80		–14.50	210.25		
65		0.50	0.25		
75		–9.50	90.25		
55		10.50	110.25		
70		–4.50	20.25		
Total = 655			**1,072.5**		

is advised to draw conclusions about the population from a sample that may be large enough to represent the population.

The distribution of various sample statistic values from all feasible, identically sized samples chosen from the population is referred to as a sampling distribution. In reality, even though we would only be using one sample from a population, we are aware that the sample statistic, say, the mean ($\bar{x}$), calculated from that sample may not equal the population's equivalent parameter (μ). Moreover, random sampling variability also causes sample statistic values to differ between samples.

However, the population parameter (μ) will be equal to the mean, or the expected value of the sample mean distribution as a random variable.

$$\text{Population mean, } \mu = E(\bar{x}) = \frac{\bar{x}_1 + \bar{x}_2 + \ldots + \bar{x}_k}{k} = \sum_{i=1}^{k} \frac{\bar{x}_i}{k}$$

where, k = number of samples.

A basic theorem in statistics for the normal distribution is that the theoretical sampling distribution of a sample taken from a population having a mean μ and the standard deviation, σ, has a standard deviation given by $\frac{\sigma}{\sqrt{n}}$ for infinite populations. This is generally called the *standard error of the mean.*

Since the variance of the sample statistics is the square of the standard deviation, the variance is given as:

$$V(\bar{X}) = \frac{\sigma^2}{n}$$

By definition, the variance of the sample statistic mean represents the spread of the sampling distribution of the sample mean and is a measure of the variability of the sample means from the parameter.

9.2.3 Normal Distribution

Normal distribution is one of the most important theoretical distributions in the theory of probability. This is the distribution for continuous random variables. It is the distribution most often found in nature in large samples, such as the height or weight distribution in a population, the size of leaves, the length of dog tails, and so on. The probability density function for normal distribution is:

$$f(x) = \frac{1}{\sigma\sqrt{2\pi}} \cdot e^{-\frac{1}{2}\left(\frac{x-\mu}{\sigma}\right)^2}$$

where,

μ = Mean

σ = Standard deviation

x = continuous random variable

π = 3.14159

e = 2.71828

With a variance of σ^2 and a mean of μ, the continuous random variable in the probability density function is distributed symmetrically on the two sides.

As shown in Figure 9.1, the probability density function of the normal distribution yields a bell-shaped curve.

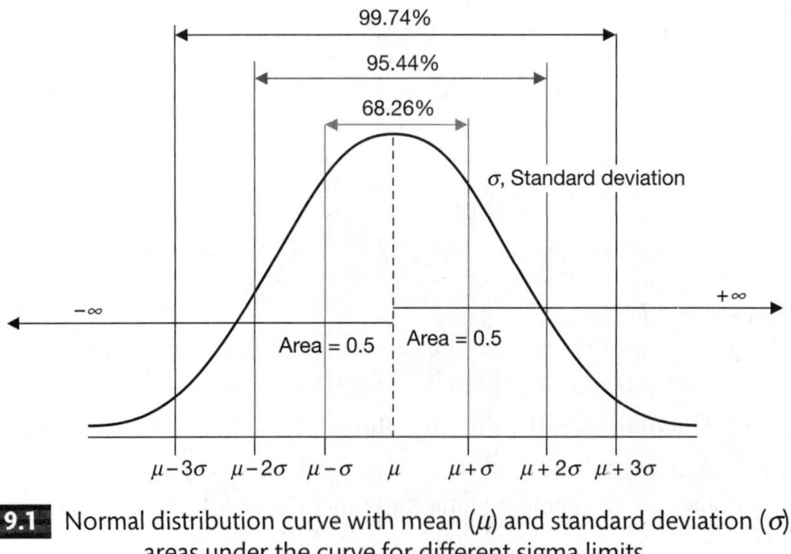

FIGURE 9.1 Normal distribution curve with mean (μ) and standard deviation (σ), showing areas under the curve for different sigma limits

This bell-shaped, symmetrical normal distribution curve, is used in the Six Sigma concept. The curve is divided into a series of segments, representing the standard deviation from the mean. The mean lies at the central point of the curve. The standard deviation, denoted by Sigma, measures how much a process deviates from its mean. Here, the mean indicates the goal to be achieved by the experimental samples. The entire area beneath the normal curve is 1.

Every process will have an upper control limit and a lower control limit of deviations within which measured values should fall. Approximately 68.26% of all values are within one-sigma deviation, 95.44% are within two-sigma and 99.74% are within three-sigma from the mean. As the sigma values increase, the values outside the boundary will decrease, i.e., fewer defects will be found.

The area within the normal curve can be found using the tables for standard normal distribution (see Appendix 1). The standard units are found by the following formula.

$$z = \frac{(x - \mu)}{\sigma}$$

The z value indicates the number of standard deviations the observed statistic x (sample mean) is from the mean μ (population mean). It can have both positive and negative values. When x is to the right of the mean, the z value will be positive and when x is to the left of the mean, the z value will be negative. When x is equal to the mean, the z value will be zero. The variance is one and the mean is zero in the standardised normal distribution, represented as $N(0,1)$.

9.2.4 Acceptance Sampling and Operating Characteristic Curve

Acceptance Sampling

During the Second World War, production volume increased immensely making it impossible to check the quality of all items. Hence, 100% inspections were substituted by inspection of samples using the sampling plans. Acceptance sampling started being widely used since the Sampling Inspection Tables were developed and distributed by Dodge and Romig in 1944 (Schilling & Neubauer, 2017).

The sample chosen must be representative of the population. The larger the population, the larger must be the sample selected. Larger samples give more information about the lot and thus reduce the risks during the decision-making. Sampling is done to determine if the lot or population conforms to specifications and, accordingly, decide whether the lot must be accepted or rejected.

For every product, specification limits are set by the customer. Sampling and inspection are done to determine if these limits are exceeded or not. Then, by applying statistical theories to the inspection results, the percentage of defectives can be determined. After the percentages of defectives are identified, it can be analysed whether there is a need to improve the processes. When the variations are more than the acceptable limits, quality improvement methods must be adopted by the organisation to reduce the number of defects. Acceptance sampling is thus a tool that can detect the production of substandard quality products or services.

Decision Making: Type I and Type II Errors

Implementing acceptance sampling over 100% inspection brings about an obvious challenge owing to the costs involved. However, a sample drawn from the lot may miss out on the defectives or may indicate a rather high proportion of defectives. Thus, there could be either of the two scenarios where an error in decision could occur:

(A) where the lot is actually acceptable, but the statistical analysis of the chosen sample will lead to the decision to reject the lot.

or

(B) where the lot is defective, but the statistical analysis of the chosen sample may lead to the decision to accept the lot.

A hypothesis is tested to determine whether there is sufficient statistical evidence in support or contrary to the researcher's claim about the population parameter. A null hypothesis indicates that two values are equal and is denoted by H_0. If H_0 is true during the hypothesis testing, the null hypothesis is to be accepted. If H_0 is true but the null hypothesis is mistakenly rejected, it is an error called the Type-I error (Scenario A). The chances of making a reasonable error when performing acceptance sampling are usually taken as 1–10 per cent. The lower the chances of making an error, the higher the accuracy. Similarly, if H_0 is false and still the null hypothesis is accepted, it is an error called the Type-II error (Scenario B). Thus, there are four logical possibilities of decision making after testing the hypothesis and they are given in Table 9.2.

TABLE 9.2 Different possibilities for decision-making

	H_0 is True	H_0 is False
Accept H_0	Right decision	Type II Error
Reject H_0	Type I Error	Right decision

Decision-making is undertaken by establishing a test statistic. The most common test statistic for samples in normal distributions is

$$z_{\text{stat}} = \frac{\bar{x} - \mu}{\sigma/\sqrt{n}}$$

Where σ = standard deviation; n is the sample size; $\bar{x}$ is the observed mean; and μ is the hypothesised or targeted mean. However, for small samples ($n < 30$), the t-statistic is used:

$$t_{\text{stat}} = \frac{\bar{x} - \mu}{s/\sqrt{n}}$$

Operating Characteristic Curve

There are circumstances when a company assumes that its process is out of control when it is actually in control and vice versa. Out-of-control indicates that the mean of a measurement is outside the acceptance limits, while in-control denotes that the mean is within the acceptance limits. As mentioned above, two errors can occur when making inferences from sample testing. Let us consider an example of a water-proofing chemical manufacturer packing bags of 1,000 g. The target weight to be packed in each bag is 1,000 g with an acceptance limit of ± 3 g.

Type I Error: When an inference is made from sample testing that the process is out of control when it is actually in control, it is called the Type I error. In the above example, if a sample has a mean different from 1,000 g ± 3 g, say 1,005 g, (while the mean of the lot is 1,000 g) and the company decides on the basis of the sample that the process is out of control, which is what acceptance sampling is, then it is a case of ***Type I error***. This basically happens because samples can potentially yield means different from the population mean, which is why we say that there is always a sampling error. Such a Type I error results in shutting down the operation in search of a problem that actually does not exist. Figure 9.2 shows the general purpose acceptance and rejection profile for a two-tail test when the lot mean is actually 1,000 g.

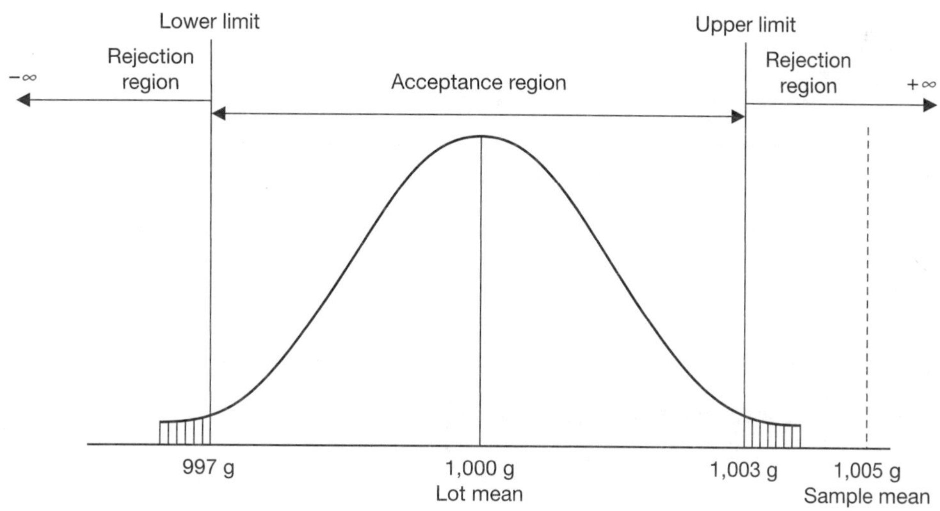

FIGURE 9.2 Case when the sample mean is 1,005 g.

Type II Error: There is another possibility of error when, in reality, the population (lot) mean (μ) has shifted and, say, has a value of 995 g, which can happen due to system malfunction. This means that the process is fundamentally not in control as the population (lot) mean is outside 1,000 g ± 3 g. However, if the sample mean is within acceptable limits, the company logically assumes that the process is in control. This is a case of ***Type II error*** when it is concluded that a process is in control when it is actually out of control.

Additionally, the actual mean due to system or equipment malfunction could be on a wide range, such as from 994 to 1,006. Here, the probability of accepting that the population mean is 1,000 g ± 3 g when the population mean has actually shifted to different values is given in Table 9.3.

TABLE 9.3 Calculating the probability of acceptance

Value of μ	Probability of accepting H	Probability of Type II error
994	0.0002	0.0002
995	0.0082	0.0082
996	0.1151	0.1151
997	0.5	No error
998	0.8849	No error
999	0.9918	No error
1,000	0.9996	No error
1,001	0.9918	No error
1,002	0.8849	No error
1,003	0.5	No error
1,004	0.1151	0.1151
1,005	0.0082	0.0082
1,006	0.0002	0.0002

Note: Standard deviation = 5, $n = 35$.

The z value is calculated as:

$$z = \frac{(x-\mu)}{\sigma}$$

Sample Calculations

Case I: When the lot mean has shifted to 996 g,

$$z_{\text{stat1}} = \frac{997-996}{5/\sqrt{35}} = 1.2$$

and

$$z_{\text{stat2}} = \frac{1{,}003-996}{5/\sqrt{35}} = 8.3$$

From the statistical tables, the area to the left of $z = 1.2$ is 0.8849 and the area corresponding to the right of $z = 8.3$ is negligible. Therefore, the area of the unshaded portion is 1 – 0.8849 = 0.1151 or 11.51%.

Hence, the probability of acceptance of mean = 996 g is 0.1151, as shown in Figure 9.3.

Case II: When the lot mean is actually 1000 g,

$$z_{\text{stat1}} = \frac{997-1{,}000}{5/\sqrt{35}} = -3.5 \quad \text{and} \quad z_{\text{stat2}} = \frac{1{,}003-1{,}000}{5/\sqrt{35}} = 3.5$$

From the statistical table, the area in each tail is 0.0002, as shown in Figure 9.4.

Hence, the probability of acceptance = (1 – (0.0002 + 0.0002)) = 0.9996.

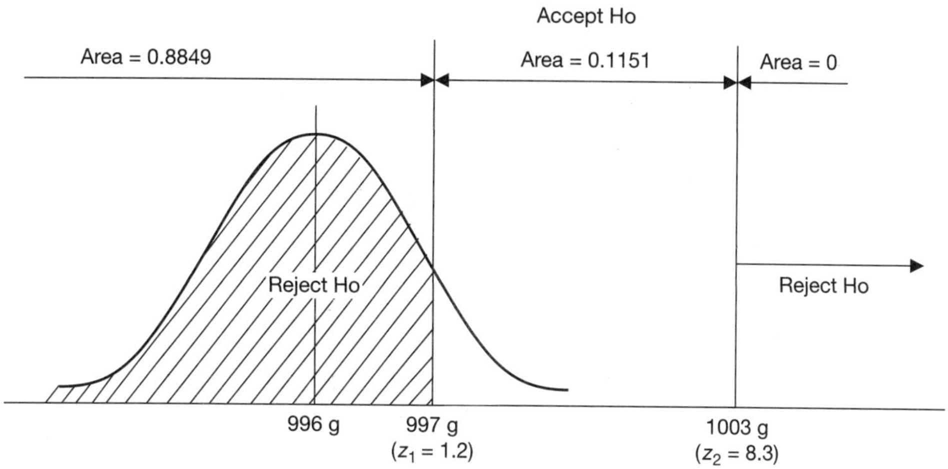

FIGURE 9.3 Test criterion when the mean has shifted to 996 g

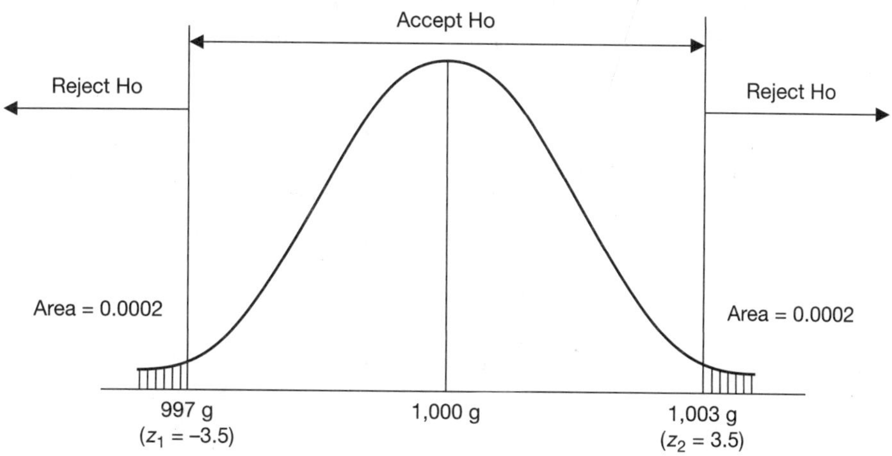

FIGURE 9.4 Test criterion when the mean is at 1,000 g

Case III: When the lot mean has shifted to 1,002g,

$$z_{\text{stat1}} = \frac{997 - 1,002}{5/\sqrt{35}} = -5.9$$

and

$$z_{\text{stat2}} = \frac{1,003 - 1,002}{5/\sqrt{35}} = 1.2$$

From the statistical tables, the area corresponding to $z = 1.2$ is 0.8849 and the area corresponding to $z = -5.9$ is negligible, as shown in Figure 9.5.

Thus, the probability of acceptance is 0.8849.

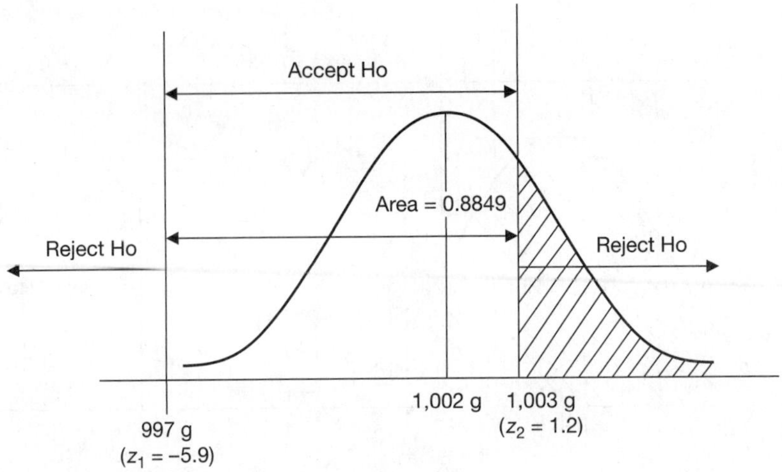

FIGURE 9.5 Test criterion when the mean has shifted to 1,002 g

The curve plotted to represent the probability of acceptance of the hypothesis is called the operating characteristic curve of the test criterion and is shown in Figure 9.6. When the shift of mean is less, the chance of acceptance is greater. In a process, when the departure from the standard is comparatively less, the process will still be likely allowed to continue. However, when the departure from the mean becomes larger in either direction, the probability of allowing the process to continue becomes smaller, which is as it should be. Hence, the probability of allowing the process to continue when the lot mean departs further from the target mean, becomes smaller and smaller as the departure increases.

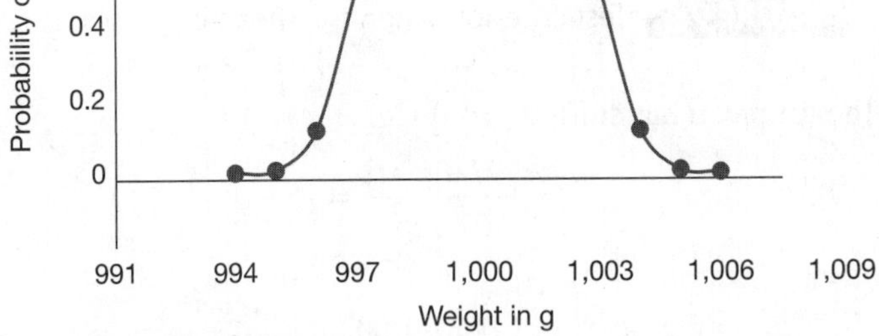

FIGURE 9.6 Operating characteristic curve (OCC)

The company can choose the desirable OC curve by perhaps changing the sample size. The OCC is used in acceptance sampling to determine the probability of acceptance of variations or defects from the targeted value. It further shows how acceptance sampling can be used to measure the risks to which one may be exposed while managing a process. Thus, it can be recognised that the number of defectives naturally increases when the process goes beyond the range of acceptable limits.

9.3 SIX SIGMA

Six Sigma (6σ) utilises statistical tools to assess how well a product or service performs in response to client demands and, it consists of methods to reduce defects or variations from processes. In order to enhance the quality, the number of variations should be restrained. If we assume that the output of a process is shown by a normal distribution curve, the area within the normal curve outside of 6σ from the mean position is two parts per billion (0.002 per million). It means that for a process operating at Six Sigma, the number of defects produced will be 0.002 per million. Table 9.4 shows the number of defects produced when a process operates under different levels of sigma.

TABLE 9.4 Defects per million opportunities for different values of Sigma

z-value	Area under the curve corresponding to z on one side of the mean	Total area under $z = 2 \times$ area on one side	Area outside the limits = 1–(2 × area)	No. of defects in one million opportunities = area outside limits x 10,00,000
1 σ	0.3413	0.6826	0.3174	3,17,400
1.5 σ	0.4332	0.8664	0.1336	1,33,600
2 σ	0.4772	0.9544	0.0456	45,600
2.5 σ	0.4938	0.9876	0.0124	12,400
3 σ	0.4987	0.9974	0.0026	2,600
3.5 σ	0.4998	0.9996	0.0004	400
4 σ	0.4999685	0.999937	0.0000630	63
4.5 σ	0.4999966	0.9999932	0.00000680	6.8
5 σ	0.4999997150	0.99999943	0.000000570	0.57
5.5 σ	0.4999999810	0.999999962	0.0000000380	0.038
6 σ	0.4999999990	0.999999998	0.00000000200	0.002

The calculation of defects is done as follows, say for 1σ:

- From the z-table showing the area of the curve to the right side of the mean, find the value corresponding to $z = 1$.
- From the z-table, the area within mean μ and $z = 1$ is 0.3413.
- Therefore, the area within the curve on both sides of μ for $z = 1$ is $2 \times 0.3413 = 0.6826$ (Refer to Figure 9.7).

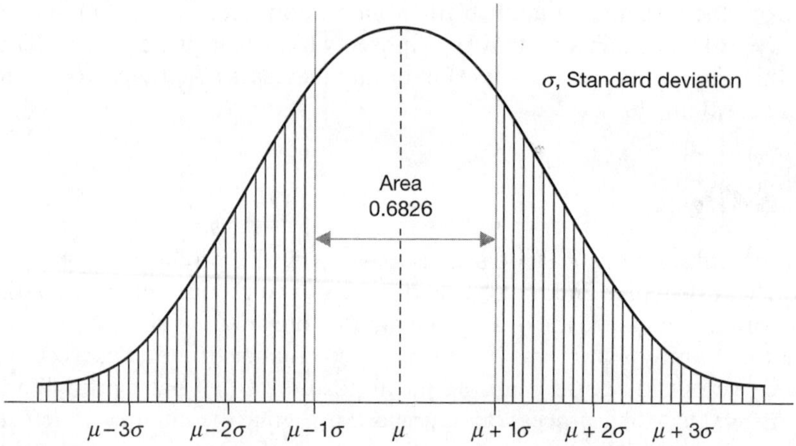

FIGURE 9.7 Normal distribution curve with mean (μ) and standard deviation (σ)

- The area outside $z = 1$ will be $1 - 0.6826 = 0.3174$.
- Hence, it shows that the percentage of non-conforming items is 31.74% for $z = 1$.
- Thus, for one million opportunities, the defects would be equal to $0.3174 \times 10{,}00{,}000 =$ 3,17,400.
- In the same way, the number of defects per million opportunities are calculated for different values of sigma and are tabulated in Table 9.4.

In real-life situations, the mean of a process may digress over a period of time due to a number of factors, such as wear and tear. Hence, while calculating the rate of failure or number of variations or defects for Six Sigma processes, we assume that the product or process performance experienced by customers during its life cycle drifts from what has been forecasted. Therefore, when estimating long-term performance, a shift of 1.5 sigma is considered to account for this fluctuation, as shown in Figure 9.8. This shift can happen in either direction. Thus, in a Six Sigma process, when the mean shifts by 1.5 sigma, the remaining region that comes within the shifted mean and the specification limit will be 4.5 sigma. The region beyond 4.5 sigma (from the shifted mean) is 3.4 parts per million on the normal curve. Or it can be said that when the Sigma level is 6 from the initial mean, the percentage of items without defects will be 99.999997 and the defects per million opportunities will equal 3.4. Six Sigma aims to operate defect-free, with 3.4 defects per million opportunities, compared to 3 Sigma, which has around 66,800 defects per million opportunities (DPMO). In statistical terms, the Six Sigma value tends to have approximately zero defects, leading to greater customer satisfaction.

Table 9.5 shows the number of defects per million opportunities for different values of sigma. Let us calculate the DPMO for a process with 2.5 sigma. To accommodate the shift in the mean of the process in the long run, we consider a shift of mean by 1.5 Sigma.

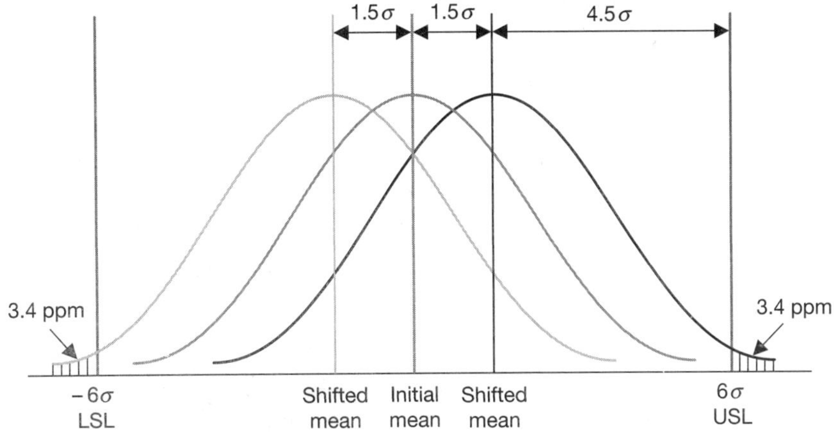

FIGURE 9.8 Six Sigma with ± 1.5σ shift

TABLE 9.5 Defects per million opportunities for different values of Sigma with 1.5σ shift

z-value	With 1.5 σ shift	Area under the curve corresponding to z on one side of mean	Area outside the limits = 1- area	No. of defects in one million opportunities = area outside limits × 10,00,000
1σ				
1.5 σ				
2 σ	0.5 σ	0.6915	0.3085	3,08,500
2.5 σ	1 σ	0.8413	0.1587	1,58,700
3 σ	1.5 σ	0.9332	0.0668	66,800
3.5 σ	2 σ	0.9772	0.0228	22,800
4 σ	2.5 σ	0.9938	0.0062	6,200
4.5 σ	3 σ	0.9987	0.0013	1,300
5 σ	3.5 σ	0.9998	0.0002	200
5.5 σ	4 σ	0.9999685	0.0000315	31.5
6 σ	4.5 σ	0.9999966	0.0000034	3.4

So, while considering a 2.5 sigma shift from the initial process mean, it corresponds to a 1 sigma shift in the current/actual process. The DPMO for 2.5 sigma is calculated as follows:

- From the z table, the area within mean μ and $z = 1$ is 0.3413 (to one side of the mean). In this case, we can see from Figure 9.9 that for processes with the sigma shift, the regions outside the specification limits are mostly on one side of the mean.

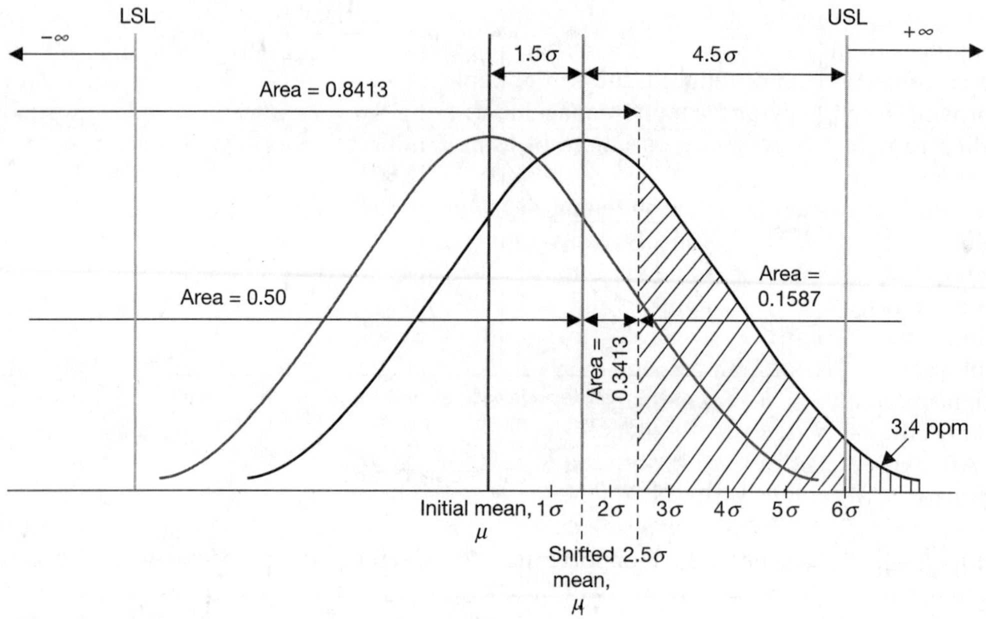

FIGURE 9.9 Mean shift of +1.5σ

- Hence, we have to add the entire area under the curve on the other side of the mean which is equal to 0.5.
- Therefore, the total area under the curve for $z = 1$ will be equal to $0.5 + 0.3413 = 0.8413$.
- Thus, the area outside the $z = 1$ will be equal to $1 - 0.8413 = 0.1587$.
- Therefore, nonconformity = 15.87%.
- Thus, for one million opportunities, the defects would be equal to 0.1587 × 10,00,000 = 1,58,700.
- Hence, when sigma = 2.5, DPMO will be 1,58,700.

Six Sigma has a multifaceted approach to process improvement. It works by reducing variations in processes and limiting defects, which leads to reduced costs and increased profits. According to the Six Sigma concept, business quality is the highest when a customer receives a product or service as per their requirements at the lowest cost. Enhancing customer happiness directs a company toward achieving world-class corporate performance. By minimising errors throughout their operations, businesses may maintain an advantage in a competitive industry. Six Sigma is a management philosophy and a paradigm shift to organisational culture and belief. Six Sigma involves something more comprehensive than traditional quality programmes, which concentrate on finding and fixing defects.

9.4 SIGNIFICANCE OF SIX SIGMA

The foundation of Six Sigma is the notion that if the number of defects in a procedure or product can be determined, then a method to fix them can be identified to achieve near 'zero defects'. To decrease the defects, Six Sigma focuses on redesigning the products and production processes rather than increasing inspection. The chances for defects during production and customer usage are reduced due to the deployment of Six Sigma. This is achieved by improving technology and supply management, using good equipment, and other factors leading to reduced processing variation. In using Six Sigma, management relentlessly puts effort into reducing defects and rigorously pursues breakthrough improvements to minimise variations in all critical processes to enhance customer satisfaction.

The application of traditional quality models was limited to manufacturing processes, whereas Six Sigma can improve all significant business processes. Six Sigma places emphasis on the needs of the stakeholders for whom the organisation is designed. It operates via various tools such as the cause-and-effect method and benefits the customers as well as the employees. The business process and the management systems in Six Sigma are ideally so well designed that the employees are happy to work to create value for the service or the product, making customers satisfied or delighted.

After organisations learned about the benefits of applying Six Sigma in the manufacturing sector, they soon used the Six Sigma methodology in other functional areas like marketing, engineering, purchasing, servicing, and administrative support (Kwak & Anbari, 2006). The large-scale adoption of Six Sigma was due to the capacity of organisations to define the advantages of Six Sigma in terms of financial returns by connecting process improvement with cost reductions.

9.5 THE SIX SIGMA MODELS

The goal, value, and specification limitations of the output of a process are established based on what customers require and expect. Specification limits that form the boundaries for acceptable tolerances are called the 'Voice of the Customer (VoC)'. The distribution of measurements of a process's outputs over a specific period is known as the 'Voice of the Process (VoP)'. The DMAIC and DMADV models are presented below.

9.5.1 Define, Measure, Analyse, Improve, Control (DMAIC)

The most commonly used model for implementing Six Sigma in an organisation for process improvement is **DMAIC**. It consists of five stages: Define, Measure, Analyse, Improve, and Control. DMAIC is an adaptation from Deming's Plan, Do, Study, Act (PDSA) cycle. DMAIC in Six Sigma offers techniques for collecting data and its analysis based on statistics helps to locate and eliminate error sources.

- **Define:** Identify the quality characteristics critical to customers (called CTQ, Critical to Quality) using a SIPOC (Supplier, Input, Process, Output, and Customer) analysis (Gitlow *et al.*, 2006). Accordingly, the project's objectives, scope, and processes are defined.
- **Measure:** Measure the performance of current processes, calculate the sigma value, and create a statistical study database. This phase aims to collect information about the ongoing processes and thus find problem areas.
- **Analyse:** Find the gap between desired and current performance, prioritise problems, and detect the causes of problems that require improvement using tools such as process maps, fishbone diagrams, and Pareto charts.

- **Improve:** Generate and identify possible solutions and check their performance on a small scale before implementing them on a broader scale to meet the required performance and financial goals. Conduct team workshops and discussions for improvement.
- **Control:** Develop, document, and implement a plan to sustain the desired improvement and monitor process improvement.

All these processes require top-down implementation as they are associated with the organisation's overall goals. Intense and focused training should be given to the employees for the successful execution of Six Sigma.

9.5.2 Define, Measure, Analyse, Design, Verify/Validate (DMADV)

DMADV is a five-step process to be followed to develop a new product, process, or service. It brings some control in organising design information, which is mostly not considered.

- **Define**: In this stage, the project charter, which will contain all essential elements, will be prepared. The scope and purpose of the project, as well as specific and measurable goals, will be identified during this phase. The availability of key players and other resources is determined and ensured for the project. A comprehensive project plan is produced, including a timetable, and completion dates. Finally, all critical participants should provide written consent and agreements for acceptance and support.
- **Measure:** By taking into account the needs of all project participants, including the Voice of the Customer (market segments), the Voice of the Business (staff segments), and the Voice of the Process, the critical project components (inputs) are measured in this phase. The voices are captured and translated into measurable project requirements in this phase. This would assist in finalising the specifications for the design.
- **Analyse:** This stage deals with producing various design alternatives likely to meet the defined requirements. Using different tools, the various design alternatives are checked against the criteria to identify the design approach that offers the most desired outcomes.
- **Design:** The specifications are finalised in this stage and the exact design requirements for the goods, service, or process are developed. Mostly, alpha testing, i.e., the initial internal testing is done at the end of this stage to verify the performance of the prototype or model with regard to the specifications.
- **Verify/Validate:** This stage determines whether the detailed design is desired and deemed acceptable by all project participants. Stakeholders are allowed to confirm the outcome and assess its suitability for the intended use. Beta testing, i.e., testing in the real-world scenario before launch, is done at this stage to ensure that the design meets the specifications as well as requirements.

Both models thus enable the delivery of the desired results from Six Sigma, reducing the number of overall defects and enhancing quality and customer satisfaction, not to mention manufacturer pride.

9.6 PRINCIPLES GOVERNING SIX SIGMA

The principles governing Six Sigma are as follows (Pheng & Hui, 2004):

- **a.** Focus on conformance to valid customer requirements. The focus of Six Sigma has to be on the requirements of the customers. When customers and their requirements are understood in detail, organisations can customise their products and services by developing new ideas and adding additional features.
- **b.** Data and fact-driven management policy. The essential components that represent and gauge the effectiveness of organisational operations are metrics or figures.
- **c.** Processes are the critical determinants of success. The focus needs to be on process improvement whenever defects or variations are detected. The processes should be controlled so that they do not go beyond the specified statistical limits.
- **d.** Proactive management focuses on defect elimination at the source rather than managing it after its occurrence. It analyses the cause of defects. People in the organisation ought to be equipped to monitor and sustain improvements.
- **e.** Teamwork has to be improved through collaboration across the organisation.
- **f.** The continuous improvement process drives perfection by accepting failures and analysing their causes. Organisations that adopt Six Sigma always keep improving. One after the other, improvements are made in all processes in the organisation.
- **g.** Being very responsive to change. Whenever the market trend changes, the organisations are required to respond to it.

It must be noted that all the above principles should be applied together. Applying one of the principles or only a few, to the exclusion of the others, will not bring the desired results. The reason is simply that it takes the entire company, from top to down, to reap the benefits of Six Sigma. Moreover, because work and tasks are so integrated and intertwined with management practices, training, and knowledge, it requires multiple directional approaches and an open mind to derive gains from the statistical practice of Six Sigma.

9.7 SIX SIGMA TOOLS

Six Sigma, being a set of tools, works best when combined with more comprehensive quality programmes like the Malcolm Baldrige National Quality Award Criteria for Performance Excellence or the European Foundation for Quality Management Award Criteria. It is not a management system by itself but consists of methods to reduce variations in processes and it provides a set of tools that can be used to improve the performance of an organisation (Raisinghani, 2005). For deploying Six Sigma, several tools that can be used at different phases of its implementation are given in Table 9.6.

Once again, it is seen that the implementation of Six Sigma is an elaborate process involving the simultaneous use of tens of tools and sub-systems. Usually, success through Six Sigma can only come through basic training, education, and practice.

TABLE 9.6 Tools used at different phases of Six Sigma implementation.

Project Phase	Tools used
Define	• Project charter • Value stream mapping • IPO (Input–Process–Output) diagram • Focus groups, questionnaires, letters, and feedback cards—to identify Voice of Customers • Process map • Kano model • Quality Function Deployment • SIPOC analysis • Affinity diagram • Benchmarking • Tools for managing and planning projects
Measure	• Analysis of measurement systems • Nominal group technique • Pairwise ranking • Process behaviour charts • Exploratory data analysis • Descriptive statistics • Data mining • Run charts • Waste analysis • Pareto analysis
Analyse	• Cause and effect diagram • Tree diagrams • Brainstorming • Process behaviour charts • Response surface methodology (RSM) • Process maps • Design of experiments • Hypothesis tests • Inferential statistics • Five whys • Simulation
Improve	• Force field diagrams • DFSS - Design for Six Sigma • Failure modes and effects analysis (FMEA) • 7M tools • Kanban • Design of experiments • Project planning and management tools • Prototype and pilot studies • Simulations

(Continued)

Project Phase	Tools used
Control	• Statistical process control • Visual process control • Failure modes and effects analysis (FMEA) • Mistake proofing • ISO 9000 • Run charts • Standard operating procedures • Change budgets, bid models, cost estimating models • Reporting system

9.8 THE UNIQUENESS OF SIX SIGMA

Six Sigma differs from TQM in terms of the level of engagement and the rate of change. It focuses on delivering game-changing results quickly. Six Sigma differs from past quality approaches in a few specific ways. The breakthrough result of Six Sigma is due to the integration of both human aspects and process improvements. Most of the other methods focus only on a subset of these elements to drive change and improve processes. Table 9.7 displays the human and procedural dimensions of improvement that Six Sigma integrates.

TABLE 9.7 Various aspects of improvement integrated by Six Sigma (Snee, 1999)

Various Aspects Improved	Remarks
Net revenue	*Human related*
Leadership	
Faster completion	
Focus on customer	
Project teams	
Change of culture	
Improvement of process	*Process related*
Variation analysis	
Disciplined approach	
Quantitative measures	
Statistical methods	
Management of processes	

Another unique factor about Six Sigma is its focus on getting bottom-line results. Six Sigma projects are not approved without considering the effect on the bottom line. In order to get beyond TQM's constraints, Six Sigma applies suitable project management methods for project selection and evaluation.

Following is a summary of the Six Sigma management approach (Anbari, 2002).

Six Sigma = TQM (or CQI)
+ Additional Data Analysis Tools
+ Stronger Customer Focus
+ Project Management
+ Financial Results

Where

TQM = Total Quality Management

CQI = Continuous Quality Improvement

Whereas, traditional quality programmes focus on investigating and correcting mistakes, Six Sigma has a wider perspective. It offers precise ways to redesign the procedure so that defects do not occur in the first attempt. It entails being observant and on-the-job all the time. Six Sigma aims to eliminate defects from every transaction by reducing variations in all processes. Hence, it is a comprehensive process that uses additional data analysis tools, focuses on the customer, applies professional project management, and has an eye on financial results, much as the entire production system is comprehensive and integrated with other activities.

9.9 IMPLEMENTING SIX SIGMA

The steps given are to be followed for implementing Six Sigma and its improvement (Pheng & Hui, 2004):

a. Set a strategic business objective.
b. Identify the most important clients, develop the supporting procedures, and delegate the tasks.
c. Define customer needs.
d. Measure the present performance.
e. Implement improvements after analysis of data.
f. Expansion and integration of the Six Sigma system into the organisation.

Identification of the variations in processes and eliminating them is the key element in Six Sigma implementation. Each process consists of a set of independent activities and with variations in each of them, the variations accumulate in the finished product or service.

For successfully implementing Six Sigma, the following activities and systems are recommended:

1. Leaders must develop a vision and convey it to all levels of the organisation. They are responsible for ensuring that Six Sigma's goals, objectives, and progress are consistent with the company's overall strategy. The philosophy, principles, and tools of Six Sigma are taught to the senior leadership. Based on requirements, new positions and departments are created, and modifications in policies for reward, recognition, incentive, and compensation systems are made. Thus, by modifying the organisation's culture, the personnel will pursue Six Sigma as a normal routine.

2. To successfully deploy Six Sigma, there needs to be an organisational infrastructure to support and manage various activities. Additional resources like machinery, new technology, or specialised personnel may be required for adopting Six Sigma.
3. It is indispensable to have proper mechanisms for communication among the various levels of management to improve the processes and to increase awareness about Six Sigma and its progress.
4. Participation of stakeholders is absolutely important and there has to be a system to collect feedback from stakeholders.
5. A process feedback system needs to be developed so that changes in processes can be immediately noticed and required improvement methods can be adopted.
6. It is necessary to select projects that are suitable for Six Sigma before attempting to implement it.
7. Six Sigma projects ought to be deployed with the necessary tools and techniques and competent personnel.
8. Decomposition of projects, i.e., breaking down projects into smaller elements is required to enable improvement at all levels.

9.9.1 Important Success Elements

Critical factors that determine the success of the implementation of Six Sigma are (Coronado & Antony, 2002):

i. Support, involvement, and commitment of top management and the availability of leaders skilled in project management.
ii. Change in organisational culture.
iii. Linking of Six Sigma processes to strategies of the company.
iv. Teamwork at all project phases, from defining project scope to product delivery.
v. Understanding customer requirements and linking Six Sigma to them.
vi. Rewarding the outstanding performers.
vii. Decision-making on the basis of facts and data collected.
viii. Selecting the appropriate resources and tools for Six Sigma implementation
ix. Training and educating the employees on the tools to be used.
x. Proper communication among the stakeholders and within the team.
xi. Continuous process control and improvement.
xii. Selection of suitable projects.

These really tie into the previous few sections that emphasise a comprehensive approach to managing Six Sigma and the company operations.

9.9.2 Roles and Responsibilities

Six Sigma deployment is possible through the involvement of the right people who have been chosen and trained in this area. There are various positions that are critical to implementing

Six Sigma management in an organisation. The following are the jobs and duties that team members at different levels have when implementing Six Sigma:

Executive Leadership/ Leadership Group/ Steering Committee

They are the top management personnel who are the inspiration and driving force of Six Sigma in any organisation. They are responsible for the following:

- To make sure that Six Sigma objectives are in line with corporate objectives.
- To create new regulations, if necessary.
- To provide resources.
- To track and control projects towards goals.
- To review the improvement of teams and the effectiveness of Six Sigma deployment.

Executive Champions

They are chosen by the CEO to look after and assist with the complete mission. It signals that the management is serious about Six Sigma implementation. Their responsibilities are:

- To manage Six Sigma infrastructure and resources.
- To oversee and assess the work of Master Black Belts and Black Belts.

Deployment Champions

They are devoted and committed leaders who have been picked by Executive Champions to execute Six Sigma across the organisation and collaborate with Project Champions to implement the following:

- establish the objectives and make sure they coincide with the priorities of the company.
- allocate resources to various initiatives.
- prepare and execute training plans.

This invariably requires being on the job all the time, monitoring progress, getting feedback, changing course, being flexible, and handling matters objectively.

Project Champions or Team Sponsors

Project champions or team sponsors are the process owners selected by the management to advance the following steps needed for quality assurance:

- manage, aid, and finance Six Sigma programmes.
- deliver manpower required to carry out the task.
- review progress.
- identify barriers and overcome them.

Hence, the tasks are never easy and challenges need to be faced on a daily basis.

Master Black Belts or Six Sigma Coaches

They are the consultants who train the task force of the company. A Master Black Belt (MBB) takes the lead role and acts as an advisor to senior executives and business unit managers.

It takes many years to study, practice, and get experience in projects to become a Master Black Belt. Eligible Black Belts within an organisation can be Master Black Belts, or they can be hired. They are certified Black Belts with additional specialised skills or experience. Their responsibilities are to:

- assist in identifying, prioritising, and coordinating key areas in a project in line with the strategic initiatives.
- teach the Black Belts and Green Belts the theory, tools, and methods of Six Sigma.
- mentor Black Belts and Green Belts within an organisation.
- improve the Six Sigma process of the organisation continually.
- administer Six Sigma across all processes within an organisation, including operations and transactions. Examples of departments in an organisation where Six Sigma can be applied are those dealing with human resources, manufacturing, information technology, facilities management, sales, call centres, and finance.

The role of coaches cannot be minimised, as they form the backbone of the new culture adopted by the company.

Black Belts/ Team Leaders/Project Leaders

They are full-time quality professionals who are mentored by MBB-trained people to implement Six Sigma in an organisation. They report to a manager of the organisation during their duty as Black Belt. The development of leaders and other potential employees inside the organisation is highly influenced by Black Belts' project management abilities and performance. The following are the responsibilities of the Black Belts:

- prepare and refine the project charter.
- inform the project progress to the champion.
- direct the team members of the project.
- arrange meetings.
- organise logistics.
- help members within the team
  - in the design of experiments.
  - in the analysis of the project's data requirements.
- impart training in Six Sigma tools that are used for improving processes and team activities.
- aid team members in preparing for the executive committee and champion's assessments.
- recommend projects for implementing Six Sigma based on their probability of success.
- guide and coach green belts.

Green Belt / Team Members

Green Belt-certified personnel/consultants may be other workers in the organisation who work on projects part-time to support Black Belts whenever required. In complex projects,

Green Belt works as team members and on less complicated ones, they work as the project manager. Essentially, the 'workhorses' of Six Sigma initiatives are Green Belts as they interface with the workers and managers. In a Six Sigma corporation, it is essential to have a Green Belt certification for advancement in career to senior manager. Green Belts are closely associated with the Black Belts across the different phases of the Six Sigma project for the smooth functioning and progress of the organisation. The responsibilities of the Green Belt are as follows:

- improve the project's charter.
- examine the project charter together with the initiative's champion.
- choose the project team's members.
- stay in touch with the process owner, Master Black Belt, and Black Belt throughout every stage of the project.
- be a facilitator of the team through all stages of the project.

The Six Sigma approach differs from other approaches and so everyone involved needs proper training. Six Sigma training focuses on four important phases: **measure, analyse, improve, and control.** They are necessary for boosting client satisfaction, cost savings, and a stronger bottom line. The training for Six Sigma includes lectures on statistics, quantitative benchmarking, and experiment design. It may last for four weeks and extend over a few months. The Black Belts go back to their organisation after each week of training and put into practice the knowledge they have acquired.

9.10 ADVANTAGES OF IMPLEMENTING SIX SIGMA

Motorola became the first organisation to receive the Malcolm Baldrige National Quality Award in 1988 following the adoption of Six Sigma (Pyzdek & Keller, 2010). Implementing the Six Sigma approach by management supports the organisation in two different ways. It is beneficial to the organisation as well as its stakeholders (Gitlow *et al.*, 2006). The organisation benefits as it attains a reduction of deviation and process centring to its targeted levels. The benefits of implementing Six Sigma for the organisation include the following:

- Better process flow.
- Reduction of defects.
- Improvement in communication.
- Reduced cycle times.
- Improved knowledge.
- Enhancement in customer and employee satisfaction.
- Better productivity.
- Decreased unit costs.
- Efficiency enhancement.
- Better flexibility of price.
- Improved designs.
- Shortening of time to market.

- Speedier delivery.
- Increased safety.
- Better quality.
- Decrease in cost of quality.
- Easier conversion of improvements and innovations into currency.

The benefits to stakeholders are due to the improvement in the organisation. The benefits to stakeholders include the following:

- An increase in revenue and a decrease in costs leads to more profit for shareholders.
- Customer delight due to improved quality of products and services.
- Reduced risk to stakeholders.
- Improvement in morale and satisfaction among employees.
- Suppliers are assured a secure source of business.

The advantages for companies implementing Six Sigma have been quantified by Harry & Schroeder (2000) as follows:

- An increase in margin of 20 %.
- Increase in capacity of 12–18 %.
- Reducing personnel needed by 12 %.
- Capital reduction of 10 to 30 %.

A three-sigma company should plan on switching to four-sigma in the starting year of execution by committing all its resources to Six Sigma. Companies should anticipate annual improvements of one sigma shift up to 4.7 sigma.[1] A business can reach up to 4.7 sigma level without incurring major capital costs. Experience has shown that moving from 3 to 4 to 4.7 to Six Sigma offers exponential financial benefits. Such businesses anticipate increasing their Sigma from 4.7 to 5 in the second year and from 5 to 5.1 in the third. The demands for improvements increase as businesses get closer to reaching Six Sigma. Companies encounter a 'wall' at 4.8 Sigma that necessitates 'Design for Six Sigma', or the restructuring of processes. Between a company with a three sigma level and one with a 4.8 sigma level, the profit margin increases measurably, making these businesses more profitable compared to their rivals such that they are able to pick and choose which plants, products, operations, or processes are to be enhanced to reach five Sigma or higher (Harry & Schroeder, 2000).

Most businesses operating between 3 and 4 Sigma led to a quality cost between 25–40 per cent of sales (Harry & Schroeder, 2000). By applying the 5 sigma strategy, the 5 sigma level can be reached, leading to reduced quality costs by around 10 per cent of sales. By improving Six Sigma performance, the cost of quality can be reduced to 1 per cent. But it takes a major rethink and proper implementation. The advantages claimed in terms of the quality cost by rising through the sigma levels are displayed in Table 9.8, although there is no explanation or study quoted to substantiate these claims.

---

1 4.7σ represents 6.0 defects per million opportunities before sigma shift, which is a reasonable defect level to tolerate in industrial processes.

TABLE 9.8 The cost of quality (adapted from Harry & Schroeder, 2000)

Sigma level	DPMO	Cost of Quality	Remarks
2	3,08,500	Not applicable	Normal performance
3	66,800	25–40 % of sales	–
4	6,200	15–25 % of sales	Average performer in industry
5	200	5–15 % of sales	–
6	3.4	< 1 % of sales	World-class performance

Note: An improvement of 10% in net income is claimed by each Sigma shift in this table.

9.11 PROBLEMS IN THE IMPLEMENTATION OF SIX SIGMA

The most identified problems during the execution of Six Sigma are:

- **i.** Refusal to change organisational culture.
- **ii.** A dearth of support from higher authorities and employees.
- **iii.** The increased initial investment that is required for setting up the infrastructure to successfully implement the change.
- **iv.** Execution takes more time and money in the beginning.
- **v.** Improper or incomplete training.
- **vi.** Not making the necessary tools available for implementing Six Sigma and doing nothing to change the organisational culture.
- **vii.** Selection of appropriate projects for execution. Adverse effects may result from its application to the incorrect project.
- **viii.** Lack of data and difficulty in analysing them.

It must be realised that enormous effort is necessary to implement Six Sigma throughout the company and its operations. Moreover, besides top-down directives, the entire company must have a quality focus and be conscious of quality. In fact, a case must be made that every company needs only a quality focus— the rest can follow. In addition, a quality approach is fundamental to have real pride in workmanship.

9.12 USE IN THE CONSTRUCTION INDUSTRY

The construction processes are less repetitive in nature than the production process and are an outdoor activity that is influenced by site conditions and topography. However, specific tasks such as wall construction, concreting, door and window installation, steel structure erection and cable prestressing, have repetitive activities. Since the productivity of an activity is directly influenced by process variation variables like resource availability, worker competency, etc., it is essential to pick relatively straightforward and recurring building operations when implementing the Six Sigma idea in construction projects. Determining CTQ, changing processes, simulating them[2] and verifying the models are only a few of the stages required for the systematic application of the Six Sigma approach (Han *et al.*, 2008). The construction industry does not have a systematic method for calculating the defect rate and tracking performance growth, as defects are usually corrected during the construction process, in contrast to the manufacturing industry. This results in incomplete data about the occurrence of defects during the construction process, which is required to improve performance and processes at the construction site. The Six Sigma concept can offer greater benefits in preserving a high standard of work by controlling numerous factors, such as safety, quality, cost, or time in various circumstances and among different project stakeholders.

When Six Sigma started being used in the construction industry, it was primarily concerned with construction materials, health and safety and had ignored the importance of management in the successful completion of the project (Sullivan, 2011). It is challenging to deploy Six Sigma in the construction industry because this industry lacks a well-defined technique for determining defects' occurrence rate and assessing performance after defects have been removed. For deploying Six Sigma in construction, the tasks are to be broken down into smaller chunks, which can be redesigned and enhanced. Using the DMAIC model, methods can be structured to improve the processes involved in construction. DMAIC may be used for detecting defects in construction and eliminating them. The improvement process will advance using a sound statistically based data analysis to comprehend 'cause-effect' linkages of problems (Mudholkar, 2008). As process changes are not always simple to implement, Champions occasionally need to take active measures to eliminate obstacles.

One of the biggest problems in the construction industry is the delay in completing projects. By suitably tailoring the Six Sigma model, it can be used to analyse the areas where improvement can be made to prevent delays. In the 'define' stage, identify the opportunity for process improvement. For instance, let us consider the problem of delay in the completion of construction work. After finding out the problem and selecting it, determine the extent of the problem if it is found suitable for Six Sigma implementation. Then, it is necessary to find out the people associated with it. Measure the process's present status and compare it with the requirements during the measurement stage. In a construction project, the baseline schedule may be taken as the benchmark. It is to be compared with the actual progress. During analysis, find out the primary causes of delay. Identify the construction activities where delays are occurring. Using statistical methods or other suitable methodologies like a fishbone diagram, analyse the root cause of delays in schedule. In the improvement stage, generate solutions that may be used to bring the project back to schedule. It may be by training the staff to improve their efficiency and thus enhance the speed of construction, using better technology to do the task, or using any method found suitable to resolve the issue. Execute the solution if it is found to be effective. Finally, in the control stage, suitable measures can be adopted to sustain the benefit. In case the solution is not successful in the long run, then measure the performance again and continue with the subsequent phases of analysis, improvement, and control.

Six Sigma may be implemented in the construction industry effectively when precast and prefabrication technologies are adopted since the chances for variabilities are comparatively

[2] Process simulation models are a different topic all by themselves. Refer Halpin, D. and Riggs, L., Planning and Analysis of Construction Operations, John Wiley & Sons, NJ, 1992.

low. The defects can be well captured in those methods, as most work happens in factories. There is always a need to improve the processes when using these technologies, as errors during fabrication can culminate in defects during their assembly.

Six Sigma can be utilised in the construction industry to reduce delays, improve quality, increase productivity, improve safety in the workplace, reduce labour costs by removing redundant processes, and develop well-defined processes for all activities.

CONCLUSION

In the construction industry, conformance to specifications is mostly determined by inspection and testing. Visual inspection with the aid of measuring devices is often adopted to determine the quality of workmanship and materials and destructive tests are done mainly to inspect the material quality. Testing all the materials for conformance is not feasible as the tests done are destructive. Hence, it is advisable to do acceptance sampling of materials to determine their quality. The probability of acceptance of the lot can be determined by developing an operating characteristic curve. OCC determines the probability of acceptance of variations or defects from the targeted value.

Six Sigma is a strategy to improve quality as it presents methods to enhance the processes so that defects or variations are reduced significantly. All businesses, including the construction industry, can use Six Sigma. A major challenge in implementing is the uniqueness of construction projects. Since the activities and resources vary with projects, the Six Sigma application requires constant tailoring to suit the needs. In the construction industry, it can help to improve processes that enable the completion of projects within the triple constraints of quality, cost, and time. It requires a thorough knowledge of the construction processes and statistical tools. Extensive training is required to equip personnel to implement Six Sigma. To succeed in implementing Six Sigma in an organisation, there should be a desire to acknowledge the change. The emphasis should shift from people and numbers to process and quality (Mudholkar, 2008). And most importantly, for staff to learn Six Sigma organisational skills, top management support is inevitable. These abilities will lead to short-term project gains as well as long-term quality and financial gains.

WORKS CITED

Anbari, F. T. (2002), 'Six sigma method and its applications in project management', *Proceedings of the Project Management Institute Annual Seminars and Symposium [CD], San Antonio, Texas.* (Newtown Square, PA: Project Management Institute).

Bertels, T. (2003), *Rath and Strong's Six Sigma Leadership Handbook.* (New Jersey: John Wiley & Sons, Inc).

Coronado, R. B., & Antony, J. (2002), 'Critical success factors for the successful implementation of six sigma projects in organisations'. *The TQM Magazine, 14*(2), 92–99.

Gitlow, H. S., Levine, D. M., & Popovich, E. A. (2006), *Design for Six Sigma for Green Belts and Champions.* (New Jersey: Pearson Prentice Hall).

Han, S. H., Chae, M. J., Im, K. S., & Ryu, H. D. (2008), 'Six Sigma-based approach to improve performance in construction operations'. *Journal of Management in Engineering*, 21–31.

Harry, M., & Schroeder, R. (2000), *Six Sigma: The Breakthrough Management Strategy Revolutionizing the World's Top Corporations.* (United States of America: Currency Book).

Kwak, Y. H., & Anbari, F. T. (2006), 'Benefits, obstacles, and future of six sigma approach', *Technovation*, 708–715.

Mitra, A. (2016), *Fundamentals of Quality Control and Improvement.* (United States of America: Wiley).

Mudholkar, V. V. (2008), 'Six-Sigma: Delivering quality to mega transportation projects', *Proceedings of Transportation and Development Innovative Best Practices 2008.* (New Jersey: ASCE).

Pheng, L. S., & Hui, M. S. (2004), 'Implementing and applying Six Sigma in construction', *Journal of Construction Engineering and Management*, 482–489.

Pyzdek, T., & Keller, P. A. (2010), *The Six Sigma Handbook: A Complete Guide for Green Belts, Black Belts, and Managers at All Levels.* (U.S.A: McGraw-Hill).

Raisinghani, M. S. (2005), 'Six Sigma: concepts, tools, and applications', *Industrial Management & Data Systems*, 491–505.

Schilling, E. G., & Neubauer, D. (2017), *Acceptance Sampling in Quality Control.* (Boca Raton: CRC Press).

Snee, R. D. (1999, September), 'Why should statisticians pay attention to Six Sigma? An examination for their role in the Six Sigma methodology', *Quality Progress*, pp. 100–103.

Stewart , R., & Spencer, C. (2006), 'Six-sigma as a strategy for process improvement on construction projects: a case study', *Construction Management and Economics, 24*, 339–348. doi:10.1080/01446190500521082

Sullivan, K. T. (2011), 'Quality management programs in the construction industry: Best value compared with other methodologies', *Journal of Management in Engineering*, 210–219.

REVIEW QUESTIONS

Multiple Choice Questions

1. How is the 'mean' calculated for a set of values?

(a) Sum of all values divided by the number of values

(b) Square root of the sum of squared deviations

(c) Difference between each value and the mean

(d) Mean squared deviation

2. What does a lower standard deviation indicate?

(a) Higher risk (b) Closer values to the mean

(c) Greater dispersion of values (d) Larger spread

3. What is the main difference between descriptive statistics and inferential statistics?
   (a) Descriptive statistics focus on the entire dataset, while inferential statistics analyse a subset.
   (b) Descriptive statistics study characteristics of data, while inferential statistics draw conclusions about the entire dataset from a sample.
   (c) Descriptive statistics analyse a sample, while inferential statistics analyse the entire population.
   (d) Descriptive statistics measure parameters, while inferential statistics measure statistics.
4. What term is used for the totality of the dataset in statistics?
   (a) Population (b) Sample
   (c) Parameter (d) Statistic
5. What is the formula for the standard error of the sample mean?
   (a) Standard Error = $\sigma/\sqrt{n}$ (b) Standard Error = σ/n
   (c) Standard Error = $s/\sqrt{n}$ (d) Standard Error = s/n
6. What does the variance of the sample statistic mean represent?
   (a) Variability of the sample means from the parameter
   (b) Variability of the sample standard deviation
   (c) Variability of the sample variance
   (d) Variability of the sample size
7. What percentage of values in a normal distribution are typically within one standard deviation from the mean?
   (a) Approximately 34.13% (b) Approximately 50%
   (c) Approximately 68.26% (d) Approximately 95.44%
8. How is the area within the normal curve typically calculated?
   (a) Using the formula $z = ((x - \mu))/\sigma$
   (b) By integrating the probability density function
   (c) By subtracting the mean from each data point
   (d) Using the variance of the dataset
9. What is the standard normal random variable?
   (a) A random variable with a mean of 0 and a variance of 1
   (b) A random variable with a mean of 1 and a variance of 0
   (c) A random variable with a mean of 1 and a variance of 1
   (d) A random variable with a mean of 0 and a variance of 0

10. What does the z value indicate in the standard normal distribution?

(a) The number of standard deviations the observed statistic is from the mean

(b) The probability of observing a specific value

(c) The variance of the dataset

(d) The mean of the dataset

11. What is the characteristic shape of the normal distribution curve?

(a) Bell-shaped and asymmetric

(b) Bell-shaped and symmetric

(c) Skewed to the right

(d) Skewed to the left

12. What percentage of values in a normal distribution are typically within three standard deviations from the mean?

(a) Approximately 68.26% (b) Approximately 95.44%

(c) Approximately 99.74% (d) Approximately 99.99%

13. How does standard deviation affect the shape of the normal distribution curve?

(a) Higher standard deviation makes the curve narrower.

(b) Higher standard deviation makes the curve wider.

(c) Standard deviation has no effect on the shape of the curve.

(d) Standard deviation determines the mean of the curve.

14. In a normal distribution, what does it mean if a value has a z-score of -2?

(a) The value is two standard deviations above the mean.

(b) The value is two standard deviations below the mean.

(c) The value is equal to the mean.

(d) The value is one standard deviation above the mean.

15. What is Type I error in hypothesis testing?

(a) Rejecting the null hypothesis when it is true

(b) Accepting the null hypothesis when it is true

(c) Rejecting the alternative hypothesis when it is true

(d) Accepting the alternative hypothesis when it is true

16. What is Type II error in hypothesis testing?

(a) Accepting the null hypothesis when it is true

(b) Rejecting the null hypothesis when it is false

(c) Rejecting the alternative hypothesis when it is true

(d) Accepting the null hypothesis when it is false

17. If the level of significance is 0.05, what is the probability of committing Type I error?
    (a) 0.05 (b) 0.10
    (c) 0.95 (d) 0.90
18. What is the level of significance of a test?
    (a) The probability of committing Type II error
    (b) When an inference is made from sample testing that the process is in control when it is actually out of control
    (c) When an inference is made from sample testing that the process is out of control when it is actually in control
    (d) The probability of rejecting the alternative hypothesis when it is true
19. What does the OC curve plot?
    (a) The probability of rejecting the null hypothesis against different sample sizes
    (b) The probability of acceptance of hypotheses for different possible values
    (c) The probability of Type I error against different levels of significance
    (d) The probability of Type II error against different levels of significance
20. What is the main purpose of the OC curve?
    (a) To determine the critical value for hypothesis testing
    (b) To determine the probability of acceptance of variations or defects from the targeted value
    (c) To plot the standard deviation of a sample
    (d) To show the probability of rejecting a true hypothesis
21. How can a company choose a desirable OC curve?
    (a) By changing the sample size
    (b) By changing the significance level
    (c) By modifying the process
    (d) By modifying the null hypothesis
22. What happens to the probability of acceptance as the departure from the standard mean becomes larger in either direction, according to the OC curve?
    (a) The probability of acceptance increases
    (b) The probability of acceptance remains the same
    (c) The probability of acceptance becomes smaller
    (d) The probability of Type I error decreases
23. What is the primary goal of Six Sigma (6σ)?
    (a) To increase the number of variations in a process
    (b) To enhance quality by minimising the number of variations

(c) To reduce the cost of production

(d) To improve employee productivity

24. What is the area outside of Six Sigma from the mean position in parts per million (ppm) when there is no sigma shift?

(a) 3,17,400 ppm (b) 31.74 ppm

(c) 0.002 ppm (d) 3.4 ppm

25. From the z-table, what is the area within the curve on both sides of the mean for $z = 1$?

(a) 0.3413 (b) 0.6826

(c) 0.3174 (d) 1.0000

26. How many defects per million opportunities (DPMO) are targeted in Six Sigma?

(a) 3,17,400 (b) 66,800

(c) 3.4 (d) 0.002

27. How does Six Sigma benefit customers and employees?

(a) By reducing product prices

(b) By creating a business process and management system that satisfies both

(c) By limiting customer service interactions

(d) By increasing marketing efforts

28. Which methods are mentioned as a tool used by Six Sigma?

(a) Cause-and-effect method and process maps

(b) Pareto analysis and run charts

(c) Brainstorming and benchmarking

(d) All of these

29. What are the 'Voice of the Customer' (VoC) and 'Voice of the Process' (VoP) in Six Sigma terminology?

(a) VoC refers to internal processes, and VoP refers to customer expectations.

(b) VoC refers to customer requirements and expectations, and VoP refers to the distribution of process outputs.

(c) VoC refers to the statistical analysis of data, and VoP refers to performance measurements.

(d) VoC and VoP are both terms used for process improvement tools.

30. Which model is most commonly used for implementing Six Sigma in process improvement?

(a) DMADV (b) DMAIC

(c) PDSA (d) SIPOC

31. In the "Measure" phase of DMAIC, what is the primary goal?
    (a) To identify and define project goals
    (b) To measure the performance of current processes
    (c) To generate and test potential solutions
    (d) To sustain and monitor improvements
32. What is the main purpose of the 'Control' phase in DMAIC?
    (a) To define project goals
    (b) To measure performance
    (c) To sustain and monitor the improvements made
    (d) To develop and test potential solutions
33. What is the primary focus of the DMADV model?
    (a) Improving existing processes
    (b) Developing new products, processes, or services
    (c) Measuring current process performance
    (d) Analysing existing customer feedback
34. What is a SIPOC analysis used for in the DMAIC model?
    (a) To develop potential solutions
    (b) To identify Critical to Quality (CTQ) characteristics
    (c) To measure process performance
    (d) To control and monitor process improvements
35. What is the purpose of the 'Verify/Validate' phase in DMADV?
    (a) To generate design alternatives
    (b) To finalise specifications
    (c) To confirm that the design meets specifications and requirements
    (d) To measure current process performance
36. According to Six Sigma principles, what should be the focus whenever defects or variations are detected?
    (a) Increasing production speed
    (b) Enhancing customer service
    (c) Process improvement
    (d) Marketing strategies
37. What is necessary for an organisation to reap the benefits of Six Sigma?
    (a) Focusing on individual departments
    (b) Top-down implementation across the entire company

(c) Limiting changes to specific projects

(d) Reducing the scope of Six Sigma to quality control

38. Which of the following tools is used in the 'improve' phase of Six Sigma?

(a) Hypothesis tests (b) Run charts

(c) Kanban (d) Affinity diagram

39. Which of the following is NOT an essential activity for successfully implementing Six Sigma?

(a) Leadership development

(b) Communication among management levels

(c) System to collect feedback from stakeholders

(d) Increasing the number of product inspections

40. What significant advantage does Six Sigma provide for stakeholders?

(a) Increased cycle times

(b) Improvement in employee morale and satisfaction

(c) Higher costs

(d) Decreased revenue

41. Which position is considered the 'workhorse' of Six Sigma initiatives?

(a) Black Belts

(a) Executive Champions

(c) Green Belts

(d) Deployment Champions

42. How can Six Sigma contribute to improving safety in the construction workplace?

(a) By increasing the number of workers on site

(b) By developing well-defined processes for all activities

(c) By reducing the amount of training for staff

(d) By ignoring environmental factors

43. Which of the following is a primary focus when tailoring the Six Sigma model to the construction industry to prevent project delays?

(a) Setting higher project budgets

(b) Identifying and selecting the most important clients

(c) Analysing areas where improvements can be made

(d) Increasing the complexity of the project design

44. Which tool can be used during the 'analyse' phase of DMAIC to identify the root cause of delays in construction projects?

(a) Run charts
(b) Fishbone diagram
(c) Project charter
(d) Affinity diagram

45. What is a critical benefit of implementing Six Sigma in the construction industry?
(a) Increasing project costs
(b) Reducing project completion time
(c) Decreasing project quality
(d) Increasing redundancy in processes

Short Answer Type Questions

1. What do you understand by mean, deviation, and variance?
2. The failure loads of ten concrete solid block samples are 50 t, 60 t, 70 t, 80 t, 90 t, 100 t, 70 t, 80 t, 60 t, and 90 t. Calculate the mean failure load and standard deviation.
3. What is the difference between statistics and parameters?
4. What do you understand by normal distribution and what is the shape of the normal distribution curve?
5. What is acceptance sampling? Write the four possibilities of decision making.
6. What is the Six Sigma concept, and how is it helpful in reducing defects in processes?
7. What are VoC and VoP?
8. What are the types of Six Sigma Models? Briefly explain each.
9. What are the principles governing Six Sigma?
10. What are the responsibilities of Executive Leadership while implementing Six Sigma?
11. What are the responsibilities of Executive Champions while implementing Six Sigma?
12. What are the responsibilities of Master Six Sigma coaches while implementing Six Sigma, and what is its other name?
13. What are the responsibilities of Black Belts while implementing Six Sigma?
14. Why is Six Sigma difficult to implement in the construction industry?
15. Distinguish between DMAIC and DMADV.

Long Answer Type Questions

1. Sketch the Bell Curve with proper labelling. Write down the characteristics of the bell curve obtained from normal distribution.
2. Write down the significance of Six Sigma and its application in the construction industry.
3. Explain in detail the types of Six Sigma models giving an explanation of each stage.

4. What are the various Six Sigma tools used in different phases of Six Sigma implementation?
5. Write down the steps involved in implementing Six Sigma.
6. What are the activities and systems required for the successful implementation of Six Sigma?
7. Explain in detail the roles and responsibilities of various team members while implementing Six Sigma.
8. How is Six Sigma implementation beneficial to both organisations and stakeholders?
9. Write down the stages for addressing the delays in construction delays.
10. What are the problems in the implementation of Six Sigma?

ANSWER KEYS

Multiple Choice Questions

1. (a)	**2.** (b)	**3.** (b)	**4.** (a)	**5.** (a)	**6.** (a)	**7.** (c)	**8.** (b)
9. (a)	**10.** (a)	**11.** (b)	**12.** (c)	**13.** (b)	**14.** (b)	**15.** (a)	**16.** (d)
17. (a)	**18.** (c)	**19.** (b)	**20.** (b)	**21.** (a)	**22.** (c)	**23.** (b)	**24.** (c)
25. (b)	**26.** (c)	**27.** (b)	**28.** (d)	**29.** (b)	**30.** (b)	**31.** (b)	**32.** (c)
33. (b)	**34.** (b)	**35.** (c)	**36.** (c)	**37.** (b)	**38.** (c)	**39.** (d)	**40.** (b)
41. (c)	**42.** (b)	**43.** (c)	**44.** (b)	**45.** (b)			

CHAPTER

10 Quality Control Tools

10.1 INTRODUCTION

In the previous chapters, we discussed about various quality control tools that are required to measure the quality of products, services, processes, and other deliverables during and after manufacturing or construction. This chapter explains in detail some of those tools and practices. Since the introduction of the concept of statistical quality control by Shewhart, several industries started to implement these tools for quality improvement. Later, as quality gained prominence across the world with rising competition among the nations, more research began to be done in this field. A few significant philosophies and practices that gained momentum have been discussed in the previous chapters. There are yet other practices that many organisations follow to attain quality and improve their performance. And many of these practices utilise statistical tools for quality management.

10.2 TOOLS FOR STATISTICAL QUALITY CONTROL

Seven basic statistical quality control tools are commonly used to analyse data regarding the quality of deliverables. Also known as the 'The Old Seven', they are listed below:

(i) Cause and effect diagram.
(ii) Control chart.
(iii) Pareto chart.
(iv) Histogram.
(v) Check sheet.
(vi) Scatter diagram.
(vii) Stratification.

They have significant applications in quality management in the manufacturing industry and a few of them in the construction sector as well. They are discussed briefly in the following paragraphs.

10.2.1 Cause and Effect Diagram

It is also called the Ishikawa diagram, as it was developed in 1943 by Kaoru Ishikawa. Since it resembles a fishbone in shape, it is often referred to as the fishbone diagram and is used to determine the causes of a problem or an effect. It is also used to sort ideas into various categories, thus helping to determine the one with the greatest impact. The causes of a process becoming out of control can be determined with the help of a fishbone diagram. As such, it aids management in determining which factors require further examination to improve the process. It is a useful technique for mapping the inputs that affect quality. The tip of the horizontal arrow, or the head of the fish, represents the problem to be investigated. Then, the major causes identified are shown by labelled primary arrows merging into the horizontal arrow. The major causes can be subdivided into sub-causes and represented by smaller arrows pointing towards primary arrows. The causes are listed on the left side of the chart, and on the right side, the problem is stated. The following are the main uses of fishbone diagrams (Mitra, 2016):

- **Cause enumeration:** The process of creating a list of all potential causes is known as cause enumeration. This list demonstrates how each cause impacts the problems (or effects) under consideration. This diagram is an illustration of the causes affecting a process, and the figure is developed by sorting out the causes and relating them to the effect. Every problem is likely to be caused by several categories of causes. It can be used to analyse the causes of poor quality of construction, delays in the completion of projects, and many others. The causes of these issues can be categorised under management, people, equipment, site conditions, material, money, and others.
- **Dispersion analysis:** The major causes are analysed in detail by investigating their sub-causes and their effects on the quality feature (or effect/problem). Each significant reason/cause goes through this procedure on a priority basis. The fishbone diagram helps to identify the reasons for variations and dispersions. It can be used to identify the reasons for construction defects/delays. Each major contributing factor to a problem is subdivided into sub-causes and studied. Thus, it will help find out the exact cause of a problem and the required rectification process.
- **Process analysis:** For process analysis, Ishikawa diagrams are created to enumerate the reasons of the problems in the sequence in which activities are performed. It can be used to perform delay analysis in construction projects.

The construction of a fishbone diagram involves the following steps:

- Identify the problem that needs to be addressed.
- Determine the causes of the problem by:
  (i) examining the processes carefully,
  (ii) using check sheets, and
  (iii) brainstorming techniques.
- Develop the fishbone diagram by placing the effect or the problem statement on the right side, in the head of the fishbone diagram.
- Draw the arrows on the left side representing the fishbone.

- Properly place the different categories of causes identified through the above techniques in the major arrows drawn to meet the horizontal arrow. The sub-categories of causes that lead to the problems are placed in the smaller bones.
- Interpret the data after determining the frequency of occurrence of causes.
- Reach a consensus by discussing the causes that require immediate rectification with the team members.

A fishbone diagram can be used in the construction industry to analyse the causes of problems. Let us consider an example to illustrate the construction of a fishbone diagram. Delays in timely completion of projects are prevalent in the construction industry. Figure 10.1 depicts the various causes for delay in a construction project using a fishbone diagram. The issue that needs to be examined is the delay in project completion, as shown in the fish's head. The branches that emerge from the main arrow display the major categories. Under numerous

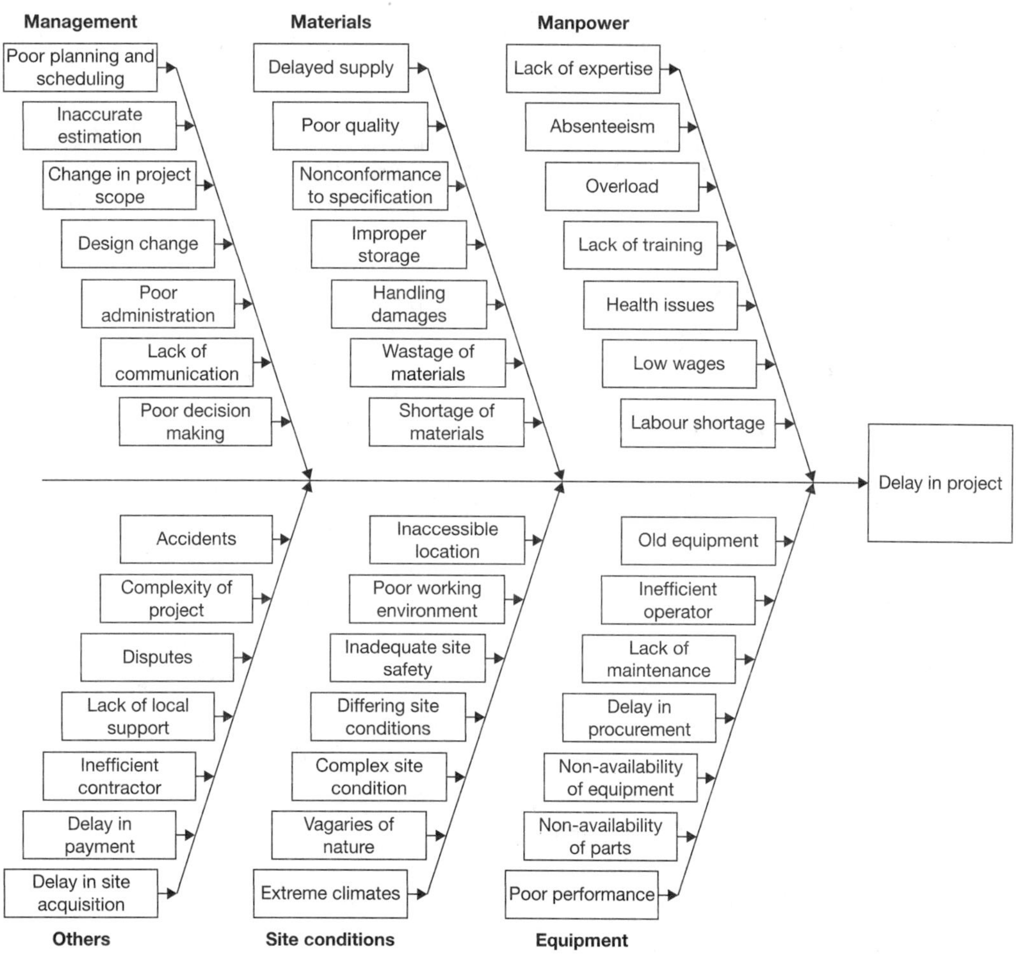

FIGURE 10.1 Fishbone diagram showing the causes of construction project delay

headings, such as management, labour, material, site conditions, equipment, and others, the reasons for the delay are enumerated in the smaller bones. By determining the intensity and frequency of various contributing factors, measures can be taken to solve the problems on a priority basis (See Singh 2017, Chapter 4). When examining causes, look for deviations that have occurred from the standards. An effort must always be made to correct the root causes of a problem and not the symptoms of the effect, as in the medical field, since it prevents the recurrence of the problem.

10.2.2 Control Chart

It is a chart that illustrates how the outcomes of a process change with time. Simple run charts plot data versus time and they are the most widely used control charts. A simple run chart showing the variations in cement price over a certain period is shown in Figure 10.2. For instance, it can be observed that between 2015 and 2017, there has been an increase, however, there was a sudden drop in the year 2018, but thereafter, year after year, the cement prices have increased. But control charts are of different types, though they follow from run charts. They can be used to represent the attributes as well as variables. Attributes are qualitative, and variables are quantitative quality characteristics. The control charts used for representing variables are the mean (x) and range (R) charts. On the other hand, the number of defective or *np* charts and the proportion of defective or p charts are used to present attributes. Many other charts, such as moving-average charts and charts for the cumulative sum (cusum), are also used for process control. These later ones are potent management tools that can be used for the identification of trends or modifications in characteristics and variable data. Even though it is more time-consuming to create a cusum chart than a typical control chart, it provides more data about a process. Cusum chart is used to control variables and attributes since it quickly detects slight changes in data.

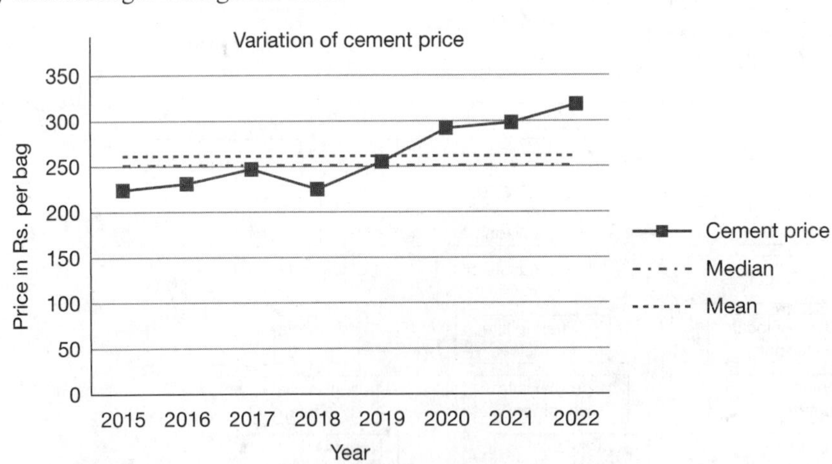

FIGURE 10.2 Simple run chart showing variations in cement price per bag from 2015 to 2022 (Jaganmohan, 2024)

A control chart will have a central line, which shows the mean, and an upper line, and a lower line representing the upper control limit and the lower control limit, respectively. The limits are determined by running a process in standard conditions, collecting samples, and inserting the mean and standard deviations into the suitable formula. Control limits set based on the process performance during a certain duration are used to fix the boundaries for variations within a process under normal operating conditions.

Variable control charts are used when quantitative measurement units of samples such as height, mass, and duration are considered. To determine the control limits in a variable control chart ($\bar{x}$-R chart), follow the steps given below:

- Calculate the mean $\bar{x}$ and range R of all subgroups

$$\bar{x} = \frac{x_1 + x_2 + \ldots\ldots + x_n}{n}$$

$$R = x_{max} - x_{min}$$

Where

n = number of samples in a subgroup

- Calculate the process mean and average range of the process.

$$\bar{\bar{x}} = \frac{\bar{x}_1 + \bar{x}_2 + \ldots\ldots + \bar{x}_k}{k}$$

Where

k = number of subgroups

$\bar{x}_1, \bar{x}_2, \ldots$ are the means of subgroups

$$\bar{R} = \frac{R_1 + R_2 + \ldots\ldots + R_k}{k}$$

Where

$R_1, R_2, \ldots.$ are the ranges of subgroups

- Calculate the upper and lower control limits

$$\text{Upper control limit of mean} = \text{UCL}_{\bar{x}} = \bar{\bar{x}} + A_2\bar{R}$$

$$\text{Lower control limit of mean} = \text{LCL}_{\bar{x}} = \bar{\bar{x}} - A_2\bar{R}$$

$$\text{Upper control limit of range} = \text{UCL}_R = D_4\bar{R}$$

$$\text{Lower control limit of range} = \text{LCL}_R = D_3\bar{R}$$

A_2, D_3, and D_4, developed by industrial engineers, are given in Table 10.1.

To illustrate the construction of a control chart for variables, let us consider the following example. A manufacturer producing waterproofing chemicals packs them in plastic bags. The weight of each packed bag is specified to be 1,000 ± 3 g. Five samples from ten subgroups have been collected for inspection. The details of the samples are given in Table 10.2.

The upper and lower limits of mean and range for a sample size n = 5 and subgroups k = 10 are calculated as shown below:

TABLE 10.1 Factors for $\bar{x}$ and R chart

Number of observations in subgroup (n)	Factors for x chart	Factors for R chart	
	A_2	Lower D_3	Upper D_4
2	1.880	0	3.268
3	1.023	0	2.574
4	0.729	0	2.282
5	0.577	0	2.114
6	0.483	0	2.004
7	0.419	0.076	1.924
8	0.373	0.136	1.864
9	0.337	0.184	1.816
10	0.308	0.223	1.777

TABLE 10.2 Details of samples collected

	Subgroups									
Sample	**8:00 am**	**9:00 am**	**10:00 am**	**11:00 am**	**12:00 am**	**2:00 pm**	**3:00 pm**	**4:00 pm**	**5:00 pm**	**6:00 pm**
1	1,002	1,001	1,002	1,002.5	1,003.5	1,001	1,000	1,000.5	1,002.5	1,003
2	1,001	1,002	999	1,004	1,002.5	1,001.5	1,000.5	1,000	1,0001	1,003
3	997	1,002	1,002.5	1,001.5	1,003	1,000.5	999.5	1,000.5	1,000	1,001
4	1,002.5	999	998.5	1,000	1,000	1,001	999	998.5	1,001	998
5	998	998.5	997	1,000	999.5	1,000	1,001	999	1,003	997
Sum	5,000.5	5,002.5	4,999	5,008	5,008.5	5,004	5,000	4,998.5	5,007.5	5,002
Average	1,000.1	1,000.5	999.8	1,001.6	1,001.7	1,000.8	1,000	999.7	1,001.5	1,000.4
Range	5.5	3.5	5.5	4	4	1.5	2	2	3	6

$$\bar{\bar{x}} = \frac{(1{,}000.1 + 1{,}000.5 + 999.8 + \ldots + 1{,}000.4)}{10} = 1{,}000.61$$

$$\bar{R} = \frac{5.5 + 3.5 + 5.5 + \ldots + 6}{10} = 3.7$$

$$\text{UCL}_{\bar{x}} = \bar{\bar{x}} + A_2\bar{R} = 1{,}000.61 + (0.577 \times 3.7) = 1{,}002.745$$

$$\text{LCL}_{\bar{x}} = \bar{\bar{x}} - A_2\bar{R} = 1{,}000.61 - (0.577 \times 3.7) = 998.475$$

Where the A_2 value is taken from Table 10.1, corresponding to $n = 5$.

$$\text{UCL}_{\text{R}} = D_4\bar{R} = 2.114 \times 3.7 = 7.82$$

$$\text{LCL}_{\text{R}} = D_3\bar{R} = 0 \times 3.7 = 0$$

Where the D_4 and D_3 values are taken from Table 10.1, corresponding to $n = 5$.

Figures 10.3 and 10.4 show the control chart for mean and range, respectively. The mean, range, upper and lower control limits of mean and range have been marked in these charts. The data of various subgroups have been plotted on the control chart. It is observed from Figure 10.3 that the means of 5 samples collected for 10 subgroups fall between the UCL and LCL, and hence, the process is in control on this account. From Figure 10.4, it can be noted that ranges of subgroups also fall within the upper and lower control limit for ranges, and hence the process is in control.

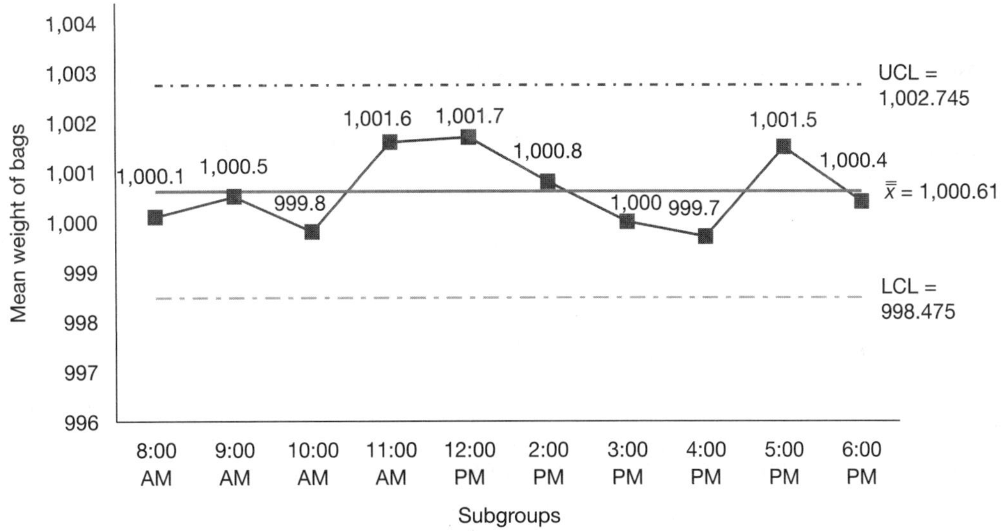

FIGURE 10.3 Control chart for mean

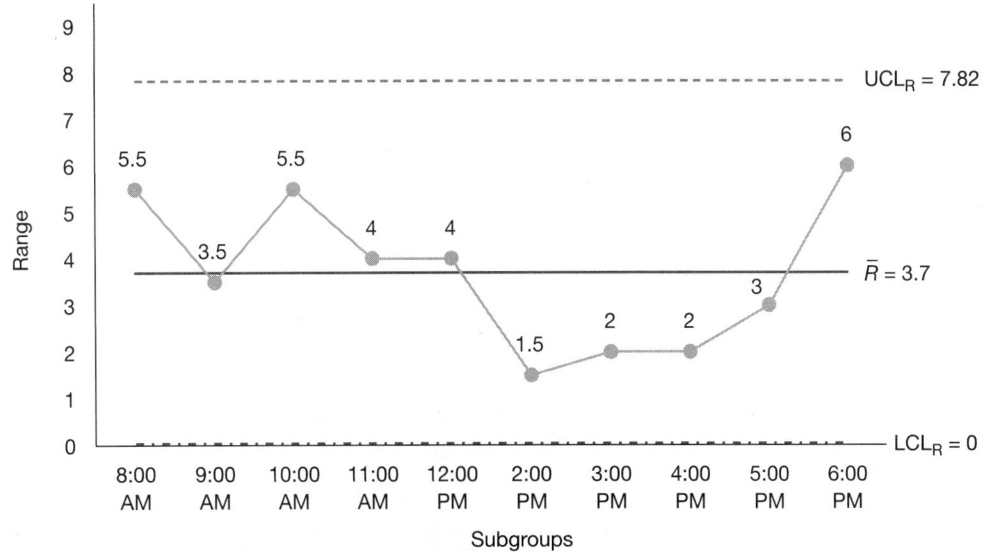

FIGURE 10.4 Control chart for range

When a qualitative characteristic such as defective/non-defective is reflected in the sample, attribute control charts are used. The steps for determining upper and lower control limits in various attribute control charts are given below:

$$p = \frac{\text{Number of rejections in subgroups}}{\text{Number inspected in subgroup}}$$

$$\bar{p} = \frac{\text{Total number of rejections}}{\text{Total number inspected}}$$

The proportion defective (*p*-chart):

$$\text{UCL}_p = \bar{p} + \frac{3\sqrt{\bar{p}(1-\bar{p})}}{\sqrt{n}}$$

$$LCL_p = \bar{p} - \frac{3\sqrt{\bar{p}(1-\bar{p})}}{\sqrt{n}}$$

The number proportion defective (*np*-chart):

$$\text{UCL}_{np} = n\bar{p} + 3\sqrt{n\bar{p}(1-\bar{p})}$$

$$\text{LCL}_{np} = n\bar{p} - 3\sqrt{n\bar{p}(1-\bar{p})}$$

The number of nonconformities with a constant sample size (*c* chart):

$$\bar{c} = \frac{\text{Total nonconformities}}{\text{Number of subgroups}}$$

$$\text{UCL}_c = \bar{c} + 3\sqrt{\bar{c}}$$

$$\text{LCL}_c = \bar{c} - 3\sqrt{\bar{c}}$$

The number of nonconformities with varying sample sizes (*u* chart):

$$\bar{u} = \frac{\text{Total nonconformities}}{\text{Total units inspected}}$$

$$\text{UCL}_u = \bar{u} + \frac{3\sqrt{\bar{u}}}{\sqrt{n}}$$

$$\text{LCL}_u = \bar{u} - \frac{3\sqrt{\bar{u}}}{\sqrt{n}}$$

Now, let us construct a control chart for the attributes. Here, the attribute chosen is the proportion nonconforming. From 10 subgroups, the weights of 100 bags of waterproofing chemicals were taken. Table 10.3 shows the details of the data collected.

$$\bar{p} = \frac{\text{Total number of rejections}}{\text{Total number inspected}} = \frac{49}{1{,}000} = 0.049$$

$$UCL_p = 0.049 + \frac{3\sqrt{0.049(1-0.049)}}{\sqrt{100}} = 0.114$$

$$LCL_p = 0.049 - \frac{3\sqrt{0.049(1-0.049)}}{\sqrt{100}} = -0.015 = 0^1$$

TABLE 10.3 Details of nonconforming (NC) bags

	Subgroups										
	1	**2**	**3**	**4**	**5**	**6**	**7**	**8**	**9**	**10**	**Total**
Sample size	100	100	100	100	100	100	100	100	100	100	1,000
Number of NC items	2	5	3	7	5	10	4	5	2	6	49
Proportion NC	0.02	0.05	0.03	0.07	0.05	0.1	0.04	0.05	0.02	0.06	0.049

Figure 10.5 illustrates the control chart for variables. Any data can be compared with these control lines to check whether they are within the limits or not. In other words, the process can be verified whether it is in control or out of control. The variations may be caused by external factors or inherent factors within the system. The locations of points in a control chart can be used to identify the reasons for variations. The different positions of the points within the limits indicate the natural variations that are inherent to the process, and they are commonly known to be the **common causes** within the system that cause a process to behave the way it does. These common causes may be due to situations such as irregularity in working conditions or system maintenance. A process is said to be in statistical control when it operates under variations only due to common causes. The occurrence of points outside the limit indicates the

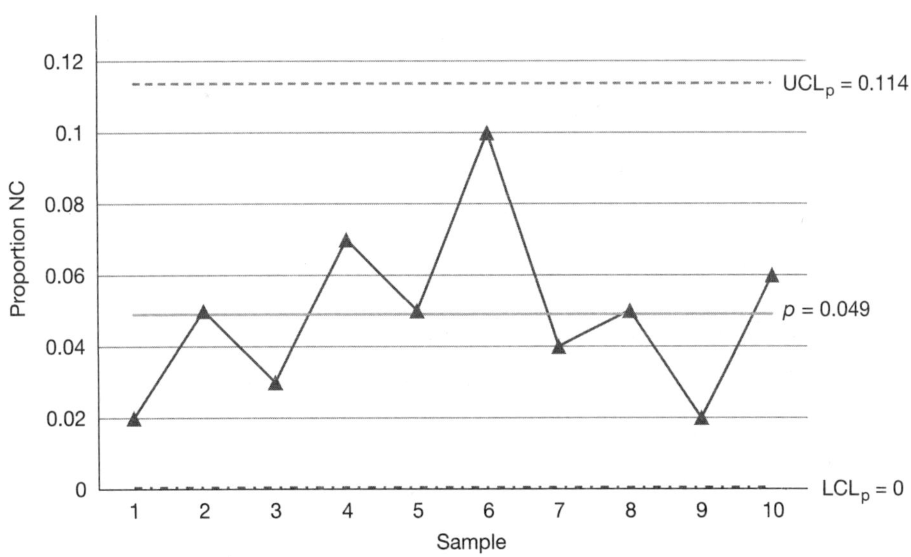

FIGURE 10.5 Control chart for attributes

[1] Since the value of number proportion defectives cannot be negative, LCLp is taken as zero.

special cause variations. It may be due to the presence of external factors such as unplanned events, equipment malfunction, improper measurements, and operator errors. It is necessary to urgently eliminate the special causes and bring the process to control before reusing the control charts for monitoring purposes, as these are not part of the designed process.

Control charts indicate the consistency of the process, and being in control does not mean that the deliverables of the process would meet the client's needs or specifications. Control limits and specification limits are different from each other. Control limits set the allowable variations in a process. However, specification limits are fixed based on the client's needs or industry standards. It defines the acceptable tolerance limits for the quality characteristics of a product or service. Control charts help track the performance of the processes and identify patterns and trends of variations. These are effective tools that management utilises to track their processes. Management must try to reduce the natural variations within the control limits. It is not enough for a process to be in control. It has also to be capable of meeting the customer's needs.

Interpreting Control Charts ('The Memory Jogger', 1994):

'The process is said to be "out of control" when:

1. One or more points fall outside of the control limits as shown in Figure 10.6.

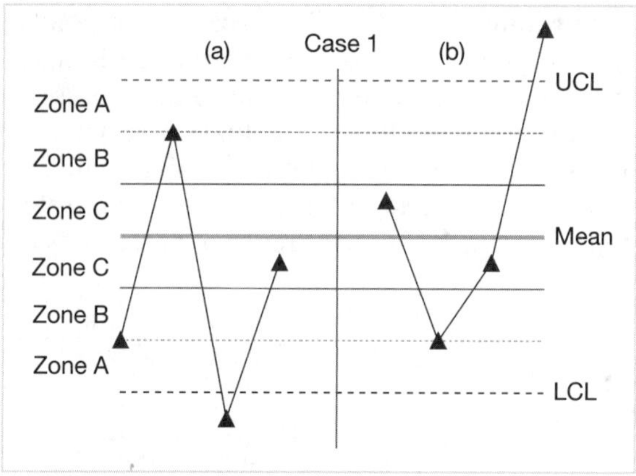

FIGURE 10.6 Control chart - Case 1

Or:

2. The control chart is divided into zones as shown in Figure 10.7, and the following situations illustrated in Figure 10.8 are encountered:
   a) There are fifteen points in a row within Zone C (above and below centreline).
   b) There are fourteen points, in a row alternating up and down.
   c) Nine successive points are on one side of the centreline.
   d) Six consecutive points in increasing or decreasing order.
   e) Four points, out of five successive points, are on the same side of the centerline in Zone B or beyond.
   f) Two points, out of three successive points, are on the same side of the centreline in Zone A or beyond.

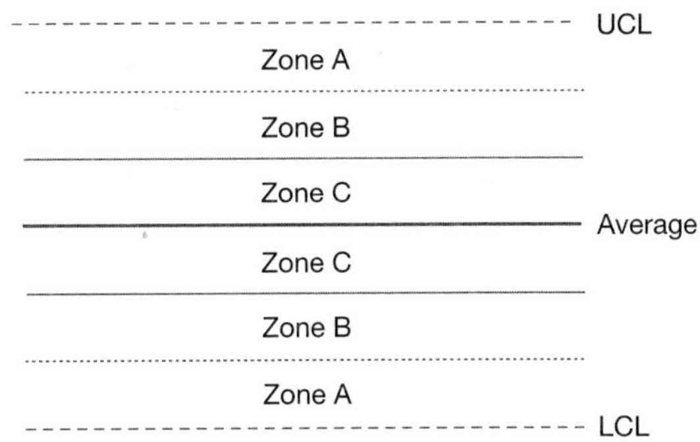

FIGURE 10.7 Zones in a control chart

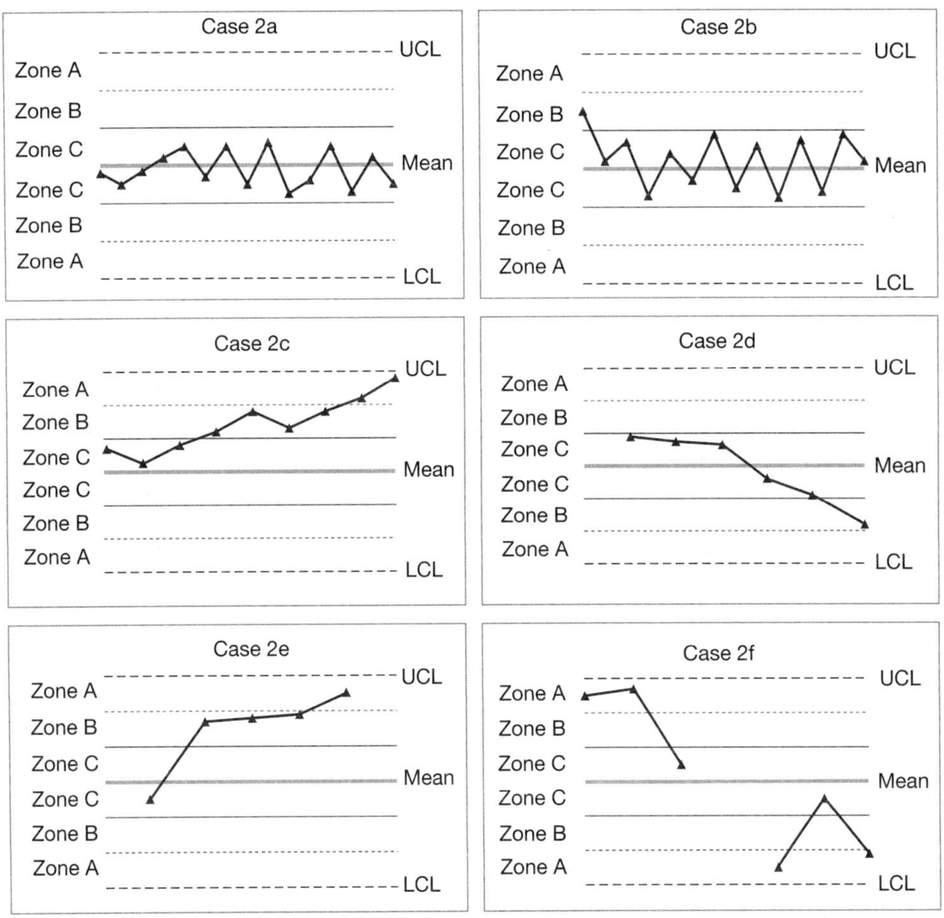

FIGURE 10.8 Control chart representing various scenarios

Process Capability

Control charts can be applied to measured parameters such as mean, standard deviations, and proportion of items when a process is in statistical control. The 'capability of a process' can be determined from these details. Process capability indicates whether a process with its natural variation can produce deliverables of the desirable specifications. It refers to the ability of a process to meet customer requirements after removing all special causes that result in variations. Capability indices can be utilised to place the process distribution with respect to the specification limits.

Process capability index, C_p, correlates the allowable spread of the specifications (i.e., the distance between the upper and lower specification limits) to the measure of process spread. The process spread is the expected distance between the measured maximum and minimum values of quality characteristics, assuming a normal distribution (Figure 10.9).

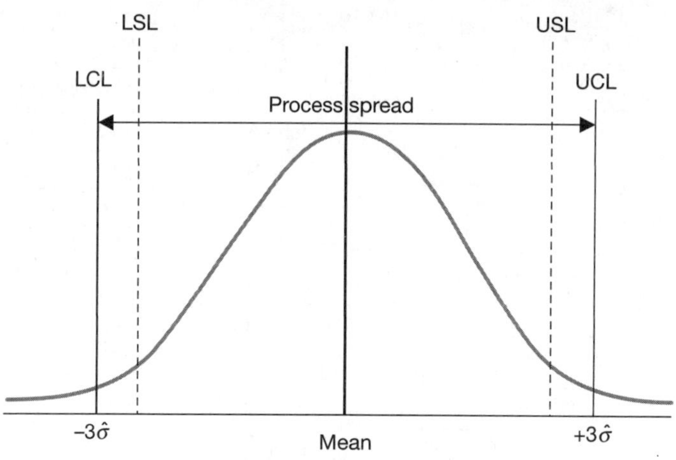

FIGURE 10.9 Process spread

It is usually considered ± 3 standard deviations from the mean. Setting the limits within ± three sigma ensures that 99.74% of the statistic falls within the control limits.

$$C_p = \frac{\text{USL} - \text{LSL}}{6\hat{\sigma}}$$

Where, USL and LSL are the upper and lower specification limits.

For a process in statistical control, $\hat{\sigma}$, standard deviation can be found from the control chart:

$$\hat{\sigma} = \frac{\bar{R}}{d_2}$$

Where, $\bar{R}$ is the average range of subgroups and d_2 is the value based on the subgroup sample size, as shown in Table 10.4.

TABLE 10.4 Factors for estimating $\hat{\sigma}$

n	2	3	4	5	6	7	8	9	10
d_2	1.128	1.693	2.059	2.326	2.534	2.704	2.847	2.97	3.078

Figure 10.10 depicts various instances of process capabilities. In the first figure, $C_p < 1$ denotes that the process is not capable of meeting the customer's specifications. The process spread exceeds the upper and lower specification limits. The acceptable control limits of the process are beyond the specification limits, and hence more defectives are made. In the second case, the process capability index = 1, which means that the process is meeting the customer's requirements/ specifications, though the chances of this scenario are as much as a coin falling on its edge. The percentage of defectives will be very low in this case. In the third scenario, $C_p > 1$, the process spread is less than the specification limits and the proportion of items that fall outside the limits will be minimal. Though the process spread is within specification limits, defectives will be made if the process is not centred. When the process is centred between the specification limits, the number of defectives will be the least.

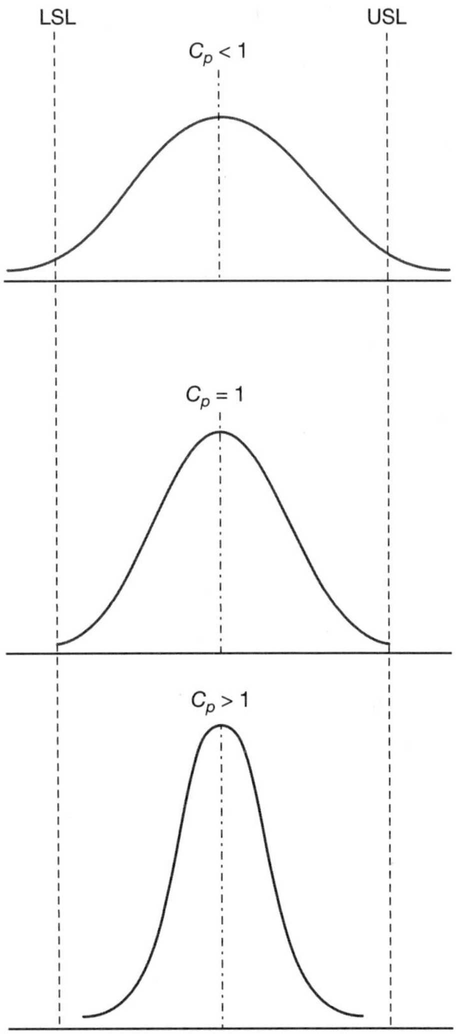

FIGURE 10.10 Simple process capability

C_p is an indicator of the potential of a process; however, it gives no idea about the centredness of the process to the targeted mean. Nevertheless, the process capabilities C_{pl} and C_{pu} (for one-sided specification limits) and C_{pk} (for two-sided specification limits) measure the process spread with regard to the specification limits and also consider the position of the process mean (Figure 10.11). The smallest of C_{pl} and C_{pu} is taken as $C_{pk,}$ which is a measure of process capability.

$$C_{pl} = \frac{\bar{\bar{x}} - LSL}{3\hat{\sigma}}$$

$$C_{pu} = \frac{USL - \bar{\bar{x}}}{3\hat{\sigma}}$$

$$C_{pk} = \text{Min.}\{C_{pl}, C_{pu}\}$$

The process is exactly centred when $C_{pl} = C_{pu}$

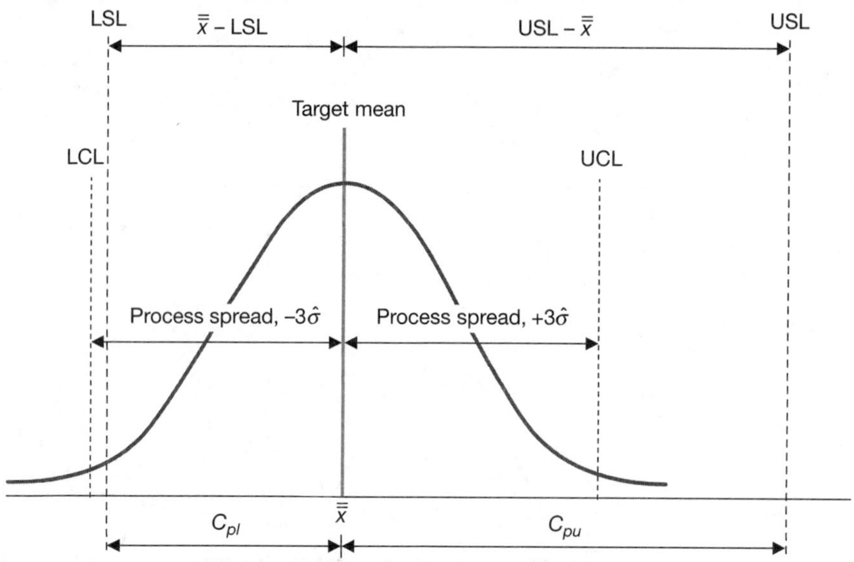

FIGURE 10.11 Measuring process capability

Let us determine the process capability index of the process mentioned previously. The manufacturer has specified the upper and lower limits of the weight of waterproofing chemical bag as 997 g and 1,003 g respectively, the same example as used in Chapter 9. The statistics of the control chart are given below:

$$n = 5$$

$$\bar{\bar{x}} = 1{,}000.61 \text{ g}$$

$$\bar{R} = 3.7$$

Specification = 1,000 ± 3 g. Hence, LSL = 997 g and USL = 1,003 g.

$$\hat{\sigma} = \frac{\bar{R}}{d_2} = \frac{3.7}{2.326} = 1.59$$

$$C_p = \frac{\text{USL} - \text{LSL}}{6\hat{\sigma}} = \frac{1{,}003 - 997}{6(1.59)} = 0.63$$

$$C_{pl} = \frac{\bar{\bar{x}} - \text{LSL}}{3\hat{\sigma}} = \frac{1{,}000.61 - 997}{3(1.59)} = 0.76$$

$$C_{pu} = \frac{\text{USL} - \bar{\bar{x}}}{3\hat{\sigma}} = \frac{1{,}003 - 1{,}000.61}{3(1.59)} = 0.50$$

$$C_{pk} = \text{min.}\{C_{pl}, C_{pu}\} = \text{min.}\{0.76, 0.50\} = 0.5.$$

Since $C_{pk} < 1$, there are defects in the process of packing of bags.

10.2.3 Pareto Chart

Pareto diagrams are useful tools in the process of improving quality because they help to identify the aspects that are most important. Italian economist Vilfredo Pareto (1848–1923) discovered that a small number of people hold the majority of the world's wealth. This is known as the Pareto principle. Problem or defect categories are distributed in a similar pattern in manufacturing or service organisations. Only a few of the issues arise frequently; the others seldom occur. The quality expert Juran generalised the concept and came up with the expression "the vital few and the trivial many" to define the Pareto principle. The Pareto principle also supports the 80/20 rule, which claims that 80% of defects, nonconformities, or other problems are due to 20% of causes. This translates to that the majority of problems are caused by only a minority of issues. By grouping issues in descending order of significance, Pareto diagrams assist in problem prioritisation. These diagrams aid businesses in determining the best sequence to solve challenges when resources are scarce. By analysing data using Pareto analysis, major causes related to a problem can be identified. It facilitates the intelligent distribution of resources to find a solution by ranking the factors that contribute to the problem. A Pareto chart is used to efficiently manage materials in construction projects where the Pareto principle applies; few materials contribute to a major part of material cost. ABC analysis, a commonly adopted inventory control method in construction, uses Pareto's Law to classify materials to determine suitable ordering strategies.

The Pareto chart consists of a vertical bar graph presented in a particular manner that assists in determining the priority in which problems are to be solved. By constructing a Pareto chart, it becomes possible to identify critical problems and focus attention on them. Better results are gained by giving more attention to the tallest bars in the chart than the smaller ones.

The following steps are to be followed for constructing a Pareto chart to determine the priority in which a problem is to be solved:

(a) Identify the problems encountered to be compared and tackled by collecting data and conducting brainstorming sessions.

(b) Determine the unit in which measurements are to be made since comparison becomes easier with uniformity in units. It can be the cost of rectification or the frequency of occurrence of defects.

(c) Choose the period in which the study is to be conducted, say in a day, a week, or a month.

(d) Collect the data of all the problems identified. For example, the frequency of occurrence of defects A, B, C, D, E, F, and G or the cost of rectification of defects A, B, C, D, E, F, and G.

(e) Compare and rank the problems based on the units selected and list them in descending order of rank, with the highest rank (highest cost or frequency) on the left and the smallest rank on the right. Problems in the lowest ranks can be combined as 'other' or 'misc' categories and are placed on the last bar on the extreme right.

(f) Each problem is represented by a rectangle, and the height shows the cost or frequency of occurrence.

(g) A line drawn from the top of the tallest bar that moves upward from left to right shows the cumulative frequencies of cost or frequency of the problems and this denotes the percentage of the total that can be accounted for in the first few bars.

Figure 10.12 shows a Pareto chart that represents the frequency of occurrences of various defect types in a system. Defect A occurs 39 times in this system compared to defect G, which occurs twice. It may be noted that this defect may not require the highest cost for rectification. Hence, the unit has to be chosen wisely to prioritise the problem. The defect occurrence frequency may be chosen as the unit of measurement when trying to eliminate the defects that occur mostly in customer complaints. When trying to reduce the cost of quality, the defect cost may be chosen as the unit of measurement.

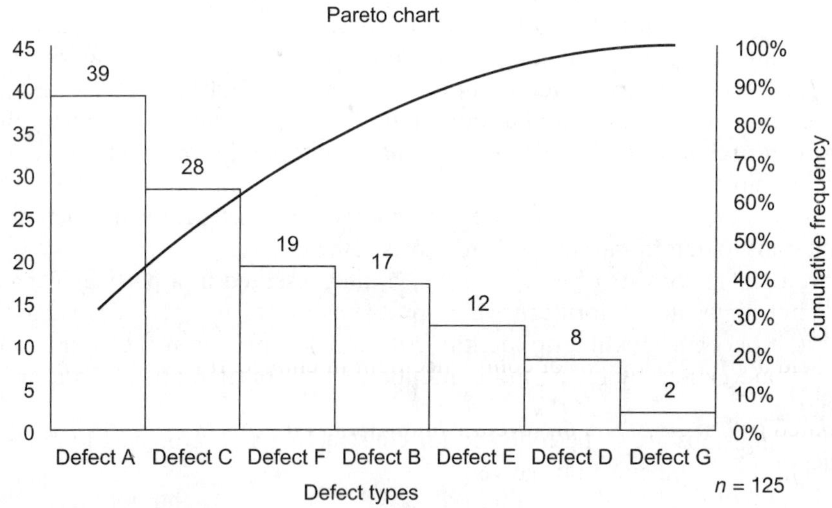

FIGURE 10.12 Pareto chart representing the defect types and the frequency of occurrences

The Pareto chart has various applications as follows:

(i) To find out the most critical problem. It may be based on the frequency of occurrence or cost of rectification.

(ii) To compare data sets of defects based on the various groups, such as the number of defects in different shifts and the number of defects produced by various categories of workers/machines.

(iii) To decompose the broad categories into smaller and specific ones.

(iv) To compare the changes that happened after modifying the processes. Figure 10.13 shows the impact of modifications made to a process. The number of defects has reduced in various categories after process modification.

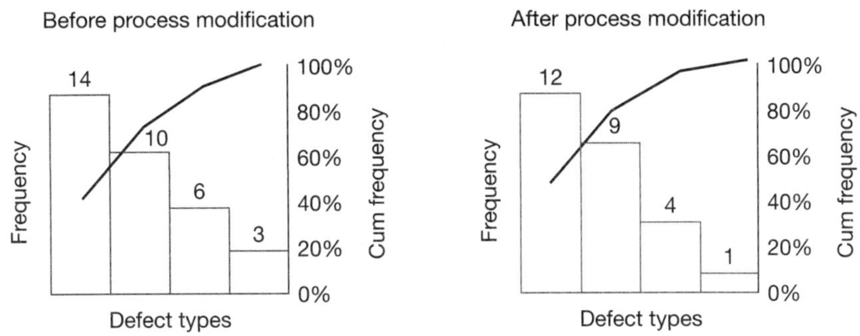

FIGURE 10.13 Number of defects before and after process modification

10.3 FORCE FIELD ANALYSIS (FFA)

Kurt Lewin developed the method of force field analysis in 1951. Force field analysis is a tool that can be used during process improvement or change management. Improvement is making something better or bringing a change or modification to enhance a process. Two forces come into action whenever an attempt is made to change something. There will be a driving force in favour of the action and a restraining force that attempts to pull the change backwards. Even while making a decision, these two forces come into play. There will be supporting positive forces and restraining negative forces. When the two forces are equal, or the restraining forces are powerful enough to resist the changes, the changes do not occur. Changes occur when driving forces are stronger than the restraining forces.

Force field analysis is a point of commencement of change. It helps in thinking creatively about a change that is required. It helps determine the various supporting and opposing factors related to a change. The involved team members reach a consensus regarding the priority of factors on both sides of the force field. The following steps are followed in conducting a force field analysis:

(i) Identify all positive and negative factors in connection with the change. It can be done through brainstorming.

(ii) Evaluate the strength of each factor on both sides.

(iii) Place the factors under the respective heads-driving forces and restraining forces. The length of the arrow representing each factor depends on its strength.

(iv) To effect a change, team members must seek ideas to increase the supporting factors and reduce the opposing forces.

Let us consider the following scenario where FFA can be used. An organisation is planning to implement quality management in their system. Hence, the management conducted brainstorming sessions to identify the factors that support and restrain the implementation of quality management. They are shown in Figure 10.14.

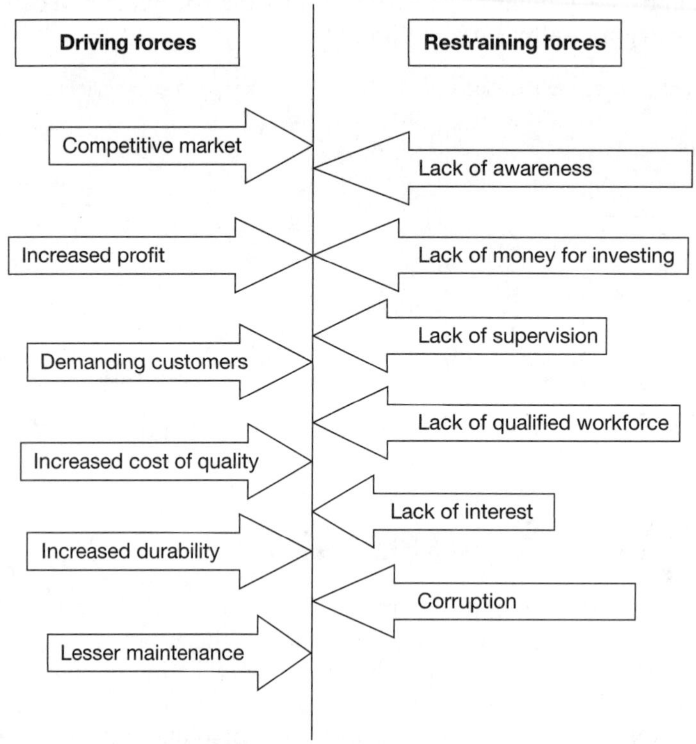

FIGURE 10.14 Force field analysis

10.4 BRAINSTORMING

Brainstorming is a useful technique for generating as many ideas as possible in the shortest possible time. It can be used to find possible solutions to a problem. It can be conducted in structured and unstructured ways. In the structured method, everyone participating in the session is forced to give an idea during their turn or in the subsequent rounds. There is pressure on everyone to contribute their idea. In the unstructured method, members share their ideas as they come. Though the second method takes place in a relaxed manner, there is a chance of not getting opportunities to present the ideas because of the dominance of the other members.

The procedure to be followed for conducting brainstorming sessions is as follows:

(i) Select participants with various backgrounds.
(ii) Specify the problem to be brainstormed.
(iii) Motivate the participants to generate as many ideas as possible.
(iv) Arrive at consensus on the most applicable ideas.

There are a few rules to be followed during the brainstorming session. They are listed below:

(a) Note down the question or the problem that is being brainstormed.
(b) All ideas are to be noted down in the exact words the speaker uses.
(c) These ideas are not to be interpreted and written.
(d) No one should criticise others' ideas or obstruct others from presenting their ideas.
(e) It has to be done quickly.
(f) Encourage participants to contribute a maximum number of ideas.
(g) 'Free-wheeling is welcomed. The wilder the idea, the better' (Osburn, 1963).
(h) Apart from contributing their ideas, participants must also suggest ways to make others' ideas better or how the ideas can be combined to make them better.

Better ideas emerge when the brainstorming is conducted in a relaxing and calming environment. Furthermore, when sufficient space is given to participants, suggestions and ideas flow, making the sessions more successful.

CONCLUSION

In this chapter, we have discussed certain tools used in quality management. These tools are required to analyse the data and make decisions for improvement. Most of these tools assist in problem-solving and quality improvement in one way or the other. Improvements can only be effective in a system when they are made based on facts and data. Quality improvement starts with the detection of the problem. Control charts aid in identifying the defectives or non-conformities in a process. It shows the existence of problems in the system. Using a fishbone diagram, the causes of problems can be determined. A Pareto chart is then used to prioritise the problems. Force field analysis is a tool that is used for process improvement or change management. It can be used to bring a change in the existing system so as to improve the process for enhancing quality. Brainstorming is a technique for generating creative ideas and solutions and is applicable during force field analysis, developing fishbone diagrams, and Pareto charts as well. All these tools thus assist in the quality management of an organisation.

WORKS CITED

Jaganmohan, M. (2024, January 2). *Price of cement in India from 2015 to 2022*. Retrieved Febraury 8, 2024, from Statista: https://www.statista.com/statistics/1301259/india-cement-price/

Mitra, A. (2016), *Fundamentals of Quality Control and Improvement.* (United States of America: Wiley).

Osburn, A. (1963), *Applied Imagination - Principles and Procedures of Creative Writing.* (New York: Charles Scribner's Sons).

The Memory Jogger: A Pocket Guide of Tools for Continuous Improvement and Effective Planning. (1994). (Salem, NH: Goal/QPC).

REVIEW QUESTIONS

Multiple Choice Questions

1. Which among the following is not a statistical quality control method among 'The Old Seven'?

   (a) Scatter diagram (b) Pareto chart
   (c) Fishbone diagram (d) Affinity diagram

2. What are the applications of the fishbone diagram?

   (a) Cause enumeration (b) Dispersion analysis
   (c) Process analysis (d) All of the above

3. Which tool illustrates how the outcomes of a process change with time?

   (a) Control chart (b) Pareto chart
   (c) Flow chart (d) Histogram

4. A process is said to be in statistical control when it operates under variations only due to ____________ causes.

   (a) common (b) special
   (c) common and special (d) unprecedented

5. Which of the following is not a special cause of variation?

   (a) Natural variations (b) Operator error
   (c) Equipment malfunction (d) Unplanned event

6. What is the application of a Pareto chart?

   (a) Determination of variations (b) Determining causes of variations
   (c) Problem prioritisation (d) Problem identification

Short Answer Type Questions

1. Under what circumstances are variable control charts and attribute control charts used?
2. Differentiate common causes and special causes of variations.

3. Distinguish between specification limit and control limit.
4. What do $C_p < 1$ and $C_p > 1$ mean?
5. What are C_{pl}, C_{pu}, and C_{pk}?
6. What are the applications of the Pareto chart?
7. What are the rules and procedures to be followed for conducting brainstorming sessions?

Long Answer Type Questions

1. Explain the steps followed in the construction of a fishbone diagram.
2. Using a fishbone diagram, determine the causes of delay in a construction project.
3. Determine the causes of poor quality in construction with the help of the Ishikawa diagram.
4. How are the limits determined in a variable control chart?
5. How are the limits determined in different types of attribute control charts?
6. From 10 subgroups, the weights of 50 cement bags were taken. The number of non-conforming items in the subgroups 1 to 10 are 3, 4, 5, 6, 3, 2, 5, 6, 3, and 4 respectively. Determine the limits of the given process.
7. Discuss process capability with a suitable diagram.
8. Discuss the process of constructing a Pareto chart.
9. Discuss in detail force field analysis.
10. How can we make use of quality control charts to improve quality in construction?
11. Prepare a run chart and apply control chart analysis to it for mean and range.
12. Prepare a numerical problem and apply process capability analysis to it.

ANSWER KEYS

Multiple Choice Questions

1. (d) **2.** (d) **3.** (a) **4.** (a) **5.** (a) **6.** (c)

CHAPTER 11 Reliability and Availability

11.1 INTRODUCTION

Different materials and products are used in the construction industry. While some products are used as fittings and fixtures, many materials and products become part of the constructed structure. Therefore, they are required to have specific quality characteristics. In other words, these products or materials are chosen for construction because of the properties they possess. Most of the constructed structures are designed for a long life span. Hence, whatever material or product that goes into construction should be durable. However, in certain situations, it can be observed that the materials/products used or the constructed facility itself fail or start to deteriorate much ahead of its expected life. This may be due to the use of materials or products that do not adhere to specifications. Even if materials or products conforming to specifications are used, defects or failure may occur at any point of time during the life, due to faulty construction or poor workmanship. For example, in pipe laying projects, even when the pipes used are of good quality, failure may occur during commissioning if installations are faulty or if the design is flawed.

For those products or systems that show failures at the beginning of their life and subsequently subside and reach a constant rate and then increase due to wear-out, the plot of failure rate versus time exhibits a bathtub curve. Similar to materials and products, some of the machinery and equipment used to make the construction process easier, faster, and more accurate may also fail. However, they are repaired and used again multiple times during their lifetime. Hence, it is required to understand its reliability and availability and to calculate the same, it is required to know the mean time between failures.

11.2 BATHTUB CURVE

The Bathtub curve is a basic tool used to analyse the failure process of products in quality engineering (Singh & Adachi, 2013). It represents the rate of failure against time. Since failure rates are high during the initial and final stages and low during the middle of its life, the shape of the failure curve, when plotted against time, has the shape of a bathtub (Figure 11.1). The early life plot, where the failure is dipping from the peak, is known as the infant region. The number of failures is high at an early age. Design errors, manufacturing mistakes, incorrect use or application, and operator ignorance result in failures in the initial period. In most cases, these can be corrected so that they do not recur.

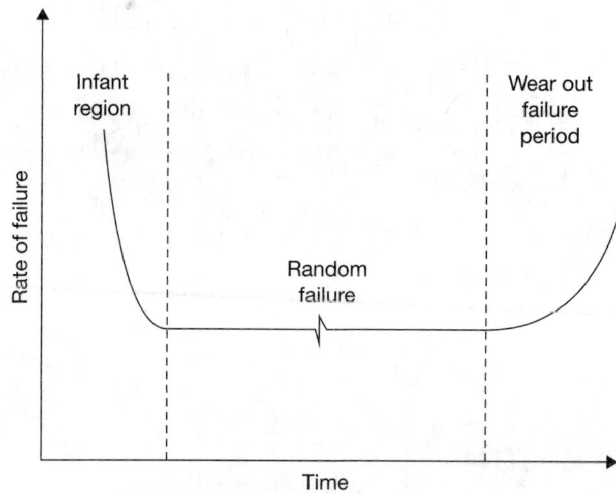

FIGURE 11.1 The Bathtub curve

During the operational period, i.e., in the middle period of life cycle, the rate of failure remains mostly constant. This region in the curve is known as the period of random failures. The failures occur in this stage due to some inherent factors in the process, variations in the environment, the occurrence of unexpected events, and changes that occur due to maintenance. The number of failures can be reduced by having proper operational control and preventive maintenance. For complex products, a redesign is basically required to decrease the number of failures.

Towards the final life stage, the rate of failure increases again and this region in the bathtub curve is known as the wear-out period. The failures during this period are predominantly due to wear and tear. In a product with many components, it is required to replace the worn-out parts to prevent a sudden failure.

The pattern of failure or defects in civil engineering structures is sometimes similar to the bathtub curve. Many defects are found immediately after construction, i.e., during its infant stage, and then they are rectified, discarded or repaired. Defects such as improper fixing of components, loose fittings, and omission of works are commonly detected after handover to the clients. Sometimes, fixtures fail due to improper handling. These are then repaired and put into use again. The failure or defect rate then reduces and becomes constant during its useful life period. The structures are prone to deterioration due to various atmospheric, environmental, mechanical and other factors, and as the structure nears the end of its life, the failure rate starts to increase again. The rate of failure or defects in a building, when plotted against time, also yields a bathtub curve.

Users become distressed as defects or failures occur during infancy. They start worrying about the durability of the product or the system and the period for which the product runs without failing. In the case of constructed facilities, early-age incidences create distress among the users, and some of them even affect their physical and psychological well-being.

The failure rates of a widget are given in Table 11.1. The bathtub curve of Figure 11.2 follows from the rate of failure per 90 days given in Table 11.1. The number of failures is 23 in the first interval of 0–90 days and 10 in the next interval of 90–180 days. The number of defects is reduced to 4 in the steady state period. The failure rate remained constant till the 900th day.

Again, it started to increase gradually till the final stage. Hence, the failure rate when plotted against time yields a bathtub curve.

TABLE 11.1 Rate of failure

	Time of failure in days												
	Infant region		Random failure rate region								Wear-out region		
S. No.	0-90	90-180	180-270	270-360	360-450	450-540	540-630	630-720	720-810	810-900	900-990	990-1,080	1,080-1,170
1	3	94	190	275	375	455	555	638	721	820	905	994	1,081
2	5	110	225	290	390	478	569	655	745	859	915	1,020	1,089
3	8	118	254	310	415	512	596	690	778	880	946	1,035	1,093
4	10	129	268	350	445	534	625	710	805	895	959	1,045	1,097
5	14	135									970	1,056	1,102
6	18	147									987	1,062	1,107
7	20	158										1,068	1,115
8	22	165										1,072	1,127
9	24	171										1,075	1,132
10	26	179										1,077	1,138
11	30											1,079	1,142
12	32												1,151
13	35												1,154
14	40												1,158
15	45												1,165
16	46												1,170
17	54												
18	60												
19	65												
20	70												
21	76												
22	85												
23	89												

Failure rate at 90 days interval

Time interval of failure (days)	0-90	90-180	180-270	270-360	360-450	450-540	540-630	630-720	720-810	810-900	900-990	990-1,080	1,080-1,170
Number of failures	23	10	4	4	4	4	4	4	4	4	6	11	16

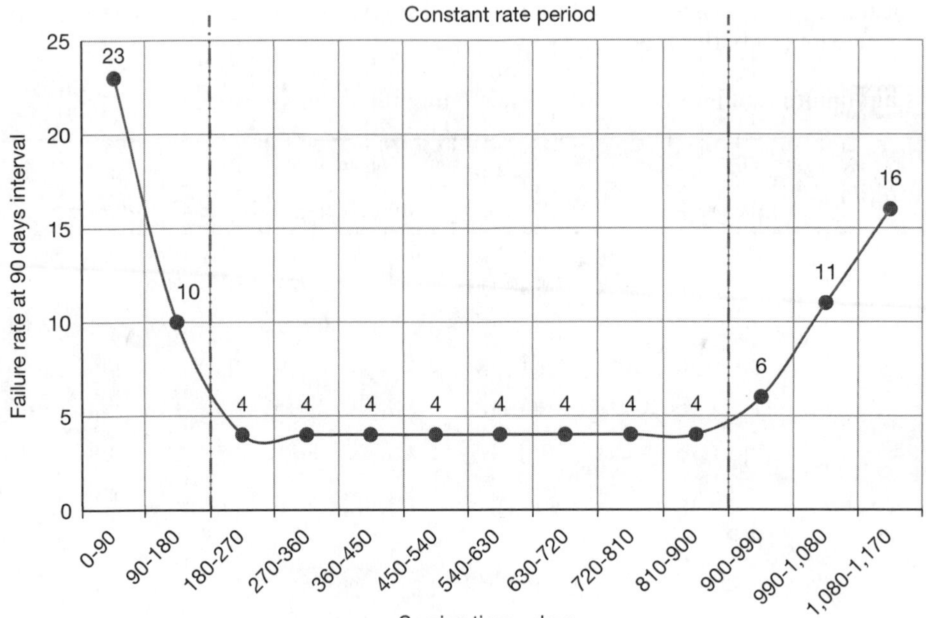

FIGURE 11.2 Rate of failure versus time

11.3 RELIABILITY

Reliability is a quality characteristic every customer wants in a product or looks forward to regarding a product. A product has to function as required by the customer or as designed by the manufacturer for the period it has been designed. Products may fail several times during their lifetime. While some are nonrepairable, others are repaired and put back to use. In many complex products consisting of various components, individual components may fail. So, they have to be replaced proactively to prevent the total failure of the system. The time between failures is an important attribute for a repairable product, whereas the time to failure is significant for nonrepairable products. The time between failures follows an exponential distribution pattern when the failure rate is constant. It implies that there exists a failure-free period for operation. The probability of failure-free operation for a specified period is known as reliability. In other words, reliability is defined as 'the probability of a product performing without failure a specified function under given conditions for a specified period of time (Juran & Gryna, 1980). It is also known as the probability of survival and is calculated using the formula:

$$P_s = R = e^{-t/\mu} = e^{-t\lambda}$$

Where

$P_s = R$ = probability of failure-free operation for a period t or longer

$e = 2.718$

t = specified failure-free operation period (operation without failure)

λ = rate of failure = $1/\mu$
μ = mean time between failures (MTBF)

A constant failure rate is assumed while calculating reliability.

Example

A 30-litre water heater takes 15 minutes to heat the water. The mean time between failures is 50 hours. The probability of the heater heating the water without failure is given by

$$P_s = R = e^{-t/\mu} = e^{-0.25/50} = 0.995$$
$$t = 15 \text{ minutes} = 15/60 = 0.25 \text{ hr}$$

There is a 99.5 per cent chance of heating the water without failure.

11.4 INDICATORS OF RELIABILITY

The mean time between failures (MTBF) is a vital indicator of reliability. It is the average time between subsequent failures in a repairable product. After every failure, the product is repaired and put back into operation.

The probability of a product operating without failure for a time equivalent to or greater than the mean time between failures is 37 per cent when the failure rate is constant. In the earlier example, if the mean time between failures is 15 minutes, then

$$P_s = R = e^{-t/\mu} = e^{-0.25/0.25} = 0.37$$

An increase in MTBF does not yield a proportionate increase in the reliability of a product, though increasing MTBF naturally results in an increase in *R*. The reliability is calculated for different MTBF when the failure-free operation period is specified as 1 hour, as shown in Table 11.2, which represents the probability of failure-free operation for one hour against the different levels of MTBF. It may be noted that an increase in MTBF from 1 hour to 5 hours results in a 46% (= 82% – 37%) increase in the probability of survival (reliability). However, at higher levels, a fivefold increase in MTBF from 20 to 100 results in an increase in reliability by just 4% (= 99% – 95%). Reliability does not improve in proportion to the increase in MTBF.

TABLE 11.2 Reliability for different MTBF

Mean time between failures (hours)	Reliability
1	0.37
5	0.82
10	0.90
20	0.95
100	0.99
1,000	0.999

Though MTBF is an essential indicator of reliability, it cannot be applied to all products. Some of the other essential indicators for reliability and their definitions are as follows:

(a) Failure rate—number of times a product fails in a specified time.
(b) Mean time to failure (MTTF)—the average time for the failure to occur in a non-repairable product, or the mean time till the first failure (MTFF) of a repairable product.
(c) Mean life—the average life when the product is operational. It is calculated as the life period till wear-out time or the major overhaul.

11.5 SYSTEM RELIABILITY

Several components or subsystems constitute a system. Each of them may have different probabilities of survival. The system reliability is calculated by multiplying the reliabilities of the constituent components. Suppose *n* components constitute a system, then system reliability, *SR,* is calculated by:

$$SR = P_1 P_2 P_3 \ldots P_n$$

$P_1, P_2, P_3, \ldots P_n$ are the reliabilities of individual components.

It is assumed that failure of any component causes the system to fail and that the reliability of one component does not affect the reliability of the other component, i.e., the component reliabilities are independent of each other. For example, in a car, the steering and transmission are two separate entities. The failure of one does not usually affect the functioning of the other. However, the failure of any of these can cause the failure of the system.

There are also situations where these assumptions are not valid. However, this formula is an approximation to determine the system reliability, which can be refined further as the relationship between various components is known. Moreover, this formula reveals the following aspects:

(a) Each component has a significant role in system reliability.
(b) System reliability reduces acutely with the increasing number of parts in a system.
(c) Reliability is affected by the complexity of the system.

Hence, when it is assumed that the components of a system are independent, the failure of any component results in system failure and each component exhibits exponential distribution, then the probability of survival or system reliability is given by

$$SR = e^{-t_1\lambda_1}.e^{-t_2\lambda_2}.e^{-t_3\lambda_3}\ldots\ldots e^{-t_n\lambda_n}$$

If time '*t*' is the same for all components, then

$$SR = e^{-t\Sigma\lambda}$$

It shows that system reliability can be predicted based on the sum of failure rates of components.

Example

A machine system has five components (A to E) with MTBF and failure-free time, as given in Table 11.3. The system reliability is determined as illustrated in Table 11.3.

TABLE 11.3 Calculating system reliability

Component	Failure free time, hr	MTBF, hr	Reliability $P_s = R = e^{-t/\mu}$	System Reliability $SR = P_1 P_2 P_3 \ldots P_n$
A	0.5	50	0.99	
B	0.25	10	0.975	
C	1	50	0.98	0.896
D	0.75	60	0.987	
E	1	25	0.96	

If the system had only components D and E, then reliability would be 0.987 × 0.96 = 0.947. If the system had components C, D and E, then reliability would be 0.98 × 0.987 × 0.96 = 0.928. Hence, it is evident that system reliability decreases with an increase in number of components.

11.6 AVAILABILITY

For a repairable product, failures may happen partly or completely several times before its major overhaul. Thus, there are times when it is operational and when it is down. When a product fails to operate, it will not be available for performing the intended function. Availability can be defined as the probability that the product will function satisfactorily when used. There are two types of availability: operational availability, A_o and intrinsic availability, A_i. The availability of a product depends on the time when it is operational, and the time required for repairs. The time when a product is not required, also known as idle time, is not considered while calculating availability. Availability is generally calculated as follows:

$$\text{Availability} = \frac{\text{Operating time}}{\text{Operating time} + \text{Downtime}}$$

Figure 11.3 gives the details of an operational cycle of a dumper used in the mining site for a certain period. The figure illustrates the operational hours and downtime in the cycle. The details of downtime – such as logistics time and active repair time – are also shown. The terms used in Figure 11.3 are defined in the note below it.

11.6.1 Operational Availability

Operational availability considers the total downtime of a product. Total downtime includes all the variables below:

- **(i) Time to repair (TTR):** the time required for diagnosis and repair of failure. This is also known as the active repair time.
- **(ii) Preventive maintenance time:** the time when routine maintenance is done.
- **(iii) Logistics time:** the waiting time for the service personnel to come for diagnosis and repair and for the spare parts to be delivered. The logistics time is counted as part of the downtime.

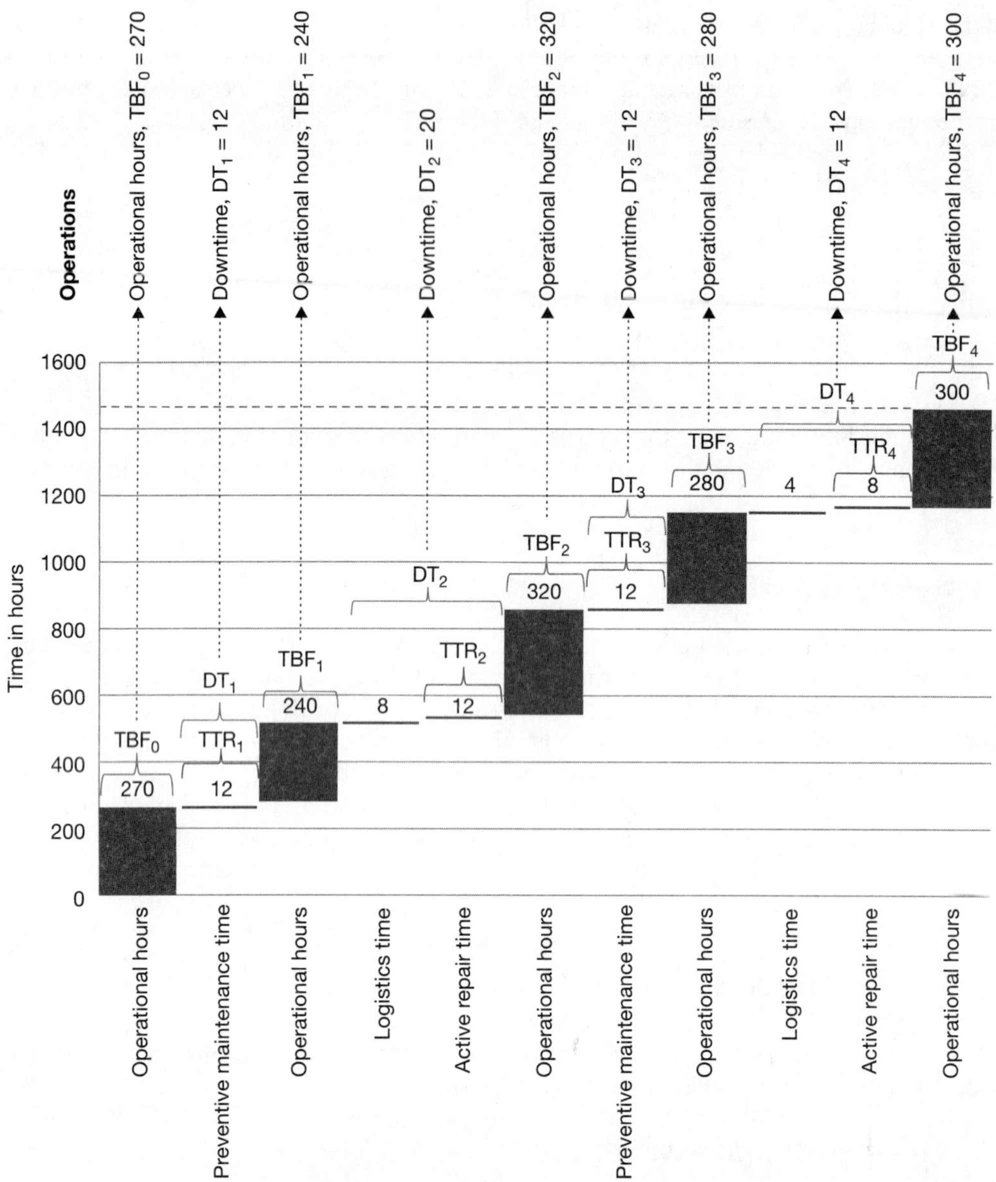

Note: Downtime (DT), Time between failure (TBF), and Time to repair (TTR)

FIGURE 11.3 Operational cycle of the dumper

From the above example, the following are calculated:

$$MDT = (DT_1 + DT_2 + DT_3 + DT_4)/4 = 56/4 = 14 \text{ hours}$$

$$MTBF = (TBF_0 + TBF_1 + TBF_2 + TBF_3)/4 = 1{,}110/4 = 277.5 \text{ hours}$$

$$MTTR = (TTR_1 + TTR_2 + TTR_3 + TTR_4)/4 = 44/4 = 11 \text{ hours}$$

In the calculation above, the last operational hours cannot be counted as either the total operation and nor can it be considered as the time between failures. That's because if the end of the activity use is reached at 1,466 hours, and the dumper has not failed, it can start on another activity thereafter.

The operating time is given by the mean time between failures. Thus, the operational availability is calculated as:

$$A_o = \frac{\text{MTBF}}{\text{MTBF} + \text{MDT}}$$

Let us determine the operational availability of the dumper above used at the mining site. Hence,

$$A_o = \frac{277.5}{277.5 + 14} = 0.95$$

implying that the operational availability of the dumper is 95%.

11.6.2 Intrinsic Availability

The intrinsic availability considers the active repair time and/or preventive maintenance time. It is determined using the following formula:

$$A_i = \frac{\text{MTBF}}{\text{MTBF} + \text{MTTR}}$$

Where

MTBF = mean time between failures

MTTR = mean time to repair, which is the active repair time when diagnosis and repair are done. Preventive maintenance time is also included here.

The formula for determining intrinsic availability is based on certain mathematical assumptions, that may not always be true in practical applications. The assumptions are (Juran & Gryna, 1980):

1. The operation of the product in the constant failure rate period is considered. The failure time follows an exponential distribution.
2. The downtime/repair time follows an exponential distribution.
3. The rate of overall system failure is not altered by the attempt to detect system failure.
4. Improvement of reliability can only be attained through design enhancement or rectifying defective or bad parts.
5. The time for preventive maintenance is considered as included in downtime for availability calculation because the machine is unavailable for use at the time it is in the garage for preventive maintenance[1].

The main difference between operational availability and intrinsic availability is that logistics time is considered for operational availability but excluded from intrinsic availability.

---

1 This is a contrary consideration compared to what Juran and Gryna (1980) use. But it is reasonable to consider preventive maintenance time of any type as downtime.

The concept of availability is very significant in the construction industry as well. It is desirable to know the availability of equipment and machinery before scheduling them for construction purposes. Most of the time, scheduling is done based on the assumed values derived from the log of failures, and it is also assumed that the service personnel and parts are available for repairs. In the case of manufacturing equipment, reliable data must be used to determine availability and prepare the production schedule accordingly. Meeting the schedule will be possible only when availability is determined accurately. To increase the availability of the equipment or machinery, the following actions may be taken.

(i) Conduct preventive maintenance as per manufacturer guidelines.

(ii) Ensure periodically the availability of spare parts and essential components.

(iii) Inspect the system periodically.

In the example above, the intrinsic availability is determined as:

$$A_i = \frac{\text{MTBF}}{\text{MTBF} + \text{MTTR}} = \frac{277.5}{277.5 + 11} = 0.96$$

implying that the intrinsic availability of the dumper is 96%.

Note that $A_o < A_i$ because MDT > MTTR. Also, note that MTTR will be always less than or equal to MDT.

11.6.3 Intrinsic Availability Example of a Batching Plant

Table 11.4 contains details of the components of a batching plant machine and their intrinsic availability.

TABLE 11.4 Availability data for batching plant

Components	MTBF, hr	MTTR, hr	Intrinsic Availability (%) $A_i = \frac{\text{MTBF}}{\text{MTBF} + \text{MTTR}}$
Mixing machine	720	5	99.31
Weighing machine	840	12	98.59
Conveyance system	320	8	97.56
Material storage	3,500	16	99.54
Control system	1,500	4.5	99.70

11.7 SAFETY MARGIN

A product failure is not always dependent on time. Failure can happen when a product is stressed beyond its strength. Strength is the inherent capability of a product, whereas stress is dependent on the operating condition to which a product is subjected. The designers adopt a safety factor to take into account the variations that exist. The safety factor is the ratio of mean strength to the expected maximum stress. It means that the safety factor considers only the mean strength and the maximum stress expected.

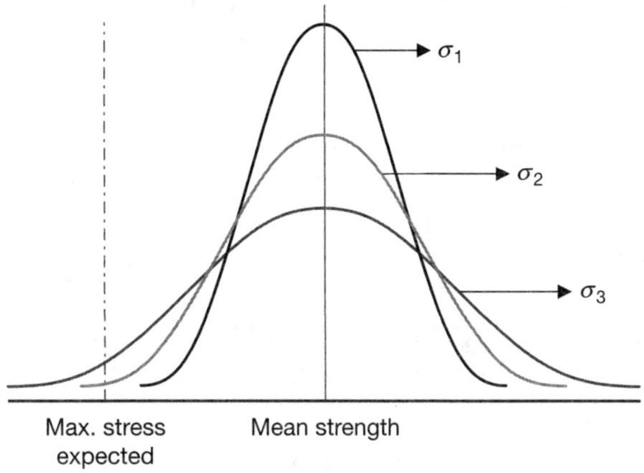

FIGURE 11.4 Variations in strength

However, while designing a product, it is essential to consider the standard deviation of strength along with the mean or target strength since the chance for variations always exists. From Figure 11.4, it can be noted that the variations in strength depend on the standard deviations. Though the three curves have the same mean strength, the standard deviations are different, which means that the extent of variations differs in each case.

Since the safety factor does not consider the variations in strength and stress, a safety margin may be used in design that partially reflects the variations. The safety margin is calculated as follows:

$$\text{Safety margin} = \frac{\text{Average strength} - \text{Worst stress}}{\text{Standard deviation}}$$

Though the safety margin does not consider the variations in stress, it considers the variations in strength. Hence, using a safety margin while designing all products is prudent.

Let us look at an example to understand this concept. The compressive strength is a critical parameter for concrete. The capability is defined by a strength distribution having 40 MPa as the mean strength and 5 MPa as the standard deviation. The maximum expected stress by design is 32 MPa. Then the safety margin can be calculated as

$$\text{Safety margin} = \frac{40-32}{5} = 1.6$$

The safety margin implies that the mean strength is 1.6 standard deviations above the maximum expected stress.

CONCLUSION

This chapter discusses the industrial reliability and availability of a product. Users always desire a reliable product at a reasonable price. Reliability is the probability that a product performs its designed functions for the specified time without failure. However, a repairable product or its components may fail several times during its service life. They are repaired and used until their end of life is reached.

Availability is the period during which the product operates without failure. It is determined by considering the mean time between failures and downtime. Knowledge about reliability and availability is essential for marketing a product and determining a work schedule. It helps improve productivity and increase profitability.

WORKS CITED

Juran, J., & Gryna, F. (1980), *Quality Planning and Analysis: From Product Development Through Use.* (United States of America: McGraw-Hill).

Singh, A., & Adachi, S. (2013), 'Bathtub curves and pipe prioritization based on failure rate', *Built Environment Project and Asset Management, 3*(1), 105–122. doi:10.1108/BEPAM-11-2011-0027.

REVIEW QUESTIONS

Multiple Choice Questions

1. Which tool is used to represent the failure rate against time?

(a) Bathtub curve

(b) Control chart

(c) Scatter diagram

(d) Affinity diagram

2. The time between failures follows __________ distribution pattern when the failure rate is constant.

(a) Poisson (b) normal

(c) exponential (d) uniform

3. System reliability __________ with an increase in number of components.

(a) decreases (b) increases

(c) does not change (d) remains constant

4. The probability of failure-free operation for a specified period is known as __________.

(a) availability (b) reliability

(c) durability (d) sustainability

5. __________ is the inherent capability of a product, whereas ________ is dependent on the operating condition to which a product is subjected.

   (a) Stress, strength (b) Strength, stress

   (c) Force, stress (d) Load, force

6. __________ is the average time between subsequent failures in a repairable product.

   (a) Failure rate (b) Mean life

   (c) Mean time between failures (d) Mean time to first failure

7. __________ can be defined as the probability that the product will function satisfactorily when in use.

   (a) Reliability (b) Availability

   (c) Durability (d) Serviceability

Short Answer Type Questions

1. What are the various regions in a bathtub curve?
2. A rice cooker takes 20 minutes to cook rice. The mean time between failures is 60 hours. Determine the probability of the rice cooker cooking rice without failure.
3. How is system reliability determined?
4. What constitutes total downtime?
5. How is availability determined?
6. What are the assumptions made when developing the formula for intrinsic availability?
7. How can we increase the availability of equipment?
8. How is the factor of safety different from the safety margin?

Long Answer Type Questions

1. Explain the bathtub curve with a suitable example from the construction industry.
2. Explain reliability in detail.
3. What are the indicators of reliability?
4. Calculate the system reliability for the following data.

Component	Failure free time, hr	MTBF in hr
A	0.25	50
B	0.5	10
C	1.5	100
D	0.85	80

5. Distinguish between operational and intrinsic availability.

ANSWER KEYS

Multiple Choice Questions

1. (d) **2.** (c) **3.** (a) **4.** (b) **5.** (b) **6.** (c) **7.** (b)

CHAPTER

12

Statistical Evaluation of Concrete Strength

12.1 INTRODUCTION

Concrete is a widely used construction material due to the quality characteristics it possesses, such as strength, durability, and versatility. The strength requirements of concrete vary with the type of its application. The difference in strength is attained by varying the proportion of ingredients used for making concrete. However, the strength attained for all samples of the same grade of concrete prepared using the same ingredients may not necessarily be the same. It varies with temperature, handling methods, type of mixing, curing, degree of compaction, and many other factors. Hence, while designing and evaluating the strength of concrete, it is very important to consider the variations that can occur. Statistical tools are used to evaluate concrete strength test results.

For construction quality control, routine sampling and testing of concrete cylinders/cubes is virtually mandatory on all public projects. In the United States, Canada, Australia, France, and New Zealand, cylindrical specimens are cast for testing, whereas in most European countries and India, cubes are cast to determine the strength of concrete. Though the tested specimens are prepared under controlled conditions, it is expected that the strength of the concrete in the structure from the same batch will be the same as that of the specimen tested. Inevitably, strength results vary and fluctuate for dozens of reasons.

12.2 VARIATIONS IN TEST RESULTS

The number of specimens tested in each sample varies depending on the test specifications. And the number of samples to be tested depends on the quantity of concrete in the work. Samples are taken from each shift/batch. A strength test result is the mean strength of all specimens in a sample. It appears that specimens from the same batch and different batches have different strengths, though they are prepared in the same manner, using the same ingredients in the same proportion.

Variations in test results are very common, and the reasons for variations are listed in Figure 12.1. However, the absence/lesser number of variations does not mean that the testing is accurate. This may be due to an error in the equipment, too.

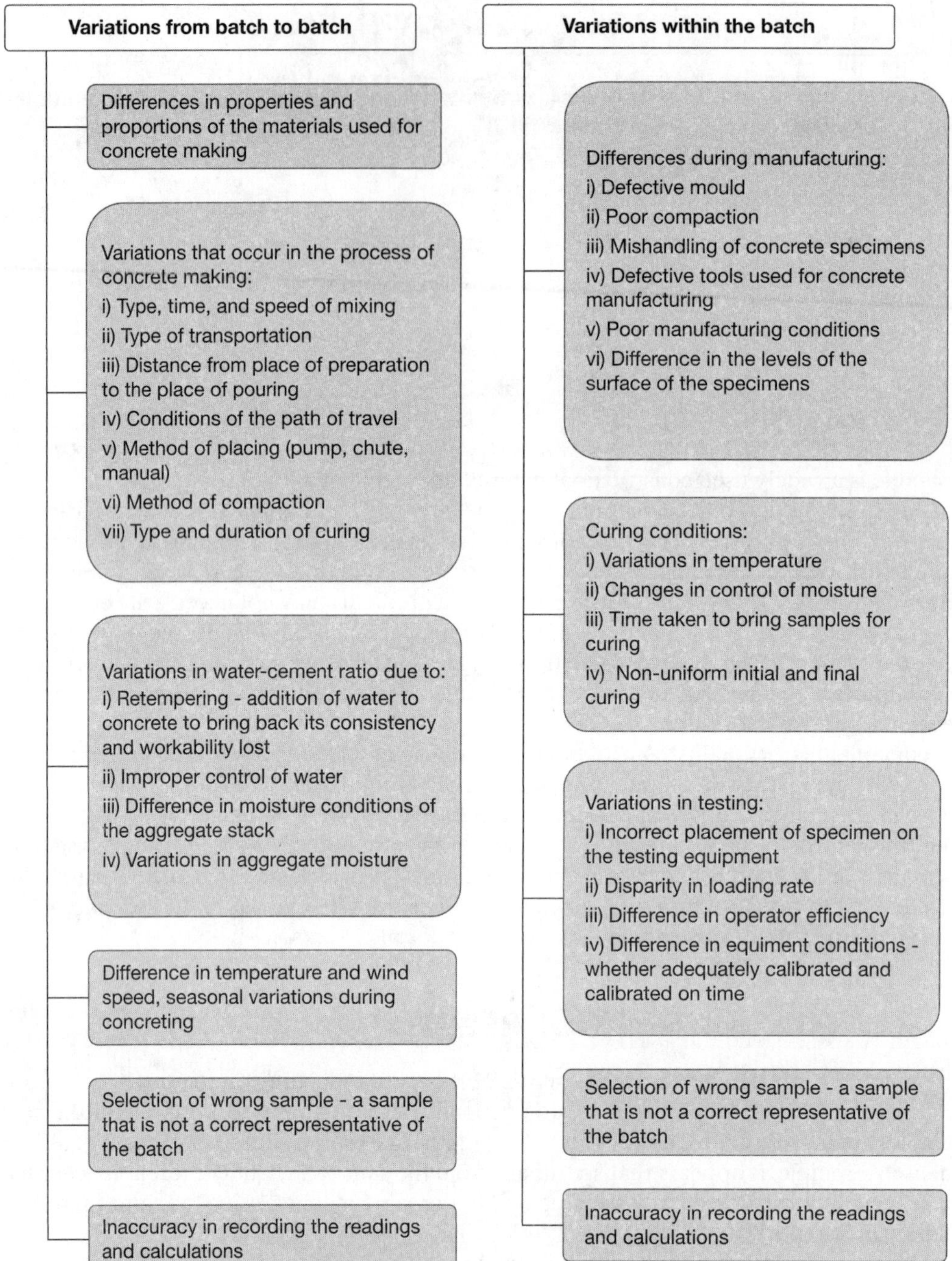

FIGURE 12.1 Causes of strength variations

12.3 ANALYSIS OF STRENGTH TEST RESULTS

To address the variations in test results accurately, it is required to have an adequate number of test results. Accordingly, suitable statistical methods can be adopted to interpret the test results. Statistical tools are a means to communicate the results in a usable form. They are used to determine the strength and quality of concrete.

12.3.1 Statistical Parameters Used in Analysis

Mean

Mean strength of test results is calculated by:

$$\text{Mean } \bar{x} = \frac{(x_1 + x_2 + x_3 + x_4 \ldots\ldots + x_n}{n} = \frac{\sum_1^n x_i}{n}$$

Where

$x_1, x_2, x_3, \ldots.., x_n$ are the values of n strength test results.

$\sum_1^n x_i$ is the sum of n test results

n is the number of tests

In the United States, the strength of concrete is determined by testing the cylinders. The number of specimens in the sample shall not be less than two when the cylinder size is 150 mm dia and 300 mm deep, and three when the cylinder size is 100 mm dia and 200 mm deep. Each strength test result is the average of the test results of the specimens in the sample. In India, the strength of concrete is determined by testing the cubes of size 150 mm × 150 mm × 150 mm on the 28th day of casting. Three specimens constitute a sample.

Standard Deviation

Standard deviation indicates the deviation from the mean. The standard deviation of a sample (a data set) is calculated by:

$$s = \sqrt{\frac{\sum_{i=1}^n (x_i - \bar{x})^2}{n-1}}$$

To combine the records of strength results of two different concrete mixtures with similar strength results, it is required to find out the statistical average standard deviation and it is calculated as follows:

When the samples are large (n_1 and n_2 are greater than or equal to 30):

$$s = \sqrt{\frac{s_1^2}{n_1} + \frac{s_2^2}{n_2}}$$

Where

s_1 and s_2 - standard deviations of test results on mixtures 1 and 2

n_1 and n_2 - number of tests in test results on mixtures 1 and 2

When the samples are small, i.e., either $n_1 < 30$ or $n_2 < 30$, we use the following formula for standard deviation, so long as the two populations have approximately equal variances.

$$s = \sqrt{\frac{\sum_{i=1}^{n_1}\left(x_i - \bar{x}_1\right)^2 + \sum_{j=1}^{n_2}\left(x_j - \bar{x}_2\right)^2}{n_1 + n_2 - 2} \cdot \left(\frac{1}{n_1} + \frac{1}{n_2}\right)}$$

Where

$\sum_{i=1}^{n_1}\left(x_i - \bar{x}_1\right)^2$ and $\sum_{j=1}^{n_2}\left(x_j - \bar{x}_2\right)^2$ are the sums of squared deviations from the means of the first and second samples, $\bar{x}_1$ and $\bar{x}_2$ respectively.

$$\sum_{i=1}^{n_1}\left(x_i - \bar{x}_1\right)^2 = \left(n_1 - 1\right) \cdot s_1^2$$

$$\sum_{j=1}^{n_2}\left(x_j - \bar{x}_2\right)^2 = \left(n_2 - 1\right) \cdot s_2^2$$

s_1 and s_2 are the standard deviations of the small samples.

Example 1 The standard deviation of cube strengths of 12 samples has been calculated as given in Table 12.1.

TABLE 12.1 Strength of concrete cubes

Sample No.	Strength of cube 1, N/mm^2	Strength of cube 2, N/mm^2	Strength of cube 3, N/mm^2	Average strength, N/mm^2	Rounded Strength (as per IS Code)	$\sum_{i=1}^{n}(x_i - \bar{x})$	$\sum_{i=1}^{n}(x_i - \bar{x})^2$
1	44.56	45.01	43.32	44.30	44.50	3.92	15.34
2	40.25	43.55	42.55	42.12	42.00	1.42	2.01
3	42.01	38.79	36.97	39.26	39.50	–1.08	1.17
4	38.27	39.25	40.44	39.32	39.50	–1.08	1.17
5	41.51	43.44	40.47	41.81	42.00	1.42	2.01
6	41.79	38.55	39.79	40.04	40.00	–0.58	0.34
7	38.1	38.47	39.11	38.56	38.50	–2.08	4.34
8	38.55	39.31	41.25	39.70	39.50	–1.08	1.17
9	43.9	39.2	38.55	40.55	40.50	–0.08	0.01
10	38.19	38.11	39.5	38.60	38.50	–2.08	4.34
11	39.19	39.3	40.24	39.58	39.50	–1.08	1.17
12	43.05	40.79	45.41	43.08	43.00	2.42	5.84
					40.58		38.92

$$\text{Standard deviation} = s = \sqrt{\frac{\sum_{i=1}^{n}\left(x_i - \bar{x}\right)^2}{n-1}} = \sqrt{\frac{38.92}{11}} = 1.88 \text{ N/mm}^2$$

Example 2 Table 12.2 shows the 28-day test results of samples of concrete cast on two different dates, 13 May 2022, 31 cubes, and 23 May 2022, 33 cubes. Determine the average standard deviation of these test results.

TABLE 12.2 Concrete sample strength on 13th and 23rd May 2022

Observations – Set I cast on 13 May 2022	**Sample No.**	1	2	3	4	5	6	7	8	9	10	11	12	13	14	15	16
	Strength, N/mm²	38.5	44.5	45	43	42	39.5	37.5	33.5	37	39	34.5	36	32	33.5	44	33
	Sample No.	17	18	19	20	21	22	23	24	25	26	27	28	29	30	31	
	Strength, N/mm²	32	33.5	34.5	34.5	36	31	42	35	35.5	34.5	43	37	35.5	38	39.5	

Observations – Set II cast on 23 May 2022	**Sample No.**	1	2	3	4	5	6	7	8	9	10	11	12	13	14	15	16	17
	Strength, N/mm²	39	45	45.5	36	38.5	42	35.5	39.5	42	45.5	33.5	38	38.5	43.5	35	33.5	42
	Sample No.	18	19	20	21	22	23	24	25	26	27	28	29	30	31	32	33	
	Strength, N/mm²	43	44.5	38.5	39.5	34	32.5	35.5	42	43.5	44	46	35.5	34.5	37	35	43	

$$\text{Here, } s_1 = 4.02, n_1 = 31, s_2 = 4.18, \text{ and } n_2 = 33$$

Since the samples are large, because $n_1 > 30$ and $n_2 > 30$, the standard deviation is calculated as:

$$s = \sqrt{\frac{s_1^2}{n_1} + \frac{s_2^2}{n_2}} = \sqrt{\frac{4.02^2}{31} + \frac{4.18^2}{33}} = 1.025 \text{ N/mm}^2$$

Example 3 Table 12.3 shows the 28-day test results of samples of concrete cast on two different dates, 12 April 2022, 12 cubes, and 18 April 2022, 13 cubes. Determine the average standard deviation of these test results.

In this case, the samples are small (n_1 and n_2 are each less than 30).

The average strength for the samples on 12 April 2022, $\bar{x}_1 = 38.42$ N/mm², and the average strength for the samples on 18 April 2022, $\bar{x}_2 = 39.12$ N/mm²

$$n_1 = 12; n_2 = 13$$

$$\sum_{i=1}^{n_1} (x_i - \bar{x}_1)^2 = 292.42$$

TABLE 12.3 Concrete sample strengths

Observation Set I - Cast on 12 April 2022	**Sample No.**	1	2	3	4	5	6	7	8	9	10	11	12	
	Strength, N/mm²	45.5	33.5	32	35.5	34	39	36.5	32	44.5	45	42.5	41	
Observation Set II - Cast on 18 April 2022	**Sample No.**	1	2	3	4	5	6	7	8	9	10	11	12	13
	Strength, N/mm²	34	36	45.5	39	39.5	38.5	35.5	38	45	34	43	40	40.5

and

$$\sum_{j=1}^{n_2}\left(x_j-\bar{x}_2\right)^2=170.08$$

Hence, the standard deviation, s, is calculated as shown below:

$$s=\sqrt{\frac{292.42+170.08}{12+13-2}\cdot\left(\frac{1}{12}+\frac{1}{13}\right)}$$

$$=\sqrt{\frac{462.49}{23}\cdot\left(\frac{1}{12}+\frac{1}{13}\right)}=1.79\ \text{N/mm}^2$$

Coefficient of Variation

The coefficient of variation, V, is the ratio of sample standard deviation and mean strength and is expressed as a percentage. It is used to compare the degree of control when compressive strength varies widely. It is determined as follows:

$$V=\frac{s}{\bar{x}}\times 100$$

Range

It is the difference between the highest and lowest values in the data set. In a sample, the range is the difference between the highest and lowest strength values. However, when there are only two specimens, range is the difference between the strength of the two. It is also sometimes known as 'pair difference'.

It is assumed that the results of strength tests follow a normal distribution[1]. As discussed in Chapter 9, a bell-shaped curve, defined by the population mean and the standard deviation, represents the normal distribution. In a normal distribution curve, 68.26% of the values are within one-sigma deviation, 95.44% are within two-sigma, and 99.74% are within three-sigma from the mean. Figure 12.2 shows the normal distribution curve with a sample size $n = 192$, sample mean $\bar{x} = 28$ MPa, sample standard deviation, $s = 2.8$ MPa and coefficient of variation $V = 10\%$.

[1] However, distribution cannot always be assumed to be normal especially when the concrete strength is greater than 70 MPa. There are chances that the test results may exhibit skewness or kurtosis.

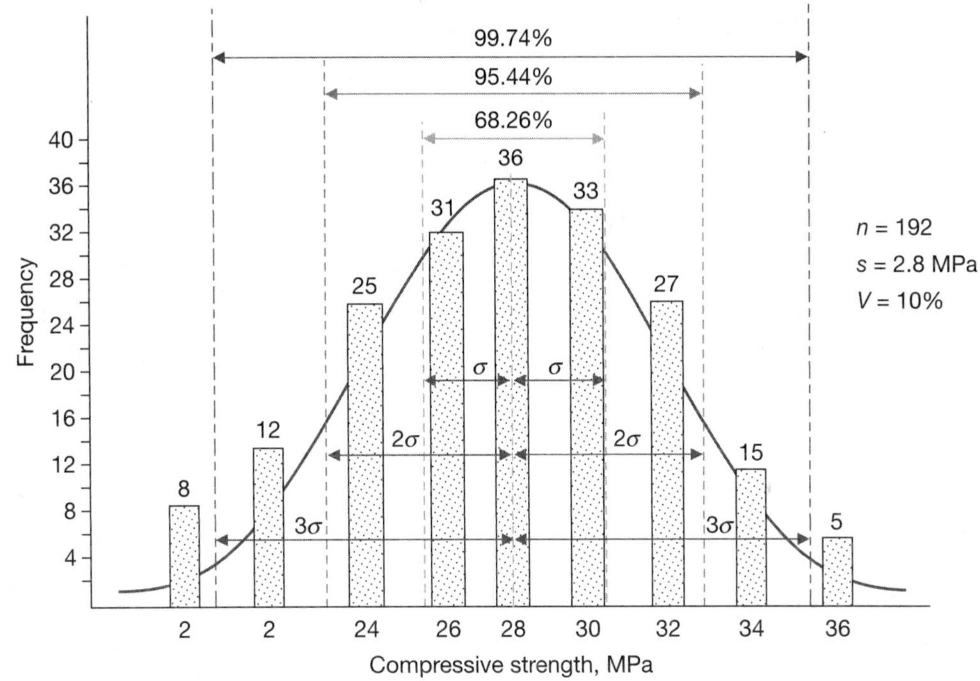

FIGURE 12.2 Distribution of strength test results

A histogram of test results arranged in the order of strength range is superimposed on the bell curve and it reveals that the data of test results are normally distributed. Various circumstances when the histogram does not fit the bell-shaped curve include a smaller number of data and errors in sampling, manufacturing, curing, and testing.

For a concrete mixture prepared under controlled conditions, most test results tend to fall near the average strength, which indicates that the variations are less, making the peak tall and narrow. However, the strength results exhibit variations from the average value when prepared under lesser control and the curve has a shorter and wider peak. There can be different curves based on differences in standard deviations for the same mean. Better control in the manufacturing process can reduce the number of variations.

12.3.2 Variations in Strength

The main purpose of applying statistical tools to concrete test results is to determine the sources of variations and thereby take appropriate action to maintain quality control. Determination of variability within the batch and from batch to batch can be done by comparing the standard deviation, or the coefficient of variation, with the earlier data. The choice between whether to consider standard deviation or coefficient of variation for comparison depends on which of these two remains constant over the range of strength. Standard deviation is found to remain constant for a limited range of strength. Many researchers have found that the coefficient of variation is a better measure to compare the strength within the batch when the strength exceeds 35 MPa (5,000 psi).

Variations Within the Batch

Variations within the batch are mostly due to variations in sampling, curing, and testing. To estimate the strength variations within the batch due to testing variability, the strengths of companion cylinders are determined. Statistical analysis is not possible with a single test result. A greater number of test results is needed to have confidence in the estimate. Though it is preferable to have 30 tests in a sample to estimate the standard deviations within a batch, it can also be determined if the average range of a minimum of 10 same-age strength test results is available. Whereas the standard deviation, $\hat{\sigma}$, can be calculated using the equation in Section 10.2.2; the coefficient of variation in a batch is given by

$$V = \frac{\hat{\sigma}}{\bar{x}}$$

Variations Across the Batch

Batch-to-batch strength variations can be determined by comparing the strength test results of different batches with each other. The sample standard deviation estimates the variations from batch to batch, which are mostly caused by constituent materials and the manufacturing process. From batch to batch, there can be changes in the properties of the materials used for concreting. This variation is attributed to the material suppliers. The variations in the manufacturing process are attributed to the concrete manufacturer. Variations in any or all of the processes like batching, mixing, transporting, pouring, compacting, curing, and sampling cause strength variations.

12.4 ACCEPTANCE CRITERIA

12.4.1 Statistical Interpretation of Design Strength and Required Strength

The quality of concrete used in the structure can be determined by testing the strength of cylinders/cubes cast from the same concrete mixture on the 28th day. The concrete cylinders/cubes to be used for acceptance testing are manufactured, sampled, cured, and tested under controlled conditions. The contract document specifies the required strength of concrete and the frequency of testing. The strength is to be specified with a tolerance limit because all products naturally vary in their test results.

It has been assumed that the concrete strength follows a normal distribution. It means that there can be some percentage of values that fall below the required strength f_c' and some values above it. Hence, statistical-based acceptance criteria for compliance with f_c' have been established by most codes, which is similar to the tolerances for other materials. To meet the standards of strength-performance requirements, the minimum required average strength of the concrete proportion f'_{cr} must be greater than the required/specified strength f'_c. The difference between f'_{cr} and f'_c is governed by the fluctuations observed by way of the standard deviation. If we want to limit the fluctuation to 'z' standard deviations, the strength requirement criterion is given by:

$$f'_{cr} = f'_c + zs$$

The allowable difference between f'_{cr} and f'_c is thus specified in the acceptance criteria. We already know from Figure 12.2 that the area (confidence) within ± 1.σ = 68.26%, while that between ± 2.σ = 95.44%, and that between ± 3.σ = 99.74%. These and in-between areas for additional values of z.σ, where z represents the standard units of the number of standard deviations of fluctuation, are given in Table 12.4. An example calculation for a confidence of 40%, which is the first row in Table 12.4, is illustrated in Figure 12.3. This follows from the z-Table given in Appendix 1.

The minimum average strength f'_{cr} increases as the variation, expressed as the coefficient of variance, increases for a required/specified strength. This is illustrated in Figure 12.4. This is done naturally to overcome uncertainty. Hence, the higher the chance of the test results going lower than f'_c, the higher should be the desired value of f'_{cr}.

TABLE 12.4 Values of z corresponding to various acceptance criteria

Confidence level/Percentage of tests within $\mu \pm z\sigma$	Probability of falling below $f'_c - z\sigma$	z
40	30%	0.524
50	25%	0.674
60	20%	0.841
68.26	**15.9%**	**1.00**
70	15%	1.036
80	10%	1.282
90	5%	1.645
95	2.5%	1.96
95.44	**2.3%**	**2.00**
98	1%	2.326
99	0.5%	2.576
99.74	**0.13%**	**3.00**

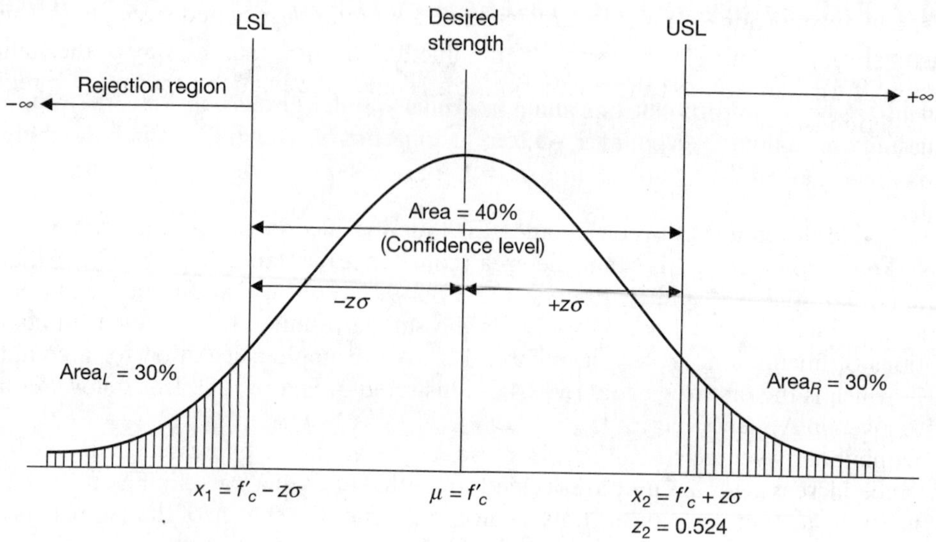

FIGURE 12.3 Graphical representation of acceptance criteria

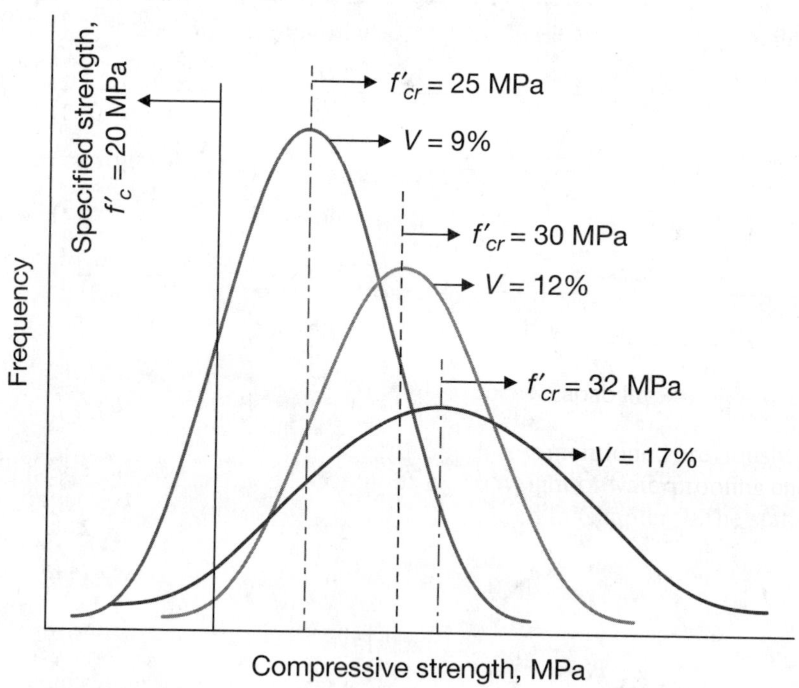

FIGURE 12.4 Normal distribution curve changing with the coefficient of variation

12.4.2 Probability Value of Test Results Falling Below the Specified Strength

Table 12.5 lists the percentage of chance by which a test will fall below f_c' when the mean strength required μ equals $f_c' + z\sigma$ for different values of z, given in Appendix 1. Figure 12.5 demonstrates how the probabilities of tests are lower than f_c' come to be in Table 12.5 for average strength = $f_c' + 2.6\sigma$.

TABLE 12.5 Percentage of tests lower than f_c' for different values of average strength equal to $f_c' + z\sigma$

Average strength	% of tests lower than f_c'	Average strength	% of tests lower than f_c'
$f_c' + 0.2\sigma$	42.07%	$f_c' + 1.645\sigma$	**5.0%**
$f_c' + 0.4\sigma$	34.46%	$f_c' + 1.8\sigma$	3.59%
$f_c' + 0.6\sigma$	27.43%	$f_c' + 2\sigma$	2.28%
$f_c' + 0.8\sigma$	21.19%	$f_c' + 2.2\sigma$	1.39%
$f_c' + 1\sigma$	15.87%	$f_c' + 2.4\sigma$	0.82%
$f_c' + 1.2\sigma$	11.51%	$f_c' + 2.6\sigma$	**0.47%**
$f_c' + 1.4\sigma$	8.08%	$f_c' + 2.8\sigma$	0.26%
$f_c' + 1.6\sigma$	5.48%	$f_c' + 3\sigma$	0.13%

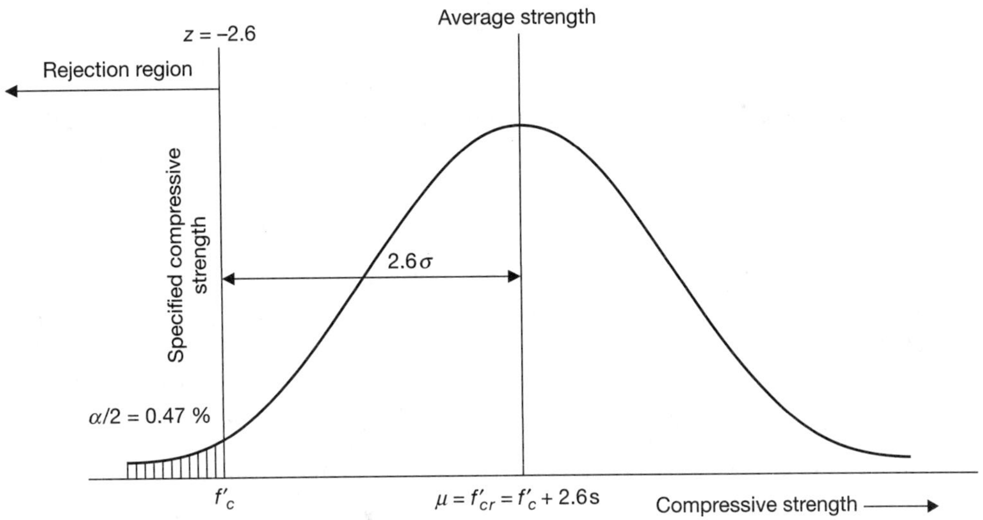

FIGURE 12.5 Graphical representation of design criteria

12.4.3 Design Criteria as Per IS Code

Before we give the terms and nomenclatures for Indian terms or use the Indian terms, we must explain how they compare to the American ACI terms used above. Table 12.6 equates the terms used.

TABLE 12.6 Terms used in IS code and ACI code

Terms used in IS code	Terms used in ACI code	Meaning
f_{ck} (Characteristic compressive strength	f_c' (Specified compressive strength)	Specified design strength
f_{ck}' (Target mean compressive strength)	f_{cr}' (Critical value of test results)	Required average minimum strength in test results

The Indian Standard IS 456 specifies the characteristic compressive strength as that value of design strength below which not more than **5 percent** of the test results should fall (BIS, 2021a). Hence, while designing as per the Indian code, the target strength of the test results (f_{ck}') is determined as follows (BIS, 2019):

$$f_{ck}' = f_{ck} + 1.645s$$

where 1.645 is the prescribed value of z; in this case for 5% of the area to be in the tail, or

$$f_{ck}' = f_{ck} + X, \text{ whichever is higher.}$$

Where

f_{ck}' = target mean compressive strength of concrete cubes in 28 days (MPa)

f_{ck} = characteristic (design) compressive strength at 28 days (MPa)

s = standard deviation in MPa

X = a factor that depends on the grade of concrete given in Table 1 of IS 10262: 2019.

Figure 12.6 is a similar representation as Figure 12.5, except that Indian terms are used and the mean is f_{ck} + 1.645s (= f_{ck}').

12.4.4 Acceptance Criteria as per IS 456

As we have seen in the previous section, concrete is designed for a strength higher than the characteristic compressive strength, and the design allows for a certain percentage (5%) of test results to fall below the characteristic compressive strength. Since it is not acceptable for concrete strength to be much lower than the characteristic compressive strength, because it affects the integrity and safety of the structure, the IS code has set a limit for acceptance of concrete for construction purposes. IS 456 has specified the acceptance criteria for valid samples.

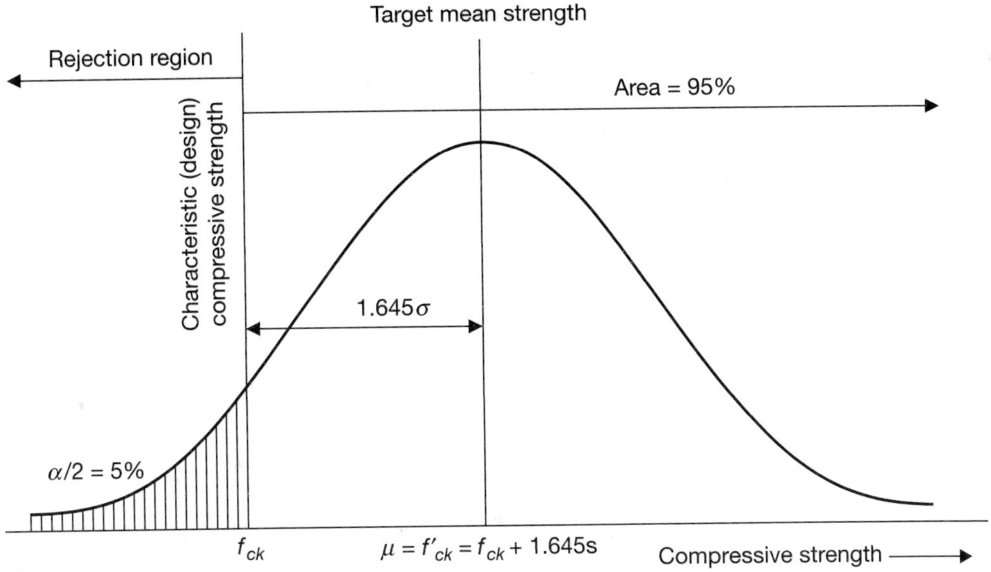

FIGURE 12.6 Graphical representation of design criteria

The following criterion checks the validity of the sample.

> 'Average of three values shall be taken as the representative of the batch provided the individual variation is not more than ±15% of the average. Otherwise repeat test shall be made, however if there is no further sample, then the average of two closest values may be taken as the average result.' (BIS, 2021b).

This criterion indicates that the range shall not be greater than 30% of the mean. The test results are invalid when the variations exceed the limits. The variations within a sample affect the consistency of results. Hence, for internal consistency and to ensure that the casting, curing, and testing processes produce valid concrete samples, the criterion that individual deviations must not exceed 15 percent of the mean has been specified. When the variations exceed 15% of the mean, fabrication processes and machine calibration must be verified.

The acceptance criteria for concrete as per Indian Standards are given below (BIS, 2021a):

- For M15 and above,
  - the mean of a group of four non-overlapping consecutive test results, f_{m4}, is to be
    - $\geq f_{ck} + 0.825 \times$ established standard deviation, or
    - $\geq f_{ck} + 3$ N/mm^2, whichever is greater,
  - individual test results $\geq f_{ck} - 3$ N/mm^2.

The illustrative distribution schematic for this condition is given in Figure 12.7.

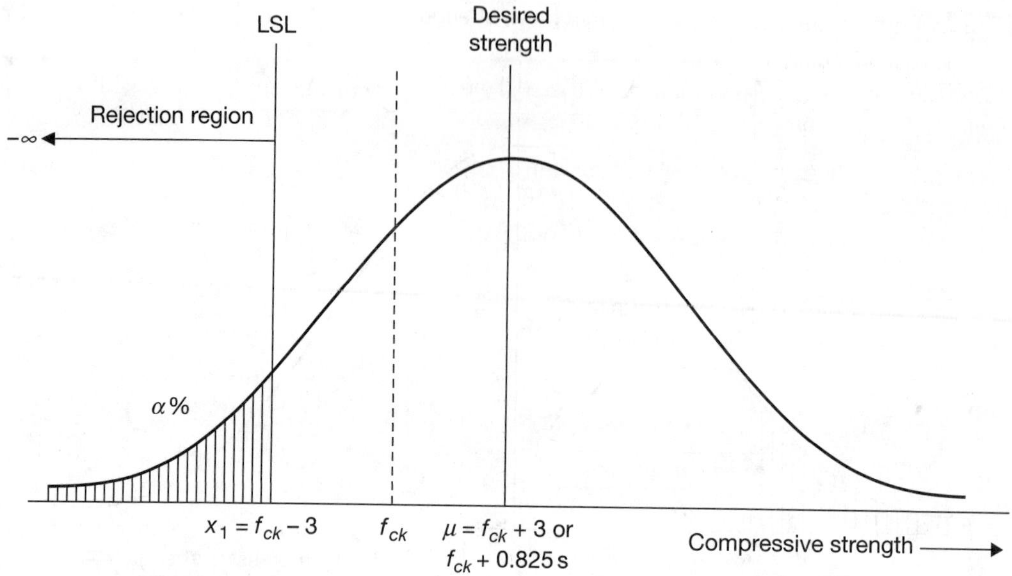

FIGURE 12.7 Graphical representation of acceptance criteria as per IS code

- **Note 1:** 'In the absence of established value of standard deviation, the values given in Table 8 of IS 456[2] may be assumed, and attempt should be made to obtain results of 30 samples as early as possible to establish the value of standard deviation.' (BIS, 2021a).
- **Note 2:** When the quantity of concrete is up to 30 m^3, the number of samples required for acceptance testing is less than 4. In such cases, the mean of test results shall be f_{ck} + 4 N/mm^2 minimum, and the individual test result must be greater than or equal to f_{ck} − 2 N/mm^2.

Example 3 At a construction project site, the following test results (Table 12.7) were obtained for the concrete done for the raft foundation. The required grade of concrete is M35. Test whether the samples can be accepted or not by applying the acceptance criteria of the IS Code.

2

Concrete grade	Value of X (MPa) (Table 1 of IS 10262)	Assumed standard deviation (Table 8, IS 456)
M 10, M 15	5.0	3.5
M 20, M 25	5.5	4.0
M 30, M 35, M 40, M 45, M 50, M 55, M 60	6.5	5.0
> M60	8.0	To be established by actual trials

TABLE 12.7 Strength of cubes of 12 samples

Sample No.	Strength of cube 1, N/mm^2	Strength of cube 2, N/mm^2	Strength of cube 3, N/mm^2	Average strength, N/mm^2, $\bar{x}$
1	44.56	45.01	43.32	44.30
2	40.25	43.55	42.55	42.12
3	42.01	38.79	36.97	39.26
4	38.27	39.25	40.44	39.32
5	41.51	43.44	40.47	41.81
6	41.79	38.55	39.79	40.04
7	38.1	38.47	39.11	38.56
8	38.55	39.31	41.25	39.70
9	43.9	39.2	38.55	40.55
10	38.19	38.11	39.5	38.60
11	39.19	39.3	40.24	39.58
12	43.05	40.79	45.41	43.08

Solution:

First, we have to check whether the samples are valid or not valid for further investigations by determining whether the individual cube strength varies by more than ±15% of the average. If any individual cube strength is more than ±15%, then the test results are rendered invalid. Table 12.8 shows the calculations for testing the validity of the samples.

Let us consider row 1 in Table 12.8. It is to be checked whether all the cubes in samples have strength within ±15% of their average strength. The cube strengths in sample 1 are 44.56, 45.01 and 43.32 N/mm^2. Their average strength is 44.30 N/mm^2, which can be rounded off to the nearest 0.5 N/mm^2, and it yields 44.5 N/mm^2. Adding 15% to the average, we get 51 N/mm^2; and 15% less than the average is 38 N/mm^2. The cubes in sample 1 have strength between ±15% of 44.5 N/mm^2. Hence, this sample is valid. Similarly, the cubes in other samples are also tested for their validity.

Now, the samples are to be verified for acceptance.

As per the acceptance criteria, f_{m4} is to be $\geq f_{ck} + 0.825s$, or $\geq f_{ck} + 3$ N/mm^2, whichever is greater, provided individual test results $\geq f_{ck} - 3$ N/mm^2. Figure 12.8 illustrates the acceptance criteria for this example.

The established standard deviation of the 12 samples yielded 1.88 N/mm^2 (as derived in Section 12.3.1). Since this standard deviation has been firmly established, we are not using the codal values of Table 8 of IS 456 that are otherwise used when $n < 30$ in the absence of an established standard deviation.

TABLE 12.8 Testing the validity of the samples

Sample No.	Strength of cube 1, N/mm^2	Strength of cube 2, N/mm^2	Strength of cube 3, N/mm^2	Average strength, N/mm^2, $\bar{x}$	Rounded strength (as per IS Code), N/mm^2	$\bar{x}$ + 15%	$\bar{x}$ − 15%	Is it valid if individual cube results do not vary by more than ±15%?
1	44.56	45.01	43.32	44.30	44.5	51	38	Valid
2	40.25	43.55	42.55	42.12	42	48.5	35.5	Valid
3	42.01	38.79	36.97	39.26	39.5	45.5	33.5	Valid
4	38.27	39.25	40.44	39.32	39.5	45.5	33.5	Valid
5	41.51	43.44	40.47	41.81	42	48.5	35.5	Valid
6	41.79	38.55	39.79	40.04	40	46.00	34.00	Valid
7	38.1	38.47	39.11	38.56	38.5	44.5	32.5	Valid
8	38.55	39.31	41.25	39.70	39.5	45.5	33.5	Valid
9	43.9	39.2	38.55	40.55	40.5	46.5	34.5	Valid
10	38.19	38.11	39.5	38.60	38.5	44.5	32.5	Valid
11	39.19	39.3	40.24	39.58	39.5	45.5	33.5	Valid
12	43.05	40.79	45.41	43.08	43	49.5	36.5	Valid

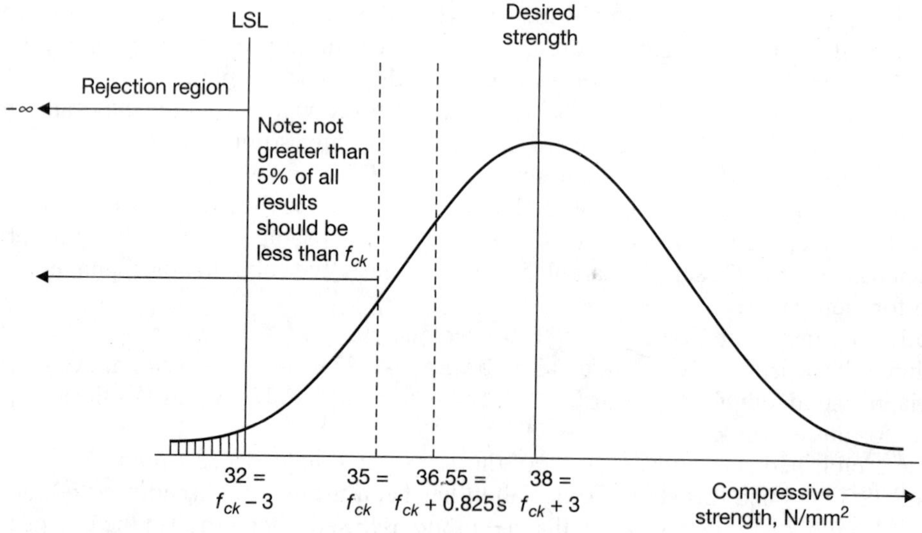

FIGURE 12.8 Graphical representation of acceptance criteria as per IS code

In addition, the mean of the group of four non-overlapping consecutive test results must be greater than f_{ck} + 0.825s (= 35 + 0.825 × 1.88 = **36.55** N/mm^2) or f_{ck} + 3 (= 35 + 3 = **38** N/mm^2), whichever is greater. Hence, f_{m4} must be ≥ 38 N/mm^2.

Table 12.9 below shows that the mean of the group of four non-overlapping consecutive test results, f_{m4}, for all the samples is greater than 38 N/mm^2. And, individual test results are greater than 32 N/mm^2. Therefore, these samples are acceptable.

TABLE 12.9 Calculation of f_{m4}

S. No.	Strength of cube 1, N/mm^2	Strength of cube 2, N/mm^2	Strength of cube 3, N/mm^2	Average strength, N/mm^2	Rounded Strength	f_{m4}
1	44.56	45.01	43.32	44.30	44.5	
2	40.25	43.55	42.55	42.12	42.00	41.38
3	42.01	38.79	36.97	39.26	39.5	
4	38.27	39.25	40.44	39.32	39.5	
5	41.51	43.44	40.47	41.81	42	
6	41.79	38.55	39.79	40.04	40	40
7	38.1	38.47	39.11	38.56	38.5	
8	38.55	39.31	41.25	39.70	39.5	
9	43.9	39.2	38.55	40.55	40.5	
10	38.19	38.11	39.5	38.60	38.5	40.38
11	39.19	39.3	40.24	39.58	39.5	
12	43.05	40.79	45.41	43.08	43	

12.4.5 Strength Criteria as per ACI 214R1-11

The strength requirement criteria are different in different countries. The ACI 214R-11 code of the USA specifies various criteria that can be used to ensure that the concrete strength meets the requirements. The criteria are usually specified in terms of standard variation or coefficient of variation. ACI 214R-11 provides the standard deviation and coefficient of variation for various control standards suitable for concrete of different strengths, as given in Table 12.10.

Though there are various criteria for acceptance, the two generally followed acceptance criteria in ACI are given below:

1 ***First criterion:*** Specifies the percentage of random individual test results that may fall below f'_c, represented by the z value. If the percentage of test results falling below f'_c is specified to be not more than 5%, then the corresponding z value is −1.645. Similarly, when mentioned that not more than 10% should fall below the required strength, then z = −1.282.

TABLE 12.10 Values of standard deviation for different levels of control *(ACI, 2011)*

Level of control of operations	Standard deviation, psi (MPa)	
	General testing	Laboratory testing
Excellent	Below 400 (< 2.8)	Below 200 (< 1.4)
Very good	400–500 (2.8–3.4)	200–250 (1.4–1.7)
Good	500–600 (3.4–4.1)	250–300 (1.7–2.1)
Fair	600–700 (4.1–4.8)	300–350 (2.1–2.4)
Poor	Above 700 (> 4.8)	Above 350 (> 2.4)

Example: Calculate the required minimum average strength of concrete, f'_{cr}, for a specified strength, f'_c, of 4,000 psi, when the contract specifies that the percentage of test results allowed to fall below f'_c is 10%.

Solution:

Assumption: Consider excellent quality control as indicated by a standard deviation of 8%.

$$\text{Hence, standard deviation} = \frac{8 \times 4,000}{100} = 320 \text{ psi}$$

Percentage of test results that fall below f'_c is 10%, implies that confidence of test result equalling the mean = 80%.

This means that the z should extend by 1.282.s from the mean to the left to ensure that the test results falling below the specification limit do not exceed 10%. From Table 12.4, the value of z corresponding to 10% falling below f'_c is 1.282.

Hence, the desired strength of concrete = f'_c + z.s = 4,000 + 1.282 × 320 = 4,410 psi (= 310 kgf/cm^2)

Figure 12.9 illustrates the above problem graphically.

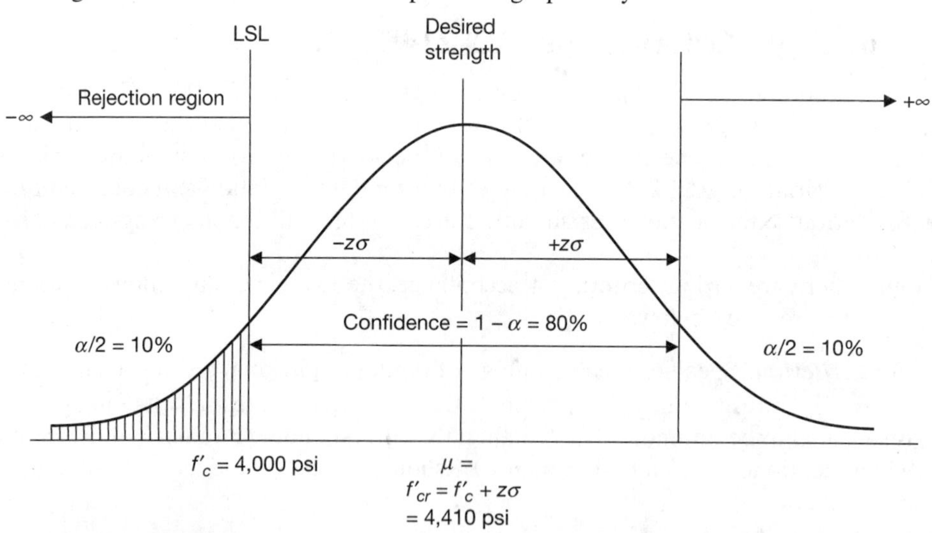

FIGURE 12.9 Graphical representation of acceptance criteria (as per ACI)

2. ***Second criterion*:** Specifies the likelihood of the average of n successive strength tests falling below f_c'. When the maximum per cent of moving average of n consecutive tests that fall below f_c' is specified, the minimum average strength of concrete is given by:

$$f_{cr}' = f_c' + \frac{zs}{\sqrt{n}} \text{ (i.e., } \frac{zs}{\sqrt{n}} = x - \mu = f_{cr}' - f_c')^3.$$

Example: Calculate the required design strength of concrete, f_{cr}', for a specified strength, f_c', of 4,000 psi, when the contract specifies that the frequency of averages of three consecutive tests below f_c' should not exceed 1 in 100.

Solution:

***Assumption*:** Consider poor quality control as indicated by an SD of 18.75%.

Thus, standard deviation $= \frac{18.75 \times 4{,}000}{100} = 750$ psi

The frequency of averages of three consecutive tests below f_c' should not exceed 1 in 100, indicating confidence = 98% → $z = \pm 2.33$

Now, the design strength of concrete, f_{cr}', should be $= f_c' + \frac{zs}{\sqrt{n}}$

So, $f_{cr}' = 4{,}000 + \frac{2.33 \times 750}{\sqrt{3}} = 5{,}009$ psi (= 352 kgf/cm^2)

The graphical representation of the above example is depicted in Figure 12.10.

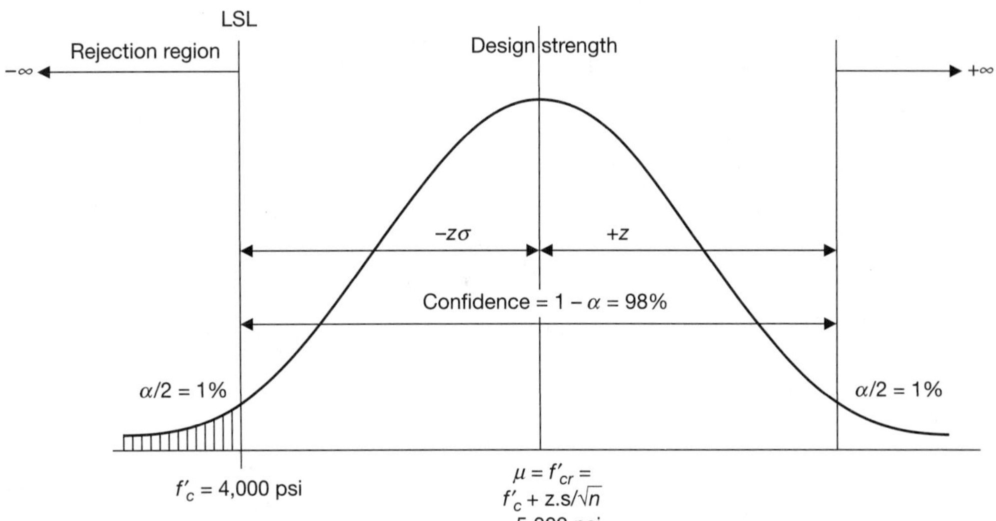

FIGURE 12.10 Graphical representation of acceptance criteria (as per ACI)

[3] Note: Standard deviation of a sample is determined by dividing the standard deviation of the individual test results (s) by the square root of the number of tests (n) in each average. This is a fundamental theorem in statistics. The value of n is generally equal to 3 in lab testing.
Furthermore, any time that $n < 30$, the t-test should be used instead of the z-test. However, even the ACI code uses the z-test as a simplification.

The other ways of specifying acceptance criteria are as follows:

- Given a level of significance, α, find f'_{cr}
- Given that f'_c should be x% less than f'_{cr}
- Given that LSL should not be less than y% of f'_c
- Given that f'_c should not be m psi less than f'_{cr}
- Given that the criterion is for average values
- Given that the criterion is for raw values

12.5 CONTROL CHART FOR CONCRETE TEST RESULTS

As explained in Chapter 10, control charts are used to identify trends in test results and, hence, determine the variability so that measures can be taken to reduce variability and increase the efficiency of the processes. When the control of the process is affected, the data gives an indication of the requirement for an action to bring back the process to control. These charts can be used to monitor the quality of concrete, especially where there is continuous production for a long period.

By way of example for illustrating the implementation of control charts in analysing concrete strength, suppose the details of the strength tests of a few concrete samples, where the strength requirement is 4800 ± 400 psi, are as given in Table 12.11.

TABLE 12.11 Details of samples

	Field Test Number (Subgroups)									
Specimen (Cube)	**1**	**2**	**3**	**4**	**5**	**6**	**7**	**8**	**9**	**10**
	Field strength, psi									
1	4,500	5,200	6,300	3,700	4,800	4,500	4,200	4,600	5,300	5,800
2	4,200	5,000	5,800	4,500	5,000	4,200	4,300	4,300	5,000	5,500
3	4,000	4,800	6,500	4,100	5,200	5,000	4,600	4,500	5,100	5,600
Sum	12,700	15,000	18,600	12,300	15,000	13,700	13,100	13,400	15,400	16,900
Average	4,233.33	5,000	6,200	4,100	5,000	4,566.67	4,366.67	4,466.67	5,133.33	5,633.33
Range	500	400	700	800	400	800	400	300	300	300

The upper and lower limits of mean and range are calculated as below:

$$\text{Sample size, } n = 3; \text{ Subgroups, } k = 10$$

$$\bar{\bar{x}} = \frac{(4,233.33 + 5,000 + 6,200 + \ldots + 5,633.33)}{10} = 4,870$$

$$\bar{R} = \frac{500 + 400 + 700 + \ldots + 300}{10} = 490$$

$$UCL_{\bar{x}} = \bar{\bar{x}} + A_2\bar{R} = 4{,}870 + (1.023 \times 490) = 5{,}371.27$$

$$LCL_{\bar{x}} = \bar{\bar{x}} - A_2\bar{R} = 4{,}870 - (1.023 \times 490) = 4{,}368.73$$

Where the A_2 value is taken from Table 10.1 of Chapter 10, corresponding to $n = 3$.

$$UCL_R = D_4\bar{R} = 2.574 \times 490 = 1{,}261.26$$

$$LCL_R = D_3\bar{R} = 0 \times 490 = 0$$

Where the D_4 and D_3 values are taken from Table 10.1 of Chapter 10, corresponding to $n = 3$.

Figures 12.11 and 12.12 show the control chart for mean and range, respectively. The inferences that can be made from the control chart are given below:

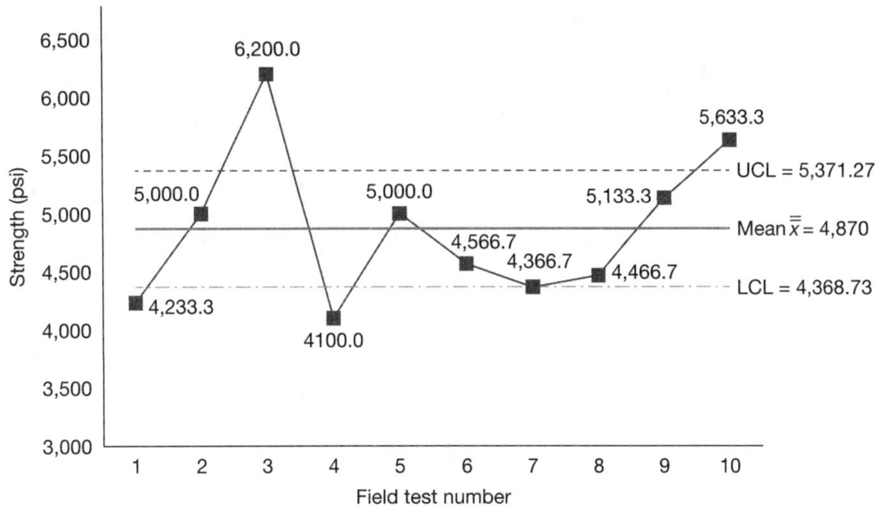

FIGURE 12.11 Control chart for the mean of strength

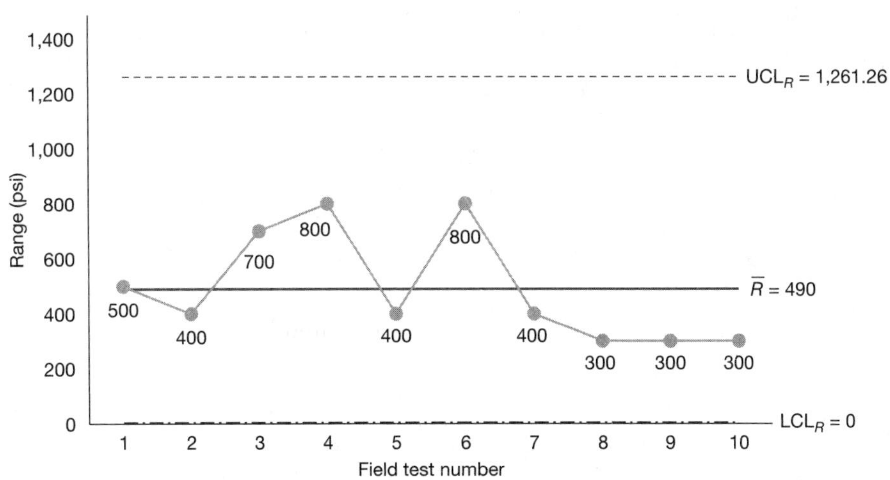

FIGURE 12.12 Control chart for the range of strength

- Defectives are being produced.
- Production is quite erratic – on both the low side and high side – as control limits for the mean are being surpassed.
- There is a significant chance of not meeting the specification.
- Exceeding specifications has drawbacks, such as extra costs for the contractor.
- Quality control is deficient.

The control chart for the range reveals no anomalies or deficiencies.

12.6 PROCESS CAPABILITY ANALYSIS FOR CONCRETE TEST RESULTS

Now, let us determine the process capability index of this process, which was introduced in Chapter 10 to discover whether the results from the control chart can be confirmed and whether we can determine additional issues and concerns with the results.

In the example of the previous section, assume that the concrete strength requirement as per the contract is 4,800 ± 400 psi. The lower side of this variation represents the minimum for the sake of structural integrity, while the upper side is a signal for the contractor not to exceed costs unnecessarily. In the previous section, we calculated the following information:

$$n = 3$$

$$\bar{\bar{x}} = 4{,}870 \text{ psi (from before)}$$

$$\bar{R} = 490 \text{ (from before)}$$

Specification = 4,800 ± 400 psi. Hence, USL = 5,200 psi and LSL = 4,400 psi; d_2 = 1.693 from Table 12.3.

$$\hat{\sigma} = \frac{\bar{R}}{d_2} = \frac{490}{1.693} = 289.43$$

$$C_p = \frac{\text{USL} - \text{LSL}}{6\hat{\sigma}} = \frac{5{,}200 - 4{,}400}{6(289.43)} = 0.46$$

$$C_{pl} = \frac{\bar{\bar{x}} - \text{LSL}}{3\hat{\sigma}} = \frac{4{,}870 - 4{,}400}{3(289.43)} = 0.54$$

$$C_{pu} = \frac{\text{USL} - \bar{\bar{x}}}{3\hat{\sigma}} = \frac{5{,}200 - 4{,}870}{3(289.43)} = 0.38$$

$$C_{pk} = \text{min.}\ \{C_{pl}, C_{pu}\} = \text{min.}\ \{0.54, 0.38\} = 0.38.$$

Since $C_{pk} < 1$, there are defects in the process. In this case, defects are being produced on both the high and low sides, but more defectives are produced on the upper side owing to the lower value of C_{pu} compared to the value of C_{pl}. This is further evident graphically in Figures 12.13 and 12.14, which show a greater area between USL and UCL than between LSL and LCL. Thus, the system is operating more on the higher side of strength implying that the contractor may be spending more on cement or water reducers than necessary, or spending more on smaller-sized aggregates than necessary. However, the client has no objection for strength results on the higher side. Such an analysis has to follow from the design mix and facts on the site.

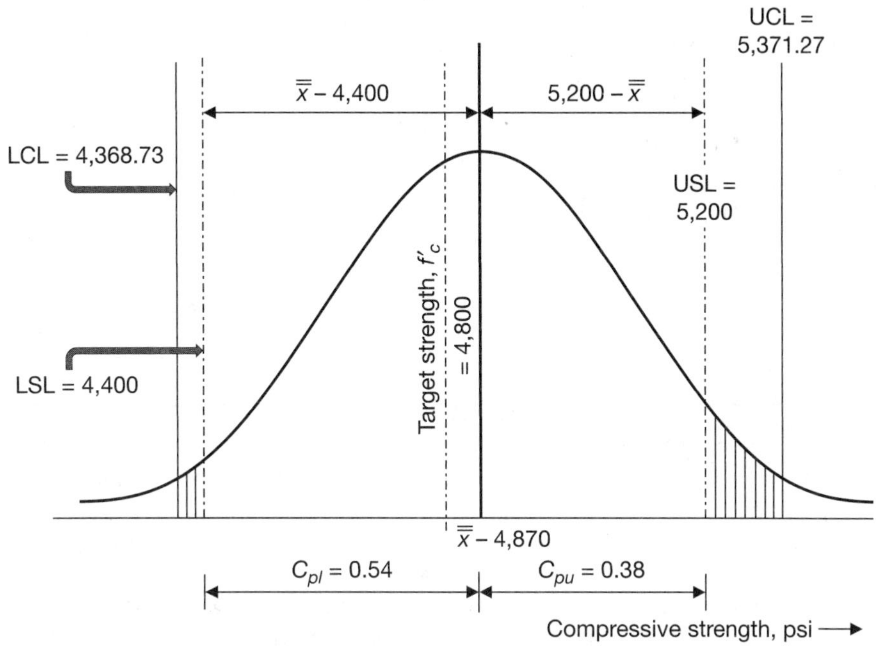

FIGURE 12.13 Process capability chart

The final process capability chart is given in Figure 12.13. It is very clear from the figure that the mean of test results is such that control limits are not aligned with the specification limits. In addition, the process variation is greater than the specification limits, which is an implication of defectives being produced.

12.6.1 Probability of Defectives Being Produced

The area between the control limits and the specification limits on either side represents the probability of defectives being produced on their respective sides. These areas are calculated as in Table 12.12 using the standard equation:

$$z = \frac{(x - \mu)}{\sigma}$$

In this case,

$$\mu = 4{,}870 \text{ (from the last section)}$$

$$\sigma = 289.43 \text{ (from the last section)}$$

TABLE 12.12 Calculation of the probability of defectives

x	LSL	LCL	USL	UCL
z	$z_1 = \frac{(4,400 - 4,870)}{289.43} = -1.623$	$z_2 = \frac{(4,368.73 - 4,870)}{289.43} = -1.732$	$z_3 = \frac{(5,200 - 4,870)}{289.43} = 1.14$	$z_4 = \frac{(5,371.27 - 4,870)}{289.43} = 1.732$
Area of the curve that falls within the mean and z (From z-tables)	0.4477	0.4583	0.3728	0.4583
Difference in the area between Specification Limit and Control Limit	0.4583 − 0.4477 = 0.0106		0.4583 − 0.3728 = 0.0855	

The areas calculated between the mean of test results and the control and specification limits are depicted in Figure 12.14. The areas between the control limit and specification limits on both the upper and lower sides of the mean are marked in the figure. The variations produced are greater on the upper side, as indicated by the larger area of 8.55% compared to 1.06% on the lower side. This means that the chances of producing a defective one on the upper side are 8.55/1.06 = 8 times more than producing a defective one on the lower side. So now, the contractor knows what to look out for. Since the variations on the lower side are less, the number of defectives produced on the lower side is less. At the same time, the higher area on the upper side may lead to an excess cost for the contractor.

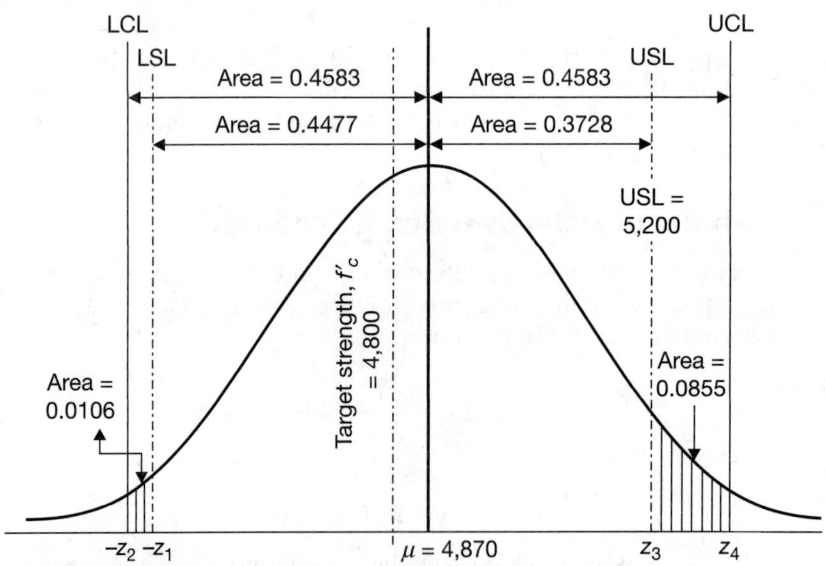

FIGURE 12.14 Area between the specification limits and control limits

Hence, action can accordingly be taken to control the process. Actions may include better mix proportioning, better mixing, better pouring, and better testing processes, as reflected in Figure 12.1. When a process is in control, the strength results will vary randomly around the mean and stay within the control limits. However, process capability determines whether the actual performance conforms to the specifications or not.

CONCLUSION

Close attention must be paid to each step in the concrete manufacturing process. However, if not manufactured properly, it can lead to the failure of the constructed structure. This is all the more important because concrete is a widely used construction material due to the strength and durability characteristics it possesses. When variations occur in the process, they may not be always recognisable during visual inspection.

Construction projects require testing the strength of the concrete to ensure that the strength meets the specifications mentioned in the contract. Testing of concrete is done on concrete specimens cast from the concrete used for construction activities. The strength of the concrete samples varies within the batch and from batch to batch for various reasons. These variations, when they exceed the specified limits, indicate that the process has gone out of control. The use of such concrete may lead to early deterioration of the structure and, in the worst case, the failure of the structure. Hence, it is very important to keep track of the strength of the concrete during construction. Random sampling and testing are, therefore, mandated in construction codes.

This chapter deals with the statistical evaluation of concrete strength test results. The various statistical parameters used for analysis have been discussed. The concrete strength test results follow normal distribution. The criteria for acceptance of concrete have been explained based on this. Variations can be calculated by determining the control limits of the process from the test result data, and the process capability found. Knowledge about the process capability helps the concrete manufacturer to take necessary action to fix the problems.

It is important to take proper quality control measures to ensure the safety of the occupants and the stability and durability of the constructed structures. Hence, the construction and building codes have stipulated criteria for quality control of various materials used for construction. The management, along with the associated workforce, has the responsibility to follow the codes and regulations and various quality practices to create sustainable, economical, and durable infrastructure for the nation and its citizens.

WORKS CITED

ACI. (2011), *Guide to Evaluation of Strength Test Results of Concrete.* (Farmington Hills: American Concrete Institute).

BIS. (2019), *IS 10262 : 2019 Concrete Mix Proportioning – Guidelines.* (New Delhi: Bureau of Indian Standards).

BIS. (2021a), *IS 456: 2000 (Reaffirmed 2021) Indian Standard Plain and Reinforced Concrete-Code of Practice.* (New Delhi: Bureau of Indian Standards).

BIS. (2021b), *IS 516 (Part I/Sec I): 2021 Hardened Concrete – Methods of Test.* Part 1 Testing of strength of hardened concrete. Section 1 Compressive, flexural and split tensile strength. (New Delhi: Bureau of Indian Standards).

REVIEW QUESTIONS

Multiple Choice Questions

1. ____________ is a better measure to compare the strength within the batch and when the strength exceeds 35 MPa.

   (a) Coefficient of variation (b) Standard deviation

   (c) Mean (d) Range

2. For a concrete mixture prepared under controlled conditions, ____________ test results tend to fall near the average strength.

   (a) all (b) most

   (c) no (d) a few

3. ____________ is the difference between the highest and lowest values in the data set.

   (a) Range (b) Mean

   (c) Coefficient of variation (d) Standard deviation

4. The Indian Standard IS 456 specifies the characteristic compressive strength as that value of design strength below which not more than ____ **percent** of the test results should fall

   (a) 10 (b) 5

   (c) 1 (d) 20

Short Answer Type Questions

1. How is the variability within the batch and from batch to batch determined?
2. How is the minimum average required strength determined when the specified compressive strength is given?
3. Illustrate the graphical representation of design criteria.
4. What is the application of a control chart in analysing the concrete strength test results?

Long Answer Type Questions

1. Explain why concrete strength varies from batch to batch and within the batch.
2. What are the statistical parameters used in the analysis of concrete strength?

3. Explain the design criteria as per the IS code.
4. Discuss the acceptance criteria as per the IS code and ACI code.
5. Calculate the required minimum average strength of concrete, f'_{cr}, for a specified strength, f'_c, of 5,000 psi, when the contract specifies that the percentage of test results allowed to fall below f'_c is 5%.
6. Calculate the required minimum average strength of concrete, f'_{cr}, for a specified strength, f'_c, of 5,000 psi, when the contract specifies that the frequency of averages of three consecutive tests below f'_c should not exceed 1 in 40.

ANSWER KEYS

Multiple Choice Questions

1. (a) 2. (b) 3. (a) 4. (b)

Appendix 1

Standard Normal Distribution Table

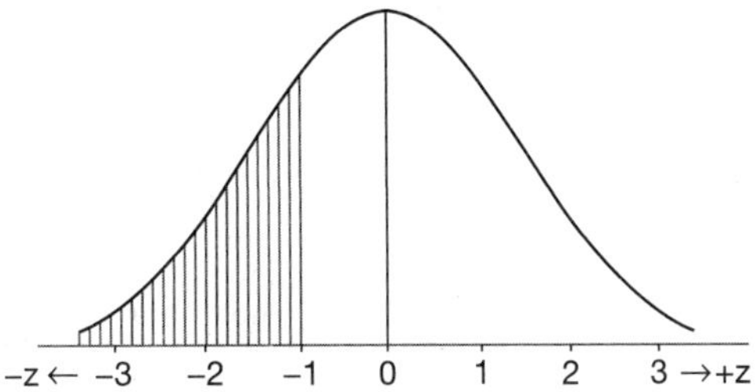

The table given below can be used to determine the area under the curve from the left tail for any value of z. The value corresponding to $z = -1$ is 0.1587, indicating 15.87% area under the standard normal distribution that is to the left of $z = (-)1.0$.

z	.00
–5.0	.000000287
–4.5	.00000340
–4.0	.0000317
–3.5	.000233

z	.00	.01	.0 2	.0 3	.0 4	.05	.06	.0 7	.0 8	.0 9
–3.4	.0003	.0003	.0003	.0003	.0003	.0003	.0003	.0003	.0003	.0002
–3.3	.0005	.0005	.0005	.0004	.0004	.0004	.0004	.0004	.0004	.0003
–3.2	.0007	.0007	.0006	.0006	.0006	.0006	.0006	.0005	.0005	.0005
–3.1	.001	.0009	.0009	.0009	.0008	.0008	.0008	.0008	.0007	.0007
–3	.0013	.0013	.0013	.0012	.0012	.0011	.0011	.0011	.001	.001
–2.9	.0019	.0018	.0018	.0017	.0016	.0016	.0015	.0015	.0014	.0014
–2.8	.0026	.0025	.0024	.0023	.0023	.0022	.0021	.0021	.002	.0019

z	.00	.01	.0 2	.0 3	.0 4	.05	.06	.0 7	.0 8	.0 9
−2.7	.0035	.0034	.0033	.0032	.0031	.003	.0029	.0028	.0027	.0026
−2.6	.0047	.0045	.0044	.0043	.0041	.004	.0039	.0038	.0037	.0036
−2.5	.0062	.006	.0059	.0057	.0055	.0054	.0052	.0051	.0049	.0048
−2.4	.0082	.008	.0078	.0075	.0073	.0071	.0069	.0068	.0066	.0064
−2.3	.0107	.0104	.0102	.0099	.0096	.0094	.0091	.0089	.0087	.0084
−2.2	.0139	.0136	.0132	.0129	.0125	.0122	.0119	.0116	.0113	.011
−2.1	.0179	.0174	.017	.0166	.0162	.0158	.0154	.015	.0146	.0143
−2	.0228	.0222	.0217	.0212	.0207	.0202	.0197	.0192	.0188	.0183
−1.9	.0287	.0281	.0274	.0268	.0262	.0256	.025	.0244	.0239	.0233
−1.8	.0359	.0351	.0344	.0336	.0329	.0322	.0314	.0307	.0301	.0294
−1.7	.0446	.0436	.0427	.0418	.0409	.0401	.0392	.0384	.0375	.0367
−1.6	.0548	.0537	.0526	.0516	.0505	.0495	.0485	.0475	.0465	.0455
−1.5	.0668	.0655	.0643	.063	.0618	.0606	.0594	.0582	.0571	.0559
−1.4	.0808	.0793	.0778	.0764	.0749	.0735	.0721	.0708	.0694	.0681
−1.3	.0968	.0951	.0934	.0918	.0901	.0885	.0869	.0853	.0838	.0823
−1.2	.1151	.1131	.1112	.1093	.1075	.1056	.1038	.102	.1003	.0985
−1.1	.1357	.1335	.1314	.1292	.1271	.1251	.123	.121	.119	.117
−1	.1587	.1562	.1539	.1515	.1492	.1469	.1446	.1423	.1401	.1379
−0.9	.1841	.1814	.1788	.1762	.1736	.1711	.1685	.166	.1635	.1611
−0.8	.2119	.209	.2061	.2033	.2005	.1977	.1949	.1922	.1894	.1867
−0.7	.242	.2389	.2358	.2327	.2296	.2266	.2236	.2206	.2177	.2148
−0.6	.2743	.2709	.2676	.2643	.2611	.2578	.2546	.2514	.2483	.2451
−0.5	.3085	.305	.3015	.2981	.2946	.2912	.2877	.2843	.281	.2776
−0.4	.3446	.3409	.3372	.3336	.33	.3264	.3228	.3192	.3156	.3121
−0.3	.3821	.3783	.3745	.3707	.3669	.3632	.3594	.3557	.352	.3483
−0.2	.4207	.4168	.4129	.409	.4052	.4013	.3974	.3936	.3897	.3859
−0.1	.4602	.4562	.4522	.4483	.4443	.4404	.4364	.4325	.4286	.4247
0	.5	.496	.492	.488	.484	.4801	.4761	.4721	.4681	.4641

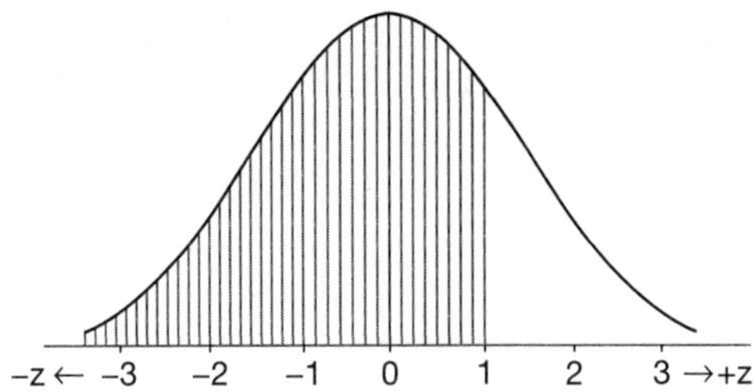

The table given below can be used to determine the area under the curve from the left tail for any value of z. The value corresponding to $z = 1$ is 0.8413, representing 84.13% area under the standard normal distribution that is to the left of $z = 1.0$.

z	.00
3.5	.999767
4.0	.9999683
4.5	.9999966
5.0	.999999713

z	.00	.01	.02	.03	.04	.05	.06	.07	.08	.09
0	.5	.504	.508	.512	.516	.5199	.5239	.5279	.5319	.5359
0.1	.5398	.5438	.5478	.5517	.5557	.5596	.5636	.5675	.5714	.5753
0.2	.5793	.5832	.5871	.591	.5948	.5987	.6026	.6064	.6103	.6141
0.3	.6179	.6217	.6255	.6293	.6331	.6368	.6406	.6443	.648	.6517
0.4	.6554	.6591	.6628	.6664	.67	.6736	.6772	.6808	.6844	.6879
0.5	.6915	.695	.6985	.7019	.7054	.7088	.7123	.7157	.719	.7224
0.6	.7257	.7291	.7324	.7357	.7389	.7422	.7454	.7486	.7517	.7549
0.7	.758	.7611	.7642	.7673	.7704	.7734	.7764	.7794	.7823	.7852
0.8	.7881	.791	.7939	.7967	.7995	.8023	.8051	.8078	.8106	.8133
0.9	.8159	.8186	.8212	.8238	.8264	.8289	.8315	.834	.8365	.8389
1	.8413	.8438	.8461	.8485	.8508	.8531	.8554	.8577	.8599	.8621
1.1	.8643	.8665	.8686	.8708	.8729	.8749	.877	.879	.881	.883
1.2	.8849	.8869	.8888	.8907	.8925	.8944	.8962	.898	.8997	.9015
1.3	.9032	.9049	.9066	.9082	.9099	.9115	.9131	.9147	.9162	.9177
1.4	.9192	.9207	.9222	.9236	.9251	.9265	.9279	.9292	.9306	.9319
1.5	.9332	.9345	.9357	.937	.9382	.9394	.9406	.9418	.9429	.9441

z	.00	.01	.02	.03	.04	.05	.06	.07	.08	.09
1.6	.9452	.9463	.9474	.9484	.9495	.9505	.9515	.9525	.9535	.9545
1.7	.9554	.9564	.9573	.9582	.9591	.9599	.9608	.9616	.9625	.9633
1.8	.9641	.9649	.9656	.9664	.9671	.9678	.9686	.9693	.9699	.9706
1.9	.9713	.9719	.9726	.9732	.9738	.9744	.975	.9756	.9761	.9767
2	.9772	.9778	.9783	.9788	.9793	.9798	.9803	.9808	.9812	.9817
2.1	.9821	.9826	.983	.9834	.9838	.9842	.9846	.985	.9854	.9857
2.2	.9861	.9864	.9868	.9871	.9875	.9878	.9881	.9884	.9887	.989
2.3	.9893	.9896	.9898	.9901	.9904	.9906	.9909	.9911	.9913	.9916
2.4	.9918	.992	.9922	.9925	.9927	.9929	.9931	.9932	.9934	.9936
2.5	.9938	.994	.9941	.9943	.9945	.9946	.9948	.9949	.9951	.9952
2.6	.9953	.9955	.9956	.9957	.9959	.996	.9961	.9962	.9963	.9964
2.7	.9965	.9966	.9967	.9968	.9969	.997	.9971	.9972	.9973	.9974
2.8	.9974	.9975	.9976	.9977	.9977	.9978	.9979	.9979	.998	.9981
2.9	.9981	.9982	.9982	.9983	.9984	.9984	.9985	.9985	.9986	.9986
3	.9987	.9987	.9987	.9988	.9988	.9989	.9989	.9989	.999	.999
3.1	.999	.9991	.9991	.9991	.9992	.9992	.9992	.9992	.9993	.9993
3.2	.9993	.9993	.9994	.9994	.9994	.9994	.9994	.9995	.9995	.9995
3.3	.9995	.9995	.9995	.9996	.9996	.9996	.9996	.9996	.9996	.9997
3.4	.9997	.9997	.9997	.9997	.9997	.9997	.9997	.9997	.9997	.9998

Appendix 2

Project Quality Plan—A Sample

A2.1 INTRODUCTION

A project quality plan (PQP) is a quality management guideline prepared for a specific project, considering all its requirements. It is developed using the directions given by ISO 10005. PQP describes how an organisation has to meet the client's needs based on the contractual requirements. It includes the scope of the project and lists the resources to be used. The personnel responsibilities and the line of communication are also mentioned in the PQP. Quality checks and inspections, as well as various controls and monitoring methods, are also included in the PQP. The following is a sample PQP for a specific project of the ABC organisation.

A2.2 DETAILS OF THE PROJECT

Name of Project:

Location:

Contractor:

Client:

A2.3 SCOPE

This project quality plan has been prepared to define the quality procedures to be followed for the construction of ______________ (Name of project) at ______________ (Location of site) for ______________ (Name of client). It has been prepared using the guidelines given by the ISO 9001:2000 series of QMS Standards.

A2.4 PURPOSE

(a) Specify the quality policy of the organisation and the objectives of the organisation.

Name of the Organisation
Vision:
Mission:
Quality Policy:
Quality Objectives:

(b) Specify the purpose of PQP.

Example: The purpose of this PQP is to facilitate the organisation to satisfy the contractual commitments of the project. It describes the quality management practices to be followed to ensure that the project is completed in accordance with the quality requirements of the client.

(c) Overview of the project – complete details of the project

(d) Specify the risks associated with the project and maintain records of response to risk mitigation measures.

(e) Documentation

Example: The documents used as reference for the preparation of the PQP are:

- ISO 9000-2000
- ISO 9001
- IS codes of practice
- Contract documents, drawings, and specifications.
- Local rules and regulations

A2.5 RESOURCES AND LINE OF COMMUNICATION

(a) Resources – List the resources according to the project requirements. Resources include manpower, equipment, plant and machinery, tools, and infrastructure for site operations.

(b) Roles and responsibilities

Example: The following table displays the roles and responsibilities of employees assigned to the project:

Position	Responsibilities
Project manager	In charge of the project Main point of contact from the organisation to the clients Organising and managing the site activities Mobilising resources Monitoring contract Coordinating with stakeholders such as clients, corporate office, consultants, planning and design team, procurement team, subcontractors, vendors, auditors, service providers, and team members, and proper communication with all of them. Employee welfare, training, and motivation Conducting review meetings Controlling finances Ensure successful completion within the budget, time, and scope as per the contract.
Planning manager	Preparing the schedule Monitoring the project Resource planning Arranging the materials on time Material reconciliation Progress review Communicating with the top management regarding the work progress Coordinating with all departments Responsible for completing the project on time
Quality manager	In charge of implementing the QMS of the organisation Preparation and execution of the project quality plan Monitoring and controlling the quality plan Material testing Site inspection and implementing test plans Identify nonconformities Documentation and maintaining records Approving the corrections made to nonconformities Monitoring and calibration of measuring equipment
Billing engineer	Preparation of bills Tracking progress based on the cost incurred Reconciliation of materials with work progress
Planning engineer	Monitor and track the progress Update the project Reconcile materials
Site engineer	Planning and schedule of construction activities on a daily basis Execute the work as per the method statement Arrange and manage the site activities Inspect the work Coordinate the site activities

Position	Responsibilities
Stores manager	Receive and store the material Track the supply of materials to the site Inspect the incoming materials
Safety engineer	Conduct HSE (Health, Safety, Environment) inspection of the work site and all other resources Carrying out awareness talks and training Planning and procurement of PPE (Personal Protective Equipment) Setting and maintaining first aid facilities in site Conducting fire drills and maintenance of fire extinguishers Analysis of accidents and near-miss cases Responsible for safeguarding the health and safety of workers and others on the site

(c) Communication – Specify the line of communication and the mode of communication.
Example: The following figure illustrates a sample of the line of communication to be followed in the project.

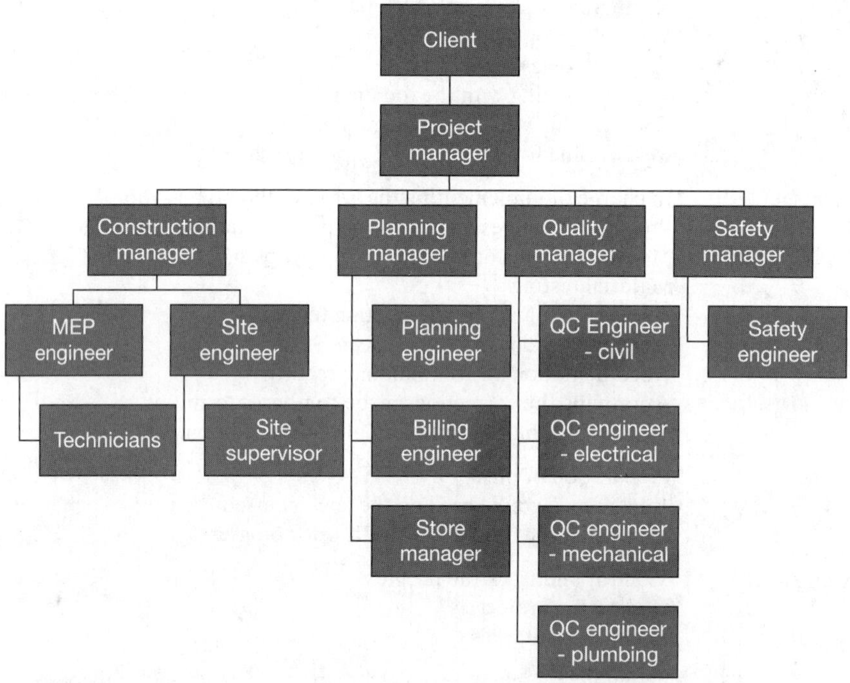

(d) Specify the competence, awareness, and training requirements for the project.

(e) Discuss the qualifications and competence requirements for various roles. Specify the types of training to be conducted for the workforce.
Example: Induction programmes are conducted to equip employees for their roles and responsibilities. Job specifications are made for all roles, and the employees are selected

based on their qualifications and competence. Whenever gaps are found, they are filled by providing necessary training to the employees. Training is to be conducted to update the employees with new technology. Different types of training are conducted to bring awareness and upgrade the skills of the workers and supervisors. Toolbox talks are to be conducted before the start of work to reinforce the knowledge about the work procedure and safety aspects at the site.

A sample training plan template is given below:

S. No.	Training area	Proposed date	Trainee department	Participant details	Duration of training	Location

A2.6 PROJECT DELIVERY

(a) **Project inputs:** Contract documents, budget, schedule, drawings, specifications, standards and regulations, available resources, work methods, quality objectives of the client and the contractor, customer feedback, audit findings, nonconformities, and cost of quality of previous projects, PQPs of similar projects and management system available, ________________.

(b) **Change management process of project scope:** Changes in scope must go through a change management process. Specify conditions when changes can be made along with the personnel authorised to request and approve changes. Inform the clients and all team members regarding the changes made. Whatever financial obligations that might arise also must be mentioned.

(c) **Control of projects:** Prepare the process maps for all activities. Specify the procedures established for quality control and assign the responsibilities to competent personnel. List the construction activities to be carried out, along with their method statements and checklists, and prepare the schedule. Enumerate the circumstances when updating is to be done during the project execution.

(d) **Managing project deliverables:** List out the deliverables based on the contract document and allocate resources for its successful completion. Prepare the progress reports on a daily, weekly, and monthly basis. Quality control procedures must be followed during the procurement process. Materials that are received should be tested for their acceptance. Materials received are to be properly handled and stored. Activities are to be carried out according to the method statements. Checklists are to be used to inspect the site activities.

(e) **Check, review, verify, and approve:** Establish procedures for verification, review and approval of design, method statements, and all other relevant documents and their approval. Prepare inspection and test plans for various stages of different activities and material test plans for materials received. They have to be mutually agreed upon by clients, contractors, and consultants.

Following are a few reports to be used in the construction site:

i. Material Inspection Report.
ii. Material Test Plan.
iii. Test Procedure.
iv. Apparatus / Equipment Verification.
v. Calibration Plan.
vi. Inspection Test Plan.
vii. Checklist.
viii. Daily Progress Report.

The sample templates for the above reports are given below:

Material Inspection Report

1. Name of the project: Date:
2. Material type:
3. Received on:
4. Receipt No:
5. Quantity as in receipt:
6. Purchase order No:
7. Other details (Make/type/batch/source):
8. Acceptability:

S. No.	Characteristics	Yes	No	Not applicable	Remarks

9. Remarks:
10. Signature of QA/QC:
11. Signature of Store Manager:

Material Test Plan

Name of the Project: Date:

S. No.	Material	Test conducted	Standards & Clauses	Acceptance criteria	Frequency of testing	Responsible personnel	To be Tested by

Test Procedure

Name of the Project: Date:

Aim:

Material required:

Apparatus/ Equipment:

Procedure:

Calculations:

Result:

Inference:

Reference:

Apparatus/Equipment Verification

Name of the project: Date:

Aim:

Apparatus/Equipment:

Procedure:

Inference:

Reference:

Calibration Plan

Name of the Project: Date:

S. No.	Name of the instrument	Part to be calibrated	Make of the instrument	Method of calibration (External/ Internal)	Frequency of calibration	Last calibrated on	Calibration due on

Inspection Test Plan

Name of the Project: Date:

S. No.	Activity	Method of inspection	Frequency of inspection	Nature of inspection	Standards & Clauses	Acceptance criteria	Responsibility

Checklist

Name of the project:

Activity:

Date:

S. No.	Characteristics to be checked	Acceptance	Observations	Remarks
		Y N NA		
		Y N NA		

Signature of Site engineer:

Signature of QA/QC:

Signature of Client:

Daily Progress Report

Name of the project: Date:

S. No.	Activity	Unit	Total Quantity	Planned	Achieved	Cumulative achieved

A2.7 DOCUMENTED INFORMATION MANAGEMENT

(a) List the documents to be controlled at the site, allocate a location for their storage, and assign responsibilities to personnel for storage and sharing. The various documents include:

- Contract documents.
- Drawings – structural and architectural.
- Specifications.
- Material receipt, inspection and approval records.
- Checklist for various activities.
- Test reports.
- Quality manual.
- Site inspection reports.
- Safety manual.
- Nonconformance reports and action-taken reports.
- Minutes of meeting.
- Site instructions.
- Installation and assembly drawings.
- Warranty cards for appliances and equipment.

(b) Documented information management process

Specify the procedures for control of various documents.

(c) Document management

Describe the procedure for intake of new documents, changing documents as per the scope change, and managing outgoing documents and other transmittals.

A2.8 AUDITING

Internal audits shall be performed to ensure that processes are carried out in accordance with the quality plan. The effectiveness of QMS can be improved by executing the audit findings. Audits are to be scheduled and performed on time. Prepare the audit calendar.

A sample template is given below.

Audit Calendar

S. No.	Audit Location	The department or function to be audited	Scope of audit	Date of audit	Audit team members

A sample template of the audit report is given below:

Audit Report/Nonconformance Report

Audit No:

Audit location:

Documents audited:

Audit summary:

S. No.	Nonconformities observed	Category of nonconformance	Standards & clauses applicable	Responsible employee	Corrective actions proposed

Name and signature of auditor:

Date:

A2.9 IDENTIFICATION AND TRACEABILITY

Specify the contractual requirements or other traceability requirements to be included in recorded information; the type of records needed to be kept showing that traceability requirements have been met and how they will be managed; and guidelines and techniques for determining the outputs' inspection and testing status.

A2.10 CONTINUOUS IMPROVEMENT

Review the progress and performance of work at different stages. Conduct brainstorming sessions to improve processes. Discuss the nonconformances during the review meeting and take corrective and preventive actions. After implementing the actions, evaluate the results, and record the accomplishment.

Index

V

W